Here's what America's top magazines and readers are saying about Skiing America. They love it.

"Loaded with facts, prices and names to help skiers cope with practically all the major ski resorts in North America."

—*The New York Times*

"Up-to-the-minute info, so accurate that even ski resort personnel peruse these pages . . . Everything skiers need to know but the weather forecast."

—*Robb Report*

"If you're planning a ski vacation . . . this guide should serve you well."

—*Ski*

"Packed with details and maps."

—*Snow Country*

"The only guidebook which describes the personality of each resort and provides an independent evaluation of the ski terrain. . . offers more extensive information than found in other ski guides."

—*Skier News*

"Get it before you ski off."

—*Endless Vacations*

"Packed with information for ski resorts across America."

—Good Morning Houston

"Lets you know where the action is . . . on and off the slopes."

—KFYI, Phoenix AZ

"Your book made the planning of the trip a breeze and my husband was thrilled with the skiing."

—JSH, Dallas TX

"Your book is, in our experience, unique and we will certainly rely upon it when we next plan a vacation."

—MIG, Burlington VT

"I hope my comments help one 100th of what yours have to me. Thanks for the book. It's a wealth of information."

—TR, Sherman Oaks CA

"Thanks for a great vacation. I used your book to great advantage when planning a two-week trip . . . keep up the good work."

—KSH, Philadelphia PA

"I have just finished reading your book, and wanted to tell you how useful and informative I found it to be. In particular, it appears (with great relief) that the information is totally reliable. For those ski resorts of which I have personal knowledge I found your comments and observations to be *totally* in accord with my own feelings."

—JLC, Toronto, Canada

"We are enthusiastically looking forward to our trip—mostly because of your book; the gracious responses to to the phone calls we made, the wonderful down-to-earth descriptions you gave us of what we should expect and the clear concise information. (The book is going with us to Colorado)"

—JR, Media, PA

5th Edition

SKIING
AMERICA 1993

by Charles A. Leocha

with
Diane Slezak Scholfield
Susan Vreeland
Katy Keck
James Kitfield
Peter Rose

WORLD LEISURE CORPORATION
Hampstead, NH   Boston, MA

Send mail to:
World Leisure Corporation
P.O. Box 160
Hampstead, NH 03841, USA

Cover design by Jutta Gork,
R&R Communications, GmbH, Leimen, Germany.
Cover photos.
Top: Bob Winsett, Jeff Andrew, Keystone Resort, CO.
Left: Grafton Marshall Smith, Crested Butte Mountain Resort, CO.
Right: Stowe Ski Area.
Back cover illustration: Jim Bennett, Hoboken, NJ

Printed in the United States of America
by Dickinson Press, Grand Rapids, MI

Distributed to the trade in USA and Canada by
The Talman Company, 131 Spring Street, Suite 201E-N,
New York, NY 10012 tel. (212) 431-7175 or (800) 537-8894

Distributed to the trade in Europe by Roger Lascelles,
47 York Road, Brentford, Middlesex TW8 0QP Tel. 081-847 0935.

Distributed to U.S. Military, Stars & Stripes Bookstores,
Mail Order and Special Sales by
World Leisure Corporation, 177 Paris Street, Boston, MA 02128.
Tel. (617) 569-1966, fax (617) 561-7654

ISBN: 0-915009-22-6

Contributors to Skiing America 1993

Charlie Leocha has been skiing worldwide for over a decade. He is author of *Ski Europe 1993*, an annually updated guidebook to the Alps' top ski resorts. He writes about travel and skiing for scores of magazines and newspapers. His most recent books are *Eastern Germany*, a guide to this once forbidden region, and *Getting to Know You*, 365 questions, activities, observations and ways to get to know another person better.

Katy Keck worked in France under chefs at Michelin-star restaurants. She owns and runs Savoir Faire Foods, a consulting company in New York specializing in food styling, recipe development and catering.

James Kitfield was awarded the Gerald R. Ford prize for distinguished reporting, and the Jesse H. Neal award for excellence in reporting. He was Editor of *Overseas!*, a travel and entertainment magazine in Europe. His articles appeared in *Newsday*, *LA Examiner*, *Penthouse*, *Omni* and others.

Peter Rose currently writes for the *Idaho Statesman*. He was selected Ski Writer of the Year by the North American Ski Journalists Association (NASJA).

Diane Slezak Scholfield writes a weekly column about skiing for *The San Diego Union*. She was selected Ski Writer of the Year in 1990 and 1991 by NASJA. She currently is president of the Southern California Ski Writers Association.

Susan Vreeland, a member of NASJA, received the 1988 Lowell Thomas Award for excellence in ski journalism and the 1990 Bill Berry Ski Journalism Award. Her articles have appeared in *Powder*, *Ski*, *Travel and Leisure*, and the *Los Angeles Times*.

Other contributors: **Mary Jo Tarallo**, with the United Ski Industries Association, contributed most of the mid-Atlantic synopses; **Tom Carter**, who writes for the *Washington Times*, wrote the Santa Fe section; **Mike Terrell**, president of the Midwest Region of NASJA, contributed the Midwest section; **Cindy Bohl** researched many of the changes in New England areas; **Paul Todd**, an instructor for Alyeska and Challenge Alaska, assisted with the Alyeska section.

Skiing America 1993 and *Ski Europe 1993* were edited by James Thompson of Old Colony Editorial Associates.

Contents

Ski Resorts in Skiing America 1993

California	Colorado	Utah	New Hampshire
Alpine Meadows	Aspen	Alta	Attitash/Wildcat
Squaw Valley	Snowmass	Snowbird	Cranmore/Black
Northstar	Aspen Highlands	Solitude/Brighton	King Pine
Heavenly Valley	Buttermilk	Deer Valley	Bretton/Cannon
Kirkwood	Vail	Park City	Waterville Valley
Diamond Peak	Beaver Creek	ParkWest	Loon Mountain
Sugar Bowl	Steamboat	**Wyoming**	**Maine**
Bear Valley	Crested Butte	Jackson Hole	Sunday River
Mammoth	Irwin Lodge	Grand Targhee	Sugarloaf/USA
June Mountain	Copper Mountain	**Vermont**	**New York**
Snow Summit	Breckenridge	Stowe	Lake Placid
Bear Mountain	Telluride	Killington	Hunter Mountain
Mountain High	Keystone	Stratton	Windham
Snow Valley	Arapahoe Basin	Mount Snow	**Canada**
Oregon	Winter Park	Stratton	Jasper
Mt. Bachelor	**New Mexico**	Sugarbush	Whistler/
Idaho	Taos	Mad River Glen	Blackcomb
Sun Valley	Angel Fire	Bromley	Sunshine/Norquay
Schweitzer Mt.	Pajarito	**Midwestern**	Lake Louise
Silver Mt.	Red River	Big Powderhorn	**Mid-Atlantic**
Brundage	Sandia Peak	Blackjack	Whitetail
Bogus Basin	Santa Fe	Indianhead/Whitecap	Showshoe/Elk
Alaska	Sipapu	Sugar Loaf	Blue Knob
Alyeska	Ski Apache	Crystal Mountain	Seven Springs
Arizona	**Montana**	Shanty Creek	Hidden Valley
Apache Sunrise	Big Mountain	Boyne Highlands	Camelback
Snowbowl	Big Sky	Chestnut	Wintergreen

Help us do a better job

Research for this book is an ongoing process. We have been at it for more than a decade. Each year we revisit many of these resorts, and every winter we speak with locals from every resort.

If you find a new restaurant, hotel, bar or disco that you feel we should include, please let us know. If you find anything in these pages that is misleading or has changed, please let us know. If we use your suggestion, we will send you a copy of next year's edition.

Send your suggestions and comments to:
Charlie Leocha, *Skiing America*, World Leisure Corp.
Box 160, Hampstead NH 03841, USA

How to get the most out of Skiing America

This is a straightforward, honest guidebook to North America's top resorts. Knowing that a ski vacation is made up of much more than skiing, we have attempted to describe the personality of each resort in addition to giving you many pages of hotel and restaurant descriptions, lift ticket and lesson prices, day care programs and nightlife activities.

The resorts described are nearly all destination resorts—those that can support five days to a week of skiing and non-skiing activity without becoming repetitious. You won't find small, local day areas described in great detail, though many are included for day skiing trips from major cities. Each of these major resorts provides a total vacation experience and has the facilities to make any skier's visit comfortable, convenient and rewarding.

Chapter organization

The resort chapters are in several sections. We begin by sketching the personality of the place, to give you a feel for the overall resort—is it old and quaint or modern and high-rise? Clustered at the base of the slopes, or a few miles down the road? Remote and isolated, or around the bend from another resort? Is it family-oriented or catering to singles, walkable with good shuttlebuses or requiring a car, filled with happy, friendly faces or packed with an aloof herd of "beautiful" skiers?

The new **Mountain Facts** box outlines the basic statistics of each resort. We note the **base and summit altitudes,** a major factor for many with altitude-related medical difficulties and an important consideration for those enjoying a sedentary lifestyle at sea level and planning a rigorous week in the Rockies. The **vertical drop** provides one indicator of how much skiing, from top to bottom, can be expected at the resort. This, combined with the total

skiable acreage and **number and types of lifts** will give you a good idea of how much skiing is available. **Uphill lift capacity** is the number of skiers the total lift system can carry up the mountain each hour—a larger uphill lift capacity normally means shorter lift lines. **Bed base** is the approximate number of people who can be accommodated overnight near the resort. Most destination resorts try to maintain a much larger uphill capacity than their bed base in order to insure short lift lines. Resorts with nearby major cities and seemingly great uphill capacity/bed base ratios may still have long lines on weekends . . . we try to let you know which resorts to avoid on weekends.

A detailed description of **where to ski** or **the skiing** is next, followed by a **mountain rating**. We suggest an approach to exploring the mountain based on your abilities, and in the mountain rating we describe what the mountain has to offer for beginner, intermediate or expert skiers; more important, this section also suggests which resorts the beginner looking for the mellow or the expert looking for the extreme may choose to avoid. (Where trail maps are included, use them only for reference when reading this book—they are not designed to be used while skiing to find your way through a ski area. Use the up-to-date official maps provided by the resorts.)

Cross-country information is included for trails that many resorts have added to their network, as well as significant cross-country and backcountry skiing opportunities near the resort.

A new section on **snowboarding** tells you whether shredding is allowed on the mountain, and where, and outlines special snowboard facilities such as quarterpipes or halfpipes, and snowboarding lessons and rentals.

The major **ski school programs** are outlined, together with prices for group and private lessons.

Lift ticket prices are listed for adults, children and seniors. The price lists in most cases include single-day passes, as well as multiday tickets and coupon books where available. Where possible we list the 92/93 prices, but in cases where no date is noted, assume the prices are from the 91/92 season.

Under **accommodations** we list the best and most luxurious places to stay in the resort as well as many of the ski area bargains. Where distance to the lifts is a factor, we note which condominiums to book and which to avoid. We also suggest affordable family hotels and inns that are particularly suited to children.

The **dining** recommendations always include the best gourmet restaurants in town, where money is no object— but we don't leave out affordable places where a hungry family can chow down and relax. In addition, there are plenty of in-between restaurants suggested for each resort. These suggestions have been compiled from dozens of interviews with locals and tourists, then combined with our own dining experiences. For a few resorts—the Aspen area, Crested Butte, Steamboat and the Lake Tahoe region—Katy Keck visited the top restaurants and writes up a Savoir Faire section.

Après-ski/nightlife describes places to go once the lifts begin to close, and where to find entertainment later in the evening. We discuss, for example, which bars are packed for immediate après-ski with loud beer drinkers, likewise where to find an inviting, cozy spot in front of a fireplace. We'll help you find pulsing disco on a packed dance floor, or soft music and quiet after dinner talk.

Details on resort **child care** facilities are given with prices, times and ages of children accepted. We describe the unique programs and any special procedures parents must follow before bringing children into the facility.

Non-skiing activities and facilities, such as tennis, racquetball and squash, fitness clubs, sleigh rides, hot-air ballooning, dog sled expeditions, snowmobiling, ice fishing and special festivals, are included under the **other activities**.

Finally, we give detailed **getting there** instructions on how to reach the resort either by plane, car, boat or train and finish with the most important phone numbers and addresses for **information/reservations**.

Types of accommodations

Let's define the major different types of accommodations available at ski resorts.

A hotel is normally located in the resort proper, is relatively large, with 25 or more rooms, and comes without breakfast or dinner. A hotel offering the Modified American Plan (MAP) includes breakfast and dinner. European plan (EP) means no meals included.

A country inn, or mountain inn, is more rustic, usually smaller, with fewer than 25 rooms. Many of these inns have packages that include breakfast and dinner.

A bed-and-breakfast (B&B) tends to be even smaller, with as few as four to 10 rooms. Many times guests share a common bath, but today most B&Bs have rooms available with private bath. Breakfast is included and some B&Bs also offer dinner arrangements.

Motels are normally located on the roads leading to the ski resorts. Where the resort has developed a good shuttle system this distance is no problem. Motels normally are excellent for families and offer some of the best budget accommodations.

Condominiums have become the most affordable and popular lodging at American ski resorts. They allow room to move around, offer a chance to save money by cooking your own meals, and are convenient, generally served by shuttlebus routes in virtually every resort. Finally, they are just as easy to book through resort association numbers listed at the end of each chapter, and normally have a convenient central check-in facility. Most condominiums will change towels and make beds daily and have a cleaning service available for everything but the kitchen.

When making reservations, especially through the resort central reservations number, ask the reservationist for suggestions. Most of the folk working the reservations lines have been on tours of the condominiums, hotels and lodges, and can make honest recommendations based on needs, budget and availability.

High vs. low season

Ski resorts have high and low seasons. The seasons are listed in descending levels of cost. The highest prices are during the Christmas and New Year's holidays. What most resorts call the "regular season" runs all of February and March. "Value season" is in January after New Year's. In most resorts "low season" represents the first weeks of December and early April.

The most noticeable change takes place in the cost of accommodations, but some resorts also lower the prices of lift tickets, especially in the pre-season and in the spring.

The lowest priced packages are normally given in the first weeks of December, with not-quite-so-low prices in

January. Shifting your ski vacation plans by just a week can often mean a major saving.

Skier ability levels

The level of skiing ability needed to negotiate a particular trail is regularly noted. Because resort and ski schools use different rating systems, we provide ours to assist you in reading the "Where to ski" sections:

Never-evers are just what the name implies and the term normally sticks with them for the first three to five days on skis.

Beginners have about a week of instruction and can turn and stop more or less when they choose, but still rely on the stem christie and wedge turns.

Lower intermediates can link stem christies and is beginning to make parallel turns.

Intermediates can negotiate any blue trail and can normally more-or-less parallel ski on the smooth stuff; they go back to survival rules when working their way down an expert trail, and definitely struggle in heavy powder and crud.

Advanced skiers can ski virtually any marked trail with carved turns, but are still intimidated by crud, deep, heavy powder and super steeps.

Experts can always ski anything, anytime, anywhere. They are few and far between.

A note about prices

Many of the prices in this book are from the current 1992/93 ski season. Where we have been unable to obtain current prices we have noted the 91/92 prices in the text. Where there is no notation, assume the prices are from last season. Unfortunately, as of late June many resorts had not announced their prices.

The prices provided in this guidebook are in no way official and are subject to change at any time; they in fact do change with the seasons. Our intention is to provide you with the best possible information for planning and comparison purposes.

Skiing for everyone

Skiers come in all shapes, sizes, sexes, builds and ages. As skiing has developed there is more emphasis on teaching people how much fun downhill skiing, cross-country skiing or snowboarding can be. This is a sport which combines the best of Mother Nature with the best of friendly people out to enjoy themselves. The first step is learing to ski—we touch on the basics of lessons, equipment and clothing. We then explore special programs for senior citizens, women and disabled skiers, which have been developed in many ski resorts.

The experience of beginning to ski

When you ski, you escape from your everyday routine. No matter what your level of expertise, you find challenge, and no matter where you ski you find beauty and a balance with nature. This is a sport that only requires you to play, a sport where everyone from beginner to expert has fun, and a sport where you not only enjoy nature, but also can easily meet and enjoy other skiers.

Learning to ski is not difficult. Toddlers can start as young as two, and you're never too old to start. If you are thinking of starting to ski—downhill or cross-country—or taking up snowboarding, the key to getting a great start is to take lessons. Ski areas are making lessons for beginners easier and more economical than ever. Many areas offer free or heavily discounted lessons for beginners. Learning to ski will not break the bank.

After only four or five downhill skiing lessons, most beginners have improved enough to negotiate their way down more than half of the marked ski trails in North America. For cross-country you need only a couple of lessons to begin gliding through the forests and across rolling meadows.

How do you get started? Call any one of the ski resorts listed in this book and ask them about their learn-to-ski packages. These include lodging, transportation, lifts, equipment and lessons. Or go down to your local ski shop and ask them about learn-to-ski programs close to home. In most cases they can give you tips and set you up with the right equipment to get started skiing.

While you are learning to ski, it is best to rent your equipment. You may be surprised at the modest fee for renting skis, bindings, boots, and poles—all of which will fit you and fit each other—for an initial weekend. A quick consideration of your height, weight, and present level of skill—let's assume the last to be never-ever—and the renters can recommend ski length and type, bindings, and adjustments. As you improve, they can suggest how to upgrade it: increasing ski length and stiffness, acquiring higher performance boots, and so forth. The two principal places to rent are ski shops near you or the facilities at the ski resorts; the choice will probably be based on the type of transportation—flying or driving—you're using to get to the resort, and how much time you're spending there. While ski resorts tend to have very complete rental inventories and will almost certainly be able to fit you with all your gear, there's a horrible time's a-wastin' feeling about standing in line to get fitted your first day there.

Besides your equipment, clothing is the next most important thing. You don't need the latest, most colorful ski fashions—what you can find in your closet should do just fine, provided you can find such basics as a pair of long johns, a sweater or two, a windbreaker or quilted car coat, wool or acrylic socks, and a pair of wool trousers or nylon wind pants—anything so long as they're not blue jeans or other cotton (cotton will get wet when you fall). If you are missing any of the basics, borrow from a friend. The secret to staying warm but not too warm is layering. A few lightweight garments are better than one heavy one, since layers trap the air and draw moisture away from your body. Remove or add layers as temperatures change.

Wear a hat—50 percent of your body heat can escape through your head! Wear gloves—not only do they keep hands warm, but also protect them; ski gloves, as you will note if you inspect a pair in a sports store, are padded and reinforced in different ways from any other gloves you're likely to have on hand—sorry about that—so these may possibly be a specific purchase. You'll probably acquire a pair of goggles as well, *vital* for discovering trail contours on overcast days. Use sunscreen—at high altitudes the sun's rays are stronger and at any altitude the reflection of rays off the snow increases the total dose you get.

Your first lessons will teach you how to walk, slide, and—not least—stop. Through several exercises you will gain more control over your movements on skis. Then the lessons focus on how to get up after falling—you may have already practiced that lesson on your own. You will then learn the basic wedge turn or snowplow turn. With this turn you will be able to manage your way down almost any intermediate or beginner slope. Your instructor will show you how to use the lifts, and you'll be on your way up the mountain. You'll be surprised how much you're enjoying it from the start, and every day you will improve.

There is no requirement to learn downhill skiing first. Many skiers go right to cross-country or to snowboarding. Just pick what sport suits you best.

Enjoy!

Skiing for senior citizens by Diane Slezak

Skiing isn't just for youngsters anymore.

Even though ski area marketing brochures depict skiers who look barely old enough to order a martini at the bar, America's ski slopes are populated by many skiers whose *grandchildren* can legally join them for an après-ski swig.

More than 200,000 of the nation's estimated 21.7 million skiers are 55 or older, according to the United Ski Industries Association. By the year 2010, that figure is expected to increase by 37 percent.

Some of those skiers learned when they were young and never stopped skiing, such as 68-year-old ski filmmaker Warren Miller. Others started late in life, such as actor James Sikking (*Hill Street Blues*) who first strapped on skis in his mid-40s.

Not all of the older skiers are celebrities. Bill Hodges is a 71-year-old retired aerospace engineer from Southern California. He first learned to ski while stationed in Korea, but quit when his children came along. He relearned the sport a few years ago at Purgatory, Colorado. Every year, he attends their SnoMasters' Classic, a five-day event specifically designed for skiers 55 and older. Skiing enables him to get away from the "hustle and bustle of southern California."

"People are so damned friendly here," he said. "Skiing is a lot easier than it used to be. The equipment is easier to turn, and the slopes are groomed so much better now. But I don't take the black runs at high-speed. My bones aren't as bendable now and I keep that in mind."

True, those who compete in the Olympic downhill are all in their teens and 20s. Racing on the edge is a young person's sport. But there is no rule that says you have to ski fast to have fun. The smile on the skier who is meandering down a bunny slope with his or her young grandchild is usually as wide as the smile on the face of a 20-year-old careening down a steep powder-filled bowl.

Thanks to programs such as SnoMasters, older adults can learn to ski without feeling intimidated. Many ski areas have started programs that cater to the upper age group. Nearly every ski area in North America offers free or heavily discounted lift tickets to skiers when they reach 60, 65 or 70.

And thanks to clubs such as the Over the Hill Gang and the 70+ Club, older skiers always have companionship. Regional and national clubs for older skiers are growing in membership rapidly. For example, the 70+ Club started in 1977 with 34 members. Now, it has nearly 7,000 members—all 70 or older—in several countries.

Here is a partial list of clubs and programs for older skiers. New programs are starting every season, so give the ski school at your area a call.

Clubs: Members of the **70+ Ski Club** wear distinctive red-and-white patches that identify them as part of this elite group. A $5 lifetime membership fee, plus a copy of a legal document that clearly shows date of birth (such as a passport, driver's license, etc.), is all it takes to join. Founder Lloyd Lambert was a pioneer in getting discounts for older skiers. About 19 members are still skiing in their 90s. For membership information, write to Lambert at 104 East Side Drive, Ballston Lake NY 12019.

The Over The Hill Gang is for skiers 50 and older. This nationwide group has local chapters all over the country whose members not only ski, but also play volleyball and tennis, go hiking and sailing and enjoy the outdoor life. For information, contact the Over The Hill Gang at 13791 East Rice Place, Suite 101, Aurora CO 80015.

Members of the **Over Eighty Ski Club** get their names inscribed on a Scroll of Distinction at the U.S. Ski Hall of Fame. The club began in 1985, and the first name on the scroll is that of Olav V, King of Norway, who still skis as often as he can. To become a member of this special group, send a minimum donation of $25 to the U.S. Ski Hall of Fame, attention: Ray Leverton, Box 191, Ishpeming MI 49849-0191.

When the **Skiing Grandmothers** take a ski trip, everyone knows it. That's because this lively group of ladies wears bright red ski suits and powder-blue cowboy hats emblazoned with ski pins. Its members are mostly from Texas, Colorado and California. Not only do they have fun skiing, but they also raise money for ski-related charities, such as the Jimmie Heuga Center in Vail. Members must ski, like to travel, enjoy charity work and of course, be a grandmother. contact club founder La Nelle Townley, 10027 Cedar Creek, Houston TX 77042.

The **Ski Meisters** is a Denver-based recreation group for those 50 and over. They ski primarily at Winter Park, Colorado, where they break into groups according to ability level, then ski with a guide who takes them on the trails best suited for them. For information, write Ski Meisters at Box 36338, Denver CO 80236.

Elderhostel offers learn-to-ski programs several times a year at Sunday River Ski Resort in Maine. The skiing is combined with other academic courses. This is the first Elderhostel campus to offer skiing. For information, call Elderhostel in Boston at (617) 426-8056.

Ski area programs: The **SnoMasters Classic** is offered at Purgatory, Colorado several times each season. For a $15 registration fee, skiers 55 and older may purchase $20-per-day lift tickets (those 65 and older can buy a season pass for $100), and receive discounts on rental equipment, lodging, food and ski lessons. They also have the use of a hospitality room, where they start the day with a continental breakfast and end it with wine and cheese. Participants can leave their belongings in the room, which is staffed during the day by volunteers. For information, call Purgatory Ski Area at (303) 247-9000.

Park City, Utah has a program for beginning skiers 50 and older called **It's Never Too Late**. A specially selected group of senior ski instructors teaches this program—not only are they selected because of their ski teaching ability, but also because they are aware of the interests and abilities of older students. Students may sign up for group lessons, which enables them to meet others in their age bracket, or private lessons. For information, call Park City Ski Area at (801) 649-8111.

Badger Pass, the downhill ski area in Yosemite National Park, California, has a **Silver Skier** program for those 60 and older. The program includes a free season pass and a beginner lesson just for senior skiers. The director of Badger Pass ski school, Nic Fiore, is nearly 70 years old. This intimate ski area has excellent learning terrain. For information, call Badger Pass (209) 372-1330.

The Silver Streak program at Waterville Valley, New Hampshire includes discounted lift tickets, parking next to the base lodge, free coffee and doughnuts, reserved seating in the base lodge and many other amenities. Call Waterville Valley at (603) 236-8311.

Aspen, Colorado has a **Fit Over Fifty** program that includes breakfast seminars on nutrition, finance and small business management as well as skiing. This five-day program costs about $1000, but includes lodging, lift tickets, lessons and the peripheral activities. Call (800) 952-1616 or (800) 826-4998 in Colorado for more details.

Stratton, Vermont, has a **Club 62** program for skiers 62 and older that includes lessons and tours on Monday, Wednesday and Friday. Club members break off into ability groups. The cost is $25, not including lift tickets. For more information, call Stratton Mountain Resort at (802) 297-2200.

Prime Time Special at Sun Valley, Idaho recognizes skiers 60 and over with this package that includes seven nights lodging, a welcoming reception, a Big Band dinner dance, a mountain hour, a race, and either a 3 out of 4 day lift ticket ($293) or a 5 out of 6 day lift ticket ($320).

Women's ski instruction: Why segregate?
by Susan Vreeland

The question is more often asked by men than women. And women ski professionals might answer it in any number of ways. Elissa Slanger, who has taught her Women's Way seminars at Squaw Valley for 20 years, says, "Women approach skiing differently than men do. They bring a different value system to skiing."

Annie Vareille-Savath, Telluride's Ski School Director, observes, "The skill level of women often drops when a man enters their ski class. Men are not asking us to do that. They are begging us not to, but even women who are strong, successful women, assertive in their own fields sometimes feel intimidated and humiliated when they are in a mixed skiing atmosphere—something they'd never feel on their own ground. They crumple into self-conscious inability or regress to silliness, stiffness or fear."

According to Toby Quinley, director of the Women's Ski Program at Breckenridge, "A major advantage of 'women's only' ski instruction is that women feel a lot freer to say what they're feeling and to declare when they're not experiencing what I've asked them to feel. I get much more feedback from women than men—and with this increased communication, more learning happens."

All agree that their aim is not to segregate women from their male friends on the slopes permanently, but to provide a temporary environment geared to eliminate learning barriers so that "women's only" instruction ultimately becomes unnecessary.

While most male instructors have dropped the condescension and macho attitude that used to be common, these women instructors feel women perform better when their goals are designed by themselves, not by any "him." Therefore, realistic goal-setting precedes division into small, homogeneous groupings of like ability levels. Because lessons feature progressive skill building and are given by the same instructor each day for each group, improvement is both dramatic and clearly recognizable.

But achievement for women skiers is far more complex than the elimination of male intimidation. Vareille-Savath, one of the few women holding the highest qualification designated by Professional Ski Instructors of America, says women might have to perfect their skills even more than a male skier of comparable success in order to compensate for strength or aggressiveness.

Most women's seminars use a holistic teaching technique involving visualization. Instructors might ask their students to imagine transferring liquid from one hollow leg to another as a way to accomplish a smooth weight shift, or riding a carousel horse to get the easy rise-and-fall motion of bending knees, or squeezing an imaginary orange placed under their arches to accomplish edging. They favor a right-brain approach of imagining one's body moving as fluidly as the instructor's. "But when the instructor is a man, women can't do imitative visualizing," says Vareille-Savath. "Our bodies are constructed differently. The center of gravity is lower, the alignment changes, so movement is different."

Discussions on and off the slopes address issues peculiar to women skiers. At Telluride, fear of speed is addressed in seminars by Marti Martin Kuntz, two-time speed skiing champion. At Aspen, Women's Program Director Pat Johannessen uses breathing techniques adapted from Aikido, the Japanese martial arts discipline, to center one's focus, get in touch with one's energy source, and erase tension. Though topics change for each seminar because of the high rate of returning students, additional seminars might be given in nutrition for the slopes, care and choice of equipment, massage and pressure points, motivation and self-esteem. Most programs incorporate video sessions.

These resorts offer women's programs:

Aspen Skiing Company offers seven seminars from December through March in Aspen and Snowmass. Aspen Mountain seminars are for strong intermediate to expert, while Snowmass seminars accommodate all ability levels. Call (800) 525-6200.

Breckenridge offers seminars December through March with three days of lessons, lift tickets and more. Contact Breckenridge Ski Area, Box 1058, Breckenridge CO 80424; (303) 453-2368, Ext. 302.

Copper Mountain's programs run Dec. to Feb. Call (303) 968-2882, ext. 6301; Box 100, Copper Mt. CO 80443.

K2 Women's Ski Adventures are directed by Kim Reichhelm, five-year veteran of the US Ski Team, at Stratton, Vermont (802) 297-2200; Heavenly Valley, CA (800) 2-HEAVEN; Crested Butte, CO (800) 544-8448; and Snowbird, UT (800) 453-3000. Prices vary according to the resort. Contact Kim at (916) 544-3671.

Park City, Utah, hosts the Holly Flanders High Performance Workshop for two-day sessions three times a season. Write Park City Ski Area, Box 39, Park City UT 84060; (801) 649-8111.

Self magazine hosts a "Peak Performance" week for women at a different ski area each year. Contact Gretel Schneider at *Self* (212) 880-8816, for more details.

Squaw Valley offers nine sessions. Call (916) 583-0119 or Ellen Beth Van Buskirk at (415) 882-7335, or write Squaw Valley USA, CA 95730.

Northstar-at-Tahoe has three-day programs. Call (800) 533-6767 or (916) 587-0200.

Steamboat Springs, Colorado hosts a Billy Kidd Racing Camp for women only. Write 2305 Mt. Werner Circle, Steamboat Springs CO 80487; (303) 879-6111.

Telluride's 5-day Women's Weeks. Sessions are December through March. Telluride Ski Resort Box 307, Telluride CO 81435; (800) 525-3455.

Skiing for the physically challenged
by Susan Vreeland

A dozen wheelchairs are lined up, empty. Their occupants are out skiing. A blue-jeaned prosthesis leans up against the wall. Its owner is out skiing. Arm in arm, with orange bibs saying "Blind Skier" or "Instructor of the Blind," pairs of skiers, bubbly with conversation, shoulder their skis and head out the door. Above it, a sign reads, "In Celebration of the Human Spirit."

Out on the slopes of Winter Park, Colorado, the world is normal again. A sit-skier in a monoski-sled beats ablebodied skiers to the chair lift, teasing them as he speeds past. An amputee skiing on one leg negotiates a sinuous slalom course with utter grace. Few people stop to stare. It's natural here, where the National Sports Center for the Disabled got its start 20 years ago.

Hal O'Leary, founder and director of what was then called Winter Park Handicap Ski Program, began with a few sets of borrowed skis and a broom closet office. Now with a full-time staff of 13 and a volunteer organization of 850, Winter Park handles 2,500 participants with 45 types of disabilities, and gives 14,500 lessons yearly.

According to O'Leary, "A limitation is not a failure. It is only temporary—until adaptive equipment is designed and methods discovered that permit success." Now, such adaptive equipment is used throughout the country.

Common among disabled skiers are outriggers, which are normally hand-held with a foot-long retractable ski tip mounted on a rocker base. This enables a skier with one good leg to have three sliding contact points with the snow. Called three-tracking, this process eliminates the weight-shifting necessary in regular parallel skiing. Four-tracking also employs outriggers and is used by people with cerebral palsy, muscular dystrophy, multiple sclerosis, or congenital defects.

For people without full control of their legs, a ski-bra, a metal brace fitted across the tips of the skis, eliminates scissoring while allowing the skier to maintain a wedge or parallel ski stance. Below-the-knee amputees use "ski legs"—protheses with the necessary forward lean built into the leg. Various sleds, one type mounted a foot above a single ski, give paraplegics and double amputees the thrill of the sport. Such sit-skiers steer and propel themselves up inclines with ski poles less than a foot long.

The blind ski with less equipment and more talk. While a beginning blind skier may use the ski-bra and straps held by a guide, before long he is guided downhill by communication skills alone, building a close trust between guide and skier.

The Winter Park facility and instructional program is foremost in the world, but programs had been germinating in other parts of the country as early as the 1950s. National Handicapped Sports now has chapters and programs in 61 cities and resorts, and reports that 12,000 individuals are in learning programs each year.

Other major, permanent on-mountain ski schools for the disabled are at the following resorts:

Tahoe Handicapped Ski School at Alpine Meadows; offices at 5926 Illinois Avenue, Orangevale CA 95662; (916) 989-0402. Onsite phone number: (915) 581-4161. With a history that goes back to the sixties running parallel with the development of National Handicapped Sports, this is one of the nation's major programs.

Bear Mountain (two and a half hours east of Los Angeles) Box 6812, Big Bear Lake CA 92315; (714) 585-2519.

Breckenridge Outdoor Education Center, Box 697, Breckenridge CO 80424; (303) 453-6422.

New England Handicapped Sportsmen's Association. Although the ski program is at Haystack Mountain in Vermont, their offices are at 26 McFarlin Rd., Chelmsford MA 01824; (508) 256-3240.

Ski Windham; offices at 1A Lincoln Ave., Albany NY 12205; (518) 452-6095.

Park City Handicapped Sports Association, Box 680286, Park City UT 84068; (801) 649-3991.

Many chapters of **National Handicapped Sports** have ambitious programs and a schedule of trips to several resorts each year. Two particularly active chapters are:

Vermont Handicapped Ski Foundation, Box 261, Brownsville VT 05037; (802) 484-7711, Ext. 3005.

Courage Alpine Skiers, 3523 Arbor Lane, Minnetonka MN 55343; (612) 938-1724.

For additional information, write or phone:

Hal O'Leary, Director, National Sports Center for the Disabled, Box 36, Winter Park CO 80482; (303) 726-5514.

National Handicapped Sports, 1145 19th St. NW, Suite 717, Washington DC 20036; (301) 652-7505. Provides a list of chapters and programs.

Doug Pringle, Education Manager, National Handicapped Sports, 5926 Illinois Ave., Orangevale CA 95662; (916) 989-0402. Pringle develops certification standards and instructional training programs.

Bill Aronson, Boston Wheelchair Tennis and Ski Association, 2 Thurlow St., Plymouth NH 03264; (603) 536-1366 or (813) 971-0047, in Florida. Provides a list of organizations that train people to work with physically challenged skiers.

How to Choose a Ski Package

For the uninformed, purchasing a ski vacation may be as complicated as purchasing a vehicle. Many considerations cloud the dream. Timing flights to coincide with ground transfers and booking lodgings unseen can be tricky. With more than 25 major resorts in the West alone, and with a variety of packagers competing for the skier's dollar, the skier had better be aware and know what questions to ask so he won't be disappointed because a resort isn't what was expected.

It's important to know what you want out of a ski vacation and to articulate it when buying a package so you can make an appropriate choice. Do you want a self-contained ski community designed for the skiing family, where every expense can be charged to the room and where nursery and teen centers free parents to enjoy the vacation themselves? Or are big-name glitz and nightlife as important as the skiing? Do you want a taste of the Old West, perhaps a mining town turned resort with Victorian relics tucked in the Rockies, remote from the fast lane and immune from lift lines? Or do you want to station yourself in the center of several ski areas where, by hopping a shuttle, you can ski a different resort each day? Knowing your own needs, particularly whether you want a family-oriented ski area or a singles resort, is probably the first step in deciding. Perusing this book will help.

The next step is to learn the options. Ski packages generally fall into three categories: resort packages covering lodging, lift tickets and possibly lessons, sold directly by the resort; ground packages covering lodging, lift tickets and transfers to and from an airport; and complete packages including air travel. These last two types are packaged by airlines   or travel wholesalers   and sold directly at consumer ski shows, through travel agencies or through a toll-free number.

Although all full-service travel agencies can book ski packages, smaller ones may book so few that they're not too familiar with the variety offered. More important, they may know very little about skiing and ski jargon— whether, for example, a mountain with 1500 feet of vertical would be challenging to an advanced skier for a week or would bore him by the second day. They may not know the importance of lift/lodging location, or may not even know the distance from lodging to lifts at a given property. (Another reason to study this guide first, before contacting a packager.)

Booking a package through a resort (see Information/reservations at the end of each chapter for the book-it-all phone number) gives you accurate answers to specific questions, but it doesn't allow you discounts on transportation, which may be a large portion of the expense, depending on your location. An advantage of working with ski packagers is that they usually offer slightly reduced airfare and lodgings because they deal in volume.

"The average savings of trip packages over individually priced items is generally five to ten percent, but that increases dramatically for trips booked far in advance or at the last minute, where there is additional discounting," said Marty Melcher, director of Advance Reservations, a Park City, Utah-based ski trip packager. According to Melcher, on a weeklong trip the average skier pays $170 per day on individually priced items, compared to $140 per day for the average package.

"But more than price, the advantage of ski packages is their simplicity," says a senior product planner for United Airlines' Instant Vacations Ski Packages. A ski trip includes many components and often requires a regional carrier to transport skiers into the mountains. There are complicated transfers—airline to airline, airport to ground transportation, resort/town to lodging—each of which must be carefully timed to get you from your home to the slopes. For an individual scheduling all this independently, the phone calls alone could be enough to discourage him before he started. A packager, especially a major airline that has coordinated schedules with mountain airlines and ground transportation, will have done the scheduling already.

Another convenience factor is the one-time check-in, which frees skiers from rechecking skis, boots and luggage on every leg of the journey.

Two major disadvantages to trip packaging have their solutions, depending on how you book:

1. Restricted time of travel. The length of trip must accord with the airline's preconceived plan. Sometimes the flights scheduled on packages take up a day of skiing. This disadvantage is eliminated, however, when the packager customizes the trip to suit the individual; for example, they can schedule a flight home after only a day's skiing.

2. Strict and limiting cancellation policies. This factor is most important. When you book with a trip packager, you enter into a contract. For the skier, the difficulty is that you enter into the contract months in advance for an activity that is weather-dependent. Although there is no industry standard for cancellations, here are some guidelines: If the major portion of the resort is not operational owing to lack of snow, the resort usually refunds the part of the package price representing lift tickets. Lodgings, however, are not so lenient and rarely accommodate cancellations without charge. Policies depend on length of prior notice. Some may not refund at all; others may charge an administrative fee of $100 and refund the rest only if they can rebook the room. Others give a credit for future use, a policy often followed by airlines, too.

To avoid these difficulties, most trip packagers advise cancellation insurance. For a nominal fee (for example, $20 on a $500 ground transportation package, a typical price for a week's trip) the insurance carrier will grant full refunds if buyer shows cause (medical or business emergency, not poor snow conditions). If airfare is included in the package, usually a credit is given rather than a full refund, even with insurance. Continental Grand Destinations, however, advertises they "refund double the difference between the component or service delivered and that promised, provided that the reason is within our operational control."

Even so, it is essential that skiers be aware of the risks when booking early or late season. According to Danny Richardson of Ski Utah, "A safe bet is Christmas to March in most areas. Of course, the better skier you are, the better conditions you expect." If you are a beginner or intermediate and are booking early or late season, one consideration is the resort's snowmaking capacity. Check our resort facts boxes to find out.

Whether you book through a trip wholesaler, an airline packager, or directly with the resort, it's important that you ask these questions:

1. Exactly what is included? Lessons? Interchangeable lift tickets? Airport to resort transportation? Lodging tax? Is the price of optional items (identified by "O" on brochures and contracts) indicated clearly?

2. If lift tickets are included and are not used each day, is there a refund? What non-ski activities are available at the resort for family members who don't ski?

3. How convenient is the lodging? (Check our listings.) Is it a ski-in/ski-out facility where no transportation is needed? If so, how far of a walk is it? Uphill? Should one rent a car? Is it part of the package? Is it winterized? Is there a free shuttle to the lifts? Does the lodging have airport pickup service included or is there a charge?

4. What amenities are available at the lodging? Ski lockers? Jacuzzi and pool? Teen game room? Maid service? Laundry? If there are kitchens, is there a grocery store within walking distance? Are there a range of restaurants close by or is there only a lodge dining room?

5. Is equipment rental included or is a discount offered with the package? The advantage of renting at the resort is the convenience of making adjustments or changes in ill-fitting equipment. However, renting equipment at the resort that first morning often cuts into precious ski time.

6. For packages including air transportation, if the plane must land somewhere other than your desti-nation, who pays the additional ground transportation? Who pays overnight lodging if any is needed? If a day's skiing is missed, is there a refund of lodging and lift tickets?

7. How reputable is the packager? How long have they been in business? Do they have a name and image so firm in the nation's mind that they would not dare risk tarnishing that good will by offering an inferior package?

It all adds up to this: the more you know, not only before you go, but before you choose where to go, the better time you'll have. Knowledge never hurt a skier.

Lake Tahoe Area

Alpine Meadows
Squaw Valley USA
Northstar-at-Tahoe
Kirkwood, Heavenly
Diamond Peak, Sugar Bowl
with Reno, Nevada

Lake Tahoe, one of the largest mountain lakes in the world, straddles the border of California and Nevada about 200 miles east of San Francisco. The South Shore is highly developed, lined by casinos and high-rise hotels cheek by jowl along the boulevard. The North Shore is less populated, with fewer and smaller casinos, mom-and-pop cabins, restaurants and occasional upscale condos.

The lake is surrounded by some of the best skiing on earth and no less than five world-class ski areas, plus a dozen smaller resorts. These areas use the whole Lake Tahoe region as a hotel base. As a resort spread, Lake Tahoe is unsurpassed—a mini-city in the wilderness, with services, restaurants and shops operating at full tilt even in summer. There are dozens of casinos on the Nevada side of the lake, scores of excellent restaurants and nightlife ranging from big-name entertainment to smoky bars and discos. Everywhere, across the lake and from the slopes, there are breathtaking panoramas.

Cross-country

The Lake Tahoe region may have the largest concentration of cross-country ski areas in the U.S.

The largest single area, without question, is in California at **Royal Gorge,** just off I-80, west of Donner Summit at the Soda Springs exit. Royal Gorge has 6,300 acres of terrain, and 280 kilometers of trail with a skating lane inside the tracks. They also make snow and use modern snowcats. Royal Gorge Cross-country Ski Area, Soda Springs, CA 95728; (916) 426-3871. Adult trail fees, $15, $8 for children; lessons, $22.

Northstar-at-Tahoe has 65 km. of groomed and marked trails. Northstar-at-Tahoe, Truckee, CA 95734; (916) 587-0273. Trail fees, $13 adults, $6 children 5-12; beginner lessons (one-and-a-half hour) including equipment, $35; $17, group track lessons; rentals, $13 for skis, boots and poles.

The Tahoe Donner Cross-country Area is also off I-80 at Donner State Park exit. This area has 65 km. of trails, all double-tracked with wide skating lanes. Tahoe Donner has California's only lighted night cross-country skiing. Tahoe Donner Cross-country, Box 758, Truckee CA 95734; (916) 587-9484. Trail fees: $12 adults; $9 juniors 13-17 and seniors 60 and over; $6 children 7-12. Lessons, $20 groups, $25 private hour, $25 skating or diagonal; rentals, $12 adults, $7 children 7-12.

Tahoe Nordic, two miles north of Tahoe City, offers 60 km. of trails at lake level (7,000 feet). Tahoe Nordic Ski Center, Tahoe City CA 95730; (916) 583-9858. Trail fees, $10 adult, $5 child 3-10; group lessons, $18 adult, $13 children; equipment rentals, $12.

Squaw Valley USA Nordic Center is at the east end of the resort parking area. Trails climb 600 feet and range from backcountry, unpatrolled trails to prepared tracks. Squaw Valley USA Nordic Center, Olympic Valley CA 96146; (916) 581-1946. Trail fees, $10 adult, $7 child; lessons, $20 group, $27 private hour; rentals, $12 adult, $8 children.

On the South Lake Tahoe end, **Kirkwood** has over 80 km. of machine-groomed track, double tracks, skating lanes and three interconnected trail systems with three warming huts, including the 1864 Kirkwood Inn, an old trappers' log cabin chockablock with nostalgia. The new White Pine trail has an environmental theme: signs along the trail discuss the flora and wildlife. Kirkwood Cross-country Ski Area, Kirkwood CA 95646; (209) 258-7248.

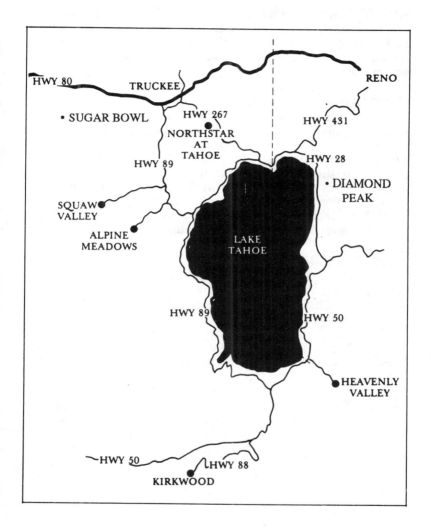

Trail fees, $12 adult, $7 children, $9 seniors; group lessons, $19-$22 adults, $14-$16 children; private hour, $23; full-day rentals, $12 adults, $8 children, $18 demos.

Interchangeable lift tickets (91/92 prices)

The Ski Lake Tahoe interchangeable lift pass is good at Kirkwood, Heavenly, Northstar, Alpine and Squaw Valley USA. Five of six consecutive days costs $180, and six of seven, $216.

Accommodations

The Tahoe basin has limitless options, from huge casino-hotels on the South Shore and large condominium projects to small, privately owned motels and even a few quaint inns. Lake Tahoe accommodations can be divided into: 1) at the resorts; 2) North Shore, 3) South Shore; 4) Reno. Skiers concentrating on Squaw, Alpine, Northstar, Diamond Peak and Sugar Bowl will find the North Shore and Reno handiest. Those skiing Heavenly or Kirkwood should gravitate to South Lake Tahoe.

Accommodations—The North Shore

The North Shore of Tahoe is relatively quiet, and from bed-and-breakfast inns and cabins on the lake, which are perfect for children, to plush condominiums and casino hotels, there really is something for everyone.

The most upscale bed-and-breakfast is the **Rockwood Lodge** (916-525-5273), originally built in the mid-1930s. There are only four bedrooms, two with private bath. The furnishings are antiques, the carpeting so plush you'll be asked to remove your shoes before walking through the house; the baths feature brass and porcelain fixtures, and the beds have down comforters. Lou and Connie run the lodge, and will prepare gourmet breakfasts to be enjoyed in the dining room or in your bedroom. The lodge is next to the base of the Homewood Ski Area, on the west shore of Tahoe about seven miles south of Tahoe City. Rates: $100 a night and $150 for the room with a lake view and four-poster bed. NOTE: This is a no-smoking inn and does not accept children. The inn is quiet and elegant.

The Mayfield House (916-583-1001), another B&B, was once a private residence in the middle of Tahoe City. The atmosphere is elegant and romantic. Breakfasts include fresh fruit and homemade pastries. There are only six rooms, none with private bath. Rates range from $70 a night for smaller rooms to $105 for the Mayfield Room with a king-sized bed.

Just to the south of Tahoe City is the new **Sunnyside Lodge** (916-583-7200, or in California only, 800-822-2SKI), located directly on the lake. There are 23 rooms, all with a lake view. If you want a room with a fireplace, make sure you ask in advance, because there are only a few. Room No. 39 makes a great honeymoon suite, but reserve early because there is a four to six week waiting list. All rooms are bright and tastefully furnished. This is an excellent property with a lively bar après-ski and a good restaurant, the Chris Craft. Rates: $95 a night for standard rooms and $130-$140 for lakefront suites.

Perhaps the most luxury for the money on the north shore of Tahoe is the **Tahoe Vista Inn & Marina** in Tahoe Vista (916-546-4819). These units are spectacular and sited directly on the lake. The Jacuzzi tubs are big, the picture windows looking onto the lake are massive and breakfast is served right at lake level on the pier. Rates here range from $152 a night or $915 a week for the smallest unit to $215 a night or $1,290 a week for a two-bedroom suite, sleeping six, with loft, two baths and giant living room.

Among the casinos just over the border, the top property is the **Cal-Neva Lodge** (800-CAL-NEVA) of Frank Sinatra and Marilyn Monroe fame. Every room has a lake view, and the best are from the deluxe suites on the top three floors. There are also honeymoon bungalows with heart-shaped tubs, round beds and mirrored ceilings. Standard rooms are $69 a night; deluxe rooms are $79; the standard suite is $129 a night, and the deluxe suite runs $159. Deluxe rooms have been redecorated.

For families or anyone looking for a great deal, **North Lake Lodge** in Kings Beach, a collection of 10 buildings only a few feet from the shore, is one of the oldest hotels on the lake but still in great shape. Continental breakfast is included in the rates and the shuttlebuses stop just across the street. The lodge rates are $35 for a queen with bath or $40 for a king or two doubles with bath. The cottage rates range from $30 a night for a queen with bath to $55 for two queens with kitchen and bath. Call: (916) 546-2731.

Two other family properties are the **Charmey Chalet Resort** (916-546-2529) and the **Franciscan Lakeside Lodge** (916-546-7234).

The North Lake Tahoe Visitors Bureau at 800-TAHOE-4 U can also suggest a list of private homes and condos which allow real family savings.

Away from the lake, in Truckee, but convenient to Northstar and Sugar Bowl is the **Truckee Hotel** (916-587-4444), which has been welcoming guests since 1863. In those days the guests had something other than skiing in mind; it was originally a brothel. It has recently been renovated, but you'll still feel like you're sleeping in the Old West. Only seven of the rooms have baths, but these feature old fashioned, claw-footed tubs and cost between $65 and $77. Others share baths, with prices ranging from $52 for a double or two singles to $73 for room enough to sleep six.

Accommodations—South Lake Tahoe

These divide into three categories and areas. The casinos just over the border in Nevada offer plenty of great rooms, views, bright lights and nonstop nightlife. At the top of Kingsbury Grade, or the base of the Nevada side of Heavenly, there is a collection of upscale condominiums and top quality hotels. On the California lake shore there are over three miles of shoulder-to-shoulder motels, hotels and other such joints—most sporting enticing signs, such as, "Our tub is hot" or "Low Low Rates."

For casinos, try **Harvey's** (800-648-3361 from outside Nevada or 702-588-2411 from Nevada) and **Harrah's** (800-648-3353 or 702-588-3515), which has everyone's highest ratings, from AAA to Mobil.

For the Nevada side of Heavenly accommodations, there are scores of condos at Stagecoach Base and Boulder Base areas.

The Ridge Tahoe is guarded like Fort Knox, so we didn't get a chance to see any of the units. We're told, however, that there's a private gondola to the Heavenly slopes. If you're that curious, try calling (800) 648-3391.

At the base of Kingsbury Grade on Highway 50 you'll find the **Lakeside Inn & Casino** (800-624-7980), which offers some of the best deals in the area. The rooms are simple and motelish but access to the mountain is excellent. Rates are $55-$65 a night.

The California side of South Lake Tahoe is a horse of a different color. Here many small motels line Lake Tahoe Boulevard for miles. Best of the lot seem to be two Best

Western properties—**The Timber Cove Lodge** (800-528-1234 or 916-541-6722), located on the beach; and **Station House Inn** (800-822-5922 or 916-542-1101), which is within walking distance of the casino area, just on the California side of the border. **Lakeland Village** (800-822-5969) is well situated and offers a hotel and collection of condominiums right on the lake with convenient shuttlebus service to the base of Heavenly and Kirkwood. Expect to pay $85 for a studio or $130 for a suite with loft in the Lodge. Townhouses cost from $130, for a one-bedroom unit that is not lakefront, to $355 for a four-bedroom, three-bath unit on the lake. **The Tahoe Chalet Inn** (916-541-3311 or 800-821-2656 in California) is three blocks from the casino area and is perhaps the best of the Tahoe Blvd. strip establishments. Finally, for those who want a room just across from Heavenly's lifts on the California side, the **Tahoe Seasons Resort** has received acceptable reviews from everyone locally (916-541-6700).

Accommodations—Reno, Nevada

Reno offers something different from the normal ski town. Here you will find nonstop nightlife and entertainment. Spend your time at the slots or playing blackjack, dance to a live band, watch your favorite stars or see a cabaret show. There are special events scheduled throughout the winter and spring. Reno also has a planetarium and two major museums.

Reno is only about a halfhour to 45 minutes from the Tahoe Area resorts and you can choose from scores of hotels at all price ranges. Call (800) FOR-RENO for room reservations and a copy of the vacation planner.

Dining—North Shore

For those not concerned with price:

Glissandi at the Resort at Squaw Creek (916-583-6300) brings New York or San Francisco class and service, all overlooking Squaw Valley. Reservations suggested.

Captain Jon's (916-546-4819) in Tahoe Vista serves excellent seafood and French country specialties. Reservations required. Closed Mondays.

La Cheminee (916-546-4322) in Kings Beach serves basic nouvelle cuisine. Reservations suggested. Closed Tuesday and Wednesday.

Le Petit Pier (916-546-4464) in Tahoe Vista presents upscale French cuisine. Reservations needed. Open daily.

Swiss Lakewood Restaurant (916-525-5211) in Homewood is Lake Tahoe's oldest and clearly its finest dining experience. Cuisine is French-Swiss and classic continental. Service impeccable. Reservations recommended. Closed Mondays, except holidays.

Wolfdales (916-583-5700) in downtown Tahoe City reportedly has supurb dining. Reservations are suggested. Closed Tuesdays.

Christy Hill, reviewed by Katy Keck in the Lake Tahoe Savoir Faire chapter, is excellent (916-583-8551).

For more moderate fare try:

Jimmy's in Olympic House at Squaw Valley USA (916-583-2614) provides a casual yet elegant setting. **Backstage Bistro** in the Opera House at Squaw Valley USA (916-581-0454) is interesting, or ride the cable car to the top of Squaw Valley USA and dine at the **Poolside Café** overlooking Granite Chief and Emigrant Peaks.

The Basque Club Restaurant (619-587-0260) on the Northstar-at-Tahoe Golf Clubhouse serves a family-style five-course meal of traditional Basque cuisine. Be sure you're hungry. There are always two entrées, plus many side dishes you just think are entrées before the real thing is served. Sleigh rides depart hourly from the clubhouse.

The former chef at La Petite Pier has opened his own restaurant, **Clementine's**, in a historic log building just south of Tahoe City on Highway 89, with gourmet dinners at less-than-$14-an-entrée prices. It is also open for breakfast and lunch.

Passage Lounge in the Truckee Hotel has good soups and interesting salads; and pleasant atmosphere with antiques; **River Ranch** at the access road to Alpine Meadows; **Jake's on the Lake** in the Boatworks complex in Tahoe City; **The Mackinaw Inn** in the Roundhouse Mall; **Col. Clair's** for Cajun cooking in Tahoe Vista. **The Soule Domain** in Crystal Bay received consistent raves from folk at both ends of the lake. **The Steak and Lobster House** in the Crystal Bay Casino also has excellent food for moderate prices. For Mexican with a big dose of margaritas and a shoulder-to-shoulder crowd on weekends, a good choice is the **Hacienda del Lago** in Tahoe City in the Boatworks Mall. **Fast Eddie's** can rustle up a side of barbeque ribs better than anyone else in Tahoe City.

For family grub (lots of good food at very reasonable prices) strike out for:

Bacchi's just outside of Tahoe City or **Lanza's** in Kings Beach, both serving good Italian fare. **The Family Tree** in Tahoe City has perhaps the best all-round family food. **Bobby's Rib Place** in Kings Beach is where country crooner Kenny Rogers used to work and rumor has it he returns from time to time. In any case, the ribs are great and only cost about $9.95. **Garwood's** in Tahoe Vista serves Mexican food with beautiful views of the lake. In Tahoe City at the Fanny Bridge some of the most reasonable meals are spooned up at **La Cuesta**, known for Tex-Mex, and **Bridgetender** for burgers and an extensive beer selection. **Sizzlers** has opened in Tahoe City at the Safeway Mall.

The casinos on the Nevada/California border all serve inexpensive breakfast, lunch and dinner specials.

For the best pizza, try **Pizza Junction** outside of Truckee, where they make their own Truckee River Beer, or the **Lakehouse Pizza** where you can enjoy a great view of Lake Tahoe, as well as **C.B's Pizza** in Kings Beach.

The best breakfasts are at the **Squeeze In** where the list of omelets requires a speed-reading course. The Squeeze In has all the atmosphere you would want in a breakfast joint built in a former alley and only 10 feet wide. On weekends expect to wait a while—this place is popular. Down the street is the **Coffee And**, which also serves up a good, basic breakfast. **The Fire Sign** about two miles south of Tahoe City has great breakfast fare as well, and for those further to the north, try the **Old Post Office** in Carnelian Bay or the **Log Cabin** in Kings Beach. If you're near Alpine Meadows, check out **The Twain Station** for breakfast and lunch.

Buy "killer fudge" in the **Ponderosa Deli** in Truckee.

Dining South Lake Tahoe

For the best restaurants in the higher priced category:

Katy Keck discusses some of the top restaurants in the Lake Tahoe Savoir Faire chapter; these include **The Summit** at Harrah's, the **Sage Room** at Harvey's. I cover the best of the rest, so to speak.

Evan's American Gourmet Café on 89th Street has become one of the best-liked restaurants on the south shore. The chef prepares California Cuisine with an unusual flair. Expect to pay for his efforts, but they are reported to be well worth it.

For good reasonable restaurants, try:

Fresh Ketch for fish, **Cantina Los Tres Hombres** or **Bueno Rico's** for Mexican, or head to one of the casinos' great buffets or fixed-price dinners. **Harvey's** has a reasonably priced Seafood Grotto with large portions. **Zackary's Restaurant** in Embassy Suites has the best blackened salmon. **Bennigan's** is in Bill's Tahoe Casino across from the High Sierra. Then there is always the **Chart House**, with a lake overlook on the Kingsbury Grade.

For great breakfasts head to **The Red Hut**, where you can pack into a small room and listen to the talk of the town a new branch opened on Kingsbury Grade handy for skiers heading to the Nevada side of Heavenly. At **Heidi's**, you can get anything from dozens of Belgian waffles to chocolate pancakes. The other two locals' gathering spots for morning gossip and breakfast in town, **Frank's** and **Ernie's**, just about face each other on Rte. 50 south.

At Heavenly, table linen lunch service is offered at **Top of the Tram** Restaurant in the $6-$7 range; fettucini Alfredo, chicken croissant sandwiches, good soups and an array of appetizers. Get there early or late.

And just in case you crave a malt "so thick it holds the straw up," head to the **Zephyr Cove Resort**. The banana-chocolate shake is highly recommended.

Après-ski/nightlife

South Shore: Head to **Carlos Murphy's** immediately after skiing or stop in the California Bar at Heavenly's Base Lodge, with its famous Grizzly Bear. If you want quieter après-ski with a flickering fireplace, stop in at **Christiania Inn** across from the Heavenly ski area.

Later in the evening, **Turtle's**, in the Round Hill Mall next to Bueno Rios, has good dancing and is the place to meet others looking to do the same. And of course, the casinos have musical reviews that are extravaganzas of sight and sound, besides top-name touring performers.

On the North Shore, try **Pete'n' Peter's** and **Rosie's Café** in the center of Tahoe City or **Pierce Street Annex** behind

Safeway near the Boatworks Mall in Tahoe City. Or head to **Sunnyside**, just a couple of miles south of Tahoe City on the lake. **Hacienda del Lago** in the Boatworks has nachos till 6 p.m. or try **Humpty's** across from the Safeway Mall. The bar at the **Olympic Village Inn** has live music every weekend. In Truckee there is occasional music at **The Passage** in the Truckee Hotel and at the **Bar of America**, both at Commercial Row. The **Hilltop Lodge** overlooking Truckee on Highway 267 has country music. The casinos on North Lake Tahoe have entertainment every night. Sure bets are the **Cal-Neva Lodge, The Crystal Bay Club, Hyatt Lake Tahoe** and the **Tahoe Biltmore**.

Getting there

By air: The major airport for the Tahoe area is Reno, served by most major airlines. The airport is only 45 miles from Squaw Valley USA, 50 miles from Alpine Meadows, 38 miles from the Northstar-at-Tahoe, 55 miles from Heavenly and 70 miles from Kirkwood.

The Lake Tahoe Airport, near South Lake Tahoe and 10 minutes from Heavenly, has service from central and northern California, quite susceptible to weather limitations. There is bus and limousine transportation to the major resorts from the Reno and Lake Tahoe airports.

By boat: That's right! The Tahoe Queen Ski Shuttle, an authentic Mississippi sternwheeler, brings skiers across Lake Tahoe from the south shore to Tahoe City Tuesday through Saturday mornings. The double-decked heated cruiser leaves at 8 a.m., arriving in Tahoe City at about 10:30 a.m. Departure is about 5 p.m. Buses pick up skiers from Squaw Valley USA and Alpine at around 4 p.m. Breakfast buffet and dinner are served; price extra. On the return trip, there is dancing and cocktails available. Call (916) 541-3364 for reservations, and confirm on the prior afternoon or evening, because departures depend on ice conditions on the lake. Cost is $16.50 for the cruise.

By train: Amtrak serves Truckee with a special ski train during the season. Call (800) 872-7245.

By bus: Getting around the lake without a car is no trouble. Shuttlebuses run between almost every major and minor hotel on the North or South Shore and from Reno to each of the major resorts several times a day. Check for schedules when you arrive. Most of the shuttles are free, but those between the North Shore and the South Shore will cost about $4 round-trip. Call: Alpine Meadows, (916) 583-4232; Heavenly, (916) 541-1330; Kirkwood, (209) 258-6000; Northstar-at-Tahoe, (916) 562-1010; Squaw Valley USA, (916) 583-6985; Royal Gorge Nordic Ski Center, (916) 426-3871; Diamond Peak, (702) 832-1177.

For skiers staying in Reno, Sierra Nevada Gray Lines operates a daily ski shuttle between downtown Reno and Alpine Meadows, Northstar-at-Tahoe (except Saturdays) and Squaw Valley USA from mid-December through the end of March. The bus departs between 7:15 and 7:55 a.m. and returns between 5:30 and 6:30 p.m. Round-trip fare is $15 for adults and $10 for those 14 years and younger accompanied by an adult. (800) 822-6009 or 329-1147.

By car Most major automobile rental agencies serve Reno and South Lake Tahoe. Driving time from Reno is about an hour to any resort except Kirkwood, which is approximately an hour and a half from Reno. It's about three and a half hours from San Francisco by I-80 to the North Shore, and three and a half hours on Highway 50 to South Lake Tahoe. When it starts snowing, the police don't let anyone up the mountains without chains or a 4-wheel-drive vehicle, so come prepared.

The Tahoe Area Ski Resorts

Squaw Valley USA

Squaw Valley USA Facts

Base elevation: 6,200'; **Summit elevation:** 9,050'; **Vertical drop:** 2,850 feet
Number of lifts: 14—1 cable car, 1 six-passenger gondola, 3 quad superchairs,
8 triple chairs, 16 double chairs, 4 surface lifts
Percent snowmaking: 10 percent; **Total acreage:** 4000 lift-served acres
Uphill capacity: 47,570 per hour; **Bed Base:** 1,600 within 3 miles

Squaw Valley USA, site of the 1960 Winter Olympic Games, is perhaps the best-known ski resort in the region. Since the 1960 Olympics, Squaw Valley has slowly been building, with a surge during the past two years, including a 405-room luxury hotel, detachable quad chair lifts and an ice skating rink at the top of the mountain.

The area undoubtedly offers some of the finest skiing in the United States. Opening the trail map of Squaw, you'll notice that there aren't any trail-cut runs—just wide open snow fields—4,000 acres of them. Basically anything in the area can be skied by anyone daring enough to challenge the mountain. This is big-bowl skiing, and where the bowls end, the chutes and tree skiing begin. Here super skiers test themselves.

From the base, access to most of the ski area, including slopes in the saddle between Broken Arrow Peak at 8,200 feet and the summit ridge at 8,900 feet, is with a six-person gondola or the 150-skier cable car. Or start with the Squaw Peak Express superchair and then connect to others. There are six separate peaks, each with every conceivable exposure, all overlooking Lake Tahoe.

Extreme skiers will be in heaven at Squaw, there is the Palisades above Siberia Bowl and Eagle's Nest at the top of KT22, with plenty of vertical air. Locals will take you to other spots where you can ski like an elevator.

Experts who like to keep their skis on the snow will find plenty of challenging terrain to explore. The entire KT22 side of the area is expert. Try Chute 75, the Alter-nates, and the Dead Tree Chute, or the National Chute off the Palisades. At Elevation 8200, on the upper mountain, try the Funnel or the Elevator Shaft, or hike to the top of Granite Chief. These are all true, very black diamonds.

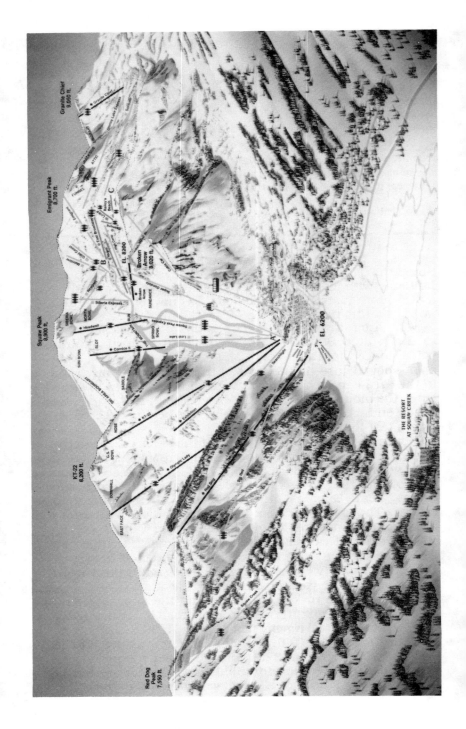

The intermediate terrain also has challenge and variety. Taking the Headwall Lift, intermediates can opt for Chicken Bowl or drop over the back of the ridge to Sun Bowl. Up Siberia Express, where experts turn to the left getting off the lift, intermediates traverse to the right. There, Newport, Mainline, Gold Coast and Emigrant serve wide-open intermediate slopes, and there are five beginner lifts just outside the Gold Coast complex. Intermediates will like the Shirley Lake area served by a detachable quad and a triple chair. The Mountain Run is a great end-of-the-day cruise: top to bottom, without stopping, a hefty 2,500 feet. Because of its reputation of being as crowded as the Hollywood Freeway in the late afternoon, a second, roughly parallel (and easier) run, Home Run, has been cut.

Snowboarding
Snowboarding is permitted on all sections of Squaw Valley USA. Squaw has a halfpipe, lessons and rentals.

Ski school
Squaw Valley USA Ski School has over 150 instructors and special courses for children, women, powder skiing, bump technique, or racing. The specific program prices are available from the school at (916) 583-0119. Group lessons cost $30 for four hours and $20 for two hours. Private lessons cost $42 an hour and $15 for each additional person. All-day private lessons run $225.

Lift tickets
All day $38; skiers under 13 or over 65, $5. Three of five consecutive days, $108; five of seven consecutive days, $170; seven-day lift passes, $224. Single cable car or gondola ride, $10, adults; $5, children.

Squaw has an unprecedented "No-waiting-in-line-or-your-money-back" program. For $1, skiers register as beginner, intermediate or expert; any one who has to wait more than 10 minutes for a lift in his ski category receives a full refund and skis free for the rest of the day. All lifts must be operating for the program to be in effect.

Accommodations

After years of almost no accommodations at the base of Squaw, some development has begun, resulting in four major lodging properties, a host of condominiums and private homes. All lodges give easy access to the slopes, but nightlife and restaurant opportunities are limited. Even if you are staying in a resort hotel at Squaw, it is best to rent a car for access to Truckee and Tahoe City, where there are plenty of restaurants and diverse nightlife.

A new deluxe hotel called **Resort at Squaw Creek** (800-327-3353; 800-3CREEK3) opened last winter after more than a decade of bitter legal maneuvering by locals fighting development. The resulting hotel blends well with the valley, especially since it's on the far side of the meadows and unobtrusive. This hotel connects with the ski area by its own lift, and is virtually a self-contained resort. No restaurant problem here: there are three. There are also three pools—a 25-meter lap pool, a beach pool with a 120-foot waterslide and a wading pool. The aquatic center is landscaped around a 250-foot waterfall. The resort has a complete fitness center. Cross-country skiing is out the door and an ice-skating rink is the centerpiece of the Plaza area. Rates start at $195 per night.

Squaw Valley Lodge (800-992-9920; in California, 800-922-9970) is on the slopes and only a few yards' walk from the lifts. The lodge boasts a fully equipped health club with four spas, sauna, steam room and heated pool. There is free covered parking, and the units are new, bright roomy studios and one-bedroom units with kitchenettes. Cost: $165 a night and up for a studio midweek.

The Olympic Village Inn (800-VILLAGE or 916-583-1501) is perhaps a bit more luxurious than the Squaw Valley Lodge, but it's about 100 yards further from the lifts. There is no health club, but five hot tubs are available, and all units have kitchens. Rates: $175 a night on weekends, $125 Sunday-Thursday.

The **Squaw Valley Inn** (800-323-ROOM or 916-583-5176) is more like a basic hotel, across from the gondola and cable car. Rates: $135 a night on weekends for deluxe rooms, $100 a night on weekdays. Standard rooms go for $120 a night on weekends, $80 Sunday - Thursday.

Squaw Valley USA also has central reservations: (800) 545-4350 or (916) 583-5585.

Child care

Squaw Valley USA has the **Ten Little Indians Infant Care** program for children six months to two years. It provides supervised activities, age-appropriate arts and crafts, and snow play oriented towards future skiing. The expanded **Papoose Snow School** is a skiing experience for children three to five years. Group activities include pre-skiing exercises and skiing instruction. Costs: all day, per child, $47; additional children from same family in the same program receive a discount; books with five full-day tickets are available. Reservations are *required* for Ten Little Indians Infant Care Center. Call (916) 583-4743.

Alpine Meadows

Alpine Meadows Facts

Base elevation: 6,835; Summit elevation: 8,637'; Vertical drop: 1,800 feet
Number of lifts: 12—1 quad super chair, 2 triple chairs,
8 double chairs, 1 surface lifts
Percent snowmaking: 10 percent, runs from 8 lifts
Total acreage: 2,000 skiable total acres
Uphill capacity: 16,000 per hour; Bed base: 10,000 (N. Lake Tahoe Area)

For every level of skier, particularly the intermediate and advanced skier, Alpine Meadows has something to offer. It has excellent expert terrain, overwhelming intermediate bowls and trails, and an excellent beginners area. Alpine may seem like a relatively small area until you take the Summit Chair and see the area unfold beneath you.

As you ride up the lift, to the right are the expert Wolverine Bowl, Beaver Bowl and Estelle Bowl; to the left spreads the seemingly endless Alpine Bowl, which is graded as intermediate.

Experts approaching Alpine Meadows have plenty of great bowl skiing and enough steeps to keep their hearts in their throats for the most part. Here's a route suggestion: take the expert bowls, to the right ascending the Summit Chair, then take the Summit Chair again and cruise down into the blue territory of Alpine Bowl. Finally, take the Alpine Bowl Chair and traverse to the Sherwood Bowls on the backside of the area or take the High Yellow Traverse to the Saddle Bowl. When you come up the Sherwood Chair, drop down Our Father—and you can say a few enroute—then head to Scott Chair and try out Scott Chute for a direct plunge, or take it easy on tree-lined roundabouts. By then your knees will have earned a cruise. Nearby, the Promised Land has great ski skiing for top skiers.

Intermediates, especially those who are better than average, will find this ski area perfect. Stay in the area all day using the Alpine Bowl Chair, or make endless runs off the Roundhouse and Kangaroo Chairs. Beginners will find themselves limited to a small but sheltered area.

In the Lake Tahoe area, Alpine Meadows has traditionally been the ski area with the longest ski season. If you are planning a trip early or late in the season, this area is your best bet.

Ski School (92/93 prices)

Alpine Meadows divides its lessons into those for beginners, and those for everyone else. The beginner program includes lifts, equipment and three hours of instruction for $50 (children 6-12, $38). Other group lessons are $34 for three hours. A book of five three-hour lessons costs $140. Private lessons are $45 an hour. An early bird special (9 a.m.-10 a.m.) goes for $38. For three or more people, add $15 a person.

Children's Ski School: The youngest age accepted by the Alpine Meadows Snow School is four years. Snow school for children between three and six costs $54 a full day or $47 for an additional child from the same family; $39 a half day or $36 for additional child from same family. Children must be toilet-trained. Registrations are at the ski school desk.

Lift tickets (92/93 prices)

Alpine Meadows: All day, $39 adults; $13, children*; afternoon, $26 adults/$9 children; three days, $108/$38; five days, $175/$55. (*90/91 prices)

Accommodations

Alpine Meadows doesn't have lodging at the base; however, there is a group of condominiums in the valley. Call the North Lake Tahoe number at the end of this chapter.

Northstar-at-Tahoe

> ## Northstar-at-Tahoe Facts
> **Base elevation:** 6,400'; **Summit elevation:** 8,600'; **Vertical drop:** 2,200 feet
> **Number of lifts:** 11—1 gondola, 2 quad super chairs, 3 triple chairs,
> 3 double chairs, 2 surface lifts
> **Percent snowmaking:** 40 percent of developed acres
> **Total acreage:** 1,700 total acres, 400 developed acres
> **Uphill capacity:** 17,500 per hour; **Bed Base:** 1,200 at resort

Unlike Squaw and Alpine, Northstar is a totally planned ski area designed to make skiing easy. Condos are conveniently near the slopes, and the runs have been planned for family skiing. Here an intermediate can feel like Tomba winning a gold medal. The grooming is impeccable—you'll have to look hard for bumps—and the entire ski area management and operations are squeaky clean.

Although Northstar's Mount Pluto is an extinct volcano, you won't find bowls and cornices as at Squaw or that other massive Western volcano, Mammoth. The skiing is all trail-cut off a gentle ridge.

Advanced skiers or those aspiring to the upper levels of intermediate will find some challenge in the drops off the East Ridge (labeled as black diamonds, but the mapmaker was being generous). Normally at least two of the runs are groomed and the others have moderate bumps. Tonini's, to the left of Rendezvous Chair, is the longest, but The Plunge, to the right of Comstock Chair, is the steepest. The only bad part is that it's over too soon. Chute, Crosscut and Powderbowl are also fun—short but sweet. If you're an air skier, you'll be disappointed; these blacks would be blues at Squaw.

Instead of getting your exhilaration by plummeting down some shaft, change your orientation and enjoy the longer rides with moderately steep and sustained pitch off the backside via Lookout Chair and the long traverse called Back Door. This run makes you feel you're in another mountain range, far away from any crowds; five stretched-out swaths provide some of the longest continuous pitches in the West, all served by the Schaffer Camp lift. Though they're all labeled as advanced runs, an intermediate will have no difficulty in good conditions.

The gem of Northstar lies between these runs: through the trees. Start down Rail Splitter, then take off into the woods to the right or left. This is an expert tree-skiing freak's delight. After a storm, Northstar is one of the prime areas where locals can enjoy powder through the trees long after Squaw's powder has been skied off.

True intermediates will feel like "real skiers" on smooth blues like Pioneer, Main Street and Logger's Loop.

Snowboarding

Shredding is allowed on all areas of the mountain. There is a halfpipe, snowboard lessons are available and boards may be rented at the Village Ski Rental Shop.

Ski School (92/93 prices)

Beginner group lessons : Intro to Skiing I gets a two hour of lessons with single lift access and equipment for $39; Intro to skiing II gets the same program but with expanded lifts for $50. Normal two-and-a-half-hour group lessons with all-day lifts for all levels are $25. Three-day programs, including lessons and lifts, are $180. The Starkids all-day program for children, five to 12 is $50 a day with lifts, lessons and lunch (add $10 for equipment).

Lift tickets (92/93 prices)

Northstar-at-Tahoe: All day, $39; afternoon, $28; two-day, $71; three of four days, $110; five of six days, $170; six of seven days, $200. There is a special seniors' rate: $26 a day for skiers 60 to 69, and only $5 for those over 70. A gondola ride will cost $5/$3. Children 5-12 get hefty discounts. Children under five with a parent ski free. NOTE: Northstar limits daily lift pass sales. In event of a sellout, no afternoon passes will be sold.

Accommodations (92/93 prices)

This area was created for condo living. The village has a convenient lodge, with rooms from $100 a night, two-night minimum. The condo rates range from $147 a night for a studio to $240 for a two-bedroom, two-bath unit. Northstar also has full-sized homes for rent, accommodating five to eight people for $300 to $450 a night. Rates are in the upper ranges during holidays. If you decide to stay at Northstar, there are special packages including lifts, rentals and lessons. Reservations: (800) 533-6787.

Child care

The licensed Minors' Camp accepts toilet-trained children two to six years old. The program combines skiing with other activities, including art, snow play, science, drama and language development. Reservations are suggested; call (916) 587-0278. Costs: all day, $35; slightly more for ski instruction. Hours: 8 a.m. to 4:30 p.m. Reservations recommended . There are learn to ski classes with lifts, lessons and lunch starting at $45.

Heavenly Ski Resort

Heavenly Ski Resort Facts
California Side—Base: 6,500'; Summit: 10,100'; Vertical drop: 3,600 feet
Nevada Side—Base: 7,200'; Summit: 10,100'; Vertical drop: 2,900 feet
Number of lifts: 25—Aerial tramway, 2 super quad chair, 6 triple chairs,
9 double chairs, 6 surface lifts; Percent snowmaking: 65 percent (650 acres)
Total acreage: 4,800 patrolled acres (1,084 skiable trail acres)
Uphill capacity: 33,000 per hour; Bed Base: 22,000 in S. Lake Tahoe

Heavenly is big. It ranks number one at Lake Tahoe for highest elevation (10,100 feet), greatest vertical rise (3,600 feet) and longest run (5.5 miles). Except for its famous face run—Gunbarrel—and Mott Canyon, the resort is most appropriate for the giant category of intermediates and advanced skiers. In short, it's tailor-made for 90 percent of America's skiers, with slope grooming, among the best in the United States, on all intermediate runs and the largest snowmaking system in the region.

There are two approaches to skiing Heavenly—from the California side and the Nevada side.

The California side, accessible up Ski Run Boulevard from Highway 50, strikes awe in the beginner because its visible face, Gunbarrel, is a straight ladder of bumps 1,700 feet high, often with dangerous-looking rocky protrusions in early winter or late spring. Leap over that by taking either the Gunbarrel Chair or the quicker aerial tramway. The mountain then has a bit of a dip down to the Waterfall Chair, which gives access to higher elevation skiing off Ridge, Canyon and Sky Chairs.

From the top of Sky the best of the California side opens up. Those looking for bumps can drop down Ellie's, or if you want the long, smooth cruising that Heavenly is known for, head to the right when you get off the chair and

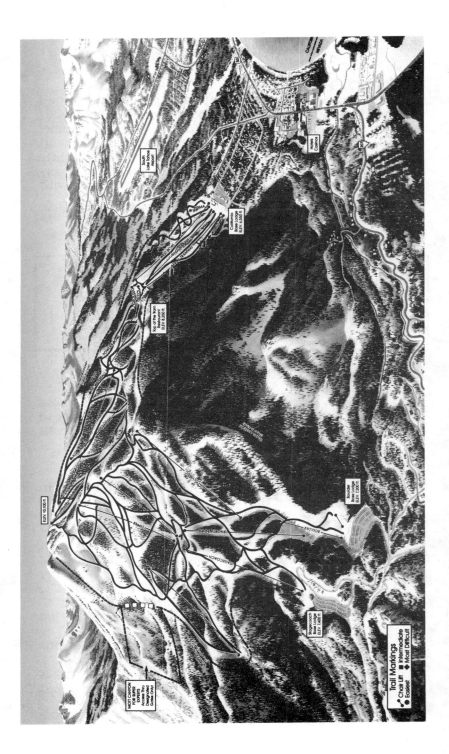

ELEV. 10,100 ft.

South
Lake Tahoe
Airport

Top of the Tram
ELEV. 8,260 ft.

California
Base Lodge
ELEV. 6,550 ft.

Harvey Casino

CALIFORNIA
NEVADA

50

50

ANGEL'S BOWN

STAGECOACH

STAGECOACH

BOULDER

Boulder
Base Lodge
ELEV. 7,200 ft.

Stagecoach
Base Lodge
ELEV. 6,600 ft.

MOTT CANYON
FOR SUPER
EXPERTS
Access Thru
Designated
Gates Only

Trail Markings
● Chair Lift ■ Intermediate
● Easiest ◆ Most Difficult

steam down Liz's Canyon, Betty's or Ridge Run. Any of those four will keep cruisers happy for hours.

When you have had enough of California, strike out for Nevada, where 60 percent of the terrain is located (and where snowboarding is permitted). Skiers entering from the Nevada side via Kingsbury Grade at either Stagecoach or Boulder Base Lodges often experience fewer crowds, but no matter where they start, skiers always want to get to the other state. You get to the Nevada side from the top of Sky; instead of turning right when you get off the chair, go left along the Skyline Trail, which does require a bit of pushing. Now here's the trick for advanced intermediates who want the best of the Milky Way Bowl: the Skyline Trail will dip a bit after you get off the Sky Chair. You then have to make a small climb and the trail starts down again. Just as you begin dropping, look to your right for tracks leading into the trees and follow them. After a short traverse you will end up at the top of the Milky Way Bowl with about twice the vertical you would have found had you stayed on the trail. The same traverse applies to skiers riding on the Dipper, which is the summit chair on the Nevada side. If you ski from the top of Milky Way to the bottom of Mott Canyon in one long run you will drop over 2,000 vertical feet through black and blacker terrain.

The Nevada side has even more intermediate cruises. From the top of the Dipper there are the Big Dipper and Orion, which runs into Jacks—all good intermediate runs. Or advanced intermediates with moguls on their minds can bump down Big Dipper Bowl or traverse a bit further and try the Little Dipper. Another good advanced run is through the ponderosa pines on either side of Little Dipper. The lower sections of the Nevada side have the Galaxy Chair with either Perimeter or The Galaxy. For a cruise that seems to take forever, go all the way down Olympic to Stagecoach Base.

Super-experts who used to scorn Heavenly now have their own playground, Mott Canyon. This north-facing wall is peppered with pines and has about a half-dozen advanced expert chutes. While nothing else at Heavenly will make the hair stand up on experts' necks, Mott Canyon surely will. The area is not served by lifts and can only be entered through designated gates. You will be brought back to civilization by a snowcat.

Home to California means taking Dipper back up to the top and traversing right to the California Run. Or take Comet and then cruise the 49er Run. The runs meander into a small depression where the three-mile, winding Roundabout with spectacular views of Lake Tahoe gets most of the beginner and intermediate traffic at the end of the day. Or with a short lift up, get to the top of Gunbarrel and East Bowl. Here intermediates normally decide to take the tramway or the chair lift down to the base area. Experts and bump-crazies tackle Gunbarrel and East Bowl, two of the longest, steepest bump runs in skidom.

Snowboarding

Snowboarding opened the entire mountain last year. There are no quarterpipes or halfpipes. Lessons and rentals are available on the Nevada and California side.

Ski School (91/92 prices)

Heavenly Valley's Ski School has a beginner special for $40 full day, $20 half day. A two-hour afternoon session costs $20. Private lessons are $50 an hour per person and $22 for each additional person. Programs are available at the California or Nevada base. "Li'l Angels" is a program for all abilities, ages 4-12. Full day ($55) includes instruction, lunch and lifts. Half day ($35) begins at 12:30 p.m., without lunch. Reservations suggested for private lessons, call (916) 541-1330, Ext. 5155.

Lift tickets (91/92 prices)

All day, $39 adult; half day, $27; children under 12 and senior citizen (65 and over) all or half day, $17; three consecutive days, $111; tram ride, $10.50/children under 12 ride free.

Accommodations

Heavenly's base area is in South Lake Tahoe, which means plenty of accommodations. The Nevada side has upscale condominiums and two lovely inns with ski-in/ski-out facilities. See South Lake Tahoe. Heavenly has its own reservation system, which can arrange an entire ski vacation including airfare, transfers, lessons, rentals, skiing and lodging. 800-2-HEAVEN or (702) 588-4584.

Child care

Heavenly has no child care program for those two to four years of age.

The the ski school has a "Li'l Angels" ski instruction program for children ages four to 12. Full day, including lunch, costs $55. Limited half days are available if reservations are made the prior afternoon for $32.

Getting there

Heavenly runs a frequent shuttle service to all the major hotels in South Lake Tahoe ranging from Lakeview on the California side to Lakeside Inn on the Nevada side. This convenience allows you to leave your car at the casino or hotel parking lot and bus on up for skiing.

Kirkwood

Kirkwood Facts

Base elevation: 7.800'; Summit elevation: 9,800'; Vertical drop: 2,000 feet
Number of lifts: 11—4 triple chairs, 6 double chairs
Percent snowmaking: none Total acreage: 2,000 lift-served acres
Uphill capacity: 15,000 per hour; Bed Base: 10,500 in S. Lake Tahoe

---

After the glitz of Heavenly and its casino-laced home town, Kirkwood is like taking a trip back into the wilderness. The lovely drive through Hope Valley to Kirkwood from South Lake Tahoe takes only about 45 minutes, but it is light-years away in altitude and ambiance. There are no bright lights, no jackpots ringing, no wide blue lake, no high-rise buildings and no noise. Instead, you have the feeling that you are entering a special secret place, known to only a select few. From the top of the Wagonwheel lift you see only pristine wilderness.

Kirkwood is a great area for the skiers who have mastered the stem christie and who are just into paralleling. And it will thrill any expert, even super-expert, with its steeps and dozens of chutes. Kirkwood's northeast exposure in a snow pocket gives light, dry conditions and produces storms that linger and dump more.

Beginners will find a great learning area served by Snowkirk Chair to the east, and on the far west there is a beginner area reached by Bunny Chair. Intermediates choose to ski either on the lower sections of the face, using

Lake Tahoe Region

Lake Tahoe Region

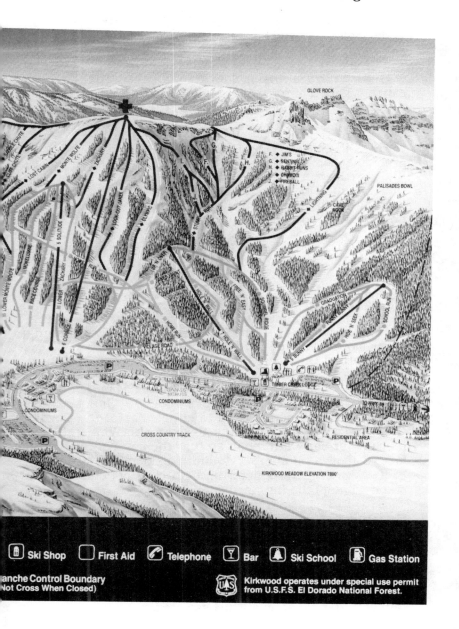

GLOVE ROCK

PALISADES BOWL

F. ◆ JIM'S
G. ◆ SENTINEL
H. ◆ RABBIT RUNS
◆ OHMIGOD
◆ FIREBALL

CAVE ROCK

TIMBER CREEK LODGE

CONDOMINIUMS

CONDOMINIUMS

RESIDENTIAL AREA

CROSS COUNTRY TRACK

KIRKWOOD MEADOW ELEVATION 7800'

🎒 Ski Shop   First Aid   📞 Telephone   🍸 Bar   🔔 Ski School   ⛽ Gas Station

anche Control Boundary
Not Cross When Closed)

Kirkwood operates under special use permit
from U.S.F.S. El Dorado National Forest.

the Hole'n'Wall and Solitude Chairs, or work their way over Caples Crest (Chair Two), then stay high on the trail (far right) and traverse to the Sunrise section. Here there will be plenty of groomed intermediate terrain to the east of Chair Four (Sunrise). This area is called The Wave because it gets a cornice that looks like a giant rounder. On the right, or west side of the chair, the half dozen runs of Thunder Saddle keep powder for three days after a snowfall because it takes two chairs to get skiers there. Watch your step along the ridge. When you get toward the bottom of the steeps, after dropping down One Man Chute, Bogie's Slide or Corner Chute, tuck and keep your speed up—for the flat run back to the Wagonwheel or Cornice chairs.

Chair Ten—Wagonwheel—had a new entry cut to eliminate the leap formerly required to get into the black runs below the Sisters. Some of the best skiing is further west, below False Peak through the chutes and trees that an aggressive intermediate could negotiate with care. But intermediates should first try the Cornice (Chair Six), which is between advanced and pure blue runs. By working the mountain from east to west, as described here, you can keep finding powder as well as new challenges. Never misjudge Kirkwood as a cruiser's mountain, even though lower slopes will suit intermediates.

The Sentinel Bowl gets groomed about every three days or so and is beautiful for anyone looking for super-smooth steeps. (Some experts complain that it needs more bumps.) If you want bumps, try Olympic, Look-Out Janek, Zack's or Monte Wolfe, which drop to either side of the Cornice Chair. Kirkwood often waits to open the Wall until late morning or early afternoon so that the sun can soften the face to allow a bit of edge. California skiers appreciate the wait; New England skiers, used to real ice, can't understand what all the fuss is about.

Snowboarding

Shredding is permitted on all areas of the mountain, however, it is limited off Chair 10 during hard snow conditions. The area has numerous naturally occurring halfpipes and quarterpipes. The ski school has private lessons but no group lessons. Boards may be rented at the Mountain Outfitter ski shop at the base area.

Ski School (91/92 prices)

Kirkwood's Ski School offers group lessons for $18 per two-hour session, which includes an $8 discount on the next lesson. Private lessons cost $50 for an hour and a half, $20 each additional person.

A guaranteed beginner special, including a full day of instruction, beginner lift ticket and rental equipment costs $40. The ski school guarantees that a never-ever will be able to ski the lift-served beginner area by the end of the day, or return for another day for a free lesson.

The ski school rates its classes by the student's preferred terrain and aggressiveness level. All one hour and 45 minute lessons are guaranteed to ski a minimum of 3,000 vertical feet. If this minimum is not met the student may take another lesson free of charge.

For expert skiers there is another Kirkwood program, called Double Black Challenge. Here you will get lessons from a guide who takes skiers "who can ski anything" out to do just that. Believe me, it's out there—friends of mine who lived in Squaw Valley used to come here to do Kirkwood's extremes.

Lift tickets (91/92 prices)

Kirkwood: All day, $35, children 12 and under and seniors 60 and over for $17; half day, $25/$11; three of five consecutive days, $99/$45; five of six consecutive days, $160/$70.

Accommodations

This resort is 30 miles from the lake and many skiers would rather stay here than put up with the 45-minute to one-hour commute from South Lake Tahoe. Of the condominium complexes, the top choice is Sun Meadows, which is directly across from the Solitude and Cornice chairs and about as centrally located as you can get in Kirkwood. The second choice is The Meadows, between Timber Creek and the Cornice Chair. The Whiskey Run condos are a favorite with families because the Mighty Mountain children's ski school is on the ground floor. Rates for all condos are the same. During regular season a standard studio costs $110 on weekends and $75 midweek. A one-bedroom unit, which sleeps up to four, runs $155 on weekends and $120 midweek. A two-bedroom premium unit will cost

$220 on weekends and $160 during the week. Reservations: (209) 258-7000.

Child care

Kirkwood Day Care accepts children out of diapers, three to six years. All day costs $35 including lunch, half day is $25. Hourly charges are $5, and lunch costs $5. The ski school has a "Mighty Mountain" program for children four to 12 which includes equipment, lessons and lifts. This program costs $50 for a full day, including lunch, and $35 for a half day.

Information/reservations

Kirkwood, Box 1, Kirkwood CA 95646; information (209) 258-6000; snow phone (209) 258-3000; reservations (209) 258-7000.

Diamond Peak

Diamond Peak Facts
Base elevation: 6,700'; **Summit elevation:** 8,540'; **Vertical drop:** 1,840 feet
Number of lifts: 7—1 quad super chair, 6 double chairs
Percent snowmaking: 75 percent **Total acreage:** 655, 300 developed acres
Uphill capacity: 7,500 per hour; **Bed Base:** 6,000

Originally called Ski Incline, this small resort was conceived 22 years ago as a neighborhood ski area serving a contented, upscale, family-oriented clientele. But during the last three seasons it doubled its size and vertical drop by its addition of Diamond Peak. It still maintains the flavor of an intimate neighborhood resort, is still small (655 acres) in comparison with other Tahoe resorts, and is still primarily an intermediate mountain. Even so, it's fun for skiers who have been coming to Tahoe for years to find something new to ski.

The skiing is in two directions: The Ridge, ending at the old octagonal Snowflake Lodge overlooking Lake Tahoe; and Diamond Peak, the recent expansion. The runs off The Ridge, served by Lakeview Chair, are gentle blacks and blues, relatively short, each with only a very short pitch that most advanced skiers would call a genuine black. Crystal Ridge off Diamond Peak is a long blue, while the canyons and gullies off it are considered advanced, with slightly steeper pitches than off the Lakeview Chair. Most of the expert terrain here, however, would be labeled intermediate at Squaw.

This is a great learner's mountain because of its friendly atmosphere and small size. For a resort as small as Diamond Peak, it's surprising to note that its ski school numbers 100 instructors—equal to Heavenly or Kirkwood—another indication that Diamond Peak is a good place to learn to ski. For children 6-12, for example, Sierra Scouts mixes ski instruction with the natural history of the Lake Tahoe region. Service clearly is a high priority, and snowmaking covers 75 percent of the developed ski area. A strong point is that even the highest chair, Diamond Peak, is sheltered, so it can run in heavy winds. In fact, when other North Shore resorts shut down because of wind, they send skiers to Diamond Peak.

Crowds will never be a problem. Ticket sales are cut off between 3,000 and 4,000. At Diamond Peak the priority is the ski experience of its guests.

Ski school (91/92 prices)

All day group lessons are $36 ; half day is $23. Private lessons are $45 an hour. A Learn-to-Ski Special, including lifts, rentals and all-day lesson is $45; half day is $29.

Sugar Bowl

Eschewing glitz and growth, Sugar Bowl is one of the oldest resorts in Lake Tahoe and the oldest chairlift-served resort in California. From the moment you step out of your car and board the gondolas to ride *down* to the lifts across a pristine valley, you feel you're stepping back in time. Most likely when you descend from the gondola, you'll see a classic red sleigh. You'll see no cars: the gondola ride is the only access.

Skiing at Sugar Bowl is full of surprises. Runs, especially those off 8,383-foot Mt. Lincoln, are a series of chutes and gullies with twists and bumps and loops and swoops, all giving the advanced skier a terrific roller coaster ride. There's constant decision-making because of interlacing routes downhill—not trails exactly, just ways to go. Confident skiers will love the g-forces unleashed when banking off the sides of narrow drainages, separating for a few moments from skiing buddies, then reconverging where the routes intersect. Sugar Bowl is not a put-it-in-neutral-and-glide kind of mountain.

Intermediates can enjoy the peak by heading far to the left when getting off Silver Belt Chair, where they will find runs like Lake View and Bill Klein's Schuss to their liking.

The other mountain, Mt. Disney, has some easier expert runs off either drainage of a ridge, with wide intermediate terrain to the far right for cruising. Beginners will find meandering routes on either side of Christmas Tree Chair, some of which take them through a quaint little neighborhood of chalets.

Sugar Bowl is recommended for a day's change of pace from the larger Tahoe resorts. The feeling of intimacy captured by the unique entry and the highly interesting swoops and gullies of Mt. Lincoln are sheer delights.

Ski school (91/92 prices)

A two-hour session is $20; two sessions will cost $32. Private lessons are $40 an hour, with each additional person $15. The beginner learn-to-ski package of lift, lesson and rental is $39 for adults, $32 for children.

Lift tickets (91/92 prices)

Day tickets are $33 for adults and $14 for children (6-12). Half day tickets cost $22 for adults and $11 for children. For seniors 65 and older, $14 weekdays. Children under 5 ski free.

Accommodations

The only lodging at Sugar Bowl is at the **Le Grand Hotel**, actually the base lodge building, cafeteria and ski services all in one, a quaint, three-story wooden structure built in 1939. Rooms have older furniture and convey the back-in-time atmosphere with historic photos and mementos. The dining room no longer has a dress code as it once did, but still preserves the grace of a former era. Call (916) 426-3651.

Child care

Sugar Bowl is establishing a day-care program this season. Contact the resort for more information.

Information/reservations

Sugar Bowl, Box 5, Norden CA 95724; information and reservations (916) 426-3651; ski conditions (916) 426-3847.

Information/reservations

South Lake Tahoe: (800) 822-5922

North Lake Tahoe : (800) TAHOE-4U

Reno: (800) FOR-RENO

Each resort also has a central reservation system for hotels in their area.

Alpine Meadows, Box 5279, Tahoe City CA 95730; Information (916) 583-4232; snow phone (916) 583-6914; reservations (800) TAHOE-4U.

Squaw Valley USA, Box 2007, Olympic Valley CA 96146; information (916) 583-6985; snow phone (916) 583-6955; admin. (916) 583-6985; reservations (800) 545-4350.

Northstar-at-Tahoe, Box 129, Truckee CA 95734; information and reservations (916) 587-0200 or (800) 533-6787.

Kirkwood, Box 1, Kirkwood CA 95646; information (209) 258-6000; snow phone (209) 258-3000; reservations (209) 258-7247.

Heavenly, Box 2180, Stateline NV 89449; information (916) 541-1330; ski conditions (916) 541-SKII; reservations (702) 588-4584 or (800) 2-HEAVEN.

Diamond Peak, Box AL, top of Ski Way, Incline Village NV 89450; information (702) 832-1177; ski phone: (702) 831-3211; reservations (800) TAHOE-4-U.

Sugar Bowl, Box 5, Norden CA 95724; information and reservations (916) 426-3651; ski conditions (916) 426-3847.

Lake Tahoe Savoir Faire

There are so many restaurants in the Lake Tahoe area from small back-alley breakfast joints to exclusive gourmet establishments that regardless of where your base is, you're sure to find something that interests you nearby. However, no matter which end of the lake you call home, there's one restaurant that is not to be missed. **Christy Hill** in Tahoe City (115 Grove Street—reservations 916-583-8551) is a real find. Just on the edge of the Lake Tahoe North Shore, Christy Hill offers superb lake views in an intimate, casually elegant atmosphere. Chef/owner Matt Adams and his wife Debbie are charming hosts, and this added hospitality makes every visit here a delight.

The menu, which changes several times each week, is loaded with the freshest fish and specialty produce. Matt's fascination with eastern flavors is evident, but his style is pure California. Start with a sashimi of fresh Hawaiian ahi, or fresh Pacific bay scallops, broiled on a skewer and served with an orange, jalapeño and cilantro butter sauce. You are almost sure to find the house-smoked chicken in one of Matt's pasta dishes—perhaps with sun-dried tomato, spinach and goat cheese as a ravioli. Or start with a salad of sesame broiled tiger prawns with spicy napa cabbage. It is served with a ginger, soy, cilantro and scallion dressing.

Entrées include fresh Hawaiian mahi, lightly blackened with three peppers and served with a southwestern style sauce of dried chilis and roasted red bell peppers. Or try the fresh California poussin, roasted with an apple, ginger, tarragon and wild rice chutney. Save room for the fabulous desserts. The hot fresh pear cobbler is outstanding! The restaurant is open for dinner only from Tuesday through Sunday from 5:30 p.m. Appetizers are $7-$8 and entrées range from $18 to $23. This is truly a meal to remember.

If you are in the mood for an adventure, also in the North Lake area, try the **Basque Restaurant at Northstar**. This family style fixed-price restaurant is run by Northstar. For $14.25 ($7 for children), you can have your fill of a hearty soup, salad, two entrées, and dessert. Menus vary daily and, not surprisingly, feature Basque specialties. The paella with saffron rice is a favorite. And the duck with an orange thyme glaze is a prize winner from a local winter festival.

Sit at long tables with your friends and order carafes of the house wine (quite a bargain at $5), or join the action outside with the specially scheduled marshmallow roasts and sleigh rides. For reservations call (916) 562-2460. The restaurant is open daily, 5 p.m.-9:30 p.m., winter only.

Harrah's Casino offers a number of dining choices, **The Summit** being the ultimate in gourmet dining. Recently it was relocated to the Star Suite for a more intimate ambiance with the feel of a private home. Executive chef Hans Limberg has put together an outstanding menu for the new Summit. Appetizers include a marinated quail with apple fritters and an American style caviar mosaic. Entrées range from chateaubriand to lobster thermidor. There is always a hot soufflé on the menu—perhaps raspberry with white chocolate crème fraîche. Appetizers are priced from $8 to $15, with entrées ranging from $24 to $32. A prix-fixe four-course dinner is $50.

The Summit is open for dinner only (6 p.m.-10 p.m.; and is closed Tuesday) reservations are strongly recommended. Call (702) 588-6611 Ext. 2196 to reserve a table.

At Harvey's, Chef Norbert Koblitz also manages to feed crowds of hungry gamblers. The top restaurant there is **The Sage Room Steak House**. For a throwback to the days of tableside cooking and great service, come to this original 1950s dining room which was rebuilt beam by beam several years ago after being almost completely destroyed. The interior, with its hand-hewn beams and redwood ceiling, is part of the original Wagon Wheel Saloon and Gambling Hall established in 1944.

Though it's called a steak house and all beef is aged on the premises, Chef Koblitz is very creative in promoting unique ingredients and inventive American cuisine. Try the beef and lobster chili with goat cheese or, my favorite, the black bean soup. The Sage Room Steak Gilroy is aged and cooked with a crust of garlic purée and potatoes. If you enjoy tableside preparation, try the roast Long Island duckling bigarade or the popular Steak Diana. There are also many tableside flambéed desserts and coffees, including bananas Foster and cherries jubilee. Entrées range from $18.50 for prime rib to $35 for Australian lobster tail. The Sage Room is open daily from 6 p.m. to 10 p.m. For reservations, call (702) 588-2411.

by Katy Keck

Bear Valley Ski Company California

No one gets to Bear Valley by accident. East of Angels Camp, California State Highway 4 climbs 50 miles to the ski area. It is the only way in. Ebbetts Pass, above the resort, narrows to steep avalanche chutes. In summer Porsche, BMW, and other car clubs make a scenic loop through this area and the Markleeville Death Ride sends humped bicyclists streaking over five passes. In winter, Highway 4 shuts down at Ebbetts Pass, just beyond the ski area—the passes are choked with snow.

Bear Valley Ski Company is the ski mountain, equipped with seven double chairs and two triples, and Bear Valley village is the crash pad, three miles away and home to a small, low-key settlement of lodges, condos, shops and restaurants. It's all about halfway between Lake Tahoe to the north and Yosemite National Park to the south, but in spirit, layout and design, Bear Valley is a lot closer to rustic backwoods Yosemite than the gaudy commercial ring around Tahoe. This is wool-shirt, fireplace, pickup-truck country.

But the residents seem backwoods by choice, not necessity: just out of sight of the tourist part of Bear Valley village is a subdivision with some 500 custom-home lots, home to symphony conductors, sculptors, company CEOs, and Hollywood refugees. Its most famous residents (of those who don't mind the publicity) are actors Lloyd Bridges and Robert Conrad. While we were in the small,

---

Bear Valley Facts
Base elevation: 6,600'; Summit elevation: 8,495'; Vertical drop: 1,900 feet
(Note: the base lodge is at 7,700 feet)
Number of lifts: 9—2 triple chairs, 7 double chairs, 2 surface lifts
Percent snowmaking: 35% Total acreage by trails: 1,280 skiable acres
Uphill capacity: 12,000 per hour Bed Base: 400

stocked-to-the-ceiling general store, another well-known face walked in; she doesn't like anyone to reveal her hideaway, but she's the star of a TV show about lawyers in a large West Coast city.

Bear Valley may not look like much on the surface, but if you dig a little you'll hit paydirt.

Where to ski

This is a skiers' mountain, like a small Squaw Valley. It has chutes, it has cliffs, it has moguls, it has bowls that fill with deep powder. And it has an unusual layout—you get out of your car and there you are at the *top* of Grizzly Bowl, which never has a lift line. Looking down rather than up at advanced terrain, you see a bowl big enough to gobble up a ton of skiers. A serious skier can get in miles and miles of skiing, and the best part is that Grizzly is all advanced and expert; you won't need to dodge any members of the Green Circle Gang.

If your sole intention is to ski Grizzly, though, check the snow conditions before you make the trip. California has had a severe drought the past few years, and Grizzly is the last part of the mountain to open, because of its lower altitude and steep terrain. But the upper mountain also has a few steep, moguled runs, as well as some dense tree skiing below Tuck's Run.

Intermediates will like the runs under the Pooh Bear and Hibernation chairs on the backside of the mountain: nearly every run is rated blue, with a couple of black diamonds thrown in to keep things lively. Back here are intermediate-size moguls and intermediate-thick tree stands, so that this level of skier can have some fun without being scared out of his or her bindings. Another great place for intermediates is the Koala Chair; the runs aren't quite so long as on the backside, making them a good choice for beginners and lower intermediates.

One warning for blue-square skiers: you may pick up a trail map showing an intermediate run snaking into Grizzly. Don't believe it: they planned to groom a trail into the bowl, and even printed the maps, but then found the terrain was too steep for a groomer. Stay out of there unless you're quite confident in ungroomed snow.

The area usually does very well with snow, averaging 450 inches a year, which is up with Kirkwood and Mammoth as best in the state.

Although the uphill capacity bed-base ratio is fantastic, Bear Valley gets *lots* of day skiers, especially on weekends; there are sometimes lift lines in good snow years, but not, so they say, as bad as at Tahoe.

Mountain rating

Good for all levels but surprisingly good for experts. The bear motif makes it easy to know which lifts will take you to trails that are right for your ability—if it's a cuddly type of bear, such as Cub or Koala, the terrain is gentle. If it's Kodiak or Grizzly, the experience will be gr-r-reat or gr-r-ruesome, depending on your ability.

Snowboarding

This is also a snowboarders' mountain. Not only do shredders have free rein, but they also have an area where no skiers are allowed. with its own rope tow.

Cross-country

Skinny-ski fans are going to love this place. Bear Valley Cross-country, across Highway 4 from the village, is the second largest cross-country area in the Western U. S. It has 120 km. of set track, 14 trails for beginners, 12 for intermediates, and five for experts. Trail huts and picnic tables are scattered throughout the trail system, and the Warming Hut Café—in the midst of the beginner trails— provides a cafeteria, restrooms, and a sundeck. They even have a heli-skiing operation for back-country excursions.

Trail fees (91/92 prices) are $12.50 for adults, $10 for those 13 to 17 and for seniors 60+, $8 for kids 8 to 12, free for those younger than 8. Rentals are $12 for adults, $8 for kids; and private lessons are $26 an hour, group lessons are $15. A beginner pass—lesson, rentals, pass—is $28.

Ski school (91/92 prices)

Group lessons begin at 10:30 a.m. and 2 p.m. Private and snowboard lessons are available by appointment. Two-hour group lessons are $20, while a double session (morning and afternoon) costs $30. A book of five lessons is $85. Private instruction is $35 per hour, $15 for each additional person. The school offers lesson-lift-equipment-rental packages for beginners for $50 an all-day lift ticket and two hours of lessons.

Bear Valley offers two programs for children 4 to 12: Kinderski, a group lesson not including equipment or lift ticket, is $20 a two-hour session, $30 a double session. The Skiing Bears program lasts all day and includes morning and afternoon lessons, lift ticket, equipment rental, lunch and indoor supervision between classes, all for $50; reservations necessary. Call: (209) 723-2301, Ext. 181.

There are also lessons by appointment for physically challenged skiers, with adaptive equipment available (795-5811). Call 753-2301 for general information.

Lift tickets (92/93 prices)

Bear Valley is offering very low lift ticket prices with midweek discounts.

	Midweek	Weekend/Holiday
Adults	$20	$25
Child (7-12)	$10	$12
Senior (65 and over)	$10	$10
Disabled	$10	$10

Child care

On weekends there is a state-liscensed Bear Care program for children two years of age and older.

For parents of younger children, the best choice for now is the baby sitters who advertise on the bulletin board outside the general store.

Accommodations

The Bear Valley village can accommodate about 400 in the 52-room Bear Valley Lodge, the 14-room Red Dog Lodge, 52 condos and 10 houses.

The **Bear Valley Lodge** is a large, rustic four-story building with wood shingles on its outside walls. Its rooms encircle a central cathedral-ceilinged lounge with a gigantic bouldered fireplace at one end. Its rooms, newly remodeled and all with private baths, range from $79 to $189. The lodge also has a dining room, bar, two hot tubs, and massage rooms. Midweek ski-lodging packages start at $68.50 per person double occupancy.

Nearby **Red Dog Lodge** has 14 shared-bath rooms starting at $50 per room for one or two people, up to $70 nightly for a four-person room.

Condo rates range from $75 to $235, with most about $100 per night.

Powderbear Accommodations features snowbound log cabins accessible by snowcat and accommodating up to eight people. After the snowcat delivers you and your luggage, you cross-country ski in and out. (Powderbear also has condos to which you can drive.) The cost is $180 a night, with a two-night minimum. Just a note: Bear Valley residents can't drive to their exclusive houses either—they use snowmobiles or skis.

The Red Dog Lodge is (209) 753-2344, and Powderbear Accommodations is (209) 753-2136. For lodging information in other towns along Highway 4, including the historic mining town of Angels Camp, call (800) 695-3737.

The only lodging within walking distance of the ski area is in skiers' RVs. No hookups are available, but RVs may park overnight in a special lot.

Reservations for the area can be made through Bear Valley Ski Corp at (209) 753-6700.

Dining

Food in Bear Valley is more hearty and substantial than gourmet. At the ski area the Hungry Bear Gourmet Café has just been remodeled and the menu has been upgraded—we haven't eaten there, you'll have to be the judge. There is also a weekend barbeque on the sun deck.

Both the **Bear Valley Lodge** and **Red Dog Lodge** dining rooms feature steak, chicken, and pasta dishes, with good wine lists. Food and atmosphere are a few steps higher than coffee shop, but not as ritzy as Deer Valley or Aspen. Entrées are in the $10 to $15 price range. The Lodge is your best breakfast bet, particularly the French toast. And coming in or out of Bear Valley, stop for a meal at the 131-year-old **Dorrington Hotel and Restaurant**. Its Italian Continental meals are served family-style, with soup, salad, antipasto and homemade bread.

Nightlife

People must ski so hard in Grizzly Bowl or at Bear Valley Cross-country that they hit the sack early. There is no movie theater; several TV channels come in clearly.

There are five bars in the area. The **Altitude**, across from the Bear Valley Lodge, is a skiers' bar and has live music ranging from soft rock to country rock. **The Red Dog Saloon** is rustic, has live music, a pool table and is a favorite with with locals. There has also a new bar in the Bear Valley Lodge.

Other activities

The closing of Ebbetts Pass to cars during the winter means great snowmobiling. In addition to miles of groomed trails, scenic areas in the Ebbetts Pass Wonderland are approved for snowmobile expeditions. There are self-guided and tour-guided options, and a permit costs $3. Rental and tour information: (209) 753-2323.

An acre-sized ice-skating rink opened last winter at Bear Valley Cross Country Ski Area. A two-hour ticket is $3, skate rentals $4.

Getting there

The resort is 52 miles east of Angels Camp and 96 miles east of Stockton on Highway 4, a spectacular drive through the Stanislaus National Forest. It is a three-hour drive from the San Francisco Bay area, two hours from Tahoe, and seven or eight hours from Los Angeles.

Information/reservations

For information, write Bear Valley Ski Company, Box 5038, Bear Valley, CA 95223; 753-2301.

For lodging information and reservations, call (209) 753-BEAR. The 24-hour snow phone: 753-2308. Lodging information: (800) 695-3737.

Local telephone area code is 209.

Mammoth Mountain June Mountain California

They said it was too high, too remote, too stormy—that it would never make it as a ski resort in the West. That was in the 1930s. Today, this resort is perhaps the busiest ski area in the nation, with 14,000 skiers swarming over its slopes on an average weekend. This is the remains of a massive prehistoric volcano, and even now with most of it missing, the surrounding ridge gives access to half a dozen wide bowls, the largest one, once the interior of the cone, a whopping 13,000 feet wide. In addition, lower peaks like Lincoln Mountain, Gold Hill and Hemlock Ridge, all carved with groomed swaths and moguled canyons, stretch six and a half miles in width. This resort's name is apt because its size is no secret.

Fifty years ago Dave McCoy strapped homemade skis on his back and hiked off into the wilderness to develop a ski resort. Against all odds—poverty, weather, timing— and in quiet defiance of doubters, he began to sculpt the mountain to his vision, this man who had never ridden a ski lift. The mountain was his passion, playground and creation, and any profits went back into it. The result was that McCoy has pioneered much of the lift equipment that is now the industry standard. Still run as a family operation, the resort bears the mark of his daily presence.

Mammoth Mountain Facts

Base elevation: *7,953';* **Summit elevation:** *11,053';* **Vertical drop:** *3,100 feet.*
Number and types of lifts: *30—5 superchairs, 7 triple chairs, 14 double chairs,*
2 gondolas, 2 surface lifts **Acreage:** *3,500 skiable acres*
Percent of snowmaking: *20 percent 22 trails, 200 acres*
Uphill capacity: *46,000 skiers per hour* **Bed base:** *30,000*

The Main Lodge is a three-level labyrinth of passage-ways for lockers and services. The output of food is stag-gering—a thousand pastries daily and, together with its two other lodges, Hut II and Mid-Chalet, 40,000 dozen eggs for breakfasts each season, which, in some years, lasts from Thanksgiving to the Fourth of July.

If size intimidates you, Mammoth's little sister, June Mountain, a half-hour drive from the town of Mammoth Lakes, will appeal. Its Old-World village atmosphere in a sheltered canyon is on a more human scale, and newcom-ers won't tend to feel lost. That is not to say it's a puny re-sort. Seven chairlifts and an aerial tram scale a 2,590-foot vertical rise (as opposed to 3,100 feet at Mammoth).

Where to ski

The mountain is crisscrossed with a network of chair lifts numbered in the order they were built. Chair 22, for example, is on a different peak from Chair 23. For those who grew up with the mountain it makes perfect sense, but it may be confusing for the first-timer who hears regulars planning their day football-quarterback style: "Take one to three, then backside to 23, down the ridge to 14, then to 13 and lateral to 19."

First-time visitors cannot conceive of the size of the mountain on their first trip: it takes years to learn the whole mountain. Regulars like to try to ski the whole mountain in one day, a project not accomplished by many. This does not mean to ski every face and every run—that's impossible. In local vernacular "ski the whole mountain" means to ride the gondola and every chair lift (26 of them) and T-bar (one of those) once in the course of a day. Calculating the route takes an engineer's planning; executing it takes an expert skier (read: "speed freak") from 8 a.m. (opening) to 4 p.m. (closing) without stopping .

One of the most popular advanced areas is the group of bowls available from Chair 3. They're great warmup runs for experts, but plan to get here early. By 9:30 a.m. or 10

June Mountain Facts

Base elevation: 7,545'; Summit elevation: 10,135'; Vertical drop: 2,590 feet.
Number and types of lifts: 8—2 quad chairs, 5 double chairs, 1 "QMC" tram.
Acreage: 500+ skiable acres
Uphill capacity: 12,000 skiers per hour Bed base: 30,000 region, 2,000 local

a.m. on weekends, the line is outrageous, although it diminishes at lunchtime. At busy times, knowing skiers head for Chair 19, which offers half a dozen runs hidden in a glen; these resist crowds and keep their grooming late into the day. Also, Chairs 22 and 25, which provide access to Lincoln Mountain and its intermediate runs and advanced chutes, rarely have lines, a phenomenon that amazes locals who know them.

Chair 1, a high-speed detachable quad, takes off from the Main Lodge. It is especially popular because experts can either plunge down Gravy Chute or weave through The Wall, a panel of bubbly moguls, while their intermediate friends can coast down the wide, smooth Broadway and meet them at the bottom.

On powder days, locals and regulars head immediately for the gondola to the summit. From there, every direction down is inside the ski area and the choices expand with the descent. Early-morning experts stick to the more central Cornice, an overhanging lip at the volcano rim with a wide apron of mogul field on the steep, but as the powder is tracked, they head to the far east Dragon's Back off Chair 9, or the far west Hemlock Ridge above Chair 14, where tree skiing and untouched powder remain. Only the uninitiated think the world begins and ends on The Cornice.

A mechanical race course is set up on Bowling Alley just to the right of Broadway.

Mountain rating

Mammoth Mountain has terrain for all levels of skier. Although that snarling lip of snow, The Cornice, looms large in every western skier's memory or hopes, it's not the most treacherous. Other runs known by ominous names like Paranoid, Drop Out, Wipe Out and Climax command that reputation. Reached from the gondola, Hangman's is an hour-glass-shaped chute hanging from the summit and bordered by wicked rocks; at its narrow part there's space for only one turn—a perfect one.

Chair 23, the summit chair, rising 1,100 vertical feet in a distance of 2,629, sucks skiers up into a steel-and-glass weather shelter, which dips down over the top and looks like a huge vacuum nozzle. The 360-degree view from the 11,000 foot ridge is spectacular—to the northeast there's Nevada, to the west the jagged Minarets and the

Ansel Adams Wilderness Area. Straight down, there's a relentless mogul field.: off the backside, a gentle summer road and somewhat steep intermediate wide-open spaces.

The mid-to-lower mountain lets the intermediate traverse vast expanses and crisscross runs. Hidden canyons like Lower Dry Creek are full of swoops and surprises, and require tighter turns.

Trails like Hansel and Gretel weave gently through evergreens, and there are sheltered slopes for learning, tucked away from the paths of mad-dash demons shooting down from the top. (Look out for these on Stump Alley, a crowded all-out raceway down to Chair 2.) Hidden gullies give even the beginning skier variety; the nursery slopes (off Chair 11 at the Main Lodge and Chair 7 from Hut II) have as much imagination as more difficult terrain.

Beginners and intermediates will find June Mountain challenging, although it has none of the high, broad bowls that make Mammoth Mountain famous. The steepest terrain at June, The Face, as steep as anything at Mammoth, is on the lower mountain so unfortunately doesn't keep the snow as long as the upper runs—intermediate cruisers and expert chutes like Davos Drop and Pro Bowl. Since June is more sheltered than Mammoth and none of its slopes is above the tree line, June tends to hold powder longer than some of the more exposed bowls at Mammoth. With snow falling more gently, not getting wind-packed, and because of the colder temperatures of the June Lake horseshoe canyon, the snow doesn't crust up so quickly. The pace at June is slower, the crowds considerably fewer and sometimes nonexistent, and the atmosphere friendly. June is less intimidating for the first-time skier for whom getting through the maze of passageways at the Mammoth Main Lodge is often the first challenge.

Snowboarding

Both Mammoth and June offer snowboarding on all runs. June Mountain is the snowboard center with a halfpipe and national competitions. Snowboarding lessons and rentals are available at both areas.

Cross-country

Ski touring in the Mammoth vicinity focuses on three main centers: Tamarack Lodge, Sierra Meadows and Rock Creek Winter Lodge.

Twenty to 25 miles of groomed trails, actually summer roads, serpentine around four of the dozen or more high alpine lakes, from which the town Mammoth Lakes is named. **Tamarack Lodge,** a 50-year-old summer hunting and fishing lodge, maintains these trails and charges $9 for access to the tracks (children under 18 free). The Lakes Basin includes many trail heads into the backcountry, where no fee is charged. Rentals are available from Tamarack Lodge at $12 for adults and $8 for children. An hour-and-a-half group lesson is $15. On weekends it's advisable to reserve ahead: Tamarack Lodge, Box 69, Mammoth Lakes CA 93546; (619) 934-2442.

Just out of town at the 8,000-foot level, **Mammoth Meadow,** a broad expanse of open area, is maintained by Sierra Meadows Equestrian and Ski Touring Center. A network of 55 kilometers of mainly flat, wide-open territory, machine groomed, gives a magnificent view of Sherwin Bowl (now under negotiation as another downhill area). Trail access is $7 for adults, $5 for children. Half day is $4 and $2. Rentals are $12 for adults, $8 for children all day. Half-day rentals are $8 and $5. Hour-and-a-half group lessons begin at 10 a.m., noon and 2 p.m. for $15 a person. Make reservations for advanced, telemark and children's lessons. A private lesson is $25 for an hour and a half. Box 2008, Mammoth Lakes, CA 93546; (619) 934-6161.

The **U. S. Forest Service** gives ski tours of Mono Lake, explaining the bizarre geological formations, at 1 p.m. on Saturdays and Sundays during heavy snow times. Reserve at (619) 934-2505.

Ski school (91/92 prices)

At peak season, Mammoth's ski school has 350 instructors. Prices do not include lift tickets (except for first-time beginners), but lift privileges ahead of lines are automatic. At either Mammoth or June, an all-day group lesson, with six to ten in a group, is $32; half day is $20. A book of five all-day group lessons is $150.

Children's group lessons for ages four to12 begin at 10 a.m. and include lunch and supervision during lunch, as well as four hours of lessons. The cost is $48 per child. Funland at Mammoth, for ages four to six, introduces children to snow walking, equipment and easy gliding; half-day sessions are $20.

Private lessons for adults or children cost $55 for one hour for one or two people. $10 is charged for each additional person.

A five-day advanced skiing clinic, conducted from 9 a.m. to 4 p.m. at Mammoth Mountain only, is $170. This clinic is offered once a month only, on the first Monday of the month; reservations required.

A weekend special just for first-time beginners includes an all-day lesson on Saturday, a half-day lesson on Sunday morning and lift privileges for $74. A three-day Learn-to-Ski package for first-time beginners includes rentals, lifts and lessons and costs $182 for adults, $131 for children (or $171 for children if lunch and lunchtime supervision are included). This package applies only to three consecutive days.

All lessons are available at both the Main Lodge and Hut II. Reservations are not necessary, but questions can be answered at (619) 934-2571, Ext. 3285 for Main Lodge, Ext. 3287 for Hut II. June Mountain Ski School number is (619) 648-7733.

Lift tickets (92/93 prices)

Adult all day, $37; half day, $27. Child all day, $19; half day, $14. Children 6 and under ski free. Seniors 65 and over ski free.

Lift tickets are interchangeable for Mammoth and June Mountains. There are free lift privileges for never-evers taking a ski school lesson.

Five-day tickets for, non-holiday periods cost $148. For information, call (619) 934-2571.

Ticket offices are located at the Main Lodge, Warming Hut II and Chair 15 access areas, as well as June Mountain. Additional satellite offices at Chairs 4, 10 and 2 are open weekends and holidays.

Accommodations (91/92 prices)

One of the nicest places to stay, **Mammoth Mountain Inn**, is also closest to the slopes—just across the parking lot. Lodging is deluxe to moderate, including hotel units with room service, motel and condominium units. Rates are $95 for rooms to $350 for a condo that sleeps eleven. There are two restaurants in the complex and a cafeteria breakfast across the street at the Yodler and the Main Lodge, but several-day visitors may wish to visit the town, four miles downhill, for dinner and nightlife. Box 353; (800) 228-4947. (All addresses conclude with Mammoth Lakes CA 93546.)

Mammoth has been called "Condo City of the Sierras." Just beyond town, **Snowcreek** is huge, wooded, spread out and posh, with athletic club including racquetball and basketball. It's actually a neighborhood at the edge of town and is the last stop on the shuttle system. Guests must drive or take the shuttle to restaurants. Units are spacious one-, two- and three-bedroom loft style, $142-$240. Box A-5; (619) 934-3333 or (800) MAMMOTH.

Closer to the slopes, in fact adjacent to Hut II, two other large condominium complexes have a range of units. **Sierra Megeve, Mountainback, 1849 Condominiums**, and **Aspen Creek** costs between $175 and $326 depending on size and amenities.

In the middle of town, where you can walk to restaurants and the shuttle to the lifts is adjacent, **Sierra Nevada Inn** offers hotel rooms starting at $65 and chalet units up to $280. **The Snow Goose Inn** is one of three bed-and-breakfast inns in town. Decorated with antiques, with breakfast served communally in a friendly atmosphere, the feel is homey and approximate price is $82, or $180 for a deluxe suite. Box 946; (800) 874-7368.

The least expensive private rooms are at **Motel 6**, but it takes no reservations. Three places offer dorm rooms: **Kitzbuhel Lodge** is good for groups and young people, with a huge dining room and group kitchen. Three to 14 beds are in each room. Cost is $20 a night for men and women. Box 433; (619) 934-2352. Besides motel rooms and large suites, **Alpenhof Lodge** has dorm rooms for $64 for men only, with three beds to a room and the bath at the end of the hall. Box 1157; (619) 934-6330; (800) 828-0371. **Ullr Lodge** is a European-style dorm for men only, mainly share-a-bath rooms, for less than $20 a night. They will rent to women if four take one room. Box 53; (619) 934-2454. The last two are on the shuttle line right in town.

At June, prices are generally lower. There are two large condominium complexes. **Interlaken** charges from $85 for studios midweek to $185 for three-bedroom units. Weekend prices are $120-$240. **Edgewater** has only one size unit, suitable for six to nine people, for $105 midweek to $165 on weekends. All other lodgings at June are small and quaint, even funky. **The Haven** has studios for $65. **Fern Creek Lodge** has cabins for $38 and motel rooms for $59. **Whispering Pines** has motel rooms for $59 and cabins for $75. **Boulder Lodge** has motel rooms for $48 and cabins for $85, some of which can sleep 17 people.

A full-service RV park is four miles from the resort .

Dining

There are more than 45 dining options in Mammoth, from gourmet French cuisine to delicatessen sandwiches and quick take-out. The top-of-the-line establishment recognized by all is **Novita's**, but expect to pay handsomely. Continental cuisine with unusual dishes, dinner. Reservations necessary; 934-4466. Mammoth Mountain Inn's **Mountainside Bar and Grill** is worth the trip up the mountain from town. Another trip from town (sort of romantic) is to the 50-year-old **Tamarack Inn at Twin Lakes**. (Take a walk in the moonlight afterward, or enjoy the lobby fireplace.) **The Lakefront** serves a light sautéed, California cuisine of fish, meat and fowl. Reservations: 934-2442.

A little less expensive in town, **Whiskey Creek**, 934-2555, is the local steak house (trendy with ferns) and **Ocean Harvest** the prime seafood restaurant. **Shogun**, 934-3970, has Japanese cuisine and a sushi bar. Ribs in abundance can be had at **Angel's**, 934-7427.

Grumpy's, 934-8587, is the locals' favorite for casual eating. **Swiss Cafe**, Old Mammoth Road; 934-6196 and **Matsu's**, 934-8277, for Chinese-American, are also popular and inexpensive. **Nik-N-Willie's Take-N-Bake Pizza**, 934-2012, is convenient for the eat-in-condo set. The best Mexican food is at **Roberto's**, 934-3667. **Berger's Restaurant**, 934-6622, is a long-time tradition for locals and the college crowd, not only for burgers but chicken, salad, Canadian stew, and homemade pastries like carrot cake and cheesecake. There is also the recognizable **Cask 'n Cleaver**, with a well-stocked salad bar.

Après-ski/nightlife

Across the parking lot from the Main Lodge, the **Yodler**, 934-2581, swings. It has a large-screen TV and a bartender who will try anything. There is no après-ski activity at Hut II, which serves families and nearby condominiums. **Josh Slocum's** in town is the après-ski hangout for ski patrol members and instructors. At **Austria Hof**, singer and guitarist Gayle Louise entertains after skiing. At the **Ocean Club**, singers Bird and McDonald entertain as much with their jokes as with their guitar, but they can get a little lewd. Locals' favorite Doug Randal plays at the piano bar at **Dry Creek Lounge**.

Dancing and general meat markets are at **Whiskey Creek** (corner Main Street and Minaret Road, a major intersection; 934-2555) and **The Rafters** (934-2537.)

There's plenty of nighttime hoopla at **Grumpy's** and its **Western Saloon and Sports Bar**; 934-8587. Featured are five giant-screen TVs, pool, foosball, shuffleboard, inexpensive chili and burgers.

Shogun, 934-3970, has an odd mix of follow-the-bouncing-ball singalong with a sushi bar and tempura, sukiyaki and teriyaki dishes.

Child care

The Small World Day Care Center at Mammoth Mountain Inn, just across the street from the Main Lodge and at June Mountain offers these services:

	Full day 8 a.m.-5 p.m.	Half day 8 a.m.-12:30 p.m.
Infants	$39	$27
Toddlers	$39	$27
Preschool	$36	$27

There is a $5 reduction for additional children. Fees include snacks and lunch, except for infants.

The combined day care/ski school rates at Mammoth Main Lodge for ages three to 12 include super vised activity from 8 a.m. to 5 p.m. and a lesson from 10 a.m. until noon. Rate is $52, including lunch. Reservations are requested. Call (619) 934-0646.

Other activities

Snowmobiles can be rented from DJs Snowmobile Rentals; (619) 934-4880. Sleds are available at Kittredge Sports; (619) 934-7566. Sleigh rides with (or without) a cozy ranch-house dinner are offered at Sierra Meadows Equestrian and Ski Touring Center; (619) 934-6161. Hot-air balloon trips take off from Mammoth Meadow. Snowcreek Athletic Club has a variety of indoor and outdoor facilities.

Getting there

By car from Los Angeles, Mammoth is 307 miles north on Highway 395; from Reno it is 168 miles south on Highway 395. From San Francisco it's 320 miles using Highway 80 to either Highway 50 or Highway 395.

Greyhound runs twice daily. Skiers' Express (213-321-1221) and other charter companies offer direct service. Mammoth Express departs daily from Los Angeles Airport and Van Nuys; (800) 446-4500.

Alpha Air has daily service from Burbank, Los Angeles, and Orang County (800-421-9353).

Although rental cars are available at the airport, once you get to town, there is little need for a car. Eastern Sierra Auto Rentals (619-935-4471) is available at the airport. The ski resort operates a free shuttle that runs throughout the town and to the Main Lodge (four miles from town) and to Warming Hut II and Chair 15 .

Information/reservations

Central reservations for Mammoth, (800) FOR MLRA or (619) 934-8006 handles accommodations, car and ski equipment rentals, airline and lift tickets, ski school, child care and even restaurant reservations. Mammoth Ski Resort reservations is (800) 228-4947. June has three booking agencies: (619) 648-JUNE; (800) 648-6835 CA only; and (800) 462-5589 CA only.

Twenty-four-hour snow report for Los Angeles is (213) 935-8866; Orange County, (714) 955-0692; San Diego, (619) 231-7785. Road information is (619) 873-6366.

Mammoth Mountain Ski Area business office is (619) 934-2571. June Ski Area office is (619) 648-7733.

Southern California Areas

Bear Mountain, Mountain High Snow Summit, Snow Valley

"It never rains in Southern California," goes the song. Not true. And when winter rain falls on Southern California's palm trees, snow falls on the mountains that ring the Los Angeles basin.

The tallest of these mountains tops 10,000 feet, and they are home to 10 ski areas, most of which lie between 6,500 and 8,800 feet Four of them -- Bear Mountain, Mountain High, Snow Summit and Snow Valley -- attract 90 percent of the skiers.

Southern Californians have a love-hate relationship with their local areas. They love them because they are so close -- about 90 minutes from surf to slopes. They hate them because they are so close -- on weekends and after a snowstorm, the slopes are as crowded as the celebrated L.A. freeways. They love them because extensive snow-making systems almost always ensure adequate coverage. They hate them because high operating costs—

Bear Mountain Facts
Base elevation: 7,140'; Summit elevation: 8,805'; Vertical drop: 1,665 feet. Number and types of lifts: 12—1 superchair, 3 triple chairs, 5 double chairs, 3 surface lifts **Acreage: 174 skiable acres** *Percent of snowmaking: 100 percent* **Uphill capacity: 14,000 skiers per hour** *Bed Base: 20,000 within 5 miles*

Snow Summit Facts
Base elevation: 7,000'; Summit elevation: 8,200'; Vertical drop: 1,200 feet. Number and types of lifts: 10—2 quad chairs, 2 triple chairs, 6 double chairs **Acreage: 230 skiable acres** *Percent of snowmaking: 95 percent* **Uphill capacity: 14,400 skiers per hour** *Bed Base: 20,000 within 5 miles*

including extensive snowmaking systems -- make lift tickets as expensive here as in the huge Colorado resorts, but with only about a third of the terrain.

Nevertheless, these four attract about 1.3 million skiers annually. They are very similar in that all have 200-250 skiable acres on largely intermediate terrain.

The differences between these four are in accessibility and visitor amenities. Mountain High is the easiest to reach, but has few lodges and restaurants (and those it does have are, well, rustic). Bear Mountain and Snow Summit are farther away, but are in the resort town of Big Bear Lake, where lodging and restaurants are pleasant and plentiful. Snow Valley falls somewhere in between.

Where to ski

Beginners, intermediates and snowboarders will have the most fun at these areas. All four have limited amounts of advanced terrain. At Bear Mountain and Snow Summit, good snowmaking systems ensure good coverage on all the slopes, but lack of snow often closes the advanced terrain at the other two areas. All four allow snowboarding, and all but Bear Mountain have night skiing.

At **Bear Mountain**, beginners have their own area under the Inspiration triple chair. They start with very flat terrain served by a Poma lift, move to an ever-so-slightly steeper slope accessed by a chair lift, then graduate to a long, gentle run.

Lower intermediates will be happiest with runs off the Goldmine or Showdown mountains, while upper intermediates will like Silver Mountain. Advanced skiers should head for the top of Bear Peak, which has the

Mountain High Facts

Base elevation: 6,600'; Summit elevation: 8,200'; Vertical drop: 1,600 feet.
Number and types of lifts: 11—1 superchair, 1 quad chair, 3 triple chairs, 6 double chairs and 3 surface lifts.
Acreage: 220 skiable acres **Percent of snowmaking:** *95 percent*
Uphill capacity: 16,000 skiers per hour **Bed Base:** *20,000 within 5 miles*

Snow Valley Facts

Base elevation: 6,700'; Summit elevation: 7,841'; Vertical drop: 1,141 feet.
Number and types of lifts: 13—5 triple chairs, 8 double chairs
Acreage: 230 skiable acres **Percent of snowmaking:** *50 percent*
Uphill capacity: 18,550 skiers per hour **Bed Base:** *20,000 within 5 miles*

area's only hair-raising run, Geronimo. When snow conditions permit, advanced skiers may go off-trail within the ski area boundaries for some of the best tree and glade skiing you'll find in Southern California.

Novices at **Snow Summit** also have a private, gentle slope, served by Chairs 4 and 8. Those with at least a few trails under their skis can head for the green runs under Chair 9. Intermediates will love Miracle Mile, a long cruiser that descends from the summit (8,200 feet) to the base (7,000 feet), and the trails served by Chairs 1, 2, 3, 5, 7 and 10. Upper intermediates will enjoy the runs under Chair 11, a relatively new section of the mountain.

Advanced skiers have the steep (but short) pitch of The Bowl served by Chair 6. The Bowl almost always is skiable, thanks to snowmaking, but also attracts a lot of hotshots who think they ski better than they can.

Snow Valley has the gentlest terrain of the four. Neverevers have several acres of flat runs at the base, strong beginners can handle the blue runs, and strong intermediates can handle most black-diamond trails. Solid intermediates especially should head for Chairs 4, 8 and 9, rated black on the trail map, but often deserted. A nice touch here: The base station of each chair has a large vertical sign on it, clearing stating the number of the chair and the symbols for the difficulty of terrain it serves.

Slide Peak is a wide face with a respectable pitch. Half the face is groomed, while the other half is left alone to build moguls. Lack of snow, its biggest drawback, closes it, off and on, during the season.

Mountain High shuttles skiers by bus between its two areas,s Mountain High East and Mountain High West. East has beginner areas at the base and at the summit; beginners who don't want to negotiate the intermediate runs that make up most of the mountain can ride back down on a high-speed quad chair, the first one in Southern California. East also has the toughest terrain, Olympic Bowl. West is largely the territory of beginner and intermediate skiers, but also has several black-diamond runs.

If you have the choice, don't ski on weekends or holidays!! The parade of cars crawling up the roads combined with the parade of skiers careening down the slopes is not conducive to a relaxing day. But if weekends are your only option, Sundays have up to 30 percent fewer skiers than Saturdays.

Even if drought continues in California, chances are that these four areas will be operating: all four have very good snowmaking systems covering much of their terrain. (Bear Mountain and Snow Summit have ample water from Big Bear Lake; snowmaking at Snow Valley and Mountain High is limited by water supply, although both of the latter areas have ambitious plans to increase that supply for 1992-93.) When snow conditions are very good, consider these smaller areas that have limited or no snowmaking— all are less crowded than the Big Four and all have lower prices: Mt. Baldy, north of Upland; Ski Sunrise, next to Mountain High in Wrightwood; Snow Forest, in the town of Big Bear Lake; Ski Green Valley, near Running Springs; and Kratka Ridge and Mt. Waterman, both on the Angeles Crest Highway north of La Canada-Flintridge.

Mountain ratings

These areas are most suitable for intermediate skiers, although beginners will find them comfortable, unintimidating places to learn on uncrowded days. (On crowded days, beginners may find them very intimidating!) Advanced skiers can be entertained if snow conditions cooperate, but experts may be bored after a couple of runs. Those who dislike sharing the slopes with snowboarders may not like these areas -- shredders often make up the majority of the lift ticket holders, particularly in the early part of the season.

A tip for upper-level skiers: After a snowfall, skip the four populated areas and head for Mt. Baldy, off the I-10 freeway north of Upland. This lesser-known area has the steepest slopes and the largest vertical drop (2,100 feet) in Southern California. Its biggest problem is very little snowmaking.

Cross-country

Although drought has made it tough for Southern California Nordic centers to operate, they do exist. The Palm Springs Nordic Center on 10,800-foot Mt. San Jacinto is accessible only by the Palm Springs Aerial Tramway; skiers with equipment may use the ungroomed trails, paying only $13.95 for the tram ticket (1990-91 price; it may go up a dollar or two in 1991-92). Rental equipment is available for $8 and hour or $18 a day. Lessons given on weekends last 90 minutes and cost $15. Call (619) 327-6002. Note: This is not near any of the downhill ski areas.

Nearer to downhill skiing is the Green Valley Lake Cross-Country Center, just beyond Running Springs. It operates only when there's enough snow, and has about five miles of set tracks, and "miles and miles" of ungroomed trails in the San Bernardino National Forest, according to co-owner Sara Williams. The longest trail is 13 miles from Green Valley Lake to Fawnskin. The 1991-92 trail fee is $5. Group lessons are $10, and rentals cost $10.60 for adults and $8 for children. Half-day rentals, after 1 p.m., are $7.50; call (714) 867-7754.

Snowboarding

It's not too surprising that the ski areas in the surf and skateboard capital of the U.S. embrace snowboarding. All four major areas not only allow shredders, but also have snowboard parks, halfpipes, rentals, lessons and many contests and competitions. Most ski and sporting goods shops near the areas also rent snowboards. Snow Summit and Bear Mountain even have a Snowboard Patrol, young ski area employees who travel on boards and watch for shredders who need a reminder on mountain etiquette.

Ski school (91/92 prices)

Bear Mountain has some of the most innovative programs, including a New Skier Center, EXCL classes that last one hour and have only three students, the only disabled-skier school in Southern California and daily racing clinics. Skiers can see themselves on videotape at the free on-mountain Skier Evaluation Center.

The beginner package for skiers or snowboarders (rentals, lifts and lessons) is $29 during the week and $39 on weekends. Each new skier also receives a coupon book good for future discounts at the area on rentals, lessons and lift tickets. Children's packages (ages 4-12) are $45 for a full day, including lunch, and $30 for a half day. Equipment rental is $9 extra. EXCL classes are $20. Racing clinics are $25. Private lessons are $50 per hour; $35 for each additional person.

Mountain High's beginner package is $25 midweek, $38 weekends and holidays ($20 and $25 for children 9-13.) It includes ski rentals, beginner lessons and a ticket good on the beginner lifts.

Adult two-hour group ski lessons are $17; group snow-board instruction costs $20. Private lessons for either sport are $48 per hour. Children 4-8 can join the Buckaroo program, $35 for the day (lifts, lessons, lunch) or $18 a half day (no lunch). Good deal: A two-hour beginner lesson (no rentals) is $8.50 but a full day costs $25. Sign up for two half days.

Snow Summit offers a beginner package for $39.50. Its two-hour group lessons are $15; snowboard group lessons are $20. Private lessons are $50 per hour. Children 5-12 who have never skied can get all-day instruction with lunch for $35, or a half day for $20. Children 9 to 12 who already ski can enroll in all-day instruction for $25; half day for $15.

Snow Valley's beginner package costs $40 for adults and $30 for children (12 and younger) and seniors (65 and older). Ninety-minute adult group lessons are $16; three hours costs $22. Private lessons are $40. Snow Valley offers the all-day SKIwee program for kids 5-11 for $35 without equipment and $40 with equipment. Lunch is included. Snowboard group lessons are $16. Snow Valley also has a midweek lift, lesson and equipment rental package, $35 for adults and $25 for kids and seniors.

Lift tickets (91/92 prices)

Bear Mountain: Adult all-day tickets: $37; children, 12 and younger, $20. Half-day (1-4 p.m.): $23 for adults, $16 for kids. Saturday-Sunday ticket: $64 for adults, $34 for kids. A three-day consecutive ticket is $101 for adults; $54 for kids. An adult and child may ski together midweek for $47; each additional child is $10. Seniors 65 and over ski midweek for $20. Students with ID ski midweek for $27 and police, fire, military and airline employees with ID ski for $30 midweek.

Mountain High: $36.75 for adult all-day tickets; $15 for children 13 and younger. Half-day (starts at 1 p.m.): $27 for adults, $13 for children. Night skiing (3-10 p.m.): $26 for adults on Fridays, weekends and holidays; $21 Mondays through Thursdays. Children ski at night anytime for $13. Seniors (60 and over) ski for $18.50; military with ID ski for $29 except on holidays. Multiday discounts available. Students with ID and young adults 22 and younger ski for $29.75 days, $18 nights. Also, one child 10 and younger may ski free with any paying adult.

Snow Summit: $35.75 for adult all-day tickets midweek; $37.75 weekends; for children 12 and younger, $14.75 midweek and $19.75 weekends. Half day, when available (12:30 p.m.): $21.75 for adults; $10.75 for kids. Beginner area only: $19.75 for adults; $11.75 for children. Seniors (60 and older) and young adults (22 and younger) can ski midweek for $29.75. Night skiing is $23.75 for adults; $12.75 for kids. 3-9:30 p.m. Multiday discounts available.

Snow Valley: $33 for adults all day, $25 for 12:30 to 9 p.m., $20 for 4 to 9 p.m. Corresponding prices for children 12 and younger, and seniors 65 and older, are $17, $15 and $12. Those who can plan in advance save big. Adults who buy a ticket five days in advance through Ticketmaster outlets pay $25 (and the Ticketmaster fee), which is good 8 a.m.-9 p.m.

Accommodations

Southern California skiing is overwhelmingly day skiing. Nearly all the skiers drive up from the urban valleys, ski, and drive home. A few come for a weekend, but very few spend longer than that. If you are a first-time visitor, plan either a day or weekend trip. Then, if you really like it, stay longer the next time.

Most of the accommodations are in Big Bear Lake, which is where you'll find Bear Mountain and Snow Summit ski areas. Many of the motels and lodges were built a few decades ago, but generally speaking, they are clean, homey and not too expensive ($70-$100 per night as a ballpark figure). Very few of the properties are slopeside.

Big Bear Lake has one major hotel, **Big Bear Inn,** a conglomeration of marble floors and walls, ornate statuary, oversize Oriental antiquities, Baroque chandeliers and a lobby ceiling with a painting of a cloud. It is the most convenient lodging to Bear Mountain, and is near Snow Summit as well. Rates for its 80 rooms run from about $75 to $250, depending on room size and time of year.

Reservations: (800) BEAR-INN. Box 1814, Big Bear Lake, CA 92315.

Forest Shores is the best appointed lakefront lodging. All units have a view. Studios and one, two, and three bedrooms. Address: Box 946, Big Bear Lake CA 92315; (714) 866-6551.

The town has a lot of mom-and-pop motels, small lodges and cottages, some on the lake, others in nicely wooded areas, still others on the single main boulevard. Be sure to ask. Two groups of cabins that are particularly quaint are **Oak Knoll Lodge** (714-866-2773) and **Cozy Hollow Lodge** (714-866-9694).

On the opposite shore of the lake, **The Inn at Fawnskin** is a contemporary log home in the tranquil setting of a private pine forest. A complete, carefully prepared breakfast and an afternoon snack are included in the rate, which varies from $75 for a modest room to $155 for the grand suite. There are only four rooms, so booking far ahead is important. Address: P.O. Box 378, Fawnskin, CA 92333; (714) 866-3200.

Another bed-and-breakfast inn, **Gold Mountain Manor**, has a triple diamond rating from AAA. It's furnished in antiques and western artifacts surrounded by spectacular fireplaces and an expansive bird's-eye maple floor. Breakfasts are feasts accompanied by tales of Big Bear history. There's an afternoon tea and sherry hour and late night desserts. Call (714) 585-6997. **Eagle's Nest B&B** is moderately priced and offers free shuttle service to ski areas. Call (714) 866-6465.

Lake Arrowhead is a small resort about 30 miles west of Big Bear Lake and about 10 miles from the nearest skiing at Snow Valley. Lake Arrowhead is a much more self-contained village than Big Bear Lake, and more modern in appearance.

The largest hotel is the **Lake Arrowhead Hilton**, with 261 rooms ranging from $85 to $225. This is a full resort hotel, featuring lakeview rooms, a health club and spa, meeting and banquet facilities. Reservations: (800) HILTONS or (714) 336-1511. PO Box 1699, Lake Arrowhead, CA 92352.

The next largest lodge is **The Saddleback Inn**, with 34 rooms spread among a central building and outlying cabins. The rest of the properties include B&Bs, cabins and condos.

Call the Lake Arrowhead accommodations and lodging information at (800) 545-5784 for more information.

Some lodging exists near Mountain High, but much of it is rustic, to be polite. If you plan to stay overnight, use this as your guideline: If the skiing is more important, stay in Big Bear Lake. If modern accommodations, shopping and restaurants carry more weight, stay in Lake Arrowhead. If you're making a very quick day trip, Mountain High is the easiest to get to.

You can make reservations and find out more about lodgings and prices through two services: Big Bear Central Reservation Service, (714) 866-5877 or 866-4601; or Visitors Information and Reservation Service, (714) 866-7000.

Dining

In Big Bear Lake: The Iron Squirrel is not only considered the finest dining by locals, it is an entirely nonsmoking restaurant.Escargots are a common appetizer, and salmon is a specialty. **Knusperhauschen** (585-8640), known locally as George and Sigi's and open only for dinner, has a continental menu of pheasant, beef Wellington and cioppino for between $16 and $19.

More moderate, **The Blue Ox** (585-7886) serves up its "Big Swede Ole Dinner," a baked potato stuffed with Hungarian goulash for $7, which is mighty good. **The Old Country Inn** (866-5600) specializes in better-than-average German, Italian and American food at moderate prices. Excellent sauerbraten. **Mandarin Garden** (585-1818) serves a fine shrimp curry and good Szechuan dishes. **Captain's Anchorage** has steak and seafood for $10-$15 (866-3997), and **The Blue Whale** is good for prime rib and seafood (866-5771).

Many places are inexpensive. For Mexican food under low lights, **La Montana** (866-2606) has entrées for $5-$7. Besides full dinners up to $13, **Maggio's Pizza** (866-8815) has Italian subs and sandwiches for $5-$6, and eight kinds of calzones for $3. **Pong's Place** serves oriental specialties (866-8688). Check out Paoli's for Italian food (866-2020) and Tio Oso (866-8099) for Mexican. **Boo Bear's Den** (866-2932) has the widest variety—from burgers at $4 to

Australian lobster at $20. The sandwiches are better than their dinners, and the hearty breakfasts are wonderful.

In or near Lake Arrowhead:

The **Cliffhanger Restaurant** on Highway 18 leading to Lake Arrowhead has Greek and Italian specialties in the $13-$30 range. Lunch runs about $7-$15, and you still get the same great views of the San Gabriel Valley (if the smog isn't too thick.)

Lake Arrowhead Village has about 20 restaurants ranging in atmosphere and price from **McDonald's** to the lakeside **Candlewood Restaurant**. The **Tulips Cafe** is especially recommended because of its homemade-style food and delicious desserts. It serves the most incredible hot chocolate you've ever tasted.

Aprè-ski/nightlife

Because these areas attract many more day skiers than overnighters, apres-ski is much more plentiful than night life. Each ski area has a bar at the foot of the slopes where skiers relax before heading down the mountain; live music is standard on weekends, recorded music during the week.

Big Bear Lake has most of the night life that exists. Places to try: **Prospector's, The Moonridge Club** at the Big Bear Inn, the **Navajo Restaurant and Saloon, Chad's,** and **the Sugarloafer.**

Child care

The only area with child care is Snow Summit, which has its Little Bear Care Center for ages 6 months to 6 years. Activities include crafts, games, videos and ski lessons for ages 3 to 6. A telephone hotline at the tops of Chairs 2 and 10 give parents access to the care center. The cost ('91-92 prices) is $45 for all day, $28 for a half day for 6 months to 2 years; $35 for all day, $20 for half day for ages 3-6. All day includes lunch. Reserve by calling (714) 866-5766, Ext. 354. On weekends, the center is often booked two weeks in advance; don't expect to walk in and be able to place your child, even on weekdays.

Advice based on experience: If your children are under 4 and you can't get them into the Snow Summit child care center, it's best to leave them at home with a baby sitter. Even if parents take turns watching a toddler at the base area, there are very few places to play that are out of the way of skiers. And toddlers get bored REAL fast! Four is the minimum age for most of these areas' children's learning programs and they enforce it.

Getting there

Carry chains. The California Highway Patrol will not let unchained vehicles past its checkpoints during snowy periods. From Los Angeles:

Bear Mountain and Snow Summit: The least crowded route is to take I-10 east to the Orange Avenue exit. Follow the signs to Highway 38, which leads to Big Bear Lake. The shorter but most crowded route is I-10 east to I-215 north, take the Mountain Resorts exit and follow Highways 30, 330 and 18 through Running Springs to Big Bear Lake.

Tip: To avoid bumper-to-bumper traffic in the city of Big Bear Lake, take Highway 38 around the north side of the lake, through Fawnskin and turn right on the Stanfield Cutoff on the east end of the lake.

Snow Valley: Take I-10 east to I-215 north, then take the Mountain Resorts exit. Follow Highway 30, then either Highway 18 through Crestline (the longer, less crowded way) or Highways 330 and 18 through Running Springs (the shorter, more congested way.) To reach Lake Arrowhead's shops and restaurants, take Highway 18 through Crestline.

Mountain High: Take I-10 east to I-15 north. Exit at Highway 138 toward Wrightwood, turn left on Highway 2.

Information/reservations

Bear Mountain: Box 6812, Big Bear Lake, CA 92315, (714) 585-2519. Snow report: (213) 289-0636 (LA number).

Mountain High: Box 428, Wrightwood, CA 92397 (619) 249-5801. Snow report: (213) 460-6911 (LA number).

Snow Summit: Box 77, Big Bear Lake, CA 92315, (714) 866-5766. Snow report: (213) 613-0602 (LA number)

Snow Valley: Box 2337, Running Springs, CA 92382, (714) 867-2751. Snow report: (714) 867-5151.

Steamboat

Winter Park

Denver

Beaver Creek Vail

Arapahoe Basin

Copper Mt.

Keystone

Breckenridge

Aspen

Snowmass Aspen Highlands

Buttermilk

Irwin Lodge

Crested Butte

• Gunnison

Colorado

▲ Telluride

▲ Purgatory

• Durango

Aspen Colorado Area

Aspen Mountain
Tiehack/Buttermilk Mountain
Aspen Highlands

Aspen is the big kahuna of ski resorts. Aspen conjures outrageous expectations. Furs and fashions flash. Style and sex sparkle. Sophisticated New York and Hollywood fashions shimmer against rustic Old West façades. Furs parade into discos with roofs rolled back to the midnight sky. Elvis's Corvette holds court amidst new-wave fashion. Learjet pilots wait patiently for parking spaces on the tarmac. Aspen's a town perfectly developed for soap opera excesses. For the nouveau riche, for the rising star, for the junior executive with new-found wealth, Aspen is the promised land. For those who dream, it is Never-Never Land and more.

Unlike most other resorts, which focus on skiing as the primary activity with all else serving as a support system, Aspen functions in an upside-down world. Skiing, for many, has become a sideline to the glitz, the gourmet dining and the pulsing nightlife. In this sense, Aspen doesn't compete with the other Colorado resorts: Aspen's main competition is the other resorts of the rich. Sun Valley, Deer Valley and Stowe draw those who have no need to see and be seen; they attract the rich without the glitz, the Aspen crowd after it tires of exposure. But there will always be a place for Aspen, a place to be discovered, a place to make a splash, a ski town where one can rub elbows with those in the middle of the action.

Aspen is also a Victorian mountain town, albeit a large one, with citizens who've escaped one ratrace only to develop a concern that another's creeping up on them:

here the competition is to see who can come up with the most original license plate or throw the most spectacular party. But there's also a side to Aspen where perfectly pouted lips, careful coiffure and cosmopolitan style are not the rule. There are women who exude a natural freshness, with almost no makeup and casually tossed or tied back hair. There are restaurants where one can eat without taking out a loan and bars that have never seen a fur coat. There are children playing tag, mothers attending PTA and workerbees who make the resort hum.

Aspen's skiing has received rave reviews for decades. There are four main mountains surrounding Aspen. Aspen Mountain, dwarfing the town, is designed to challenge intermediate and advanced skiers. Tiehack/Buttermilk, in contrast, is just a nub, but serves as the perfect beginner terrain and cruising mountain. Aspen Highlands is the most varied of the mountains, with skiing for experts and beginners, cruisers and bumpers. Snowmass, itself the third-largest ski mountain in America, although included with the Aspen lift ticket, is really a resort of its own, covered in the next chapter.

There is simply more to do in this bustling town in winter than anyplace else. Action is the driving force and Aspen thrives on it. Make no mistake: money is the fuel that determines how much action you can get and how long you can keep running in Aspen. But with beauty, the right clothes and a touch of mystery, anyone can be invited almost anywhere.

Where to ski

To help skiers get oriented, there are free mountain tours. The tours lasts one and a half hours and give a sense of the history and nature of the area, as well as pointing out different runs. The Tiehack/Buttermilk and Snowmass tours are given on Sundays at 9 a.m. from the ski school meeting place and on Aspen Mountain Monday morning at 9:30 a.m. at the base of the gondola.

Aspen Mountain Facts

Base elevation: 7,945'; **Summit elevation:** 11,212'; **Vertical drop:** 3,267 feet
Number of lifts: 8—1 gondola, 1 quad superchair, 2 quad chairs, 4 double chairs
Percent snowmaking: 33 percent **Total acreage:** 625 skiable acres
Uphill capacity: 10,775 per hour **Bed Base:** 10,000

Aspen Mountain is one of skidom's best intermediate and expert playgrounds. Beginners shouldn't even think about tackling this terrain, but with Tiehack/Buttermilk so close they don't need to. The Silver Queen Gondola whisks skiers to the summit of Ajax, as the mountain is known to locals. From here there are 3,267 feet of uninterrupted vertical back to the gondola base. That's the skiing that has brought generations of skiers back to Aspen.

The basic rule for Aspen Mountain is that intermediate terrain is found on the top knob around the summit and in the gullies nestled between the ridges. The expert stuff drops from the ridges down into the gullies. The gentlest terrain, Dipsy Doodle, Pussyfoot and Silver Bell, funnels into Spar Gulch. Ruthie's Road along the ski area boundary connects with Ruthie's Run, and Copper Bowl is a long intermediate run, serving a dozen expert trails from the Bell Mountain Ridge and Gentleman's Ridge.

Tiehack/Buttermilk Mountain Facts
Base elevation: 7,870'; Summit elevation: 9,900'; Vertical drop: 2,030 feet
Number of lifts: 7—6 double chairs, 1 surface lift
Percent snowmaking: 27 percent Total acreage: 410 acres
Uphill capacity: 6,600 per hour Bed Base: 10,000

Tiehack/Buttermilk Mountain is all the name implies. Beginners will have a chance to experience top-to-bottom runs with mastery of the wedge turn or halting stem christies. Intermediates will start to qualify themselves as expert, and wise experts will let their skis go and enjoy no-stress, no-crowd cruising.

The beginner terrain concentrates under the Tiehack/Buttermilk West chair. Tom's Thumb, Red's Rover, Larkspur, Westerward Ho and Blue Grouse will keep beginners busy and improving in the West Tiehack/Buttermilk area. The Homestead Road turns back to the Savio chair and lazily winds its way to the Main Tiehack/Buttermilk area.

Intermediates with confident turns will have fun on Jacob's Ladder and Bear, which drop from the Cliff House to the Main Tiehack/Buttermilk area. But the real playground is Tiehack. This area surprisingly has black runs on the trail map; don't get too excited—they are only black on the map. Explore them with skis under your feet and you'll discover only good, solid intermediate trails, but they make inspiring cruisers. In one day on the mountain you can ride the Upper Tiehack chair a dozen times, taking a different cruise on each run. Buckskin, Ptarmigan, Sterner, the Glades, Tiehack Parkway and Racer's Edge (where the Mahre brothers trained) all offer variations on the cruiser's theme—every one is 1,500 feet of dipping and sweeping curves. Smile in the evening when you overhear others scoffing about what a waste Tiehack/Buttermilk is for real skiers, and savor memories of 15,000 feet of vertical—just in an afternoon.

Aspen Highlands Facts

Base elevation: 8,000'; **Summit elevation:** 11,800'; **Vertical drop:** 3,800 feet
Number of lifts: 11—9 double chairs, 2 surface lifts
Percent snowmaking: 20 percent **Total acreage by trails:** 552 skiable acres
Uphill capacity: 10,000 per hour **Bed Base:** 10,000

Aspen Highlands is the odd man out. It is not part of the Aspen Skiing Company, but it is a major factor in Aspen skiing. Aspen Highlands is the best-balanced mountain, with slopes for every level of skier, and it's the locals' favorite. This is a slope where you can be comfortable if you appear for lunch at mid-mountain in jeans and gaiters. The vertical rise is the highest in Colorado, but it takes three lifts and a half hour to reach the summit. From the top of Loges Peak Lift, the run back to the base is an uneven series of steeps, catwalks and gentle runouts. This mountain has some fantastic long cruises. The ridge, knifing directly to the summit, has thrilling pitches down both sides.

Beginners will find themselves plying the trails served by the Exhibition II chair and the Grand Prix Poma. These open Prospector, Norway, Nugget, Exhibition and Apple Strudel. Intermediates will want to take the next series of lifts: Cloud 9, Olympic and Loges Peak. (The easiest of the intermediates are off Cloud 9.) Experts will have all the steeps they need from the top of Loges Peak with Kessler's Bowl, Snyder's Ridge, Sodd Buster, Garmisch and St. Moritz. Dropping from Cloud 9 are The Wall and Le Chamonix, which will test any skier. Off the backside of the Olympic chair, the Olympic Bowl area has expert and intermediate terrain. After short, steep drops you traverse back to Robinson's Run.

In addition to this cluster of runs, check out the lower mountain. The Nugget Chair will take you to the top of Bob's Glades or Upper Stein, or you can drop into Thunderbowl and ski virtually anywhere you want. The Thunderbowl area is served by a chair from the base and a Poma for its upper reaches.

The Merry-Go-Round restaurant at the top of the Exhibition II lift is one of the better cafeterias you'll find on a mountain. The apple strudel here is the real thing and an Aspen tradition, made with Gretl Uhl's original recipe. Freestyle competitions are held Fridays at noon on Scarlett's Run facing the Merry-Go-Round. At the Cloud 9 restaurant the ski patrol members do aerials over the deck when they have time and conditions cooperate.

Mountain rating

There is something for everyone. Beginners will have the most expansive experience at Tiehack/Buttermilk. Intermediates will probably have a more varied day at Aspen Highlands than on Aspen Mountain, but the longest runs sweep down Ajax, and it's hard to beat the exhilarating cruising on Tiehack/Buttermilk. Experts have a tossup between Aspen Highlands and Aspen Mountain.

Snowboarding

Unlimited snowboarding is permitted at Aspen Highlands and on Tiehack/Buttermilk Mountain. Shredding is not allowed on Aspen Mountain, and is controlled, based on snow conditions at Snowmass.

Aspen Highlands, Snowmass and Tiehack/Buttermilk all have halfpipes. All areas offer special snowboard lessons following a similar format to their ski lessons. Tiehack/Buttermilk has a two-day Snowboard Special for $99 including rentals, lessons and lifts.

Aspen Highlands offers two-hour beginner snowboard lessons twice a day (10:15 a.m. to 12:30 p.m. and 1:30 to 3:30 p.m.) for $30 per session which includes lesson and rental.

Rentals are available throughout the Aspen area.

Cross-country

Craig Ward organized the most extensive free Nordic trail system in America, 80 km. of groomed trails. The system is accessible from Aspen or Snowmass and includes easy golf-course skiing as well as more difficult trails rising up to Snowmass.

In addition to the free trails provided by Aspen's Nordic Council, Ashcroft Touring Unlimited has 30 km. of groomed and set trails, and backcountry skiers can strike out along summer hiking trails. There is also a hut system connecting Aspen with Crested Butte over the Pearl Pass. And the Tenth Mountain Trails Association has developed a Vail-to-Aspen hut system.

Cross-country contacts and centers (R=rentals, L=lessons, G=guides, F=food, T=trail fee, TL=telemark lessons): Aspen/Snowmass Nordic Council (925-4790); Ashcroft Ski Touring (R,L,T,F)—925-1971; Aspen Touring Center (R,L,TL,G)—925-7625; Snowmass Touring Center (R,L,F)—923-3148; Ute Nordic Center (R,L,F)—925-2145; Fred Braun Hut information on trials to Crested Butte—925-7345; Tenth Mt. Trail Association—925-5775.

Ski school

Aspen offers everything from the state-of-the-art Vic Braden Ski College and the holistic Magic of Skiing workshops, to basic first-timer lessons and expert clinics. In all, there are more than 25 different programs to choose from. Prices are for 91/92 unless noted otherwise.

The Vic Braden Ski College uses extensive video analysis, bio-mechanical research and positive psychology to move first-time skiers to breakthroughs. The emphasis is on making ski lessons easy and fun. All programs are four days long and cost $595 per person, including lift tickets, four days of instruction, equipment rentals, and videos of your progress. Make reservations through the Aspen Skiing Company (920-0784).

The Magic of Skiing approaches skiing from a mind/body perspective. Theoretically, the approach to skiing should permeate your entire lifestyle. The cost for the one-week program is $1,595, which includes lift tickets, ski instruction, videotaping, seven-day health club pass, group discussions and, most important, training in relaxation, relationships, fitness and health, awareness and mind/body coordination. For reservations and information, call 925-7099.

The Aspen Skiing Company ski school offers an extensive traditional lesson program. For reservations and information, call (303) 925-1220 or (800) 525-6200.

Group lessons are given at Aspen Mountain, Tiehack/Buttermilk and Snowmass. When you enroll you are assigned a meeting place either on the mountain or at the base lodge. Adult group lessons cost $40 a day. First-time programs for adults are held only at Tiehack/Buttermilk and Snowmass, and are free if you buy a multiday lift ticket on the first day of ski school. Lessons meet daily at 11 a.m. in both Snowmass and Tiehack/Buttermilk.

All teen and children's programs are held at Tiehack/Buttermilk or Snowmass. For children seven to 12 the fee is $45 a day (four hours) and five days cost $190. The same programs are available for teens. Special kids' and teens' ski weeks comprise five-day programs that include lessons, fun races, a picnic and video. The price for both is $190.

All children three to six are enrolled in either "Powder Pandas" at Tiehack/Buttermilk or "Big Burn Bears" at Snowmass. Children from 18 months to four years are enrolled in "Snowcubs" at Snowmass. The programs cost $55 a day including lunch and lifts and $255 for five days.

Private lessons start at $65 an hour for one student; $85 an hour for two to five. Two hours of lessons cost $120 for one and $165 for up to five. Full-day lessons run $340 for one to five people. A book of coupons for five full-day lessons costs $1,575 for up to five students.

Three-hour racing clinics cost $40 a day or $114 for three days. Bump, powder and video clinics all cost $35 for each two-hour session. The "Mountain Masters" program for intermediate and advanced skiers provides a guide who will run you for four days, until your legs feel weak, for $250. A special women's seminar costs $195 for three days and $260 for four days.

Aspen Highlands Ski School (92/93 prices)

Group lessons are $42 for a full day; $30 for half days; $70 for two days; $105 for three days; $175 for five days.

Private lessons are $70 an hour, $130 for two hours, $195 for three hours and $295 full day. There is no limit on the number of students in private groups.

Four-day never-ever packages with lifts, lessons and rentals cost $200. Three-day skier's packages with lifts, lessons and rentals cost $195 or $165 without rentals.

Aspen Highlands has a two for one ski school special based on a strange formula and depending on the phase of the moon. Call the area for details.

Snow puppies (three and a half to six years) have a program that includes lessons, lifts and lunch for $55 a day, or $220 for five days.

Lift tickets (91/92 prices)

Lift ticket coupon books are available for all four Aspen Area mountains: Aspen Mountain, Tiehack/Buttermilk, Snowmass and Aspen Highlands. These coupons can be exchanged for day tickets at the area of your choice. Four of five day coupon books for adults cost $156, six of seven day coupon booklets are $228.

One day (three mountains), $41 adults/$25 children (12 and under); four out of five day (three mountains), $160 adults; five day (three mountains), $200 adults/$110 children.

Those 70+ and children under 6 ski free.

Aspen Highlands (92/93 prices)

Full day, $30 adults/$15 children 12 and under, and seniors 65 to 69; half day (morning or afternoon), $22; two days, $58; three days, $78; five days, $115. The student rate for skiers 13 to 18 or with a college ID (to age 25) is $22 a day. Skiers over 70 pay $15 a day.

Accommodations

Accommodations in Aspen range from luxurious to inexpensive. The town surprisingly had few top-scale properties in the past, but formerly fatigued hotels have been creatively restored in the past few years to bring glamour back to Aspen's lodging. The condominiums in the town are consistently old; you won't find soaring three-story living rooms as at Snowmass or Deer Valley. Most of Aspen's are products of a bygone era, but they are well-maintained and comfortable. Reservations for virtually all properties are available through the Aspen Chamber Resort Association, (800) 262-7736, in Colorado (800) 421-7145 or (303) 925-9000.

Hotel Jerome 330 East Main Street, (800-331-7213) is the other place to be seen. This once run-down historic hotel has been brought back to more elegance than the silver barons ever knew. The lounges are filled with overstuffed chairs and framed by etched glass. Rooms are filled with antiques, and each has a brass or carved wooden bed. Baths feature private Jacuzzis, marble counters and telephones. Rates during regular season are $319-$549.

For those searching out a smaller, more intimate hotel, the **Sardy House** 920-2525 on East Main Street is a restored Victorian mansion. A more modern addition has been tacked onto the rear, but we suggest you attempt to get one of the original rooms in the main house. Rooms during regular season are $220-$285; and relatively small suites range between $350 and $500.

The Little Nell Hotel (800) 525-6200 has 92 rooms and suites, only steps from the Silver Queen Gondola at the base of Aspen Mountain. All rooms have working fireplaces, down-filled sofas, oversized beds with comforters, and marble bathrooms. There is a spa and heated outdoor pool. Doubles with mountain view run about $325, and with town view about $300 a night. There is a three-night minimum for weekend stays.

Other top-rated luxury hotels are the **Aspen Club Lodge** (800-882-2582), the small **Hotel Leñado** (800-321-3457), the **Gant** (800-345-1471), **Hotel Aspen** on Main Street (800-527-7369) and **Molly Gibson Lodge** (800-356-6559). The new **Ritz Carlton Aspen** opens this winter.

Aspen room rates drop dramatically from this stratospheric level to $85-$130 a night for a double.

My favoriteplace in Aspen, a lodge of a kind that's disappearing all too fast, is **The Mountain Chalet** (925-7797). This place is just plain friendly to everyone including families. If you can't stand the sight of a three-year-old crawling over a lounge chair in the lobby or of families howling over a game of Monopoly, then don't stay here. Rates are reasonable and include a hearty breakfast served family style. Call for rooms early, folks reserve space here years in advance.

Other places that treat their guests very well are the **Alpine Lodge** (925-7351), **Mountain House** (920-2550), and **Crestahaus Lodge** (925-7081).

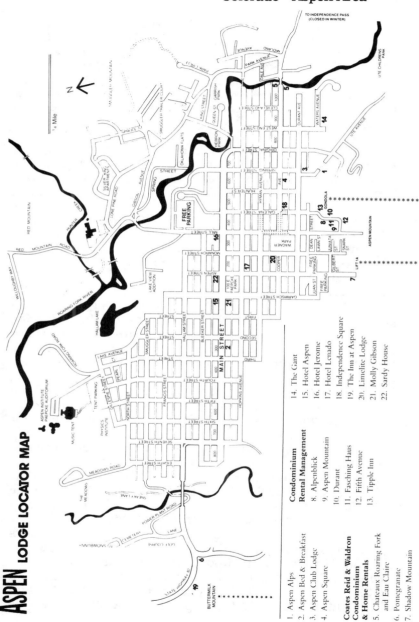

Colorado - Aspen Area

ASPEN LODGE LOCATOR MAP

1. Aspen Alps
2. Aspen Bed & Breakfast
3. Aspen Club Lodge
4. Aspen Square

Coates Reid & Waldron Condominium & Home Rentals
5. Chateaux Roaring Fork and Eau Claire
6. Pomegranate
7. Shadow Mountain

Condominium Rental Management
8. Alpenblick
9. Aspen Mountain
10. Durant
11. Fasching Haus
12. Fifth Avenue
13. Tipple Inn

14. The Gant
15. Hotel Aspen
16. Hotel Jerome
17. Hotel Lenado
18. Independence Square
19. The Inn at Aspen
20. Limelite Lodge
21. Molly Gibson
22. Sardy House

TO INDEPENDENCE PASS
(CLOSED IN WINTER)

¼ Mile

Try **Skier's Chalet** (920-2037) across from the finish line of the World Cup (Lift 1A), the **Christiana** (925-3014) at 501 West Main Street and the **St. Moritz Lodge** (925-3220), only five blocks from the center of town.

Good rooms are also available for $59 to $90 each night at the **Little Red Ski Haus** (925-3333), the **Christmas Inn** (925-3822), **Innsbruck Inn** (925-2980), **Ullr Lodge** (925-7696) and budget champion, **Tyrolean Lodge** (925-4595).

Both the **Maroon Creek Lodge** (925-3491) and the **Heatherbed Lodge** (925-7077), opposite Aspen Highlands, are wonderful places to stay out of the bustle of Aspen.

Several management companies rent condominiums. For luxury condos right on the slopes, try Mountain Queen Condominiums (925-6366); all are three-bedroom units. The Aspen Club Management (800-443-2582 in Colorado, 800-882-2582 nationwide) controls two luxurious condominiums, the Aspen Club and the Clarendon. Expect a unit with two bedrooms and two baths to run $162 to $488 during the regular season.

Coates, Reid and Waldron, 720 East Hyman Ave. (925-1400 or 800-22-ASPEN), is the largest management company in the area. Chateau Eau Claire and Chateau Roaring Fork are two of their most popular units. Two-bedroom, two-bath units run $260 a night during regular season. Shadow Mountain is not so luxurious, but has a ski-in/ski-out location. Its two-bedroom, two-bath unit is $235 during the regular season. Pomegranate, near the base of Tiehack/Buttermilk, is perfect for cross-country skiers, who will pay $227 a night during regular season for a two-bedroom, two-bath unit. There are units in every corner of town, but none would be rated luxurious. Coates, Reid and Waldron also handles home rentals.

Condominiums directly on the slopes with similar prices are the Fasching Haus (925-5900), Fifth Avenue (925-7397) and Durant condominiums (925-7910). They are available through the Aspen Resort Association.

Just outside of town, the **T-Lazy-7** (925-7254) offers apartments. You'll pay $50 for a double bed in a small studio and $175 for five bedrooms and living area that easily sleeps 10. If you can fill these apartments, they are a deal that's hard to beat, and they're on a real working ranch where kids have no end of exploration. A shuttle service takes skiers to town, Tiehack/Buttermilk and Aspen Mountain.

The nearest RV park is at Basalt KOA, 20 miles away.

Dining

I'll start with *the* place to eat breakfast, **The Wienerstube** at 633 E. Hyman and Spring. Come here for eggs Benedict, Austrian sausages and home-made Viennese pastries. **Pour la France!** at 411 E. Main is good for croissants and pastries, quiches and waffles, with superb coffee in a high-tech coffee shop atmosphere. **Main Street Bakery** has homemade baked goods, granola, fruit, eggs and great coffee for reasonable prices.

For the best gourmet-level dining, Katy Keck, who spent a year working with the top chefs in France, visited Aspen. Her observations follow in the next chapter, Aspen Savoir Faire, for those who want more details.

A trip to **Krabloonik** (923-3953 in Snowmass) is a real adventure. Although a bit pricey, you can arrive by dog sled and the menu offers the only wild game menu in the area. **Chez Grandmère** in Snowmass has splendid French meals in a restored Victorian farmhouse with one seating per evening for a fixed price of $50 per person.

There are plenty of dining choices for considerably less money. Among them are some of Aspen's excellent specialty restaurants. **Pepi's Hideout** (925-8845) at the corner of First and Cooper is an elegant little place with many European and American dishes. **Smuggler Land Office** (925-8624) at 415 E. Hopkins in the historic Brand Building has tasty Cajun and Creole food, including Cajun popcorn with a spicy rémoulade. **Cache Cache** (925-3835) on the lower level of the Mill Street Plaza is highly recommended by locals for Mediterranean cuisine. The polenta niçoise, wild mushroom canneloni and perfectly grilled yellowtail were favorites. **The Golden Horn** (920-3373) at 320 S. Mill has good veal and Swiss specialties. **New York's Mezzaluna** at 600 E. Cooper (925-5882) serves authentic Northern Italian cuisine, including exotic pizzas from a wood-burning oven.

La Cocina (925-9714), 308 E. Hopkins, is a very popular Mexican place with locals, but **The Cantina** (925-FOOD) at the corner of Mill and Main is a newer, trendier alternative. **Boogie's Diner** at 534 E. Cooper (925-6610) is a real 50s diner with oldies like Elvis's favorite "Hound Dog," blue plate specials and meatloaf as only Mom could make it. **Little Annie's Eating House** (925-1098) at 517 E. Hyman is still the ribs, chicken, hamburger and potato pancake champ. **The Skier's Chalet Steak House** (925-3381) across from the base of lift 1-A has been around since 1951 and is a great food institution, and very inexpensive. **The Steak Pit** (925-3459) at the corner of Cooper and Original also has some of the best steaks in Aspen, though its location in the basement of a grocery store makes that hard to believe. **Racine's Home Plate,** (925-1986) 333 East Durant in the Mountain Chalet, after all these years, is the best family restaurant in town. It has undergone a big menu change, now has a wine license and serves reasonable wines. It is also a good spot for filling breakfasts. **Asia,** 132 W. Main Street, was recommended for the best Chinese (Szechuan, Mandarin and Hunan) food in town. It is located in an opulent Victorian setting, but there is free delivery if you prefer (925-5433).

For eating experiences, Aspen goes all out. **The Pine Creek Cookhouse** (925-1044) is located on the cross-country trails of Ashcroft. Don a miner's lamp, put on cross-country skis and head out for a great evening meal. Prices are $40 per person, plus drinks, and include the cross-country equipment and guides. **The T-Lazy-7 Ranch** (925-7040) organizes a Western night every Wednesday and Thursday. It includes ragtime piano entertainment, cheese and crackers, sleigh rides, cooking your own steak and chicken on an open grill and a Country & Western band cookin' up some footstompin' music. The price is $35 for adults, $20 for children.

Après-ski/nightlife

The old standby, Little Nell's has been replaced by **Shlomo's** in the "new" Little Nell. If you don't find what you want there, the crowd is spread out to **Little Annie's, Cooper Street Pier,** the **Ute City Banque,** the **Red Onion** and **O'Leary's. Legends of Aspen,** a sports bar, **The Cantina,** with its very happy hour (have a margarita in the compadre size) and the **Hotel Jerome Bar** are all great après-ski meeting places—the Legends filled with locals, the Cantina loud, the Jerome quiet.

At night, well after 10 p.m., when the disco beat begins to take over, the town inside its bars and clubs is alive. The new high-energy place to find out who's in town is **Mezzaluna**, with its brassy, horseshoe-shaped bar. The newest addition to Aspen's bar scene is **Caribou Club** ostensibly requiring membership and packed with celebrities. On the Mall, head to **Tatou**, the hot spot to be seen these days. **Ebbe's**, together with its glitter and light show, has skylights that roll back to expose the night sky over the dance floor. The downstairs bar is quieter, but has a better view of comings and goings than the upstairs. A slightly lower-keyed dancing place is the **Tippler**.

For a good singles bar, head to the **Ute City Banque** for the best in upscale people-watching. A relatively mixed crowd with normal pedestrian tastes congregate in the **Red Onion**, **Little Annie's** and **O'Leary's**. The **Cooper Street Pier** is very much a local and college student hangout. **Shooter's**, down the stairs across Hyman Avenue from the Ute City Banque, is a very dark and smoky Country & Western bar with great deals on shooters and beer and great dancing. For the best "last call," try **Mother Lode**.

Child care (91/92 prices)

At Tiehack/Buttermilk children from three to six years can be enrolled in the **Powder Pandas** with a facility at the Main Tiehack/Buttermilk base area. The program runs from 8:30 a.m. until 4:30 p.m. It includes homemade lunches and toddler instruction on kids-only slopes. Costs are $55 a day; five-day programs cost $255. Rental equipment is $15 a day. For reservations call 925-1220.

At Snowmass the **Big Burn Bears** program handles three to six year olds. The program includes lunch, ski lessons and arts and crafts. Costs are $55 a day and $255 for five days. Reservations are suggested. Call 923-1220. There is also a snowplay program for children 18 months to four years at Snowmass called "Snowcubs."

Aspen Highlands has the **Snowpuppies** program for children three and a half to six years. Lessons, lunch and lifts run $46 a day or $195 for a five-day program. For reservations, call 925-5300.

Aspen Mountain does not have a company program for children. However, children can be enrolled in the Snowmass programs, a bit out of the way.

There is a local preschool, the **Aspen Sprouts** (920-1055), which accepts children two to five years and concentrates on preschool activities. Call for reservations.

Little Feet Day Care in Aspen (920-1548) has programs for infants six weeks to 18 months. It is open year-round 7:30 a.m. to 5:30 p.m., Monday through Friday.

Other private day-care and babysitting services are available in both Aspen and Snowmass through the Aspen or Snowmass reservations offices, Supersitters (923-6080) or the Chamber of Commerce (925-1940).

Other activities

The Aspen Historical Society organizes a two-hour walking tour of old Aspen for $5. Call 925-3250. The Wheeler has film classics on Monday and Tuesday evenings, as well as a continuing program.

There are dog sled rides at Krabloonik Kennels in Snowmass (923-3953). Full-day rides cost $160 and include lunch prepared in a tent in the wilderness.

The Aspen Center for Environmental Studies has snowshoe tours for $24 a person. There is also a Hallam Lake Snowshoe Tour on Mondays, Wednesdays and Fridays; cost is $15 a person.

Go for a hot-air balloon ride with Unicorn Balloon Company (925-5752) for $160 a person, which includes continental breakfast with champagne. There are daily departures, weather permitting, from Aspen and Snowmass. Other balloon companies are Adventures Aloft II (925-9497) and Aspen Balloon Adventure (925-5749).

Sleigh rides, part of the Western party night noted in the dining section, take place at the T-Lazy-7 Ranch. The ranch also hosts private sleigh rides for $10 a person, with a five-person minimum. Call 925-7040. The Aspen Carriage Company (925-4289) offers one-hour sleigh rides. Adults pay $15 and children pay $8, with a $40 minimum.

The Aspen Athletic Club is open to the public from 7 a.m. to 10 p.m. on weekdays and 8 a.m. to 8 p.m. on weekends. There is a $10 daily fee.

Getting there

United Express offers nonstop connecting into Aspen airport with service from Chicago, Dallas and Los

Angeles. Continental Express and United Express both have frequent flights from Denver.

Vans to Vail, Skiers Connection and Aspen Limousine all operate a van service to Denver Stapleton Airport.

There is Amtrak service to Glenwood Springs. Greyhound bus offers daily bus service between Glenwood Springs and Denver's Stapleton International Airport.

Information/reservations

For any Aspen area information, bookings of transfers, hotel rooms and lift tickets, call Aspen Chamber Resort Association at (800) 262-7736 nationwide or (303) 925-9000/1940.

Aspen Skiing Company Reservations: (800) 525-6200.

Aspen Highlands Sales, (800) 356-8811 handles information and reservations at Aspen Highlands.

Aspen Savoir Faire

This mountain town with Victorian roots has enjoyed an unparalleled culinary revolution that has bypassed sole meunière for a more exotic "beach party" shellfish. There are black trumpets and white truffles, edible nasturtiums, a veal dish called "@*#?&!", and just everybody is into lemon grass. After a year in California, the leader of the revolution is back! Gordon Naccarato, in partnership with Charif Souki, owner of Mezzaluna, is scheduled to open ZG this Thanksgiving at the newly refurbished Aspen Cliff Lodge (709 East Durant, 925-4400) after a trial run this summer. With superb views and Naccarato's inimitable style (remember the tequila-marinated "Kick-Ass Swordfish" and lobster lasagna?), this restaurant is sure to add intrigue and sound a wake-up call on Aspen's dining scene.

Another long-time favorite had a culinary rebirth a few years back. **The Little Nell** at 675 E. Durant (920-4600) specializes in—no, invented—American Alpine Cooking. Chef Richard Chamberlain arrived from Texas to install a Provençal menu at this rebuilt, elegant institution, took one look at the mountains and hot tubs out the window, and realized Mediterranean was the wrong fit. Faster than the flip of a flapjack, he created the concept of American Alpine. The menu is a delight: smoked tomato and corn chowder; fruitwood-smoked duck in a wild rice pancake with sun-dried cherry sauce; wild mushroom strudel and salad with roasted pepper vinaigrette; all original . . . all perfectly executed. But the only starter you need remember, as far as I'm concerned, is the pecan-fried oysters, served with a spicy rémoulade. Shucked to order and flash-fried in a nutty crust, this dish will bring me back every time.

Chamberlain's approach, drawing inspiration and technique from Alpine cooking, while using his individual style and creativity in choosing the ingredients, carries throughout the menu. A favorite entrée is the oven roast salmon with a potato and basil crust, served with a warm tomato chutney. Save room for the crème brulée tart. The restaurant, in The Little Nell hotel, serves three meals daily. Dinner starters range from $5.50 to $12, and entrées from $19.50 to $28. For fine dining, it's one of the best values in town.

Like the Liittle Nell, the Snowmass Lodge & Club is owned and operated by Aspen Skiing Company. Their restaurant, the **Four Seasons Grill**, offers food as distinctive and flovorful as Chamberlain's, with a more southwestern flair. Chef Scotty Philip, formerly of Cowboys, offers a prix-fixe $29 four-course menu that is one of the area's better bargains. Start with the roast cumin seed chicken in paper bread or the black bean cakes with tomato salsa and fresh mozzarella. Entrees range from the chili-crusted trout with a pineapple peanut salsa and jicama cilantro cakes to filet of beef stuffed with spinach, garlic and goat cheese. Starters are reasonably priced between $4.50 and $6.75, while entrees range from $14.50 to $24.50 for the stuffed filet. Call 923-5600 for reservations.

Syzygy, now in its sixth successful season, is well established as a favorite among locals. Chef Jean Dwyer uses her New York and Aspen experience to combine French, southwestern, Oriental and Italian cuisines.

Don't be put off by the hard-to-pronounce name (Siz i je) or the obscure explanation of its meaning on the menu (the conjuction or oppostion of three or more heavenly bodies—for us earthlings, that's fine food, good service, and elegant atmosphere.) At 520 E. Hyman Avenue on the second floor (925-3700, reservations required); the atmosphere is intimate yet casual. The menu consists largely of specials that change frequently, but a few menu staples continue to sell out. Get there early if you want the pineapple scented sage crêpes with pheasant onions and garlic, served with a kumquat relish—it's rarely there by the last seating.

Start with the ahi tartare . . . sashimi of ahi with oriental flavors on tamari seed cakes and chili pesto. For an entrée, try the sauteed sea scallops with guava barbeque and wasatch potato chips. Plan on spending about $11 to $12 for appetizers and $27 to $34 for entrées, a meal well worth remembering. Open daily from 6 to 10 p.m.

Piñons (second floor at 105 S. Mill; 920-2021), decorated in a cozy western ranch style, with aged stucco walls, a big leather bar and huge brass bowls filled with corn tortillas, specializes in Colorado Cuisine. The wild pheasant quesadillas with sour cream, salsa and guacamole were rivaled only by the lobster strudel, a flaky combination of phyllo dough, morels and chanterelles. While other appetizers are not nearly so inspired in design, they are all perfectly executed. Try the potato pancakes with pan-seared scallops and caviar. Entrées range from a simple roast chicken with natural juices to pan-seared local pheasant breast with foie gras and truffles! The ahi is sautéed with a macadamia nut crust and lime butter, and the elk tenderloin, served with ginger and pink peppercorn sauce, is perfectly grilled. In fact, all meats and fish are grilled on a mesquite and cherry wood grill, perfectly. Desserts vary daily, but will usually include the white chocolate macadamia nut tart. You may need a chain saw to get through it, but it's worth every effort for its nutty caramel taste. Prices are steep, but you didn't come to Aspen to save money.

If you think, at these prices they should entertain you and clean your apartment for a year, there is a man who will at least do the former. Mead Metcalf has been playing to the Crystal Palace's two sellout crowds per evening (6:00 and 9:15 p.m.) for the last 34 years. At 300 East Hyman Avenue (925-1455; reservations may be necessary several weeks in advance), **The Crystal Palace** adds wit and satire to the old notion of barbershop quartets. Amid stained glass and crystal chandeliers, the talented staff not only cranks out a full dinner and bar service, but then belts out a cabaret revue spoofing the media's latest victims. Last year added skits on Mike Tyson and John Sununu to hits about Jim and Tammy and Fergy and Di. For $45 per person ($35 at the later show), you can choose from perfectly pink beef tenderloin with Madeira sauce, roast duckling with sauce bigarade (a piquant sauce flavored with Cointreau and brandy), rack of lamb or prime rib. The food doesn't have to be good, but it is.

For additional entertainment, try New York's **Tatou**, new last season. Located at 419 East Hyman (920-9091), Tatou offers an early show of live jazz and blues with a prix-fixe dinner for $28.50. Dinner is served from 6 to 7:30, with the music beginning at 7. The three-course dinner includes starters such as lobster chowder or wild mushroom casserole, followed by honey mustard salmon, grouper braised with Zinfandel, or crispy duck, and a selection of home-made desserts. After 9 p.m., there is a $10 music charge.

On the outside chance there's still a platinum card burning a hole in your parka, try Aspen's latest in exquisite dining: **Renaissance**, 304 East Hopkins (925-2402). Chef/owner Charles Dale claims to be one of three restaurants in the world to have a daily changing degustation or tasting menu (six courses), as well as offering course-by-course wine pairings by the glass. The menu itself is $85, or with wine, $125. Dale's menu offers modern French cuisine, with a touch of Colorado. The wine selection alone offers impressive choices for a by-the-glass listing. A leader in ecological awareness in Aspen, Dale's menu reflects his concerns: all fish are line-cught or farm raised. Start with tuna carpaccio, then proceed to perfectly grilled ahi à la Pekinoise with Thai beach rice. His game specialties often include roast Colorado pheasant with pear-onion marmalade and polenta. Don't miss the Renaissance grand dessert—it's got more chocolate than Switzerland! A la carte menu entrées cost $26 to $31. Open daily, 6 to 10:30 p.m. Reservations recommended.

The Golden Horn Restaurant, downstairs at the corner of Mill and Cooper dates back to a 1949 nightclub. Klaus Christ, chef/owner since 1972, has always offered savory Swiss specialties with a wine list cited by The Wine Spectator for seven consecutive years as one of the top 100 in the country. But recently Christ introduced a new lighter menu, a radical departure from many other menus in town, in addition to offering the traditional Swiss fare. Called Cuisine Minceur, from a style developed in southern France, it offers three full-flavored courses for less than 450 calories. The menu changes daily, but generally begins with a soup, such as fresh tomato basil, followed by an entrée such as grilled veal chop or swordfish, and completed with fresh berries. Open daily and reservations are advised (925-3373).

The hottest new place in Snowmass is **Cowboys** in the Silvertree Complex. Open après-ski from 2:30 p.m. for appetizers, Cowboys also serves dinner daily from 5:30 to 10 p.m. Chef Philip Kendzior has fired up a menu sure to thrill even the boldest cowboy. The Colorado loin of lamb is stuffed with achiote and roast garlic pesto and served with a rosemary tomato cream. The mesquite-grilled T-bone is served cowboy-style, branded with a sweet and mild barbeque sauce. Shrub dusted tournedos are saddled on a corn-bread crouton and served with campfire tomatoes. They claim on the menu to be able to meet special dessert needs, but no one could tell me if they serve S'mores. For reservations call 923-5249.

For a real adventure, head out to the **Ashcroft Pinecreek Cookhouse** (925-1044) for a casual evening and solid fare. At an elevation of 9,725 feet, this rustic log cabin is among the Elk Mountain peaks and towering pines, near the ghost town of Ashcroft, some 12 miles from Aspen. Turn left in front of the church at the Aspen Highlands turnoff and drive to the end of Castle Creek Road. From here at the Ashcroft Ski Touring Center, the Cookhouse is accessible by a one and a half mile cross-country trek, or by a sleigh drawn by a team of Percherons. Reservations are essential, as the logistics of running a kitchen not reached by road during the winter is no small matter. Between the 12:00-2:30 luncheon service, featuring a skier's buffet, and the 6:30 dinner service, the Cookhouse feeds several hundred people each day. And all that food must come in by snowmobile. Meals are prepared right in front of you in the open kitchen.

Food will be served by one of your cross-country guides. Dinner is a prix fixe meal for $50 ($10 extra if you are one of the 29 who chose to take the sleigh). The menu changes daily, but includes choices of venison, lamb, fresh trout, or a pasta dish, such as fettucine with artichokes, sun-dried tomatoes and shrimp. After the 40-minute trek or the nippy sleigh ride, the cozy cabin with tables adorned with deerhorn and candle centerpieces seems perfect. After the meal and a bit of wine, the trip back to the Touring Center doesn't seem nearly so long or cold. What better way to end your escape from an urban existence than under the clear Colorado skies?

Dining on the Mountain

Unlike the majority of U.S. resorts, the Aspen Skiing Company puts restaurant contracts up for public bidding, so real live restaurateurs end up with these contracts. And what you'll find is a far cry from the typical ski-joint burger line where all meals are made at the base cafeteria resort-operated kitchen, then trucked up the mountain for your dining pleasure. Sit-down dining has not yet been approved by the masses who come to the mountain for a more obvious reason, but when you want to take it easy, it's a nice alternative.

Cafe Suzanne, formerly at the bottom of Buttermilk West, is now at the bottom of Elk Camp Lift 10 at Snowmass and specializes in French Country Cuisine. Also a cafeteria, the food is a pleasant surprise, with a daily assortment of entrée crêpes, such as buckwheat crêpes with spinach, mushroom or chicken, and of dessert crêpes. Suzanne McPherson has taken her classical French training and customized it to the fast-food needs of the mountain. There is a daily hot entrée special, generally a Provençal or Norman dish, and a special soup with a homemade sourdough boule. You won't find a Parisian hot dog with gruyère and Dijon in any other area mountain restaurant. Also, some menu items, such as chicken breast marinated in herbes de Provence, are flagged with a heart logo, indicating AHA heart-healthy selections. Open daily 9 a.m. to 3:30 p.m.

Also at Snowmass, try **Gwyn's High Alpine Restaurant**, at the top of Alpine Springs (Lift 8), for fine dining. Gwyn offers a sit-down breakfast daily from 9:30 until 10:30 a.m. Lunch is served from 11:30 a.m. to 2:30 p.m. Reservations are essential (923-5188). If you take the first chair up, but aren't quite ready to brave the cold, you can relax with an orange blossom and enjoy a zucchini frittata, fresh fruit pancakes, or alpine potatoes with mushrooms, zucchini, green onions, tomatoes and Alouette, Monterey Jack, and cheddar cheeses over a cup of Kona coffee. At noon, you can warm up with the special appetizer—New Zealand green lip mussels, steamed and served with a roasted red pepper; a fresh garden vegetable fondue, a pasta special, the catch of the day—perhaps Rocky Mountain ruby red trout, pan-fried in citrus flour and served with a cranberry orange butter, or the warm vegetable strudel, such as zucchini, mushroom, tomato, or smoked cheddar.

While not a sit-down restaurant, at **Bonnie's** just above Lift 3 on Aspen Mountain, owner Bonnie Rayburn feeds some 1,500 hungry skiers per day between 9:30 a.m. and

2:30 p.m.. Go before noon or after 2:00, unless you love lines. (If you do find yourself there at peak hours, there's a new outdoor fajita express line for $3.50 that will get you on your way in a hurry.) At $3.25 per slice, Bonnie's gourmet pizza on freshly made crust is a huge crowd pleaser. Choose from smoked chicken with pesto, spinach with goat cheese, or spicy mushroom and eggplant. Home made soups are served with large crusty pieces of freshly made French bread. The apple strudel, with homemade pastry and local apples, is legendary. Relax on the sunny deck—there's no better mountainside people watching.

At **Ruthie's**, top of Lift 1A, Aspen Skiing Company has created the Aspen View Room, where you can relax over lunch and enjoy a great scope of the town below. Start with a mesquite-grilled onion soup, topped with Swiss and parmesan. The entrée listing specializes in grilled items, such as the Aztec grilled chicken breast with black beans and corn salsa and pepper jack cheese, or the ski patrol trout, mesquite charred with toasted almond-lemon pesto sauce. Reservations are accepted—call 920-0728.

by Katy Keck

Snowmass Ski Area

Often treated as part of the Aspen complex because it's owned by the same corporation, Snowmass is a formidable mountain in its own right. Even with the jostling among ski areas for first rank in total acreage and lifts, Snowmass is one of the top five resorts in America in size. It covers over 2,000 acres, more area than Aspen, Mt., Buttermilk and Aspen Highlands combined! It has four mountain peaks and a vertical of over 3,600 feet. Now, with three high-speed quad superchairs, the lift system can move over 20,000 skiers an hour.

Snowmass is the perfect intermediate and advanced playground, the promised land for cruisers. Some 62 percent of the terrain is labeled as intermediate. The Big Burn allows you to put it on autopilot and let go, and the run from the top of Elk Camp to Fanny Hill is nearly a four-mile cruise. But Snowmass has steeps and areas like Hanging Valley Glades and Hanging Valley Wall that pucker up intermediates and delight advanced skiers.

The village of Snowmass seems to stretch forever. This is a purpose-built ski resort à la Keystone, Copper Mountain and Steamboat. There is a village mall area with a cluster of shops, restaurants, bars and ski administration facilities. Most of Snowmass, hundreds of condos, is spread out around the lower part of the ski area. At Snowmass over 95 percent of the accommodations are slopeside, where skiers only have to wander from their doors to the slope and ski down to the first lift. It doesn't get much more convenient than Snowmass.

Snowmass Ski Area Facts
Base elevation: 8,220'; Summit elevation: 11,835'; Vertical drop: 3,615 feet
Number of lifts: 16—3 quad superchairs, 2 triple chairs,
9 double chairs, 2 surface lifts
Percent snowmaking: 3 percent Total acreage: 2,099 skiable acres
Uphill capacity: 20,535 per hour Bed Base: 6,000 in resort

Where to ski

Beginners have a wide, gentle area parallel to the village. Fanny Hill eases down by the mall, Wood Run lift opens another easy glide around the Wood Road side of the village, and further to the left, a long straightaway, Funnel, will give the beginner the feeling he's really covering terrain. Beginners who get antsy and want to see more of the mountain can head up to Sam's Knob, eat lunch, enjoy the view and take the easy way down a meandering trail bearing the names Max Park, Lunchline and Dawdler, which softly turns its way back to Fanny Hill. (Make sure you avoid the blue runs on the face of Sam's Knob because they are not for beginners.) The next step up would be Elk Camp, which is labeled blue but is very gentle.

Intermediates will be in their element. The Big Burn is legendary cruiser's fun. It's an entire side of a mountain that was reportedly set aflame by Ute Indians in the 1880s as warning to advancing white settlers. The pioneers settled anyway, but the trees never grew back thickly, so the run, dotted by a few spruce trees, is a mile wide and a mile and a half long.

If the pitch there is not quite to your liking, head over to High Alpine, which is perhaps five degrees steeper. (Once on the mountain, the lift system will keep you at the higher altitudes until you decide to come in for a landing.)

Advanced skiers and experts ready to burn up well-pitched cruising will think they've found nirvana when they make the first descent into the Campground area. A wonderful long run for solid intermediates or advanced skiers is to come off the top of Big Burn on Sneaky's, then schuss to avoid the uphill stretch at Sam's Knob, cut south around the Knob and head into the blacks of Bear Claw, Slot, Wildcat or Zugspitze to the base of the Campground lift. All offer great cruises and patches of moguls normally of the mellow, sand-dune variety.

Advanced skiers will have a chance to keep their hearts in their throats by dropping through the trees in the Hanging Valley Glades or enjoying steep open-bowl skiing on the Hanging Valley Wall, longer and more intriguing—both labeled as double black diamonds. To get there quickly on powder mornings, take Wood Run, Alpine Springs and High Alpine Chairs. There are no signs and it has a remote feel. The ski school offers guided tours back here. Check at the ski school desk at High Alpine.

Another playground for the extreme skier is the drops into the Cirque, a scooped-out place between Sheer Bliss and High Alpine lifts. Don't try them unless you're comfortable on Hanging Valley Wall. You'll have to be deft of foot on Rock Island and KT Gully.

Even more challenging is AMF at the top of The Cirque. It's not on a trail map, but a local resident says it's "awesome" and stands for "Adios, My Friend."

Mountain Rating

This is an intermediate mountain even though it has pockets of advanced terrain and beginner smoothies. Skiers who love cruising will think they have arrived in heaven. Few competent skiers who have returned from Snowmass have been heard complaining. That's the best recommendation of all.

Snowboarding

Snowboarding is allowed on the mountain. However three chutes are controlled based on snow conditions. Just below the Naked Lady chair on the Funnel trail there is a 500-foot long, 50-foot wide halfpipe with eight-foot-high sides. Private and group lessons are available through the ski school. Boards are rented at The Boardwalk in the village.

Cross-country

See the Aspen section.

Ski school

See the Aspen section.

Lift tickets

See the Aspen section.

Accommodations

Snowmass is a modern condominium village. There are few hotels but thousands of condominium rooms, and the condos are new and luxurious. Their positioning on the slopes cannot be beat, and the modern touches like soaring cathedral ceilings and wide-open, glassed-in living rooms will make this seem like a vacation in paradise. All rates below are for the regular season with double occupancy. All reservations are through Snowmass Accommodations (800-598-2004).

There are more economical times to visit than the regular season listed here. The "value season" is normally before Christmas, in January and in early April.

Hotel accommodations are relatively limited:

The Snowmass Lodge and Club is below and outside the village, but posh. It serves as the Nordic center and has a deluxe athletic club. There are regular shuttles to the slopes. Rates, including lift tickets: $190-$275 a night.

These two are the class acts in Snowmass Village. The **Silvertree** has rooms as low as $130 during low season, regular season rates are $280-$355. **Wildwood's** rates are as low as $103 in low season and then $192-202 during regular season. Both are comfortable, with beautiful rooms, and close to everything in Snowmass.

Mountain Chalet costs $179-$188 during regular season with rooms as inexpensive as $100 during low season. The **Pokolodi** normal season rates are $130-$140 with low season costs as low as $56.

Condominiums are everywhere in Snowmass. The rates given here are unit per night rates for two-bedroom units designed to accommodate four during regular season. The **Woodrun V** units are the most luxurious and roomiest, with multilevel units, private hot tubs and elegant furnishings. Rate: $520-$620. **Shadowbrook** is probably the best in the village area with two bedroom and den condos costing $375 and four bedrooms ranging up to $750.

The **Top of Village** two-bedroom units run $375-$425 in regular season. The **Timberline** three bedroom condos cost $420-$450 during regular season. Both of these are a good 5- to 10-minute climb above the village mall.

The **Stonebridge** in the center of the village has two-bedroom units for $350-$390. The **Terracehouse, Willows** and **Lichenhearth** are clustered together two levels below Village Mall; two-bedroom units range between $200 and $330. The Willows are unusual because they are separate buildings, either cozy studios with kitchenettes ($119-$180 for two) or two bedrooms for $238-$330. Above the village is the **Sonnenblick,** with three-bedroom/loft units only, for $380-$475, which may be good for hefty-sized families.

Dining

Snowmass mostly attracts a cook-in-the-condo crowd. But the choices for dining in Snowmass are excellent for anyone deciding to head into the village . . . and remember that Aspen is only 20 minutes away.

But the resort claims two of the best restaurants in the area. **Kranbloonik** (923-3953) has become an institution, even when measured against the more trendy competition in Aspen. It's a formal dining experience featuring wild game and seafood amid spectacular views and the howling of sled dogs in the kennels outside. With a bit of imagination you can imagine yourself in "Doctor Zhivago" country. **Chez Grandmere** (923-2570), has only seven tables and offers a fixed-price meal in a Victorian setting for around $50. Other top quality spots are **Cowboys** on the Village Mall with gourmet Colorado cuisine. **La Boheme, Il Poggio** and **The Conservatory.**

Midrange dining can be found at **The Tower, Hite's** (with unusual breakfasts), **Pippins Steak and Lobster, Moguls, Brother's Grill** and **Mountain Dragon** for chinese.

For the family, **The Stewpot** features soups, tasty and unusual stews and sandwiches, or try **S'No Beach Café** (featuring "eggs S'no Beach" for breakfast). A popular hangout is **La Pinata** for fair Mexican food at fair prices, where sombreros and wild art line the walls and locals play darts and table shuffleboard.

Snowmass excels with mountaintop cookery. See Katy Keck's recommendations in Aspen Savoir Faire.

Après-ski/nightlife

The **Timbermill** and the **Brother's Grill** are the hubs of immediate après-ski with live music. The Timbermill tends to be more crowded and rowdier. Brother's has five different draft beers and almost a dozen hot drinks for quick warmups. **Hite's** has also begun jazz for après-ski.

At night Snowmass is quiet. The hottest action in town is in the **Tower** (923-4650), where Doc Eason performs continuous magic throughout the night. For those with dancin' boots, head to **Cowboy's** where theuy strike up western music and dance country swing.

Child care

At Snowmass the Big Burn Bears program handles children three and a half years through kindergarten for snow play and ski instruction. The Snow Cubs program accepts children 18 months to three-and-a-half, and offers indoor and outdoor play and nap time. Both include lunch and cost $55 a day, or $255 for five days. Evening rates are $5 an hour per child, dinner included. Reservations suggested: call 925-1220 or (800) 525-6200.

Little Red School House (923-3756) offers fully licensed day care for children from two and a half to five years; the Little Red School toddler Center (923-5020) offers day care for those from one to two and a half years. Snowbunnies (923-2809) provides sitters for three to six year olds.

Other activities

The Anderson Ranch Arts Center in Snowmass Village exhibits work by visiting and resident artists throughout the winter. The center also offers a series of workshops in ceramics, woodworking and photography from January through April. Call 923-3181 for current events.

Getting there

See the Aspen Section.

Information/reservations

Snowmass runs one the best reservation systems in the country. Staff members will take care of your entire ski vacation from air transportation and transfer to lodging and lift tickets, lessons and child care. Call (800) 598-2004, or (303) 923-2010.

Breckenridge Colorado

Breckenridge is a town with a split personality, but don't blame it on modern development; it's been that way from conception. Breckenridge was named for a man who became a Confederate brigadier general, but its streets are named for Union heroes—Lincoln, Grant and Sherman. This is the town that first welcomed a hearty former slave, Barney Lancelot Ford—who went on to create the most successful saloon between St. Louis and San Francisco—and then unceremoniously ran him out of town. Breckenridge, eager to become Summit County's capital, reportedly "obtained" the county records from neighboring Parkville though an infamous midnight requisition.

The Victorian buildings lining the streets of town have witnessed wild revelry during gold and silver booms and the discovery of Colorado's largest gold nugget, but they also stood silent over windswept, vacant streets when Breckenridge joined the list of Colorado Ghost Towns.

Today, reborn, Breckenridge still displays its inherited division. Modern developments around the base area rise in stark contrast to the restored Victorian town. The ski industry brought economic life back to Breckenridge, but the born-again fervor of the locals has preserved the town's Victorian gingerbread soul. Thus, visitors may submerge themselves in modern condos, pulsating spas,

---

Breckenridge Facts

Base elevation: 9,600'; Summit elevation: 12,998'; Vertical drop: 3,398 feet.
Number and types of lifts: 16—4 superchairs, 1 triple chair, 8 double chairs and 3 surface lifts
*Acreage: 1,600 skiable acres **Percent of snowmaking:** 43 percent*
***Uphill capacity:** 24,430 skiers per hour **Bed base:** 23,000*

modern fitness facilities, glitzy discos, and three mountains. They also have in Victorian Breckenridge hundreds
of boutiques, scores of pubs and dozens of restaurants
packed into restored buildings.

The wooden gingerbread kingdom and the concrete
and glass slopeside developments are tethered by an old-
time trolley bus, which shuttles visitors from the restored
town—where it seems at home—to Beaver Run, the Hilton
and the Village at Breckenridge.

Breckenridge is now the second most popular ski area
in Colorado and the third in the nation. Because it's relatively close to Denver, weekend skiers stream into the
town. The installation of high-speed four-seat chair lifts
on Peaks 8 and 10 and two high-speed quads on Peak 9
normally makes for a wait of less than 10 minutes. And
with the skiing spread over three mountains, there is
plenty of room for skiers even on peak days.

You'll find your fellow skiers are a mixed bag, generally down-to-earth. You'll see very few of society's upper
crust, and you won't be overwhelmed with teens and pre-
teens bombing down the mountain. Regular ski jackets
predominate, with almost no furs to be seen. The
Breckenridge crowd definitely is not as upscale as that of
Aspen or Vail, nor is it as laid back as Crested Butte. Here,
you'll find a balanced, middle-of-the-road, comfortable
atmosphere and plenty of great skiing.

The skiing

Breckenridge, on three peaks covering 1,600 acres, is
the largest of the Summit County ski areas. At the main
base facility, at the bottom of Peak 9, the Quicksilver
high-speed quad chair powers skiers from the village up to
the higher lifts connecting to the Peak 10 sector. Another
superchair takes skiers up from the Beaver Run area to
either Peak 9 or a Peak 8 connection.

Originally this was known as an excellent beginner
and intermediate resort, but the opening of the back bowls
off Peak 8, and the North Face of Peak 9 and Peak 10,
added hundreds of acres of expert terrain. Today,
Breckenridge boasts a very high percentage of expert terrain and the highest in-bounds skiing in North America,
and still maintains its wide-open, well-groomed runs for
beginners and intermediates.

Imperial Bowl, crowning Peak 8, which tops out at nearly 13,000 feet, creating a total vertical of 3,400 feet. This bowl adds 60 acres to Breckenridge's terrain.

Beginners will probably stick to the front side of Peak 9 area unless they are enrolled in the Peak 8 ski school, which has excellent beginner facilities. Peak 9 offers the most extensive intermediate and beginner terrain. The easiest runs are Silverthorn, Eldorado and Red Rover, all skiable from the top of the Quicksilver lift. For more challenge, intermediates should take Lift B to the summit and ski down Cashier, Bonanza and Upper Columbia. More advanced intermediates enjoy American, Gold King and Peerless, which might be rated black at a smaller resort.

The North Face on the back of Peak 9 is expert territory. Plenty of good skiers have begged for a rest after playing with Tom's Baby, and even prayers won't help lower intermediates who accidentally find themselves in Hades, Devil's Crotch or Inferno—once you drop down the face from Chair E, there is no escape or easy traverse.

For the best cruising, head to Peak 10 and alternate between Centennial and Crystal. These runs are slightly easier than American and friends off Mercury Superchair, but the combination of a high-speed lift with the rest of the mountain being expert terrain makes the crowds lighter. Everything else on Peak 10 is in the expert category, with Mustang, Dark Rider and Blackhawk boasting monstrous bumps. The Burn, dropping to the left of the high-speed lift, offers limited short-but-sweet tree skiing.

Peak 8, where skiing at Breckenridge began, is the most varied of the mountains. Beginners practice snowplows and stem christies near the base facility; intermediates have a chance to ski alongside the high-speed Colorado lift down Springmeier, Crescendo and Swinger; experts and advanced skiers can play in Imperial Bowl and drop down a half dozen runs, such as Spruce and Rounders to the left of the Colorado lift, or play in the Back Bowls. Experts can take the T-bar up to wide-open Horseshoe Bowl and the smaller, steeper Contest Bowl. (These bowls are wide—solid intermediates can ski them.)

The Breckenridge Skier Services staff provides a free guided skiing tour of the three peaks Monday through Friday at 10 a.m. by an appointment only. Stop in at the ski school for sign-up, or call 453-5000.

Mountain rating

Breckenridge could be one of the world's perfect resorts if it found somewhere to grade a long beginner slope: the current facilities for beginners are adequate but could be improved. For intermediates the resort is heaven, with plenty of varied terrain and excellent access. There is plenty to keep any expert busy and happy. The bowls, the North Face, the short mogul runs between Peaks 8 and 9 and the bulk of Peak 10 are designed with advanced and expert skiers in mind.

Cross-country

The Breckenridge Nordic Center, near Peak 8 base, is the base facility for 23 kilometers of groomed, double-set trails for all skiing abilities. Ski rentals, lessons, guided and moonlight tours are available. Call (303) 453-6855.

Ski school (92/93 prices)

Breckenridge has 300 instructors, teaching all levels. There are bump courses, and racing and powder classes.

Group lessons cost $36* for a one-day lesson; $73 for two-days' lessons. Private lessons are $70 for one hour, $165 for three hours and $295 for six hours; $20 extra for additional students. (* one-day price is from last season)

The children's ski school handles students from never-evers to advanced skiers. Ticket prices are the same as those for the adult program, but child supervision and lunch are included for $5, or send the kids along with a sack lunch. There are children's programs at both Peak 8 and Peak 9, and there are differences between the two. Peak 8 has a nursery for children from ages two months to two years and a junior ski program for kids three to five. Peak 9 is for beginning, intermediate and advanced child skiers from three to five years. Reservations are required for the children's program.

A series of special women's seminars include three days of lessons, lift tickets, videos, wine and cheese party, a group dinner and picnic for $260; it runs occasionally through the year. Call (303) 453-5000 for exact dates.

NASTAR races are held daily, 11 a.m. to 3:30 p.m., on Country Boy on Peak 9 and on Freeway on Peak 8. Register at the top of the course. Fees are $5 for two runs and $1 for

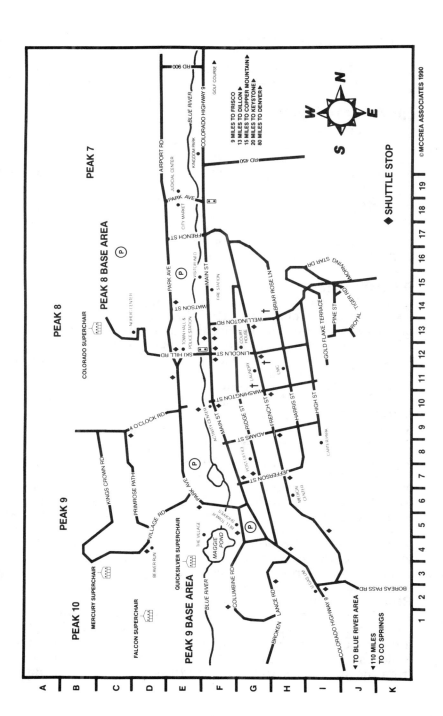

PEAK 7

PEAK 8

PEAK 8 BASE AREA

PEAK 9

PEAK 10

PEAK 9 BASE AREA

COLORADO SUPERCHAIR

MERCURY SUPERCHAIR

FALCON SUPERCHAIR

QUICKSILVER SUPERCHAIR

KINGS CROWN RD

PRIMROSE PATH

VILLAGE RD

BEAVER RUN

4 O'CLOCK RD

THE VILLAGE

BELL TOWER SQUARE

SILVER SQUARE

MAGGIE POND

COLUMBINE RD

BLUE RIVER

BROKEN LANCE RD

COLORADO HIGHWAY 9

▼TO BLUE RIVER AREA

▼110 MILES
TO CO SPRINGS

BOREAS PASS RD

NORDIC CENTER

PARK AVE

CITY MARKET

PARK AVE

JUDICIAL CENTER

AIRPORT RD

KINGDOM PARK

BLUE RIVER

RD 900

GOLF COURSE

COLORADO HIGHWAY 9

RD 450

FRENCH ST

MAIN ST

WATSON ST

TOWN HALL &
POLICE STATION

SKI HILL RD

FIRE STATION

WELLINGTON RD

BRIAR ROSE LN

COURT
HOUSE

LINCOLN ST

CMC

LAUNDRY

WASHINGTON ST

MAIN ST

RIDGE ST

ADAMS ST

FRENCH ST

HARRIS ST

HIGH ST

GOLD FLAKE TERRACE

PINE ST

ROYAL
TIGER RD

MORNING STAR DR

JEFFERSON ST

MEDICAL
CENTER

LARTH PARK

ACTIVITY CENTER

PARK AVE

ILLINOIS GULCH

LOMAX

9 MILES TO FRISCO ▶
13 MILES TO DILLON ▶
15 MILES TO COPPER MOUNTAIN ▶
20 MILES TO KEYSTONE ▶
80 MILES TO DENVER ▶

N
W   E
S

◆ SHUTTLE STOP

©MCCREA ASSOCIATES 1990

additional runs. A self-timed course is open on Peak 8 at Freeway and on Country Boy on Peak 9 for 50 cents a run.

Lift tickets (92/93 prices)

Full day—$36* adults / $15 children (12 and under) and seniors (60-69); two of three days—$73/$30; three of four days—$99.75/$45; four of six days—$130/$60; five of seven days—$157.50/$75; six of eight days—$180/$90. (* prices from last season)

Seniors 70 and older, children 5 and younger ski free.

A Ski the Summit pass is available for four and six days. A coupon book is good at Keystone, Arapahoe and Copper Mountain, as well as Breckenridge: four days— $132 adult/$68 child and senior; six days—$198/$102.

Accommodations

Breckenridge boasts the most extensive ski-in/ski-out accommodations of any resort in the U.S. There are no super luxury ultra-expensive accommodations in the resort, although if you require such amenities private homes can be found tucked along the trails back in the trees. For the basic skier, the best of Breckenridge is right on the slopes.

The Village at Breckenridge (reservations and information: 800-321-8552; in Colorado: 800-643-2997; local: 303-453-2000) surrounds the Peak 9 base area. Try to get into Plaza 1, 2 or 3, which are the most spacious units. The three-bedroom units here are giant-sized. Liftside has studios with Murphy beds, and the Hotel Breckenridge rooms are medium-sized, well-appointed studios. All amenities are available: on-site health club facilities, indoor/outdoor pools, hot tubs, racquetball, steam, sauna and exercise room. Approximate per person rates— (regular season): $115-140; (value season): $85.

Beaver Run (reservations and information: 800-525-2253; in Colorado: 800-331-1282; local: 303-453-6000). This complex is built alongside Mercury and Quicksilver super chairs serving Peak 9. It is also home to Spencer's Restaurant, Tiffany's disco and the Copper Top for après-ski. There are seven outdoor hot tubs, indoor/outdoor swimming pools, a giant indoor miniature golf course and a great game room for kids tired of skiing. The Kinderhut child care center, located in the hotel, will take children from the ages of one to three; kids three to six can take ski lessons. Deluxe rooms with fireplaces and spas cost about $50 a night extra. Normal rates for two-bedroom condo— regular season: $295; value season: $240.

The Breckenridge Hilton (reservations and information: 800-321-8444; in Colorado: 800-624-4433; Denver: 303-825-3800; local: 453-4500) This hotel is almost but not quite ski-in/ski-out: it's only 50 yards from the slopes. The rooms here are massive, about 40 feet by 12. There is an indoor swimming pool, whirlpool spas and a fitness and exercise room. Rates per room with two queen beds or a king with sofabed—normal season: $140; value season: $105.

The River Mountain Lodge (800) 325-2342; in Colorado (800) 553-4456; local (303) 453-4711. This collection of studio and one-bedroom suites is in the heart of Breckenridge, only steps away from Main Street. The ski bus stops across the street with excellent access to any area of the slopes. This is one of the most reasonable accommodations in Breckenridge.

For most other lodging, call **Breckenridge Resort Chamber**, (800) 221-1091, (800) 800-BREC or (303) 453-2918. Explain exactly what you want to the reservationist and he will attempt to match you to the best property. Remember that the major tradeoff is between price and distance to the slopes. NOTE: Trail's End and The Cedars, both condominiums, have every bit as good a location as Beaver Run, the Hilton or the Village; only the amenities are different.

Dining

Breckenridge has not gained a reputation for gourmet dining, and it probably won't in the near future. The best restaurants in town won't set a Michelin taster's tongue to quivering, but they still can rustle up acceptable vittles.

Our top choices where price is no object are:

Webers Restaurant, 200 N. Main Street (tel. 453-9464), with the best Victorian ambiance in town and some of the best food. Cuisine is German, featuring sauerbraten and schnitzels, and traditional American. Meals cost between $12 and $22, excluding drinks. Entrées include soup, salad, veggies, dessert and coffee. Reservations suggested.

St. Bernard Inn, 103 S. Main Street (tel. 453-2572), has what most consider the best Italian food in town. Entrées are priced $14-$24, with pasta dishes ranging $8-$11. Reservations suggested.

Best of the moderate restaurants: **Tillie's**, 213 S. Ridge Street (453-0669), has good basic food. Menu is limited but so are the prices. The hand-carved bar, the tin ceiling and the stained glass provide a good period effect. Some nights Tillie's crowd could be quorum for a town meeting.

The Hearthstone, 130 S. Ridge St. (tel. 453-6921), in one of the best Victorian houses in Breckenridge, which served as a bordello in the old mining days. Prices are reasonable, food acceptable and ambiance hard to beat. One-pound steaks for $17. Most entrées priced from $10 to $15.

Some locals have recommended **Pierre's** for fine dining. Try it at your own risk. Tex-Mex food is reliable and always a bargain. Try it in **Mi Casa**, 600 Park Ave, across from the base of Peak 9, or **Sol Iquano**, 306 N. French Street, (a bit out of the way), where the emphasis is on Mex more than Tex. **Colt's Sports Bar and Eatery**, 401 S. Main, has satellite TV for the big events and good, inexpensive food 'til late. For fish, head for **The Whale's Tail** at 323 Main Street (453-2221).

Breakfast: For one of the best breakfasts at any ski resort, the hands-down winner in Breckenridge is **The Prospector** at 130 S. Main Street. The Huevos Ranchero will be memorable and they should test your facial sweat glands. The best bargain breakfast is found at the **Copper Top** in Beaver Run, where for about two bucks skiers get eggs, bacon or sausage, hash browns and a muffin.

Après-ski/nightlife

Breckenridge's liveliest après-ski bars are **Tiffany's** and **Copper Top**, depending on the hour and season in Beaver Run, the **Village Pub** in the Bell Tower Mall, and **Mi Casa**, with great margaritas-by-the-liter, across the street from the Peak 9 base.

Tiffany's at Beaver Run rocks until the wee hours, but after dinner most of the action moves into town. **The Mogul**, downstairs at 109 Main Street, has a raucous younger crowd with loud, live music and long lines on weekends. A slightly older group with plenty of locals gathers at **Shamus O'Toole's**, 115 S. Ridge Street, a wide-open roadhouse with live music on most evenings and an eclectic crowd, ranging from absolute blue-collar to those yuppied-up for the evening. Some nights the mix is intoxicating, and on others merely intoxicated, which often sets off fireworks. **Horseshoe II** on Main Street gets packed and there is dancing at **Josha's** on Park Avenue across from the Village at Breckenridge. For a non-dancing, quieter time, wander down to the **St. Bernard** on Main St.; a cozy bar in the back is often packed with business-class locals. Try it after midnight for local gossip at its best.

The old **Gold Pan**, 103 N. Main Street, is the legacy of Barney Lancelot Ford. It is the oldest continuously operating bar west of the Mississippi. It's hard to imagine, but this was once one of the jumpingest places in the Wild West, with a miner or two known to be thrown through the saloon doors. A long, 100-year-old mahogany bar presides over a now worn, dimly lit room with a pinball machine tucked into the back corner and a couple of well-utilized pool tables. The crowd has shifted to yuppie pool players from the former group of truckers, pool sharks sporting earrings, and the temporarily unemployed.

Child care

The Kid's Castle is located at Peak 8 and has been expanded. It accepts children as young as two months. Infant care for children from two months through two years is $45 a day, $30 a half day. Parents must provide diapers, formula, food, change of clothes etc.

Toddler care for those 18 months to two years costs the same. Provide diapers for children not yet potty-trained.

Child care for three to five year olds is $38 a day and $26 for half days.

The Junior Ski School offers classes for children between three and five years. An all-day child care/ski school costs $44. A half day of lessons is $30, three-day packages $120. An hour of private lessons together with a day of child care costs $80, with a half-day of child care, $70. Call 453-5000.

The Kinderhut, at Peak 9 in the Beaver Run Resort, accepts children between one and three years in a child care program with outdoor activities as well as indoor play. Older children between three and six have programs that include a full day of instruction, equipment and snacks. The daily 90/91 rate was $45; $35 for a half day. There are also multiday packages that range up to around $250 for six days. Call 453-0379 or 453-6000.

Other activities

Breckenridge is full of opportunities for exploration of the old town. There is a historical tour, over 100 restaurants and bars and scores of boutiques with everything from jewels and furs to hats and T-shirts.

Heli-skiing is available to back-country locations. Call 668-5600 for details.

Ice skating is centered on Maggie Pond. Snowmobiles can be rented from Tiger Run Tours at 453-2231. Sleigh rides leave every evening for a starry drive out to a steak dinner in a heated tent. And best of all is a dog sled ride (453-0353). Just the experience of seeing the bounding dogs and a dozen puppies is worth the effort.

Getting there

Breckenridge is 85 miles west of Denver's Stapleton Airport by I-70 to Exit 203, then south on Highway 9. It is a 90-minute drive. Resort Express has regular vans connecting the resort with the airport. Telephone: (800) 334-7433.

In Breckenridge, nearly everything is within walking distance. The town is served by a three-tiered transport system. The town trolley and town buses cruise the streets regularly and the Summit Stage links Breckenridge with Keystone, Copper Mountain and Frisco.

Information/reservations

The Breckenridge Resort Chamber central reservation office handles transfers, lodging and lift tickets. Call (800) 221-1091 or (303) 453-2918.

Breckenridge snow conditions: (303) 453-6118.
Breckenridge switchboard: (303) 453-5000.

Copper Mountain Colorado

Copper Mountain Resort rests on the Gold Coast of Colorado skiing, a series of closely bunched resorts that tap into a Rocky Mountain skiing mother lode. Although not as quaint as nearby Breckenridge, as extensive as Vail or as challenging as the gut-wrenching Arapahoe Basin, Copper stands out for its accessibility and versatility. Denver lies less than an hour and a half away on I-70, a ribbon of highway visible from just about everywhere on the mountain. Add to that short commute Copper's meticulously laid out mountains—divided into perfect sections for beginners, intermediates and advanced skiers, reading right to left as you face the mountain—and you have one of the favored day-skiing destinations for Denver folks.

Don't expect to find any old copper mines or even a miner's turn-of-the-century saloon: Copper is strictly a creature of the modern-day master plan. Its purpose-built condominium villages are divided into three sections. The heartbeat of the resort thumps from the Village Center, where you'll find the high-speed American Flyer quad and the American Eagle quad as well as most of Copper's dining and nightlife. The condos in this section tend to be the more upscale, and there's the Athletic Club for off-slope exercise. The East Village, centered at the base of the B lift, offers less expensive accommodations, as well as a few bars and restaurants. The West Village is home to Club

Copper Mountain Facts

Base elevation: 9,600'; **Summit elevation:** 12,360'; **Vertical drop:** 2,760 feet.
Number and types of lifts: 20—2 super quad chairs, 6 triple chairs, 8 double chairs, and 4 surface lifts
Acreage: 1,330 skiable acres **Percent of snowmaking:** 20 percent
Uphill capacity: 28,250 skiers per hour **Bed base:** 2,800

Med, two upscale properties and the cross-country center. Shuttlebuses connect the various sections.

Where to ski

Beginners and intermediates should hop directly on the high-speed American Flyer lift, or Union Creek in the West Village. Nearly the whole side of the mountain under Union Peak consists of sweeping runs ringed by trees, perfect for the advanced beginner and lower intermediate.

For a long run to the bottom, beginners should bear left and take Copper-Tone connection for an easy cruise. Bear right down Copperfield to the shorter J lift, and you can take the equally sweeping Soliloquy to Roundabout connection to the bottom. The K and L lifts, which you pass near the bottom—and constitute the far right border of the resort—are also custom-made for the beginner. In fact, this side of the resort offers one of the most extensive network of runs for the beginner that we've seen.

Intermediates should exit just to the right of the quad and try the American Flyer, I-Beam and Windsong runs under the I and J lifts. Better yet, take the new American Eagle quad chair from Village Center and dart down any of the runs bordering this lift. If you're patient enough to follow the quad with the E lift, you'll have the best intermediate runs of the resort at your feet. Both Collage and Andy's Encore are worthy challenges for the intermediate, offering good grade without the heavy moguls or tight funnels that can turn a blue run black (and an unwary intermediate black and blue).

Expert skiers need not despair. The powder monkeys among you can find a virgin slate—and the best views the resort has to offer—at the top of Union Peak. All that doesn't come without a price, however. Take the S chair after exiting the high-speed American Flyer, then *walk* more than 100 yards up the ridge to whatever spot above Union Bowl strikes your fancy. All three runs that parallel the E lift are also short and steep, and Brennan's Grin in particular will bring a smile to a serious bump skier's face. Bear far right off the E lift and you can find serious tree skiing on Enchanted Forest (even more serious tree skiing, albeit unmarked, is available if you bear left about halfway off the Collage run). If you take the Storm King drag lift instead of heading down Enchanted Forest, you'll come to the side of Copper reserved strictly for experts. After you take the steep drop into Spaulding Bowl (lose a ski here and you'd better hope to have an uphill friend), there are four very worthy expert runs to the bottom of the Resolution lift. Because this lift is approached only by expert runs, there's rarely a wait.

Mountain rating

This is one of the best-divided mountains in America. There is a wonderful beginner area, plenty of intermediate and enough expert terrain to keep most experts busy. Copper is also part of Ski the Summit, which means virtually limitless terrain.

Snowboarding

Shredding is permitted on all sections of the mountain. Copper Mountain has a permanent halfpipe and an annual snowboard race series. Both snowboard lessons and rentals are widely available.

Cross-country (91/92 prices)

Copper Mountain, squeezed between I-70 and the mountain, has created an excellent and varied cross-country trail system. Some 25 kilometers of tracks fan out from the Union Creek cross-country center. Some of the trails are set tracks and others are open to skating. The center offers rentals, lessons and clinics.

Track fees for adults are $8; for children and seniors 60-69, $6. Those 70 and over ski free. A complete package for cross-country first-timers, including half-day lesson, track fee and all-day waxless equipment is $30. The newcomer telemark package includes a half-day lesson, telemark equipment rental and a beginner lift ticket for $40.

Normal cross-country group lessons are $22 for a half day. The telemark program costs $42 and includes all lifts. Private lessons are $33 an hour per person, $15 per hour for each person additional.

One innovative twist is that skiers with multiday lift tickets may trade a day of Copper Mountain downhill skiing for the Newcomer Track Package.

Daily cross-country rentals cost $13 for adults and $10 for children. Telemark rentals are $18 for adults per day.

The Copper Mountain Cross-Country Center phone is (303) 968-2882, Ext. 6342.

Ski school (92/93 prices)

Adult classes for those 12 and over are 10 a.m.-1:30 p.m. and 12 noon-3:30 p.m. Costs are $37 a day if you have a lift ticket or $59 including lifts.

A special introductory package, including a full day of classes, lifts and rentals, is $52 for adults. Children pay $52, but this includes lunch.

An excellent package program includes lessons, lifts and rentals for the seasoned skier. Adults pay $64 and children, with lunch included, pay $52.

Private lessons from 8:30 a.m. or 2 p.m. and 2:30 p.m. cost $65 per hour for one or two skiers. One-and-a-half-hour private lessons taken anytime between 9 a.m. and 2 p.m. are $80 for one or two. Half-day private lessons run $155 and full-day lessons for up to four skiers are $285.

There is also a specialty program for expert skiers called the Diamond Cutter Workshop and a NASTAR workshop, both costing $32 per session. For racers, two runs in NASTAR races cost $6, with $1 for each additional run. A self-timing race course is also available on Loverly Trail.

Copper Mountain ski school doesn't ignore the children—there is a Junior Ranch program for ages four to six and a Senior Ranch for those seven to 12. Both all-day programs include lunch. Lessons with lunch are $43; three days with lessons, lunch and lifts, $135.

Lift tickets (92/93 prices)

Full day—$37 adults/$16 children (under 12); half day—$26*/$13*; two of three days—$70 for adults only; three of four days—$102/30; four of five days—$132/$40; five of six days—$160/$50; six of seven days—$180/$60. Seniors from 60 to 69 years ski for $23 a day and seniors over 70 ski free. Beginners pay $16 for limited lifts.

NOTE: Children's lift tickets are now only $10 a day, one of the best bargains in the industry. There are also Kids Ski Free/Stay Free packages during December, January and April that allow children 12 years and under to ski and stay free.

Ski the Summit passes good four consecutive days are $132 for adults and $68 for children. Six-day Ski the Summit passes cost $198 for adults and $102 for children.

Accommodations

Copper Mountain Lodging Services has one-stop shopping for accommodations. Call (800) 458-8386. The Copper Mountain Resort Chamber provides information and reservations in the Copper Mountain area at (800) 525-3891 or (303) 968-6477 in Colorado. All Copper Mountain Lodging Services properties include membership in the Athletic Club, with swimming pool, Jacuzzis, steam bath, two indoor tennis courts and weight training facilities.
Lodging is split according to the village—Village Center, East Village and West Village. All condos are in the same general price range; those managed by Copper Mountain Lodging Services are the newer properties and are concentrated in the Village Center and West Village area. Top choice for condos is the **Spruce Lodge** because it's so close to the lifts. The **Telemark Lodge** in West Village is another favorite with its small bar and crackling fireplace. It also sits equidistant from the downhill lifts and the cross-country area. The **Mountain Plaza** is basically made up of hotel rooms.

The **Westlake Lodge** and **Bridge End**, both costing the same as Spruce Lodge, are significantly further from the lifts. The Lodging Services properties are $99-$170 a night for a normal hotel room; $135-$240 a night for a one-bedroom condo; $215-$385 a night for a two-bedroom unit; and $275-$444 a night for three-bedroom units.

In the East Village section the condominiums are a bit older than the Village Center units. They are slightly less expensive and just as convenient to the lifts for the intermediate and expert areas. However, they will be a bit out of the way if your group is made up of beginners. Of this group, the **Peregine** is perhaps the most luxurious and **Anaconda** follows. The other units have the same amenities. These Carbonate Property Management units cost $95 for a hotel room; $145-$155 for one-bedroom units; $210 for two-bedroom condos; and $270-$280 for three-bedroom units. The **Best Western Foxpine Inn** is the distant poor cousin of Copper Mountain properties.

There are excellent packages available that combine lodging and lifts. From January 3 through February 12, 1993 packages, including lodging and lifts, start at $93/day/person. From February 13 to April 3, 1993 programs will start at $105 per day per person based on double occupancy. Call (800) 458-8386 or (303) 968-2882.

Club Méditerranée is the first Club Med built in North America and still its only U.S. winter club. Rooms are small, à la Club Med. The programs and activities are nonstop, and everything is included in the price except drinks. There are ski lessons, dancing, and sumptuous spreads for breakfast, lunch and dinner. In fact, Club Med guests rarely venture outside of the Club Med world except to ski—even then they are still lesson-wrapped in the Club Med cocoon. For reservations, call (800)-CLUB MED.

Dining

Copper Mountain's range of restaurants is fair for a resort of compact size. **Pesce Fresco** (968-2882, Ext. 6505) in Mountain Plaza is the most upscale restaurant in the town. Reservations are suggested. **O'Shea's** in the Copper Junction building has great bargains, especially the dinner buffet, and the best breakfast buffet for miles.

Rackets Restaurant (968-2882, Ext. 6386) located in the Racquet and Atheletic Club offers a southwestern menu and a great salad bar.

The East Village has the best restaurants. Virtually everyone's favorite was **Farley's** in the Snowflake building, which serves up heaping portions of prime rib, steaks and fish. Reservations are a good idea; call 968-2577. (Don't hesitate to ask for the table next to the fireplace.)

Another favorite for light fare and great burgers is the **B-Lift Pub**, which has a breakfast, lunch and dinner menu and is by far the best bar in town.

Après-ski/nightlife

This is one of Colorado's better immediate après-ski resorts. At the base of the B-Lift, the **B-Lift Pub** rocks from 3 p.m. to 5 p.m. It's a great spot to meet people, and most of the skiers you find here are real skiers because the bar anchors the expert and intermediate sections of the mountain. **Copper Commons Bar** gets overflow après-ski, and **O'Shea's** hums as well.

While the best laid-back food is found in East Village, there's dancing only in the Village Center. O'Shea's gets a good crowd as well for drinking and dancing.

If you are having dinner in the East Village and don't want to move far, Farley's has a good bar downstairs, and the B-Lift Pub is always a good time.

Child care

The Belly Button Bakery and Belly Button Babies are two of the most innovative child care programs in Colorado. In-room babysitting services are also available. Sitters are limited and cost $6/hr., plus $1 for each child.

Belly Button Babies accepts children two months to two years. Full day costs $44 and includes lunch. Parents should provide diapers, extra change of clothing, a blanket and a favorite toy.

The Belly Button Bakery, for kids over two, has ski programs and indoor activities. One day with lunch is $44.

Call 968-2882, Ext. 6344. Reservations are required. A $10 deposit each day guarantees the reservation.

Other activities

The Copper Mountain Racquet and Athletic Club is the primary focus of nonskiing activity. Membership is included when you stay in Copper Mountain Lodging Services properties. Enjoy a 25-yard lap pool, Nautilus and free weights, sauna, steamroom, exercise classes and two indoor tennis courts. Call Ext. 6380 for info.

Getting there

Copper Mountain is 75 miles west of Denver's airport. The drive is a straight shot on I-70 to the Copper Mountain exit. Resort Express runs vans between Stapleton and your lodge, with 13 daily departures. One-way fare is $35, round trip, $62. You can make reservations when you reserve lodging, or call Resort Express at (303) 468-7600 or (800) 334-7433.

Information/reservations

Call Copper Mountain Resort Chamber at (800) 525-3891, (303) 968-6477 or 825-7106 (Denver direct). Copper Mountain Lodging Services is at (800) 458-8386.

Crested Butte Colorado

The big news at this resort is the addition of a quad superchair which will replace the old Silver Queen. This new lift and the additional terrain opened last season combined with downhome western friendliness makes Crested Butte one of my favorite resorts.

You won't find flashy ski outfits, you won't hear talk of yesterday's movement in 30-year bonds, you won't be caught in the middle of a disagreement between a movie star and his agent, and you won't hear much griping about slow lifts or cruddy snow. Crested Butte has a laid-back attitude and the locals, many 1960s refugees, have a way of looking at the better side of life, and after a few days in Crested Butte it's contagious.

Entering the town, which has been designated a National Historic District, is like stepping back to the turn of the century. A walk down Elk Avenue, the main street, takes you past the old post office, built in 1900; the hardware store, where old cronies still reminisce around a pot-bellied stove; and The Forest Queen, reputed to have once been a bordello. More than 40 historic structures are tucked in and around the town.

In contrast, the ski area, about three miles away, is surrounded by modern condominiums and a giant hotel, with more in the planning stages. With the shuttlebus system there is no need for a car once you cruise into town.

Crested Butte Facts
Base elevation: 9,100'; Summit elevation: 11,875; Vertical drop: 3,062 feet
Number of lifts: 13—1 quad superchair, 3 triple chairs, 5 double chairs,
4 surface lifts_Percent snowmaking: 35 percent
Total trail acreage: 1,150 acres Uphill capacity: 16,010 per hour
Bed Base: 3,500

Crested Butte has also made a major commitment to snowmaking, which has insured excellent coverage for early season skiing. Last season the resort increased its snowmaking capacity by 25 percent to improve the early season snow quality. The snowfall statistics speak for themselves. Crested Butte has one of the highest average snowfall of any ski town in Colorado.

The skiing

The Crested Butte skier seems to like his terrain just as nature left it. There are plenty of trails for intermediates and beginners, even some for experts. But you'll notice immediately that almost half of the Crested Butte area doesn't even have a lift or a trail painted onto the trail map. There's just a huge area called the North Face with a series of double diamonds punctuating the mountainside; and on the far right side of the resort are another grouping of double diamonds, hard against the area boundary, to the right of the new quad superlift.

Let's make sense of it all: beginners have extensive terrain, served by the Keystone lift. However, this is not stuff you want to attempt with the skiing ability you learned from a book on the plane: never-evers should head to the Peachtree lift. After a day or two of wedge turns and a practiced snowplow position, strike out for Keystone.

Intermediates in search of long cruising runs should go up Keystone or Silver Queen, and spend time perfecting GS turns down Treasury, Ruby Chief, Forest Queen, Bushwacker, Gallowich and variations of the same. The Paradise Bowl at the top of the Paradise lift gives intermediates a taste of powder on good days. For advanced intermediates any of the runs down from the Silver Queen are manageable. The short and steep Twister and Crystal both have good bail-out routes about halfway down the run. The new tree skiing at various locations off the Teocalli and the new superchair lifts gives intermediates a chance to test themselves on natural slalom courses.

Upper Forest, Hot Rocks and Forest have always technically been part of Crested Butte's lift-served terrain. But in 1987 the resort linked the huge North Face area with the other lifts. The resort installed a short Poma lift to drag skiers to the crest of the North Face and the Phoenix Bowl. This area offers what experts claim is the best extreme skiing in Colorado, comparable to Utah steeps. The resort has free tours of the North Face daily at 10:45 and 12:45, and will add guides for the new Teocalli Bowl area. The North Face normally opens in mid-January.

Mountain rating

Crested Butte has plenty of terrain for every level of skier. It needs it, because there are no alternatives in the near vicinity, with the notable exception of 2,000 acres of snowcat powder skiing at nearby Irwin Lodge, the largest such operation in North America. Beginners will end a week carving a good stem christie, intermediates will have had a chance to explore almost every marked trail if they are adventurous, and experts will leave already making plans for the next chance to challenge the North Face.

Cross-country

Crested Butte is linked with one of the most extensive cross-country networks in Colorado. For those on skinny skis, the adventures are virtually limitless. Crested Butte was the pioneering resort in the rediscovery and popularization of telemark skiing; it has more telemark skiers per capita than any other big-time ski resort.

In April hundreds of free-heel skiers scramble up the North Face and drop 1,200 vertical feet through deep snow competing in the Al Johnson Memorial Uphill/Downhill Race. Johnson used to deliver mail on Nordic skis to 1880s mining camps. Every month the Crested Butte Nordic Center sponsors a different race event, ranging from citizens' races to team relays and the Alley Loop race.

The Crested Butte Nordic Center is located at the edge of town, on 2nd St. between Sopris and Whiterock Streets. Call (303) 349-6201. The town maintains about 30 km. of Nordic tracks, which begin a few yards from the Nordic Center. After skiing, the center also has hot tubs and racquetball courts for après-Nordic activity. There are more than 100 miles of backcountry trails.

The trail fee is $8 a day. A half-day tour costs $20 and a full day is $40. Private lessons are $150 for a full day; ask about the hourly rates—they should be about $50 an hour. Half-day lessons are $34. Rentals for touring skis are $12 a day. Children and seniors pay half price.

A picnic tour with lunch, rentals and guide costs $46 and overnight hut tours are also available.

Snowboarding

Snowboarding is allowed on the entire mountain including the double-diamond Extreme Limits. Snowboard lessons are available from the ski school for $26 per two-hour lesson. Classes are given Tuesday, Thursday, Saturday and Sunday at 1:30 p.m. Special lessons and rental package, including a two-hour lesson and all-day rental, is available on Tuesdays and Thursdays for $38.

Ski school (92/93 prices)

The ski school offers everything from beginning lessons to race camps, bump and powder workshops and snowboard instruction. Registration and reservations are at the ski school desk in the Gothic Center, (303) 349-2252.

Group lessons: Adult regular group lessons range from $26 for a half-day (two-hour) lesson to $100 for five half-day lessons. There is a three-day introduction to skiing package for $146, which includes an all-day lesson, two 2-hour lessons and lifts.

Private lessons: One and a half hours are $68 for one, with each additional person costing $18; two hours costs $85 per person with additional students costing $30 apiece; three hours are $125 for one; and six hours cost $230 for one with additional skiers costing $30 apiece.

Special programs for bump and double-diamond powder skiers cost $37 a day. Two hours of snowboard lessons are $26. NASTAR races cost $5 a person for two runs. Race clinics include coaching and a race for $34 a person. A private racing coach can be arranged for $68 an hour. For children between seven and 12 the Butte Busters Ski School has been organized. Group lesson rates including lunch are: all day, $39; two days, $74; three days, $105; five days, $170. Lesson rates do not include lifts or rentals.

Lift tickets (91/92 prices)

Crested Butte opens this season (92/93) with **FREE SKIING** from November 20 through December 19. That's right. Lift ticket prices for the entire period will be zero dollars and zero cents ($0.00).

Regular season prices are in effect from the Christmas season through early April. Special reduced prices are available in April until closing.

Full day, $36 adults/$22 children (12 and under); half day, $27/$16; two days, $72/$44; three days, $108/$66; five of six days, $165/$95; six of seven days, $180/$99.

Senior citizens over 70 ski free.

Kids Ski Free: Children 12 years of age and younger ski free when accompanied by parents or guardian, except in the Christmas to New Year's period December 20-January 3, and during Easter. This program is on a one-to-one basis, that is, one child per parent.

Accommodations (92/93 prices)

Most of the accommodations are clustered around the ski area in Mount Crested Butte. There are a handful down in the old town area, not as modern nor as convenient to the slopes. They are, however, closer to the nightlife and offer a taste of more rustic Western atmosphere.

The mountain accommodations are either ski-in/ski-out, walking distance or shuttlebus distance. The prices drop as you get further from the mountain. (In Crested Butte, walking distance means less than five minutes, and shuttlebus means about a five-minute ride at most.)

Crested Butte Vacations can take care of everything from your plane tickets to hotel room, lift tickets and lessons with one phone call. It also offers some of the best packages available. Before you make any arrangements, call (800) 544-8448 and ask for the best possible deal.

The following prices are for the Regular Season, mid-February through the end of March. January rates are lower and holiday rates are higher.

Grande Butte Hotel (800-341-5437 or 303-349-7561), a ski-in/ski-out lodging, is the only real hotel. Mountain hotels don't get much better than this. Room rates start at $150 per night and special rates will drop as low as $90 such as the Ski-Free period

Crested Mountain Village is perhaps the top luxury group of properties at the mountain. It has a series of spectacular penthouse suites that open onto the slopes.

The Buttes are also well-appointed condos. Rooms start at $159 for studio accommodations. Two-bedroom condominiums are $293; three-bedroom units run from $354 for a ski-in/ski-out.

The Gateway, across from the Peachtree lift and about a two-minute stroll from the Silver Queen, is perhaps the best value of any condo on the mountain when you trade price for space and amenities. Two bedrooms go for $255 a night, three bedrooms $340. Gateway units are managed by several competing agencies. It is best to book through through Crested Butte Vacations; call (800) 544-8448.

The Plaza, across from the main lifts, is one of the most popular condo projects on the mountain. It gives excellent value and is especially popular with groups because special functions can be easily arranged. Two-bedroom condos cost $225 a night, three-bedroom units are $305.

Wood Creek and **Mountain Edge** are convenient to the lifts, but not particularly well appointed. The **Columbine** is an excellent ski-in/ski-out property. These three properties, together with nine others within shuttlebus distance of the lifts, are managed by Crested Butte Accommodations at (800) 821-3718 or (303) 349-2448.

The Crested Butte Club, on Second Street, is the upscale old-world elegance champion of the area. Seven suites have been individually furnished with Victorian furnishings including his & hers sinks and a copper and brass tub, as well as beautiful four-poster or canopied beds and a fireplace. The amenities include the fitness club, with heated swimming pool, two steam baths, three hot tubs, weight room, and racquetball courts. This is a no-smoking property. Room rates range from $115-$125. 349-6655.

The Claim Jumper, 704 Whiterock Street; 349-6471, a restored bed-and-breakfast, is the class act in town. Jerry and Robbie Bigelow took it over a year ago and filled it with a collection of memorable antiques. Bedrooms have themes and are furnished with brass or old iron beds. There are only seven rooms, two with private bath. Room rates are $79 or $89 including a full breakfast. Children are not encouraged; no smoking.

The Cristiana, 621 Maroon Ave.; 349-5326, is only a block from the ski shuttle and a five-minute walk from downtown. This has a mountain inn atmosphere and most of the guests manage to get to know one another. The rooms are small, but everyone lives in the hotel's living rooms so the smaller sleeping areas are not noticed. Rates

VILLAGE AND TOWN MAPS

MT. CRESTED BUTTE
(Base Area Map)

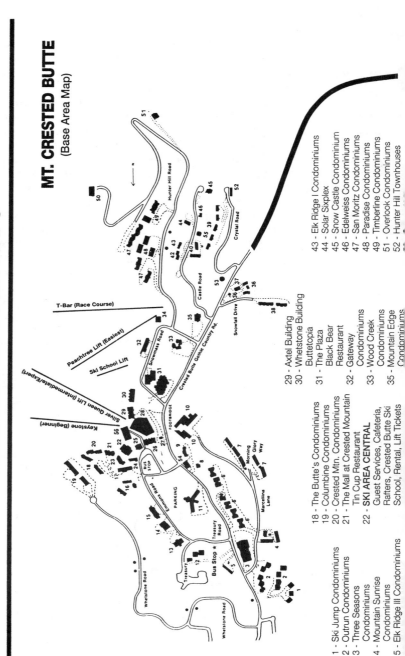

1 - Ski Jump Condominiums
2 - Outrun Condominiums
3 - Three Seasons Condominiums
4 - Mountain Sunrise Condominiums
5 - Elk Ridge III Condominiums

18 - The Butte's Condominiums
19 - Columbine Condominiums
20 - Crested Mtn. Condominiums
21 - The Mall at Crested Mountain
     Tin Cup Restaurant
22 - **SKI AREA CENTRAL**
     Guest Services, Cafeteria,
     Rafters, Crested Butte Ski
     School, Rental, Lift Tickets

29 - Axtel Building
30 - Whetstone Building
     Buttetopia
31 - The Plaza
     Black Bear
     Restaurant
32 - Gateway
     Condominiums
33 - Wood Creek
     Condominiums
35 - Mountain Edge
     Condominiums

43 - Elk Ridge I Condominiums
44 - Solar Sixplex
45 - Snow Castle Condominium
46 - Edelweiss Condominiums
47 - San Moritz Condominiums
48 - Paradise Condominiums
49 - Timberline Condominiums
51 - Overlook Condominiums
52 - Hunter Hill Townhouses

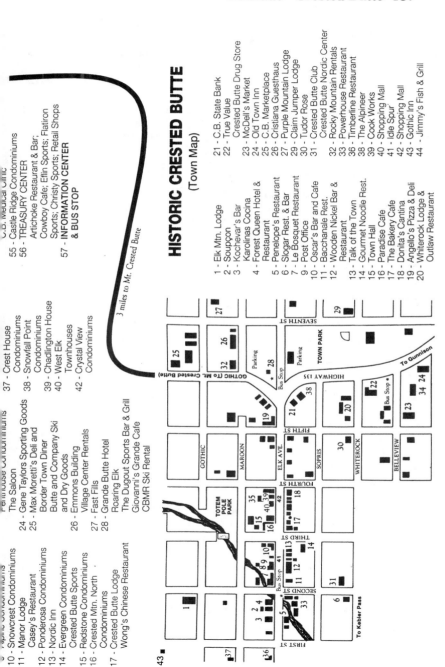

HISTORIC CRESTED BUTTE
(Town Map)

1 - Elk Mtn. Lodge
2 - Soupçon
3 - Kochevar's Bar
    Karolinas Cocina
4 - Forest Queen Hotel &
    Restaurant
5 - Penelope's Restaurant
6 - Slogar Rest. & Bar
7 - Le Bosquet Restaurant
8 - Post Office
9 - Oscar's Bar and Cafe
10 - Bacchanale Rest.
11 - Wooden Nickel Bar &
     Restaurant
12 - Talk of the Town
13 - Gourmet Noodle Rest.
14 - Town Hall
15 - Paradise Cafe
16 - The Bakery Cafe
17 - Donita's Cantina
18 - Angello's Pizza & Deli
19 - Whiterock Lodge &
20 - Outlaw Restaurant

21 - C.B. State Bank
22 - True Value
     Crested Butte Drug Store
23 - McDell's Market
24 - Old Town Inn
25 - C.B. Marketplace
26 - Cristiana Guesthaus
27 - Purple Mountain Lodge
29 - Claim Jumper Lodge
30 - Tudor Rose
31 - Crested Butte Club
     Crested Butte Nordic Center
32 - Rocky Mountain Rentals
33 - Powerhouse Restaurant
36 - Timberline Restaurant
38 - The Alpineer
39 - Cook Works
40 - Shopping Mall
41 - Idle Spur
42 - Shopping Mall
43 - Gothic Inn
44 - Jimmy's Fish & Grill

55 - Castle Ridge Condominiums
56 - TREASURY CENTER
     Artichoke Restaurant & Bar;
     Cowboy Cafe; Eflin Sports; Flatiron
     Sports; Christy Sports; Retail Shops
57 - INFORMATION CENTER
     & BUS STOP

C.B. Medical Clinic

37 - Crest House
     Condominiums
38 - Snowfall Point
     Condominiums
39 - Chadlington House
40 - West Elk
     Townhouses
42 - Crystal View
     Condominiums

The Saloon
24 - Gene Taylors Sporting Goods
25 - Max Moretti's Deli and
     Border Town Diner
     Butte and Company Ski
     and Dry Goods
26 - Emmons Building
     Village Center Rentals
27 - Fast Fills
28 - Grande Butte Hotel
     Roaring Elk
     The Dugout Sports Bar & Grill
     Giovanni's Grande Cafe
     CBMR Ski Rental

10 - Snowcrest Condominiums
11 - Manor Lodge
     Casey's Restaurant
12 - Ponderosa Condominiums
13 - Nordic Inn
14 - Evergreen Condominiums
     Crested Butte Sports
15 - Redstone Condominiums
16 - Crested Mtn. North
     Condominiums
17 - Crested Butte Lodge
     Wong's Chinese Restaurant

3 miles to Mt. Crested Butte

are $65 for a one-bed room, $75 for a room with two beds (double occupancy). Add $10 during Christmas season.

The Forest Queen, corner of Elk and 2nd, 349-5336, has a reputation for being inexpensive, with bunks going for only $15 and a double with bath for only $30. Breakfast is included!

The Elk Mountain Lodge around the corner from the Forest Queen on 2nd Street has simple rooms, all with private bath, for $60 to $75 per room a night. Call 349-7533. If you decide to stay, ask for Room 20 on the third floor with lots of space, a balcony and a great view.

Red Lady Rentals at 214 6th Street, 349-5354, offers rentals in private homes in the area as well as in many special condominiums. If you are looking for something out of the ordinary, check with them for help.

Dining

Crested Butte is blessed with more excellent, affordable restaurants than any other resort in the West. You can dine on gourmet French cuisine or chow down on platters of family-style fried chicken and steaks.

The top of the line gourmet restaurants are **Soupcon** (349-5448), located in a tiny old historic building and tucked into an alley off Second Street, **Le Bosquet** (349-5808) on Elk near Second, and **Timberline** (349-9831) at the end of Elk. Call for reservations at both before expecting to sit down during the ski season. **Penelope's** (349-5178) on Elk Avenue has improved its menu dramatically and serves up dinners in a beautiful dining room.

For hard-to-beat group and family dining, head to **The Slogar** (349-5765). It used to be the first bar the miners hit when returning from the mines and is decorated in old bordello decor. Slogar's offers an all-you-can-eat (more or less) skillet-fried chicken dinner with mashed potatoes, biscuits, creamed corn, ice cream and even some other extras for a flat price of $9.45 each. It also offers a family-style steak dinner. Reservations recommended.

For other substantial meals, head down Elk Avenue to **Donita's Cantina** (349-6674), where the margaritas are giant and strong and Mexican food comes in heaping portions. Be early or be ready to wait. No reservations.

The Powerhouse Bar and Grill (349-5494) presents Mexican food at Elk Avenue and Second Street. This converted powerhouse offers a unique atmosphere and more Mex than Tex-Mex. For something special try the cabrito, goat cooked with a spicy sauce.

The Idle Spur (349-5026) on Elk Avenue is a restaurant and bar housed in a log barn building with its own micro brewery. The suds are potent and mix with moderate prices and live music (and steep covers) on weekends, but forget the grub.

The best pizza in the area is found in the **Black Bear Bar** at the Plaza on the mountain. And for a quick down and dirty meal, try **Angello's** as well.

The best breakfast by far is served in the **Forest Queen**. The atmosphere is Old West and turn of the century. Ask for the *"baggins."* You won't find it on the menu—it has developed as a specialty for most of the locals.

For breakfast on the mountain head to **The Tin Cup** or **Max and Moretti's Deli and Croissant Factory.** For a good lunch try **Rafters,** the **Cowboy Café** in the Treasury Center, or for a more elegant setting head to **The Artichoke** and start off with artichoke soup.

Après-ski/nightlife

Here nightlife means wandering from bar to bar. The immediate après-ski action is centered in **Rafters** at the base of the lifts. Then it begins to move downtown to the **Wooden Nickel,** with some wild drinks, and **Oscar's,** which has a very happy hour from 10 p.m. to 11:30 p.m. Oscar's also offers karaoke. The **Eldorado** has dancing, live music and welcome munchies. **The Talk of the Town** is a smoky locals place with video games and a shuffleboard table. **Kochevar's** is another favorite of locals, but watch out, the shuffleboard table is horrific. The **Idle Spur** normally has dancing, sometimes even a polka or two, but watch your step when you arrive and leave—the owners allow too much dangerous ice to build up.

Rafters has dancing and good singles action most nights in Mount Crested Butte, plus it is within stumbling distance of most of the lodging.

Child care

The Buttetopia Children's Programs take care of teaching, feeding and caring for your children.

Registration and information are in the Whetstone Building; 349-2259. Hours: 8:30 a.m. to 4 p.m.

Nursery for children between six months and three years costs $38 for a full day and $28 for a half day.

Day care for children between three and six years is available for $38 per full day and $28 per half day. ABC's on skis, which includes lessons, lunch, snacks and activities, costs $46 a day. Private lessons are $58 an hour. A full day advanced group lesson with rentals, lesson and lunch but no lifts will cost $46.

Other activities

These include snowmobiling, snowmobile dinner tours to Irwin Lodge, snowcat dinner tours to a Paradise Warming House mountain hut on Crested Butte Mountain, winter horseback riding, sleigh rides with and without dinners, and ballooning—weather permitting. Call Mt. Crested Butte or Crested Butte Chamber of Commerce at 349-6462 for brochures and information. For winter horseback riding, call the Fantasy Ranch at 349-5425.

Getting there

Crested Butte is one of the most convenient ski resorts to reach in Colorado. There are ten daily nonstop flights from Denver with United and Continental; from Dallas with American; Saturday flights from Houston with Continental; and Wednesday, Saturday and Sunday service with Delta from Atlanta. Flights arrive in Gunnison, only a half-hour drive from the resort.

There is regular airport-to-resort transportation, $30 round trip, by Alpine Express, which meets every arriving flight and takes you direct to your hotel or condo. For reservations, call Crested Butte Vacations at (800) 544-8448 or (800) 822-4844 or (303) 641-5074.

Information/reservations

Crested Butte Mountain Resort, Box A, 12 Snowmass Road, Mount Crested Butte CO 81225; (303) 349-2333; Crested Butte Vacations: (800) 544-8448 or (303) 349-2222. Snow reports: (303) 349-2323.

Crested Butte Savoir Faire

For a town of its size, Crested Butte has an impressive number of fine dining choices, most within steps of one another. At the far end of Elk Avenue is **The Timberline Restaurant**. Chef Tim Egelhoff spent five years as sous chef at Creme Carmel in Carmel, California before opening the Timberline a little over a year ago. He combines the freshest seasonal products to create a Cafe French Cuisine, whose roots derive from classic French, with a pinch of California and a dash of the Rockies. Served in a quaint old private home, the menu changes weekly. Start with the roasted garlic crêpes, filled with spinach, mushrooms, walnuts and feta, and topped with a creamy lemon caper sauce. Or try the goat cheese Napoleon—layers of fluffy puff pastry crammed full of eggplant, sun-dried tomatoes and chèvre. There are six entrées nightly, and I fell in love with the roast pork loin, oven-roasted with rosemary and honey. The duckling with two preparations, served with ginger and cherries, was prepared to a cracklin' perfection. Timberline does not stand on ceremony, yet continually turns out impeccably prepared, creative meals. It also offers a wide selection of reasonably priced boutique wines. Open nightly from 5:30 p.m. For reservations, call 349-9831.

A stone's throw from the Timberline is **Soupcon Restaurant**, hidden in the alley behind Kochevar's Bar. This log cabin started at half its current size in 1916 as a private residence to the Kochevars. While there have been several restaurants over the past 30 years, Soupcon itself dates back almost twenty years. Current owners Maura and Mac Bailey have created an innovative French cuisine, with menu items posted daily on a chalkboard. This small restaurant fills quickly. Reserve early for one of two seatings, 6 and 8:15 p.m. (349-5448.)

A special appetizer often on the menu is oysters aioli, served with a spicy paprika sauce, with fresh thyme, basil and peppers. There is also frequently an oyster soup hollandaise. Entrées range from $16 for a roast duckling with lemon garlic sauce to $24 for rack of lamb with port and mustard. Save room for Mac's special desserts—the Orient Express chocolate torte is always a hit.

Le Bosquet, another fine French restaurant, is now in its 15th year in this casually elegant setting. Chef/owner Victor Shepard and his wife Candy offer dishes such as hazelnut chicken in an orange thyme cream sauce, as well as home-smoked trout served with caviar. Many of the menu items are also served in a heart-healthy version, minus the cream, butter, salt, and wine, and are identified with an American Heart Association seal. Tournedos au Bosquet is available in a 4- or an 8- ounce size, with either a fresh rosemary béarnaise, black peppercorn, or red wine sauce. The 4-ounce size is served plain, with steamed potatoes and fresh vegetables with lemon juice. Perhaps after steamed potatoes, you can indulge in a double chocolate moussecake. Cost is about $30 per person for three courses, without beverage, tax or gratuity. Call 349-5808.

For gourmets with a sense of adventure, join a snowmobile tour to the **Irwin Lodge**. Perched on a remote and unspoiled ridge high above the village, the Irwin Lodge is Crested Butte's answer to Twin Peaks' The Great Northern . . . well, without Audrey. Complete with great room and roaring fires, this immense cedar structure is maintained in an 1890s tradition. Each night snowmobile tours from the town below arrive to join guests of the lodge for some of the Curtis family culinary tradition. Start your meal with the legendary toasted raviolis, served with a trio of sauces: red pepper and balsamic vinegar; garlic, ginger, and orange, and a pesto piñon sauce. Entrées range from tournedos au poivre to grilled halibut with raspberry cream sauce. There is an eclectic 28-item rotating menu, with four new selections each day of the week. After one visit, you'll realize that a week's stay is needed to sample all the chef's greats.

Snowmobile tours and the dinner are priced separately, so call 349-5308 to inquire about prices and make arrangements to join a tour. Trips fill up rapidly so plan at least one week in advance.

by Katy Keck

Irwin Lodge, Colorado

Irwin Lodge at Lake Irwin, twelve miles west of Crested Butte, is Colorado's most exclusive and remote recognized ski area. Virtually unlimited skiing stretches over 2,200 acres with an overall 2,100-foot vertical drop. The lodge was originally built by an eccentric millionaire with a vision of building the perfect ski lodge. The only way in is on snowmobile, snowcat or cross-country skis. There are no lifts, no phones (the only contact with the outside world is two-way radio), no network television, and only one massive lodge; the crowds are underwhelming, averaging only about fifty skiers at a time.

Inside, the lodge is even more impressive. The 120-foot-long lobby stretches almost the length of the building and soars to the center ceiling two stories above. The lobby is the most important room of this lodge: in fact, it takes up 60 percent of the structure with only 40 percent dedicated to the guest rooms.

Mornings begin with breakfast from 8 to 9:30 a.m. Snowcats make their first climb to the ridge at 9:30 a.m. loaded with skiers, and cross-country skiers take off on organized tours a bit later.

The skiing

There is skiing here for every level of ability. Naturally, beginners will have their problems but beginner powder skiers will have the time of their life. There are two groomed slopes—one for intermediates and one for beginners. The top of Dan's Delight leads to the advanced areas as well as a groomed beginner and intermediate slope. 70 MPH Basin dropoff opens more difficult terrain.

One run to the left off Dan's Delight starts in a relatively tame bowl, then offers a choice of continuing down through the gladed Central Park area or turning to the left and dropping down an expert chute into the wide-open

Banzai Bowl. Twenty-five or thirty turns later you enter the trees to begin running nature's slalom gates through the Lumber Yard, where some of the Ponderosa pines are only three to five feet apart. The 70 MPH Basin offers real advanced terrain which bottoms out at the West Wall, where skiers have a choice of almost a dozen chutes and runs down the face, starting with open glades and then ending through tightening trees.

Normally, skiing starts at 9:30 a.m. and continues until 4:30 p.m. From 12:30 until 1:30 p.m. everything stops for the lunch buffet while the snowcats are serviced and the skiers fuel up for the afternoon.

Irwin also offers snowmobiling and guided cross-country skiing as well as ice fishing and snowshoeing.

Snowboarding

Shredding is permitted but it is difficult if you need to traverse in deep, deep powder. A problem referred to as post holing occurs when the free leg sinks into the snow. Closest board rentals are available in Crested Butte.

The costs (91/92 rates)

The way to do Irwin is to purchase a package that combines lodging, meals and activities (but not transfers). The three-day/three-night package will run $634.50, the four-day/three-night package will cost $726, seven days and six nights will cost $1,399. These packages include snowcat skiing, snowmobiling and/or cross-country skiing.

Folks coming up to ski from Crested Butte pay $160 a day for the same snowcat skiing, including transportation from Crested Butte and lunch.

Getting there

Round-trip transportation from Crested Butte, $40.

Information/reservations

Contact Irwin Lodge, PO Box 457, Crested Butte, CO 81224, tel. (303) 349-5308, or (800) 2-IRWIN-2.

Keystone Arapahoe Basin Colorado

Keystone is one of those resorts where everything works. Keystone Mountain is one of the best intermediate playgrounds in Colorado, and with the advanced skiing on North Peak and the Outback plus the expert terrain of Arapahoe Basin, it has something for every ability level. The resort management has created a smoothly humming community with buses shuttling to every corner, a state-of-the-art ski rental organization, foot-of-the-mountain child care, the Rockies' largest snowmaking system, the nation's largest maintained outdoor ice-skating center and one-number central reservations. Keystone has one extra magic ingredient that radiates from everyone, including bus drivers and lift attendants, cafeteria workers, instructors and management—Service, with a capital S and normally with a smile.

Physically, Keystone is different from other resorts in Colorado: it was planned from the ground up. With no old

Keystone/North Peak/Outback Facts
Base elevation: 9,300'; **Summit elevation:** 11,980'; **Vertical drop:** 2,680 feet
Number and types of lifts: 19—2 gondolas, 3 quad superchairs, 1 quad chair,
3 triple chairs, 6 double chairs, 3 surface lifts.
Acreage: 1,104 skiable acres **Percent of snowmaking:** 71 percent
Uphill capacity: 32,817 skiers per hour **Bed base:** 5,000

Arapahoe Basin Facts
Base elevation: 10,780'; **Summit elevation:** 13,050'; **Vertical drop:** 2,270 feet
Number and types of lifts: 5—1 triple chair, 4 double chairs
Acreage: 490 skiable acres **Percent of snowmaking:** none
Uphill capacity: 6,200 skiers per hour **Bed base:** 5,000

town that the resort could anchor to or build around, Keystone is the product of continuous condominium buildup. Without a town center or resort center to speak of, and townhouses and condos grouped in clusters radiating from the main base facilities, Keystone has a spread-out, homogenized feel. The closest attempt at a social gathering place is the collection of shops, restaurants and condos grouped around the pond and called Keystone Village. But the "village" has no pulse—it is too far from the base area to be a center for après-ski activities and too isolated to be much more than a promenade for guests at the Keystone Lodge and the closest condominiums.

Even without the flavor of an alpine resort or western mining town, Keystone is a phenomenal success. It is a tribute to service, great organization, and creative, affordable packaging; and, of course, its proximity to Denver. The resort is perfect for family vacations and couples or small groups of friends who want to spend time alone. Those searching for excitement, nightlife or a singles scene will be better pleased elsewhere.

The skiing

The Outback A new gondola, two new lifts, a gorgeous new $6 million mountain- top lodge and restaurant facility, $6 million in snowmaking, 17 trails and 256 acres on new terrain make it one of the most ambitious expansions in the country last year. The skiing on the Outback is mostly upper-intermediate and advanced tree and glade skiing. For the most part, the trails are ungroomed, giving rise to Volks wagen-sized bumps. It is not exactly wilderness, but neither is it the comforting close to home skiing found on the tamer parts of Keystone.

Keystone Mountain is one of the better intermediate mountains in Colorado, maybe in America. Snowmaking covers 100 percent of the mountain, and the slope grooming may be surpassed only by Utah's elite Deer Valley. The Mountain House base area has three chair lifts taking skiers up the mountain, and the other base area, River Run, is the lower station of the gondola that reaches the Summit House, 2,340 feet higher, in 10 minutes.

One of the gondolas serves the night-skiing area until 10 p.m. This is the largest single-mountain night ski operation in the United States and covers 13 runs.

If you see a trail going up and down the mountain, you can be assured that it is intermediate. These are not pansy-level intermediates—they are great cruises with enough twists, turns and dips to entertain the most jaded skier. Paymaster, the Wild Irishman, Frenchman and Flying Dutchman are runs that play with the mountain's terrain. The bumps, twists and steps offered by these cruises represent nature at its best, and obviously did not have the character bulldozed out of them.

Trails cutting across the mountain are principally for beginners. You can take most of them traversing from the top of the Peru Chair, or take Schoolmarm along the ridge and drop down Silver Spoon or Last Chance.

Advanced intermediates and experts have really only one trail on Keystone Mountain that develops pitch—Go Devil, dropping down the far right edge of the area served by Packsaddle lift. This relative lack is easily remedied by taking a lift up to the Summit House, then dropping down the super-long, groomed Mozart cruise to the base of Keystone's **North Peak**. The descent to the North Peak base can also be negotiated down Diamond Back, which maintains a steeper pitch and is infrequently groomed. These North Peak runs are almost all advanced expert and are a great playground for skiers working on technique and steeps. Warm up on Starfire or Last Alamo. The two intermediate runs then plunge into Ambush, Powder Cap or Bullet. On the other side of the lift Cat Dancer and Geronimo offer a challenge, and experts can break their own tracks through the trees directly beneath the lift.

Arapahoe Basin, long a legend with real skiers, was folded into the Keystone package about 10 years ago, so skiing at Arapahoe is included in the Keystone lift ticket. This stark ski area is only a short five-mile shuttlebus ride from Keystone, but it's another world when it comes to skiing. Arapahoe is the highest lift-served skiing in North America, topping off at 13,050 feet. Arapahoe Basin's above-timberline terrain is subjected to howling winds, plummeting temperatures, and white-out conditions: this is the closest thing Colorado has to skiing the high Alps.

Arapahoe has an area for true beginners, called Molly Hogan, but it is small. Beginners who've gone beyond the absolute basics have Chisholm, Wrangler and Sundance

Keystone/Arapahoe - Colorado

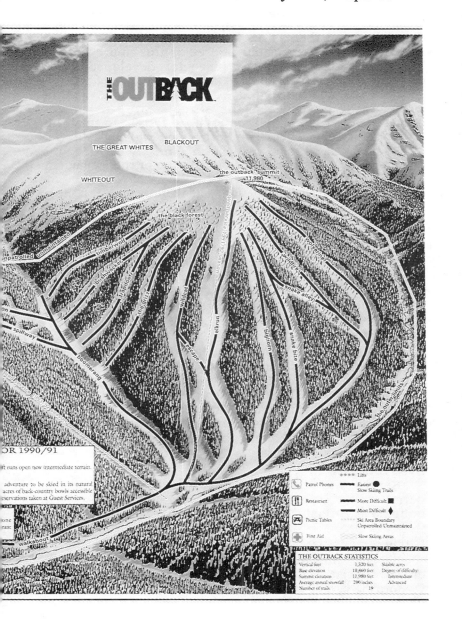

THE **OUTBACK**

THE GREAT WHITES   BLACKOUT

WHITEOUT

the outback summit
11,980

the black forest

unpatrolled
unmaintained

timberwolf
bushwacker
dunkley
algene
wildfire
treeline
elkrun
bighorn
snake bite
snake alley
the outback summit
spillway
boomerang

OR 1990/91

t runs open new intermediate terrain.

adventure to be skied in its natural
acres of back-country bowls accessible
servations taken at Guest Services.

walkabout

Patrol Phones		Lifts
Restaurant		Easiest
		Slow Skiing Trails
Picnic Tables		More Difficult
		Most Difficult
First Aid		Ski Area Boundary
		Unpatrolled Unmaintained
		Slow Skiing Areas

THE OUTBACK STATISTICS

Vertical feet	1,520 feet	Skiable acres
Base elevation	10,460 feet	Degree of difficulty:
Summit elevation	11,980 feet	Intermediate
Average annual snowfall	200 inches	Advanced
Number of trails	19	

winding down from the top of Exhibition Chair. Intermediates can test themselves from the top of either the Lenawee or the Norway Chair and enjoy this above-timberline bowl skiing. It is the place for developed intermediates to push their abilities and get a change of pace.

It is the advanced and expert skier that Arapahoe seems to be created for—the strong, hardy skier who braves weather, wind and super-steep terrain to push his envelope of experience. The entire east wall has chutes, gullies and steeps regularly searched out by experts, and dozens of expert runs drop from the top of the Pallavicini Lift. When all is said and done the heart of Arapahoe for experts is the "Palli," a legendary avalanche chute, a steep stamped in nature. It used to be that skiers had to drop off the cornice and then hike about five minutes to the north-facing run, but the new Pallavicini Chair rising from the parking lot opened this drop to anyone willing to jump.

Thanks to its elevation and unusual nature, Arapahoe doesn't hit stride until late January when the gullies fill in and the rocks have sufficient cover. It's skiable until the end of May, sometimes, as last season, until mid-June.

Mountain rating

These mountains break easily into categories, with some exceptions as noted above. Keystone weighs in as great beginner and cruising terrain. North Peak is for advanced skiers with expert tendencies. Arapahoe Basin is for strong intermediates, advanced and very expert experts. The new Outback is for upper intermediates and expert skiers. The night skiing is for everyone.

Snowboarding

Keystone is not open to snowboarders. Shredding is permitted at Arapahoe Basin without limits. There is a halfpipe at A-Basin, lessons and rentals.

Cross-country

Keystone has also developed one of the most extensive cross-country touring areas in Colorado. The cross-country touring center (468-4275) at the Ski Tip Lodge services 24 km. of groomed trails around the resort and is open from 8 a.m. to 5 p.m. There are an additional 57 kilometers of extensive backcountry skiing trails to mining ghost towns in the Montezuma area. Make sure to request Keystone's cross-country brochure.

Trail fees are $7 a day or $6 for a half day. Lesson packages range from $32 to $35. There are special children's classes for $28. Rentals are available from the touring center. Cross-country activities include moonlight tours for $28 and mountain tours. A women's cross-country seminar is held every spring, focusing on total development for the cross-country experience.

Ski school (92/93 prices)

Keystone's ski school is as smoothly running as its shuttle system, and the mountain is perfect for lessons of every type.

Group lessons meet daily from 10:25 a.m. to 1:30 p.m. for a two-and-a-half-hour session at all three locations (base of Keystone, River Run Plaza and Arapahoe Basin). These sessions cost $27 each. Beginners have a lesson that includes lift tickets during the same period for $36, or $47 with rentals included. The Keystone ski week with five days of instruction costs $450.

Private lessons provide the chance to work on personal skiing quirks and move at your own pace. One hour is $60 and one and a half hours are $80. Additional skiers will be charged $20. A private half-day lesson (three and a half hours) for one to three people is $185. Full-day lessons (seven hours) are $275.

Five Key Ski Weeks will provide five days of three hour lessons from 9:30 a.m. to 12:30 p.m. Price including instruction, lifts, video awards and orientation is $260. Programs start on December 14, January 4 and 18, February 1 and March 1, 1993.

For ski school reservations, call (800) 255-3715; in Colorado, 468-4170.

For children there is a special Minor's Camp Program for five-to-12 year olds with all-day supervision. The best skiers are enrolled in the Mountain Mashers program. The rates include rental equipment. One day is $60 and includes lift ticket, lesson, lunch and rental equipment. The Mini-Minor's is a program for kids three or four years old. Full day with lunch is $60, half day with lunch $50.

The Mahre Training Centers are now held exclusively at Keystone. These are five-day and three-day sessions conducted by either Phil or Steve Mahre. The skiing, for all levels, teaches fundamentals. In the evening there is a classroom session where on-slope activities and techniques are reviewed, and one of the Mahre brothers is available to answer questions. The three-day program costs $355 and the five-day program costs $575. Both include lifts, six hours of instruction daily, video, races and time for fun. Lodging is not included. The Mahre programs run through late February. A spring training program at A-Basin starts may 9 and costs $825 with lodging.

Lift Tickets (92/93 prices)

Keystone, because of its night skiing, has a somewhat different arrangement of prices. Note carefully the times when the pass is valid. Children get discounted full-day and multi-day lift tickets, but no discounts for afternoon, twilight or night tickets. Seniors 60-69 pay $21 a day, and 70 and over ski free. Also note: lift tickets are valid on all four mountains, including Araphoe Basin, however, a lift ticket limited to Arapahoe Basin is $33 a day.

Full day all mountains (8:30 a.m.-10 p.m.): $38 adults/$17 children (5-12); three-days of lifts cost $96/$45; six days will run $180/$90.

Twilight (2-10 p.m.) $28; night (4-10 p.m.) $22; and late night (7-10 p.m.) $15.

Accommodations

Keystone, a condominium community, has two hotels within the system. One is the modern **Keystone Lodge**, which also houses the main restaurants and dozens of conference rooms for business meetings. The other embodies the only "past" Keystone exhibits, the quaint **Ski Tip Lodge**, a perfect ski lodge. Rooms are rustic, the dining room elegant and the sitting room warm and inviting.

The Ski Tip Lodge only rents rooms with breakfast and dinner included. Private rooms have baths, and the dorm rooms share one. The rooms are not giant but are comfortable and the food is reported to be wonderful. Private rooms during regular season based on double occupancy are $110 per person a night; dorm rooms cost $84 per person a night. Call 468-4242 for reservations.

Other than the Keystone Lodge, which has normal hotel rooms, accommodations are broken into ratings of

Bronze, Silver, Gold and Slopeside. Each group has a central swimming pool and, except for the slopeside units, all have about equal access to the lifts, thanks to the excellent shuttle system.

Slopeside condominiums are virtually ski-in/ski-out—they are right across the street from the Keystone Mountain Base Area. The **Chateaux d'Mont** condos are spectacular, by far the most luxurious and worth every penny. We strongly recommend trying to get one of these units. Those renting at the **Keystone Mountain Inn** are paying mainly for location.

Gold condominiums seem to be priced in a higher category because of more lavish decoration and because they are closer to the Keystone Village and Keystone Lodge. This is logical because they would be the best locations for any company planning a meeting at Keystone. However, they are not worth a premium to a skier or his family.

The Silver condominium grouping offers the best value for money and are considered more "homelike." **The Sts. John** units have spectacular views and were built with just about every amenity. In the Silver category these units are clearly the leader. In the deluxe group we also highly recommend the **Pines** condominiums.

Kids 12 and under stay free in the same lodge room or condo with their parents, providing minimum occupancy is met and the maximum occupancy is not exceeded.

Dining

There are three eating experiences visitors to Keystone should try to include during their stay—**The Keystone Ranch** (468-4161); the **Ski Tip Lodge** (468-4202); and the **The Alpenglow Stube**, perched at 11,444 feet at the top of North Peak.

They all require reservations. The Keystone Ranch is a restored log ranch house of the 1930s. Reportedly, the only completely original part of the house standing is the original fireplace. The Ski Tip Lodge exudes a homey, rustic flavor. The Alpenglow Stube is located in The Outpost which features rough hewn timbers, massive fireplaces, vaulted ceilings and expansive windows. The restaurant, seemingly inspired by Heidi and elegantly decorated by a Victorian Martha Stewart, features a menu of such non-traditional skiing fare as roasted salmon with leeks, veal chops and wild mushrooms and pumpkin soup. It is reached by a ride on the Keystone to North Peak gondola and serves meals until 10 p.m.

Another experience is **Der Fondue Chessel** at the Summit House. Ride the gondola to the top of Keystone Mountain then enjoy fondue and wine by candlelight with music by a Bavarian band. Call 468-2316 for reservations.

In the Keystone Lodge there are two main dinner options. **The Garden Room** offers fanciful gourmet fare, while the **Bighorn Steakhouse** serves up hefty portions of buffalo or beef steaks and seafood. Reservations are suggested for the more formal Garden Room (468-3740).

Après-ski/nightlife

Keystone will never be mistaken for Aspen or even Park City. The nightlife is very limited unless you consider a night curled in front of a fireplace sipping brandy an acceptable alternative to leaning on a bar, knocking back a few brews and dancing.

The best bet for a good night out dancing and meeting the other nightlife denizens is at the **Last Chance Saloon**. Across the highway you will find the **Snake River Saloon**, which has good action with a slightly older crowd.

For immediate après-ski activity, try the **Last Lift Bar** in the Keystone Village or the **Snake River Saloon**.

Child care (92/93 prices)

Keystone has made major efforts for children's skiing. (Minor's Camp programs are described under Ski School.) The resort has designated "Children Only" skiing areas and classes have an average 5:1 student/teacher ratio.

The Children's Center at Keystone Mountain base accepts infants as young as two months, and the nursery at Arapahoe accepts children from 18 months. Reservations are required; call 468-4182.

Child care for children two months and older is $44 for a full day and $34 for a half day, either a.m. or p.m. Both include lunch. From 5-10 p.m. cost is $6 an hour. The Snowplay Program, designed for children three and older, costs $44 for a full day of activities and lunch, and $34 for a half day of fun.

Other activities

Keystone has a good athletic club with two indoor tennis courts. Tennis lessons are available for $45 an hour.

Sleigh rides to the Soda Creek Homestead, including a dinner with all the fixins, will cost adults $48; children under 12, $30. The sleigh ride without dinner is $10 a person. Call (800) 451-5930 or (303) 468-4130.

Ice skating in the middle of Keystone Village is open each day and night. The rink, which is smoothed twice a day, has a fee of $6, ice skates can be rented for $6.

Getting there

Keystone is 75 miles from Denver. Transportation can be booked between the airport and the resort with central reservations number, (800) 222-0188 or (303) 468-4242.

Keystone is a 90-minute drive by I-70 and over the Loveland Pass or through the Eisenhower Tunnel. By shuttle the trip is hassle-free. Resort Express has 13 round trips daily from Denver's Airport to Keystone. Call (800) 334-7433, or check in at Door #6 when arriving in Denver.

The Summit Stage provides free transportation between Dillon, Silverthorne, Frisco, Breckenridge and Copper Mountain all day. Call 453-1241 for information.

Within Keystone a free shuttle system runs continuously from 7:30 a.m., passing every 15 minutes. In the evenings the shuttles run every 20 minutes until midnight on weeknights, until 2 a.m. on Fridays and Saturdays. Bartenders and hotel doormen will call the shuttle to ensure pickup in the evenings and late at night, 468-4200.

Information/reservations

For all reservations except air, call Keystone Condominium Reservations at (800) 222-0188 or 534-7712 (toll free from Denver); or the Keystone Lodge at (800) 541-0346.

General information: 468-2316 or (800) 222-0188.

Current ski conditions: (303) 468-4111

Denver-direct ski conditions (303) 733-0191

Activities information/reservations (800) 451-5930.

Purgatory-Durango Colorado

If you are ever banished to Purgatory, don't fret—at least if your exile is to this ski area in southwestern Colorado, 25 miles north of the town of Durango.

Purgatory draws heavily from Arizona, New Mexico, Texas, and to a growing extent, Southern California. One attraction for skiers from these states is that they can drive here without crossing any major mountain ranges. Another attraction is Purgatory's undulating terrain: millions of years ago glaciers scraped this valley, leaving narrow natural terraces on the mountainside. Purgatory's runs plunge downward for a bit, then level off, then plunge, then level off—all the way to the bottom; the effect is rather like a roller coaster ride. Skiers who love to get air go bananas here, and those who don't can use the flat areas to catch their breath before the next steep part.

Like many of Colorado's ski resorts, Purgatory helped a dying 19th century town get back on its economic feet. Unlike some of the others, the ski area is 25 miles away from the town. For years skiers stayed in Durango and drove the 50-mile round trip, but fortunately quite a bit of development has taken place here in the past decade. The resulting Purgatory Village has hotel rooms, condos, restaurants and shops—fewer than Durango, but enough so that the visitors who aren't that big on nightlife and fine dining won't have to leave Purgatory during their stay.

Purgatory-Durango Facts
Base elevation: 8,793'; **Summit elevation:** 10,822'; **Vertical drop:** 2,029 feet
Number of lifts: 9—4 triple chairs, 5 double chairs
Snowmaking as percent of area: 22 percent
Total acreage: 640 acres skiable terrain accessed by lifts
Uphill capacity: 12,700 per hour **Bed base:** 3,120 near resort, 7,000 in Durango

About that name: it's inspired, along with many trail names, by the Divine Comedy, and since Dante Alighieri's 14th century epic described an imagined journey through all three realms of the other world—Hell, Purgatory, and Paradise—you'll see runs named Hades, Cherub, Divinity, and 666, as well as an elegant on-mountain restaurant called Dante's. The area founders thought of the Divine Comedy because Spanish explorers had christened the river that flows through Durango "Rio de las Animas Perdidas," River of Lost Souls.

Where to ski

This season there are four new trails and 35 new acres of terrain. One of the new intermediate trails will take skiers down to Dante's midmountain restaurant and connect with the Legends. Another adds to the expert stuff and a beginner trail provides new skiers the chance to ski a new part of the resort. The resort has also added thirty new acres of snowmaking on the front side of the mountain—now man-made snow is served by five lifts.

At Purgatory, skiers can enjoy a nice progression from beginner to expert terrain. Never-evers have their own learning area, Columbine Station. An intra-area shuttle-bus takes beginners here after they have bought their rentals and lift tickets. After a couple of lessons on the terrain under Lift 9, they are ready to board Lift 7, which takes them back to the base area. Purgatory offers *free* beginner lessons to adults, and over 11,000 skiers take advantage each season. The management figures that if beginners have a good time, they'll be back.

Beginners will like the runs under Lift 4. The easiest of these is Walk-a-Lot, a gently winding catwalk trail. Divinity and Angel's Tread are wide, gentle runs, and Columbine winds through stands of trees, giving beginners a feel of being deep in the woods. As they progress, they may want to head down Salvation toward Lift 3, which goes straight for the summit. From there, they can descend The Bank or Silvertip to Westfork, where they have many choices for getting back down.

The next step is the intermediate runs off Chair 2. Snowmaking on these runs ensures a good surface. After skiers feel comfortable on What, Limbo, and Westfork, they should make for Peace and Boogie, two wide intermediate runs off Chair 3. Still not enough of a challenge? Then head down blue-square The Legends toward Dead Spike, the widest of Purgatory's runs, or continue on The Legends to the mid-loading station on Chair 8. Sally's Run is not so steep as Chet's, but both are advanced runs.

Still not enough to make your heart leap into your throat? Go for Wapiti, a black run under Lift 5. Or try Catharsis or 666, two short black runs under Lifts 1 and 6.

If evn this is insufficient challenge, then you're ready for Bull Run, a double-black trail that starts just below Dante's Restaurant off Lift 5. It has a tough pitch as well as funnels and moguls (and once you're on it, you're stuck). Other advanced areas include the short steep runs at the bottom of Lift 8, and Styx and Hades off Chairs 1 and 6.

Purgatory's runs are quite long. Although many stretch from summit to base, they twist and turn, passing islands of trees and picnic tables.

Mountain rating

Purgatory may be a place where souls suffer before being allowed into Paradise, but that's in Dante's poem. Intermediates get to bypass the limbo stage and head straight for nirvana, such are the variety and plenitude of trails for this level. The resort also offers a lot for beginners and advanced skiers. Only experts looking for extremes may feel that they are somewhat in Purgatory.

Cross-country

The Cross-country Skiing Center is across Highway 550 from Purgatory. It maintains 16 km. of track, which winds through trees and glades. Rentals are available. Trail fees: $5 a person. Group lessons are $20 for a half-day; with rentals, $25. Your downhill lift tickets can be swapped for a day of cross-country.

Snowboarding

Purgatory has welcomed snowboarders since 1985. "Dude Ranch" is a half-pipe near the top of Chair 2 off the Westfork run. Also, the trail called "What" is a naturally shaped half-pipe, so snowboarders like to use it. Snowboarders tend to avoid the Legends area, served by Chair 8, because they have to take BD&M Expressway, a long flat run, back to the main area. (Area employees say the initials stand for Boring, Dull, and Monotonous; actually, the run is named for three of Purgatory's pioneers.)

The Purgatory Village Center houses the San Juan Snowboard Company, a shop devoted to the sport. It sells equipment and clothing, rents equipment, does tuning and repairs, and arranges backcountry tours led by experienced snowboard guides.

Ski School

Purgatory has long been known as a leader in teaching beginners the basics. The Start 'Em Off Right program offers two half-day adult beginner lessons Free with the purchase of two all-day or any multiday adult lift tickets. That means a savings of $50. Purgatory Ski School also offers a free half day of beginner-only adult lessons with the purchase of one adult lift ticket.

Purgatory also has lessons and special workshops for other skier levels. Group lessons cost $36 for a full day, $26 for a half day. Private lessons are $260 for a full day. Private lessons lasting 90 minutes are $70 per person, with each additional person an extra $20. If you can time your private lesson for 9 a.m. or 3 p.m., the cost goes down to $45 an hour, $15 each additional skier. Further discounts on private lessons are available for half and full days. A one-run, 12:30 p.m. private lesson is $25.

Purgatory also has some innovative special programs. The Big Three gives you three half-day lessons, three lift tickets, and three days of rental equipment, $165 for adults and $135 for children. The Sundays Are Fundays program includes a free clinic with the purchase of a lift ticket every Sunday in January and February. The lessons rotate between snowboarding, telemark skiing and mogul techniques. At selected times throughout the season, men and women can register for gender-segregated workshops. The men may choose between the eight-week, one-afternoon-per-week Men's Day program ($160) or three-day workshops ($250 including lift ticket and $160 without). Women have a three-day workshop, or the eight-week program. The three-day program costs $250 including lift tickets and $160 without. All workshops include instruction, video critiques, a NASTAR race clinic, and extras, such as wine-and-cheese parties and sleigh ride with dinner.

The "Ski Demons" program is for kids 6-12. An all-day program including lift ticket, lessons, and lunch is $46 for the first child in a family and $39 for additional kids. Half day, starting at 12:45 p.m., is $26.

Children three and a half through six can enroll at Teddy Bear Camp, a combination ski lesson and child care program. The costs are $45 for two lessons and lunch, $40 for full day with one lesson and lunch, and $30 for half day with one lesson and lunch. Rental equipment is $7 extra, but may be used only during the program. Purgatory also has a 90-minute private lesson costing $60 that teaches parents the dos and don'ts of skiing with their kids while the kids are learning.

One of the nation's outstanding instruction programs for disabled skiers is here at Purgatory. For information, call 247-9000, Ext. 3217, or 259-0374.

Lift tickets

Full-day price for adults is $35, for children $18. For a half day, the costs are $26/$14; for two days, $68/$34; for three days, $99/$51; for additional days, $30/$16 each.

Accomodations

Purgatory-Durango has three lodging areas. The condos at the base are the most expensive; hotels and condos within 10 miles of the ski area are a little less so, and lodging in Durango is dirt cheap, but 25 miles away.

Base-area condos at the **Purgatory Village Hotel, Angelhaus Condominiums, Brimstone Condominiums, East Rim, Edelweiss, Sitzmark** and **Twilight View** have full-service units (kitchens, fireplaces, common-area Jacuzzis and laundry facilities) from $85 for a studio $310 for a three-bedroom. Prices vary slightly for similar-size units in the various complexes.

Several other complexes are two to ten miles from the ski area. The prices at **Cascade Village, Needles, Silver Pick, Tamarron** and **Whispering Pines** range from $82 for a studio at Cascade Village, one mile north, to $258 for a three-bedroom at Tamarron, nine miles south. Most of the outlying condo complexes have free shuttles to and from the ski area. (Even if you brought your own car, leave it behind and take the shuttle: it will get you closer.)

Durango may be the only ski town in America where the winter lodging prices are lower than the summer ones. Winter rates are as low as $18 a night for a one-bed unit in a clean, comfortable, but unadorned motel, and several motels have this low-end rate. The high end in town is $175 per night for a suite at the **Red Lion Inn**. The average rate is around $45 a night.

Dining

Purgatory base area offers **Sterling's, Mesquite Bar and Grill**, and **Farquahrt's** for local eateries. For some of the best fish in Colorado, flown in daily, and for local game, try the **Cafe Cascade**, two miles north of Purgatory (259-3500), elegant dining in a rustic setting with entrées $10-$15; everyone who has eaten here raves about it.

Dante's, midway on Chair 5, offers sit-down gourmet dining at lunch, only for skiers. **The Powderhouse**, also on the mounain, has more mundane fare. Down the hill are the **Tamarron's** three restaurants: in the Tamarron's San Juan Dining Room, the piñon nut waffles with chokecherry syrup are so good I had them three breakfasts in a row.

Durango is where we find most of the restaurants. **The Palace Grill**, 1 Depot Place (247-2018), has continental cuisine such as honey-glazed duck, with most entrées $14 to $20; it's been one of Durango's top restaurants for years. **Ariano's**, 150 East 6th St. (247-8146), serves north Italian specialties for $8 to $15. **The Ore House**, 147 6th St. (247-5707) is an Old West steak house, rustic and casual with entrées in the $10-$15 range; it's become the favorite gift certificate in the weekly Purgatory good-employee gift drawing. **The Red Snapper**, 144 East 9th St. (259-3417) also has fresh seafood in a saltwater aquarium setting. Entrées are about $10-$15, and they have wonderful vegetables and salads. **Pronto Pizza and Pasta**, 160 East 6th St. (247-1510) is good for families and those looking for a bargain, and features thin-crust pizza and fresh pasta. They even deliver, if you're staying in Durango, and they have an all-you-can-eat pasta buffet every weekend. **Carver's Bakery and Brew Pub**, 1022 Main Ave. (259-2545) is the best place in Durango for breakfast; muffins and bagels are fresh daily. It's a hangout for locals and on some weeknights there's an open mike for Durango performers. **Olde Tymer's Cafe**, 1000 Main Ave. (259-2990) in the restored Wall Drug building claims the best hamburgers in town and huge margaritas. Daily specials include $2.95 burgers Monday nights, $1.25 taco night on Friday—Purgatory employees jam the place these nights. Mexican food on weekends. **The Golden Dragon**, 992 Main Ave. (259-0956) serves Chinese food in huge portions. Sunday brunch at the **Red Lion Inn** is outstanding and a good choice for skiers departing on Sunday, since the inn is between the ski area and the airport.

Après-ski/nightlife

Skiers congregate in three places after the lifts close: **Farquahrt's**, where the music is the liveliest; **Mesquite's**, slightly more sedate; or **Sterling's**, which is the quietest. Nightlife at the ski area is limited to Farquahrt's, which has live bands Thursday through Sunday—they play two sets: 4 to 6 p.m. and 8:30 to 11.

A popular après-ski spot is the **Trimble Hot Springs**, about 20 miles from the ski area toward Durango. Natural mineral springs bubble into an Olympic-size outdoor pool, heated to 90 degrees, a 105-degree outdoor therapy pool, and several private tubs.

If you really want to tango, you gotta go to Durango. Catch the Durango Lift from the base area, $5 round trip; everything in town is in walking distance. Depending on the time of year, Durango is either jumping or mildly hopping. Spring Break, which goes on for several weeks in March and April brings thousands of college students, and the bars schedule lots of entertainment.

Durango has quite a variety of musical entertainment. Try **Farquahrt's** downtown for dancing, or the **Sundance Saloon**. Farquahrt's has an eclectic clientele—hippies, neo-hippies, yuppies and college students. The music ranges from reggae, to blues, rock'n'roll, and oldies. The dance floor is small and crowded. The Sundance Saloon is a cowboy bar with Country & Western music and dancing.

The audience becomes the entertainment at three places: **Carver's Bakery and Brew Pub** has an open mike for folk singers—bring your own acoustic guitar. The bar on the second floor of **The Pelican's Nest** restaurant (658

Main Ave., 259-2888) has live jazz on the weekends and a jam session on Thursdays—bring your own trumpet or sax and join local amateur jazz musicians. **The Back Stage Saloon** (128 East 6th St., 247-7775) has a karaoke machine with some 1,500 songs. The Back Stage is very popular with ski clubs, who sing until the wee hours.

The other popular hangouts are the **Old Muldoon**, furnished in a dark Victorian style, and the **Solid Muldoon**, which is worth a visit just for the decor. Everything imaginable—typewriter, kayak, bubble gum machine (with gumballs), and the kitchen sink—hang from the ceiling. They spin a wheel of fortune every so often, setting the price of drinks for the next few minutes. Over at the **Diamond Belle Saloon** in the Strater Hotel, a piano player plunks out hit tunes from the Gay 90s—1890s, that is.

Child care

Purgatory has a full range of programs, including infant care and ski lessons for the little ones. Ski Demons is for children six to 12. Full day, including lunch, lessons, and lifts, is $46; half day, $36.

Teddy Bear Camp is for children two to six, and has snow play, storytime, and other activities. Child care without ski lessons: full day with lunch, $30; half day with lunch, $22; half day only, $20; hourly rate available. Ski lessons for children three and a half to six, with two lessons and lunch, is $45; one lesson with lunch, $40; a half-day lesson and lunch, $30; half-day lesson only, $30.

Cub Care, for children two months to two years, is $40 for a full day, $30 for a half day.

Purgatory will babysit children two to 12 years on these holidays—Christmas through New Year, Martin Luther King weekend, Presidents' weekend in February, and Spring Break, several weeks in March and April. The $25 cost includes dinner and runs from 6 to 10 p.m.

Other activities

Buck's Livery has evening sleigh rides with dinner included. Departures are at 4:30 and 7 p.m., and the cost is $31 for adults, $19 for kids 6 to 12, and $10 for kids under 6. Buck's also has hour-long daytime sleigh rides when enough people sign up, $12 for adults, $8 for kids; prices subject to change, reservations necessary.

High Country Snowmobile Tours offers guided snowmobile trips including one-hour rides and backcountry tours. Rates are $25 per hour, $40 for two riders on the same snowmobile. Make reservations for at 247-9000, or visit the Purgatory Activities Booth on the second floor of the Village Center.

Getting there

The Durango-La Plata County Airport, 44 miles south of Purgatory, is served by America West, Continental Express, United Express, and Mesa Airlines.

By car, the resort is 25 miles north of Durango, 330 miles southwest of Colorado Springs, 350 miles south of Denver, 232 miles north of Albuquerque; 470 miles northeast of Phoenix, and 825 miles northeast of Los Angeles. There are no major mountain passes from the south or west. If you don't have four-wheel drive or snow tires, chains are highly recommended.

The Durango Lift shuttle service runs four to five times a day between town and resort for $5 round trip.

RVs may park in the Purgatory parking lot, but there are no hookups. RV campgrounds are closed in winter.

Information/reservations

With one call you can arrange lodging, transportation, lifts, transfers, ski rentals, and lessons. Call Purgatory-Durango Central Reservations at (800) 525-0892. Ski area information is 247-9000. Telephone area code is 303.

Steamboat, Colorado

Its ad campaign would have you believe that horses outnumber the cars in the ski area parking lot, that cowboy hats and sheepskin jackets are the preferred ski wear and that you should watch out for tobacco plugs on the dance floors. In reality, this is a big, sleek, modern ski area with very little Day's Work or Red Man in sight.

Steamboat Village, the cluster of condos, shops and restaurants next to the ski mountain, is unpretentiously upscale. Boutiques offering elegant high-priced goods are intermixed with T-shirt shops; gourmet restaurants are within steps of ribs-and-hamburger eateries. You will see an occasional socialite swathed in fur, but right behind her will be someone wearing a 15-year-old ski parka. Everyone looks right at home.

In Steamboat Village, the only cowboy hats you're likely to see grace the heads of Steamboat's resident celebrity, Billy Kidd, and the ticket punchers in the gondola building. Venture into downtown Steamboat Springs, though, and you may see cowboys sauntering down Lincoln Avenue. Northwest Colorado still has many cattle ranches, so they'll probably be the real thing.

The downtown area—about 10 minutes by car and about a half hour by shuttlebus—squeezes into its dozen blocks a hodgepodge of old Victorian buildings, 1950s storefronts and a gas station or hardware store here and there. Good restaurants and nightlife havens will be found

Steamboat Facts

Base elevation: 6,900'; **Summit elevation:** 10,585'; **Vertical drop:** 3,685 feet.
Number and types of lifts: 20—1 gondola, 2-quad superchairs, 1 quad chairs, 6 triple chairs, 7 double chairs, 1 ski school chair, 2 surface lifts
Acreage: 2,500 skiable acres **Snowmaking:** 24 percent of groomed trails.
Uphill capacity: 29,327 skiers per hour **Bed base:** 15,500

at the village, downtown and on the stretch of highway linking the two. A shuttlebus runs between the slopes and the town every half hour with a series of stops along the way, making it easy to enjoy the village, town and everything in between.

Steamboat is a particularly great place for non-skiers. In addition to the aforementioned shopping, Steamboat has many, many activities that go beyond the usual sleigh rides and snowmobile tours. Some of the best are detailed below: see Other Activities.

This season Steamboat will be be adding two new quad superchairs to replace the chairs at Storm Peak and Sundown. The Four Points lift will also be replaced with a triple chair.

The skiing

Expert skiing here means trees, and lots of them. Steamboat has only a few extreme steeps, but the runs from the Priest Creek and Sundown chairs are tree skiing developed to an art. These trails have been expertly thinned, trees about 50 feet apart along the center, and as close as 10 feet at the edges. That may sound like a lot in the safety of your living room, but when you're gathering speed with not much room to bail out, those trees will seem inches apart.

Such trails produce gallons of adrenalin, even for the best of the best skiers, who now have to cope with a natural slalom course where the "poles" ain't spring-loaded. To avoid a trip down in a ski patrol sled, skiers must substitute excellent control and technique for simple daring: few skiers wish to repeat an intimate encounter with a silver aspen.

Other good areas for advanced and expert skiers is "The Meadows" area off to the north of Storm Peak. There, Chutes 1, 2 and 3; the Christmas Tree Bowl, the Ridge and Crowtrack provide great challenges.

Many of the black-diamond runs aren't so intimidating as you might think. Though the terrain gets steep in spots and the moguls pretty high, the trails are generally wide, allowing ample room for mistakes and recoveries. Westside, a black trail off Rendezvous Saddle, is steep but usually groomed. It's a good starting point for intermediates wondering if they can handle the other black runs.

Among the great cruisers are all the blue trails from the Sunshine Chair (locals scornfully call this area "Wally World"), Sunset and Rainbow off the Four Points lift and Vagabond and Heavenly Daze off Thunderhead Peak. If the crowds build, head for the short intermediate runs reached by the Bashor chair, which often is deserted.

Although Steamboat has plenty of terrain marked with green circles, it ranks somewhere in the middle as a place for never-evers to learn. Beginners start on gently sloping terrain at the bottom of the mountain. Two problems with this terrain: the natural fall line is perpendicular to the direction you to ski to return to the lifts, and this is the area all the skiers on the slope funnel into at the end of the day. Steamboat gets more than a million skiers a year, so that's a lot of people whizzing by the slow-going snowplowers.

With the exception of some gentle terrain served by the Bashor and the two Christie chairs, most of the green trails higher on the mountain are catwalks. Although they have a gentle grade, they are narrow in places, they intersect advanced runs (where bombers are likely to use the intersection as a launching pad for the next black section), and they have some very intimidating dropoffs on the downhill side. An example of this is Steamboat's longest run, a three-mile winder called Why Not? If beginners are part of your group, *insist* that they enroll in ski school so that they will have a pleasant experience.

Mountain rating

Excellent tree skiing for experts, nice mogul runs for advanced intermediates, great cruisers for intermediates. Passable for beginners.

Cross-country

The Steamboat Ski Touring Center at 2000 Golf Course Rd. (303-879-8180) has about 30 kilometers of groomed, set tracks winding along Fish Creek and the surrounding countryside. The touring center has group and private instruction for all ability levels, rentals at $10 per full day or $8 half day, a restaurant, and backcountry guided tours. Trail fees are $9 a full day; $7 a half day after 1 p.m.

Track skiing also is available at Howelsen Hill in downtown Steamboat (303-879-2043) and at Vista Verde and Home Ranch, both guest ranches in Clarke County, about 25 miles from Steamboat.

Rabbit Ears Pass has many marked backcountry ski trails ranging from 1.7 to 7 miles for cross-country skiers, intermediate and above. Call or visit the U.S. Forest Service Ranger Station (57 10th Street in downtown Steamboat, 303-879-1870) to get current ski conditions and safety tips. Other popular backcountry areas are Buffalo Pass, Pearl Lake State Park, Stagecoach State Recreation Area and Steamboat Lake State Park.

Snowboarding

Snowboarding is allowed on all lifts and trails. Lessons are offered daily and cost $35 for three hours.

Ski school (92/93 prices)

In addition to the normal ski-school classes, Steamboat has special classes or clinics for telemark skiing, snowboarding, bumps, powder, skiers 45 and older, women, disabled skiers— even a style clinic to teach skiers who can parallel how to look good when they ski. Group clinics last three hours and cost $30 to $35.

Steamboat also has the **Billy Kidd Center for Performance Skiing** for intermediate and higher-level skiers. The clinics, which are offered only on specific dates throughout the season, refine the skier's technique in the bumps, through race gates and on tough terrain. The two-day camp is $300 for adults; $230 for kids. Three days cost $450 and $345 respectively.

Regular adult group lessons are $32 for two hours; $45 for all day, with multi-day discounts available. Lift/lesson packages start at $200 for three two-hour lessons and four days of lifts. Private lessons are $60 for one hour, $110 for two and $145 for three.

Children have the **Rough Rider program** (ages first grade-15) or **Kiddie Corral** (ages 3 1/2-kindergarten). The

Rough Rider group lessons are $28 for two hours and $48 for all day (no lunch). Kiddie Corral is $32 for half day; $48 for full day and lunch.

A special Ski Week package for adults is offered Monday through Friday and costs $132 for five two-hour lessons, an on-mountain barbecue, video analysis, NASTAR racing and a Ski Week pin. A similar children's program is $200, but the lessons are all day and all lunches are included. Lift tickets are extra.

Lift tickets (92/93 prices)

Prices are divided between a regular season and the value season, which runs from the ski area's opening through mid-December. Multi-day discounts don't apply until you buy at least four days, and you only save $2 per day on the six-of-seven-day pass.

Children don't get multi-day discounts, but can qualify for the Kids Ski Free program, which works like this: One child skis free when a parent buys a lift ticket valid for at least five days and stays in a participating Steamboat property. If the parent rents skis, the child gets free rentals. The program is not available during the Christmas vacation period.

Seniors aged 65-69 pay $23 per day, and those 70 and older ski free.

	Regular Season	Value Season
One day	$39	$34
Half-day	$31	$26
Two consecutive days	$78	$68
Five of six days	$192	$165
Six of seven days	$222	$192
Youth (12 and under)	$23	$23

Accommodations

The **Sheraton Steamboat Resort**, the only luxury full-service hotel, sits at the center of Steamboat Village. The gondola building is about 25 yards from the front door. Christmas reservations require a minimum seven-night stay. Nightly rates range from about $129 for a hotel room in January to $439 for a two-bedroom suite at Christmas or February/March.

Nearly all the other lodging at the ski area is in condominiums—hundreds of them surrounding the base area. The quality is quite good in the units that we inspected. Many properties have varying rates depending on when you come. Before mid-December and after March 31 are the cheapest; January comes next, and Christmas and Presidents' Weekend in February are most expensive.

Torian Plum (800-228-2458 or 303-879-8811) is one of the best, with spotless rooms and facilities, an extremely helpful but not overbearing staff and the ski area out one door and the top ski-area bars and restaurants out the opposite side. Prices range from $190 per night for a one-bedroom in early or late season to $415 for the same unit during Christmas. A three-bedroom unit goes for $270 per night early and $720 at Christmas.

Torian Plum's sister properties, **Bronze Tree** and **Trappeur's Crossing** start at $165 and $130 in early season and top out at $605. Bronze Tree has no one-bedroom units, so the price is for a two-bedroom. Trappeur's Crossing is about two blocks from the lifts.

Generally, prices are based on how close the property is to the lifts. Those in the expensive category ($150 per night and up) include the **Best Western Ptarmigan Inn** (close to lifts, but farther from shopping and night life), **Norwegian Log Condominiums, Storm Meadows Resort** and **Thunderhead Lodge and Condominiums.**

More moderate facilities ($95-$150, generally) include **Timber Run Condominiums** (three outdoor hot tubs of varying sizes), **the Harbor Hotel** in downtown Steamboat (free bus pass is included with your stay), **The Lodge at Steamboat**, and **The Ranch at Steamboat** (great views of the ski hill and the broad Yampa Valley).

Economy lodging includes **the Alpiner Lodge** (downtown), **Shadow Run Condominiums** (500 yards from lifts), **Alpine Meadows Townhomes** (800 yards away) and **The Rockies** (one mile away).

The Steamboat Bed and Breakfast, (879-5724) new last season, is located at 442 Pine Street. The B&B has rooms filled with antiques. Winter rates are $70-$80 per double room with breakfast. No children, no pets.

In the nearby town of Clark is one of only a handful of U.S. Relais and Chateau properties, **The Home Ranch**.

Cabins are nestled in the aspens of the Elk River Valley. A stay here includes three gourmet meals per day in the main house and a shuttle to the ski area. Call 879-1700.

Steamboat Reservations Services will make suggestions to match your needs and desires. Let the reservationist know the price range, location and room requirements (quiet location, good for families, laundry or other special amenities). The number is 800-922-2722.

Dining

Steamboat has a great variety of restaurants—varied menus, varied atmosphere and varied prices. The area has more than 50 restaurants, including one or more Cajun, Chinese, French, Italian, Russian and Scandinavian. Look for the Steamboat Dining Guide in your hotel or condo—it has menus and prices.

Katy Keck covers some of Steamboat's finest dining in detail in her Steamboat Savoir Faire chapter—here are some that have moderate prices ($15-$20 per meal, including drinks) and a casual atmosphere:

At the ski area or close by:

Dos Amigos (879-4270) serves large portions of Tex-Mex food and sandwiches and is part of the infamous "Steamboat Triangle" apres-ski circuit along with **Tugboat** and **Mattie Silks'** bar, and **The Cathouse Cafe**.

La Montaña (879-5800) see Katy's Savoir Faire section.

Grubstake (879-4448) serves hamburgers, steak sandwiches and the like.

Anderson & Friends, with locations on the mountain (879-8080) and downtown (879-0208), has fresh salads, homemade soups and sandwiches.

Downtown:

Old West Steakhouse (879-1441) is somewhat expensive, but packs in the crowds for steaks and seafood.

Giovanni's (879-4141) has not only Brooklyn-style Italian fare, but also what may be the largest collection of Brooklyn memorabilia this side of the borough.

BW-3 (879-2431) has several "flavors" of beef and buffalo burgers, and **The Cantina** (879-0826) is downtown's equivalent of Dos Amigos in food and bar.

Between ski area and downtown:

Mazzola's (879-2405) has the best pizza in the area.

You never need to leave the mountain for lunch, as several excellent restaurants are operated by or near the ski area. **Hazie's** and **Ragnar's**, both on the mountain, are wonderful for lunch as well as dinner. **The Grubstake** and **Tugboat** are both good base-area spots to grab lunch, and **Buddy's Run** in the Sheraton Resort is another good spot.

If you're in town for breakfast or lunch, try the **In-Season Bakery and Deli** (879-1840), which serves homemade soup, sandwiches and salads. Soothing classical music is played on the stereo system, and the pastries are incredible.

Good breakfast spots are **The 5th Street Cafe** or **The Shack Cafe** downtown, or **The Tugboat** at the base area. Avid skiers can board the gondola at 8:15 and have breakfast at **Charlie's Breakfast Club** at the top of the gondola until the slopes open at 9 a.m. Biscuits and gravy are a specialty, with other high-fuel fare also served, cafeteria-style.

Après-ski/nightlife

For immediate, relatively rowdy apres-ski, the place to go is the **Inferno**, just behind the base of the Silver Bullet gondola. Skiers pack into the bar where each hour the bartender spins the "shot wheel," setting prices anywhere from 35 to 95 cents. When 35 cents comes up, revellers buy shots by the tray.

Dos Amigos, as noted, is one leg of the "Steamboat Triangle." You have margaritas here, then head for the **Cathouse Cafe** and **Tugboat** for beer or mixed drinks. Friday is "Zoo Night" at the Cathouse, where any beer that has an animal on the label or in the name is $2.

Downtown, the **Old Town Pub** and **The Blue Bayou** are popular après-ski locations.

Quieter apres-ski locations on the mountain include the **Conservatory** at the Thunderhead Lodge with its 45 different beers of the world and crackling fire, **HB's** in the Sheraton or **Innerlinks**, which had a guitar player singing folk/pop/country tunes the week we were there.

Late-night places include **Inferno, Dos Amigos** and **Tugboat**, all with live music and lots of people. Another place with live music but not as big a crowd (probably because you have to walk up three or four floors) is the **Clock Tower Saloon**.

Downtown, the lively spots include **BW-3, The Steamboat Saloon** (where you'll find many cowboys who drink long-necked beers and dance the two-step) and **The Old Town Pub**. On Wednesdays, head for **the Steamboat Yacht Club** to watch the ski jumping on Howelsen Hill, and anytime, try one of the dozen vodkas at **Gorky Park**, with Russian (and neighboring republics) entertainment.

Steamboat has two movie theaters downtown and one at the mountain, if that's your idea of nightlife. A night trip to Strawberry Park Hot Springs is great fun; see Other Activities. **Buddy's Run** usually has comedy Tuesday through Friday night, and occasionally, a big-name artist, such as Lyle Lovett, will perform at the Sheraton.

Child care

Steamboat has a well-deserved reputation for building a family-friendly ski resort. Day care has been a serious commitment for several years.

The Kiddie Corral takes children from six months to first grade. The ski program for children 3 1/2 to first grade is detailed in the ski school section of this chapter. "Buckaroos" aged 2 1/2 to 3 1/2 get all-day child care and a one-hour ski lesson for $80. Nursery care covers six months to six years who will not be skiing or playing in the snow. They get games, puppet shows, movies, crafts, rest time and stories for $36 all day or $28 for half day. Three or more days costs $34 per day, and lunch is $4 extra. Parents must bring a lunch for children under 2.

KC's Nite Club is an evening care program for children 2 1/2 to 12 years every Tuesday through Saturday from 6 to 10:30 p.m. Snacks, games, video and rest time are included for $6 per hour. A second child is an additional $3 per hour, and three or more children are $10 per hour for the group.

Reservations are required for all care programs, plus a deposit of $25 per day is required when reservations are made. That deposit is refundable provided changes are made 24 hours or more in advance. Call the Steamboat Reservations Service (800-525-2628) or the Kiddie Corral, 879-6111, Ext. 469.

Other activities

Steamboat has so much to do *off* the mountain, it's tempting to skip the skiing. Here is a mere sampling of what you can do:

• Soak in the natural thermal waters at **Strawberry Park Hot Springs,** about 10 miles north of the ski area, where it comes out of the ground about 160 degrees. Fortunately it then combines with cold creek water to form three pools of varying temperatures. Admission to the hot springs is $5; a tour (transportation and admission) is $20. However, unless you have four-wheel drive or chains, spend the extra for the tour—the road to the springs is narrow, slick and winding. Strawberry Park is open from 10 a.m. to 10 p.m. during the week and stays open a couple of hours later on weekends. Helpful info: After dark, many bathers forgo suits (unless it's a clear, moonlit night, you won't see much). The only place to change is an unheated, dirt-floor tepee, so wear your swimsuit under your clothes, but take dry clothes. You will also need a large trash bag to put your clothes in; otherwise, steam from the pools will freeze them.

• Ride in a hot-air balloon. Four balloon companies offer rides, and a fifth specializes in bungee jumping. **Balloons Over Steamboat, Ltd.** (879-3298) is the oldest company in town; others are **Pegasus Balloon Tours** (879-9191), **Eagle Balloon Tours** (879-8687) and **Aero Sports Balloonists** (879-7433). **Downward Bound, Inc.** (879-8065) does the balloon bungee jumps. A half-hour balloon ride runs about $75—sounds steep, but the view and experience is spectacular. Winter flights usually go twice in the morning, 8 and 10 a.m. and again just before sunset.

• Learn to drive on ice. Now in its ninth season, the **Jeep-Eagle Ice Driving School** (879-6104) teaches how to drive skillfully and confidently on ice and snow. French race-car driver Jean-Paul Luc and his staff give half-day, full-day and multi-day lessons on a specially constructed course. The school office is in the Torian Plum shopping mall at the ski area.

• **Bobsledding** down a 5,000-foot lighted track is available from 6 to 10 p.m. every night, weather permitting, at Howelsen Hill in downtown Steamboat Springs. Helmets and sleds are provided, and rides cost $7 each, or $50 for a 10-ride punch card.

• A **ParaPlane** is a single-rider, powered parachute steered with the feet. The pilot, who receives about an hour of instruction before takeoff, sits in a frame with three wheels on the bottom. This company shares space with a fur shop in the Torian Plum shopping center.

• The Steamboat Activity Center, with a location at 720 Lincoln Avenue and another in Gondola Square at the ski area, is a one-stop information and reservation center. Call 879-2062, or (800) 488-2062 toll-free.

Getting there

Steamboat Springs has two airports: the closer, Steamboat Springs, is serviced by Continental Express from Denver. Yampa Valley Airport at Hayden, about 20 minutes away, handles jets—American, United, United Express and Northwest have direct flights there from more than 100 North American cities.

Panoramic Coaches' Steamboat Express is available daily from Denver's Stapleton International Airport. For schedule and information, call (800) 525-2628.

Steamboat is 157 miles northwest of Denver via I-70 through the Eisenhower Tunnel, north on Highway 9 to Kremmling, then west on U.S. 40 to Steamboat Springs. Plan on at least three hours by car.

Steamboat has an excellent bus system between town and ski area running every 20 minutes. The fare is 50 cents each way. Exact change is necessary, but a buck will pay for two people.

Information/reservations

Steamboat Reservations Services is a one-call service that can book airlines, lodging, lifts, transfers and many activities. The number is (800) 525-2628.

Steamboat Savoir Faire

Without a doubt, the most impressive evening in Steamboat starts at Gondola Square at the Silver Bullet terminal. It is here that you set off on the complimentary journey into the stars on the Silver Bullet. This roomy 8-man gondola (in New York, we would call it an apartment with a view) is complete with blankets for the crisp nighttime ride to the top of Thunderhead. The view into the valley is breathtaking.

Once on top your reservation will be waiting at **Hazie's** (879-6111). Named for Hazie Werner, mother of Buddy Werner, Hazie's offers exquisite nouvelle continental cuisine, with unbeatable views. The Steamboat Mountain executive chef, Danish-born Morten Hoj, has created a menu that will intrigue any palate. Choose from one of five delicious appetizers—escargots with garlic herb butter and French brie were delicious, as was the cheese and chive ravioli. The second course allows a choice of the soup du jour or shrimp bisque, or the Hazie's salad with mixed greens, artichoke hearts, Bermuda onions and mushrooms.

Try the very popular beef tenderloin roasted with garlic and crushed peppercorns. Seafood entrées might include charbroiled yellowfin tuna with fresh pineapple salsa. There are also several daily specials, which have included grilled swordfish and veal prime ribs, both cooked to perfection. Dessert offerings vary, but are sure to include the ethereal white chocolate mousse. Let the sommelier help you choose from Hazie's list of over 90 wines. Open from Tuesday to Saturday, Hazie's offers this prix fixe four-course dinner, including the gondola ride and an after-dinner drink, for $45 (discounts for children aged 6 to 12, those 5 and under eat free).

Hazie's also serves lunch (reservations recommended) from 11:30 a.m. to 2:30 p.m. There is an assortment of soups and salads, and entrées like Maryland crab cakes, chicken crepes, or the popular Hazie's burger.

If you find your skiing keeps you over in the Sunshine Peak area, however, try **Ragnar's** at Rendezvous Saddle featuring Scandinavian and continental cuisine in an atmosphere reminiscent of Steamboat's earlier days. Lunch is served from 11:30 a.m. to 2:15 p.m., and reservations are suggested—879-6111. Start with a smørrebrød platter, an assortment of Scandinavian herring, salami, ham, Danish paté and Nordic cheeses. There are several Scandinavian salads, including a shrimp salad on romaine with tomato, onion, celery and cucumber, or a pickled herring, potato and beet salad. Entrées range from daily specials such as mesquite-grilled chicken Florentine to a pork tenderloin with glazed onions. Prices range from $7.95 for a mesquite-grilled hamburger to $12.95 for Norwegian salmon.

At night, five times a week (Tuesday through Saturday), Ragnar's offers a prix fixe Scandinavian menu at $60 for adults. This evening also starts at Gondola Square, but once off the Silver Bullet at the top of Thunderhead, you climb into a sleigh to continue your journey to Rendezvous Saddle. You'll want at least one mug of hot spiced glögg before relaxing to music and enjoying the meal. For reservations, call 879-6111, Ext. 320.

For Steamboat's pinnacle of French dining, try **L'apogee** (911 Lincoln Avenue, 879-1919). Chef/owner Jamie Jenny has created a casually elegant ambiance where he serves some of the area's finest French food, with an unparalleled award-winning wine list. Start with the fresh shucked Apalachicola oysters simmered in white wine and served on a citrus and herb beurre blanc, or try the goat cheese tart with garlic rosemary breadsticks. Several specials, often wild game, are offered each day. Menu staples include the filet of beef chargrilled with a horseradish bordelaise sauce. Appetizers start at $6.50 and entrées range from $15.95 for charbroiled breast of chicken in a red wine sauce to $24.95 for two double-cut Colorado lamb chops in a Dijon herb crust.

While the food cannot be too highly praised, it is the wine list that is truly impressive. There are over 500 wines, ranging from $12 to $1,000 a bottle, all maintained in three temperature-controlled cellars. L'apogee also features Steamboat's only cruvinet system, serving over 30 vintage wines and ports by the glass.

This talented kitchen crew also services the more casual **Harwig's Grill** (same address, no reservations). Jenny has traveled extensively in Southeast Asia, and his grill menu reflects his passion for their flavors. Start with the Shau Lin Szechuan marinated chicken, chargrilled with orange coriander yogurt sauce or the ginger and veggie dim sum. The menu offerings range from bouillabaisse to Down Under lamb burgers, but it is the chalkboard that will tell the real story of the day. All fish can be ordered sauteed, poached or grilled, with a choice of any of the sauces: hollandaise, newburg, cranberry orange or citrus butter. First-time clients are often surprised when they see jackalope on the board, but will take Jenny's humor more seriously after trying the delicious mignonette of rabbit tenderloin and émincée of elk, with a chasseur sauce. Prices in the grill range from $3.50 for appetizers to $7 - $11 for entrées. The list of 60 wines here is offered for under $21 per bottle.

As if Jenny et al weren't busy enough with L'apogee and Harwig's, last season they took over **Cipriani's, The Conservatory** and **The Grill**, located in the base of the Thunderhead Lodge at Ski Times Square. These restaurants are open daily, with Cipriani's and The Conservatory serving fine cuisine in the evenings only (5:30 to 10:30 p.m.) and with The Grill serving more informal food for breakfast starting at 7 a.m., lunch and dinner. Call 879-8824 for reservations.

For more than Mex, don't miss **La Montaña**, located at 2500 Village Drive. Chef Michael Fragola has created an inventive menu that goes way beyond tacos and fajitas. Start with the award-winning grilled braided sausage, a trio of elk, lamb and chorizo sausages, braided together and mesquite-grilled. For the entrées, there is one I will remember for many meals to come. Years later, I can still taste every bite of their grilled elk tenderloin with a pecan crust and bourbon cream sauce, served with grilled polenta and roasted sweet pepper relish, one of the most incredible combinations of textures and flavors. The chef's keen understanding of southwestern ingredients is reflected well in an ever changing list of specials. Try mesquite grilled sea scallops on smoked corn salsa with a guajillo prickly pear sauce or the grilled swordfish with a tomatillo and sun-dried cherry compote.

Fragola has also recently implemented a light cuisine menu, with such greats as sweet pepper relleño, stuffed with corn, chilis, mushrooms and low fat mozzarella. Appetizer prices are about $6 and entrées about $10 for Tex-Mex taco dinners and $14 to $17 for the southwestern specials. Save room for the fried ice cream with three sauces—caramel, chocolate and prickly pear cactus.

New last season was the **Steamboat Smokehouse** at 912 Lincoln Ave. Here midst a no credit card, no reservations, no nonsense atmosphere are some of Colorado's best Texas-style hickory smoked barbequed anything . . . you name it . . . brisket, sausage, turkey, chicken, ham and even a daily road kill special (open 11 a.m. to 10 p.m.).

For Creole cooking try the **Blue Bayou** which has crawfish, jambalaya, oysters, grilled and blackened fish. Appetizers start at $2.50 and entrées are $12.95-$19.95.

A popular seafood restaurant is the **Steamboat Yacht Club**, found at 811 Yampa Avenue on the banks of the river itself. The greenhouse dining room overlooking the water is a great place for watching night skiing or Wednesday night ski jumping across the river on Howelson Hill. Offering both lunch (11:30 a.m. to 2:30 p.m.) and dinner (5:30 to 10 p.m.) daily, there is a wide selection of fresh fish. The menu is designed to mix and match fish, cooking techniques and sauces to suit your tastes. Try the yellowfin or mahi mahi, grilled or blackened, then choose from a citrus mango butter, a Szechuan style or Sante Fe style sauce. Prices are a reasonable $15.50. The Yacht Club also has a full selection of meat and poultry. For reservations, call 879-4774.

If you are unable to choose between these excellent dining spots, plan a trip back for next September and sample your way through some of the best grilling you'll find. All these great chefs will be together under one big tent competing in the Annual Sizzlin' Chefs Classic, a grilling contest sponsored by the local culinary association.

by Katy Keck

Telluride, Colorado

Far away from the major skiing hoopla of Colorado, tiny, picturesque, Victorian Telluride is tucked into a narrow, deep and spectacularly beautiful valley. The town, huddled beneath the soaring peaks of the San Juan Mountains, is packed with history and legend. Appropriately, surrounding it is some of America's most legendary expert skiing. And this season it celebrates 20 years as a ski resort.

You probably wouldn't imagine anyone sticking a ski resort way out here, starting from scratch—that would be crazy. No, Telluride is the creation of the era of gold and silver mining: that's why the road was built, and why they put in a railroad, one of the great stories of the American West. The energies poured into digging out precious metals also created the world's first practical alternating-current electrical system for mine equipment, and one of the best town water supplies. But gold meant money, money meant banks, and banks attracted bank robbers: it was here that Robert Leroy Parker, a.k.a. Butch Cassidy, robbed his first bank. He reportedly practiced his getaway over and over before the robbery, timing his escape down main street.

Jack Dempsey worked here as a bouncer and dishwasher before becoming famous. Telluride was even witness to politics (of a relatively harmless variety): in 1903 William Jennings Bryan delivered one of his renowned renditions of the "Cross of Gold" speech from the front of the New Sheridan Hotel.

Today, Telluride has been declared a national historic landmark *in toto*. The main street still appears much as it

---

Telluride Facts

Base elevation: 8,725'; **Summit elevation:** 11,890'; **Vertical drop:** 3,165 feet.
Number and types of lifts: 10—1 super quad chair, 2 triple chairs, 6 double chairs, and 1 surface lift
Acreage: 1,050 skiable acres **Percent of snowmaking:** 15 percent.
Uphill capacity: 10,000 skiers per hour **Bed base:** 4,100

did when Butch Cassidy began his career, the homes around the town have remained unchanged as residents work to restore the old Victorian finishes. And the mountains surrounding the town remain as imposing, beautiful and majestic as ever.

What has changed is the skiing. Telluride will celebrate its 19th year as a ski resort, changing from a place dedicated to the extremely steep to an all-round area with some of the best beginner terrain in Colorado.

Another continuing change is the emergence of the modern, condoesque Telluride, being built on the mountain side, above the beautiful valley. This development offers excellent access to the mountain, but it doesn't have the soul of original Telluride which created the mystique that brought skiers and celebrities to the town; these condo buildings might be found at any modern resort—Beaver Creek, Snowmass, Stratton—and they are definitely not part of the legendary historic town of Telluride in feeling, in experience, in shopping, or in nightlife, though they do share the same ski area.

The skiing

Start with what put Telluride on the skiers' map—The Plunge and Spiral Stairs. This duo, where left ungroomed, is as challenging a combination of steep bumps as you can find anywhere. If you manage to get down in any condition, you can savor some sense of accomplishment. Mammoth is an alternate trail but not any easier. Formerly untamed Bushwacker is just as steep, but these days its massive bumps have succumbed to winch-cat grooming. Even skiers dropping down below the base of Chair 9 will find a very narrow trail, about two or three moguls wide, which requires better than intermediate skills to negotiate well. For the basic intermediate skier who glides off at the top of Chair 9, the only real alternative is to follow See Forever around to Lookout or to the Gorrono Basin. New trail maps have listed The Plunge as a double-square advanced skiers run since mountain operations began grooming sections of the run to open it to advanced intermediates. Groomed, this run is a thrill, allowing experts to play on a steep cruise not found on many other mountains in North America, and letting advanced intermediates gingerly ski down.

Telluride - Colorado

Ski Patrol | N NASTAR | R Restaurant | Restrooms | Free Bu

RIDE

R   A   D   O

**Gold Hill
Elevation:
12,247'**

SILVERGLADE
6 APEX
QUEEN
IS ALLEY
DEW DROP
11
12
13
ALTA
SILVER TIP
POLAR
BOOMERANG
BIRGO
5
GATEWALK
PALMYRA
SUNDANCE
EEK A BOO
DRAW
COMPETITION
2
VILLAGE BYPASS
BOOMERANG
DOUBLE CABIN
SAN
JOAQUIN
VILLAGE
10
WORLD'S
LONGEST
SUPER QUAD
BRIDGES
GALLOPING GOOSE
MEADOWS
MEADOWS
1

	Existing Lifts
───O───	Proposed Lifts
	Proposed Gondola Transit
	Easiest
───■───	More Difficult
───◆───	Most Difficult

**Day Lodge
Elevation: 9,160'**

Artist rendering not to scale

Nordic   Telluride Ski Resort Rentals   Religious Services   Child Care/Nursery   Base Area

Perhaps the drive to label The Plunge and its sister super-steep trails as intermediate has been spearheaded by Telluride's limited intermediate terrain. The only true intermediate terrain is in the Gorrono Basin, but Telluride Face is with its grooming now acceptable for advanced intermediates. In fact, even without adding terrain, increased grooming is making more and more runs acceptable for intermediates each year. At the other extreme, Sunshine Peak is underwhelming. The most fun for an intermediate, besides a careful exploration of the Plunge and Spiral Stairs face, would be repeated trips up the Chair 4 and down Peek a Boo, Humbolt Draw, Pick and Gad and Tomboy. Even the "expert" runs off Chair 6 are manageable because they are relatively short.

Telluride is strengthening its expert hand with the opening of an additional 400 acres of glade and above-timberline skiing in the Gold Hill area.

Beginners, on the other hand, will find this one of the best places in the world to learn to ski. The Meadows has for years been considered a perfect beginners' area, and with the construction of the world's longest super quad chair lift, Telluride has four of the longest and best teaching slopes in skidom.

Mountain rating

Telluride is a rite of passage for experts. It's a chance to test oneself against the most consistent steeps and monstrous bumps most resorts allow to grow. For intermediates, Telluride is making a serious effort to groom more formerly expert slopes, and there are plenty of challenges for anyone trying to graduate to the expert level. If you are an intermediate whose trademark trails are down long mellow cruising terrain, head elsewhere. For beginners, there is virtually no better place to be introduced to skiing. The slopes are perfect and the visuals unsurpassed.

Snowboarding

Shredding is allowed on the entire mountain with a halfpipe located in Gorrono Basin. Ski school beginning snowboarding lessons cost $50, including lift and rentals.

Cross-country

Here again the spectacular scenery makes cross-country a joy to experience. For high mesa, cross-country skiing this area is difficult to beat. The Telluride Nordic Center offers a 50-km. network of groomed trails around town and the ski area.

Lessons are also available. Track fees are $10. Adult and children's group lessons are priced at $25. Full day back-country tours cost $45. Equipment rentals—skis, boots and poles—for a full day are $14 for adults and $13 for children. A day on your downhill ski pass can be exchanged for a day of cross-country, including equipment, a two-hour clinic and track fees.

Cross-country guides in the area have organized a Hut Tour through the San Juans. The guides have established several tour programs around the five-hut, 45-mile network. Huts are approximately six miles apart and each is equipped with padded bunks, propane cooking appliances and a big potbelly stove. The same rates apply to all programs: about $19 per person cabin fee and $25 a day for provisions, which covers breakfast, lunch and dinner. The $100 a day guide fee is split between the members of the group. Groups are held to a maximum of eight skiers.

Helicopter skiing, one of the ultimate skiing experiences, offers access to untracked powder and gorgeous views. Helitrax takes skiers on a full day outing of five runs and approximately 12,000 vertical feet; and a cross-country heli-tour of remote mesas is also available. For reservations and more information: Telluride Helitrax, Box 1560, Telluride CO 81435; 728-4904.

Ski school (92/93 prices)

Telluride's Ski School, run by Annie Vareille-Savath, has introduced a grouping system for students. The breakdown of ability is not based only on level of skiing, but on the skier's style (some define this as "guts").

Type One skiers are hesitant about speed and don't want to be pushed—the instructor will work more slowly with this group. Type Two skiers are more interested in developing the "right look" on the slope (the ultimate yuppie approach). Type Three skiers are aggressive and eager to learn new skills rather than develop a pretty style. The school's philosophy is that grouping these types of skiers together will increase their enjoyment of the courses.

Group lessons cost $35 for a half day clinic (two and a half hours). You can combine clinics, with three costing $70 and five for $120.

Private lessons are $65 an hour, with each additional skier paying $25. A full day of private lessons is $325, $75 for each additional skier.

Workshops on powder and bumps and courses on the steep and deep, as well as gate racing clinics and a video analysis of your skiing, cost the same as normal clinics.

Telluride's Women's Week is a program that deals with both psychological and physical approaches to skiing. The price, which includes lifts, races, video analysis, seminars, and wine and cheese parties, is $370 for five days or $300 for three days. Concurrent men's weeks have identical prices to the women's program.

Ski school also offers telemark instruction. NASTAR two-and-a-half hour courses costs $35, or practice on your own for $5 (two runs) and $1 for each additional run.

Lift tickets (92/93 prices)

Telluride's early season discounted rates, good November 21-December 18, are $29 per day, $24 per half day and $20 for children between 6 and 12 years of age.

Normal season rates are: all day, $39; half day (a.m. or p.m.), $30; all day seniors 65-69, $23; all day children 5-12, $22; four days, $144; five days, $175; six days, $204. Seniors 70 and over and children five and under ski free.

Accommodations

In Telluride you can stay down in the old town, in the Mountain Village, or clustered around Coonskin Base. The accommodations in the new mountain village are at the end of this section.

The San Sophia Bed and Breakfast (800-537-4781) the upscale property in town, near the Oak Street Lift. Rates are $125-$195. This cozy B&B has received rave reviews since it opened several seasons ago. It is considered one of Telluride's best with exceptional service.

The venerable, historic **New Sheridan Hotel** (728-4351) is a step back in time. It's right on Colorado Avenue, the main drag, close to everything, with a skiers' shuttle stopping right outside the front door. This is a chance to experience a bit of history. Rates $35 to $119.

Other downtown properties are the **Dahl Haus** (728-4158), originally built in the 1890s as a boarding house for miners. All rooms have shared bath but the condominiums have all amenities. Condominium prices per night are $80 for a studio, up to $190 for a two-bedroom condo and about $120 for a one-bedroom unit. **The Johnstone Inn**, recently renovated B&B has eight small, quaint rooms with private bath and a full breakfast every morning for $70 to $145 per night. The **Manitou Hotel** (800-237-0753 or 800-233-9292 in Colorado) has recently been redecorated with country fabrics and antiques. It is near the Oak Street Lift and is only a two-minute walk from the center of the town. Each room has a double bed, and the price includes continental breakfast. Rates: $85-$175. **The Ice House Lodge** has been turned into a luxury hotel located a block from the Oak Street Lift. You'll get 6-foot tubs, comforters, balconies, and custom furniture. Rates are $90 to $350 a night.

The Riverside Condos are perhaps the nicest in town and located near the base of the Oak Street lift. Rates range from $120 to $370. **The Manitou Riverhouse** is just as near to the lifts but be ready for lots of stairs if you rent here. Rates are $100-$320.

Around the Coonskin Base check into **Viking Suites Hotel, Etta Place** and the **Cimarron Lodge**, where you can almost literally fall out of bed and onto the lifts, and the **Tower House** about two blocks from the lifts. During regular season they cost approximately: two people—$85 to $215; two to threebedrooms—$155-$355.

More moderate units are **West Willow** and **Coronet Creek**, where rates range about $20-$25 less than in the more luxurious units described above.

In the Mountain Village

This section of Telluride, as I have already mentioned, is new, but they are connecting it with the historic downtown by a three-stage gondola which will run from morning to the evening hours linking the modern condos with valley tradtion with about a ten-minute ride.

Pennington's (800-543-1437) is the B&B of choice for the utmost in elegance. The rooms are giant and the views magnificent. The only problem is that you are not *really* in Telluride. Prices are $150 to $260 per room with breakfast.

The most luxurious property is the massive **Doral Telluride Resort and Spa**. This $75 million edifice has 177 rooms and a 42,000 square foot spa. Rates for deluxe accommodations start at $310 per night. Call

For the most deluxe accommodations on the mountain, check out the newly developed mountain village and try the **Telemark Condominiums** for $535 to $775 for a group of eight to ten people, **Columbia Place Lodge** for $180 to $300 for four persons, or **Kayenta Legend House** costing $380-$525 for six people.

Telluride has also organized a **Regional Half-Price Program** with the towns of Cortez, Montrose, Ouray, Ridgway, Mancos and Dolores. If you stay in one of these spots, you can get half-price lift tickets—$14.50 during bargain season and $19.50 during regular season. Call Teluride Central Reservations for more information.

Dining

Telluride's pitch to upscale dining is found in these three downtown restaurants. All are expensive, with entrées in the $15-$24 range. **Athenian Senate**, 123 S. Spruce; 728-3018, built in a restored saloon/bordello/senate building and featuring basic, consistent Greek-American food. **La Marmotte** located near the Ice House Lodge serves French cuisine; 728-6232. **Silverglade**, 115 W. Colorado; 728-4943, menu dedicated to California and a grill. There is plenty of fresh fish, Mahi Mahi to blackened salmon and tasty desserts.

For more casual and moderate dining: **Leimgruber's** serves German cooking and beer imported from Munich with Gemütlichkeit: 728-4663. **Eddie's** serves up great pizzas. **The Floradora** claims the best burgers in town. **Excelsior Cafe** is the breakfast spot. **Baked in Telluride** does fresh bagels each morning. **Gregor's Bakery & Cafe** serves tempting pastries, fresh baked bread, custom cakes and the *best* cup of coffee in town. **The T-ride Country Club** offers cook-your-own steaks and seafood. **Sofio's** serves good Mexican cuisine but be prepared for a long wait—it's worth it. Have a Margarita. The **Powderhouse** serves local specialties as well as their secret Powderhouse Cocktail.

The San Juan Brewing Company provides good basic chicken, fish and beef to be washed down by local brew.

In the mountain village try one of the new restaurants in the Doral Telluride Resort and Spa (728-6800)—the **Alpenglow** with American/Alpine cuisine or the **Sundance** with southwestern cuisine. **Evangeline's** (728-9717) also gets good reports for Cajun Creole cooking.

If you are staying in a condo and feel couch potato-ish just call up for deliveries. Eddie's delivers pizza—728-5335. **Telluride Room Service** (728-4343) delivers gourmet meals from the town's top restaurants. I'm sure somebody delivers Chinese, and you can even have someone do all your shopping for you, from soup to nuts to wine and beer, before you arrive at your condo: call **Details** at 728-6048.

Nightlife

Here Telluride makes up in spirit what it lacks in number of bars. For immediate après-ski, stop in at **Leimgruber's Bierstube** near the Coonskin Lift for a selection of great beer and a sure shot at meeting folks. When there is live music the place to be is the **Fly Me to the Moon Saloon**. It normally has live entertainment, especially Thursday through Saturday. **The Last Dollar Saloon** has the best selection of imported beer in Telluride, plus pool tables and dart boards.

Legends Tavern is a new spot with live music and dancing. You can get sandwiches and burgers as well. The old Victorian **New Sheridan Bar**, after renovation is one of the "must sees" in Telluride to experience the essence of the Old West.

Child care

Children's programs have been consolidated in the Village Nursery and Children's Center—it's in Le Chamonix condominium complex, within walking distance of the Mountain Village Base Facility, and has day care, infant care, lessons, nursery and rentals.

The Children's Ski Center (728-4424) open 9 a.m. to 4 p.m., takes ages 3 to 12. Lessons and lunch cost $40 per half-day; $50 full-day; $135, three days; $225, five days.

Lift ticket rates for children in Children's Ski School are $12 a day for those from 6 to 12 years and free for those 5 and younger. Rental equipment per day costs $10.

The Village Nursery takes children from two months and up, it is open 8:30 a.m.-4:30 p.m. Cost: infants under one year, $7 an hour and $40 for a full day; one year and up for all day with lunch, $35, half day, $25; multi-day rates available from 728-8000.

Getting there

Telluride has an airport only five miles from town. Continental Express and United Express serve the resort from Denver; Mesa Airlines has flights from Phoenix and Albuquerque; and Delta Connection has flights from Los Angeles three day a week.

Montrose, 65 miles from Telluride, is served by United Express and Continental Express from Denver as well as Continental from Houston.

Ground transport is provided by Telluride Transit (728-6000); Skip's Taxi (728-6667); and Western Express (249-8880). All require 24-hour advance reservation for Montrose pickup.

Information/reservations

Telluride central reservation system can handle reservations and lodging, lifts, lessons, nursery programs, ski school, transfers and air transportation. Call (800) 525-3455 (nationwide) or (303) 728-4431.

For the Telluride Mountain Village Resort Management Company call (800) 544-0507 or (303) 728-8000.

The following independent agents can help with lifts and lodging: Telluride Accommodations—(800) 233-9292 or 728-3803; Resort Rentals—(800) LETS-SKI or 728-4405; Lodges at Telluride—(800) 446-3192 or 728-6621; Telluride Lodging Company—(800) 852-0015 or 728-4311.

Vail
Beaver Creek Resort
Colorado

In man's many endeavors, there is always one standard against which all others are measured. If only for the sake of comparison, someone has to be considered King of the Hill, Le Grand Banana. In the realm of U.S. skiing, that mantle is worn, for the most part graciously, by Vail.

Vail lays claim to that lofty position largely because it is such a *complete* area, lacking none of the essential ingredients that form the magical stew of a world class ski resort. There is quaint village atmosphere, raucous nightlife, fine dining and pizzeria snacking. There is horse-drawn sleigh riding and helicopter skiing. But above all, there is The Mountain.

This is not a crammed-together area of craggy peaks and deep valleys, the type of mountain range that makes Utah and the European Alps so stunning. Rather, Vail Mountain is a single stoop-shouldered behemoth so massive that every crease and wrinkle in its cape becomes an-

---

Vail Facts
Base elevation: 8,200'; Summit elevation: 11,450'; Vertical drop: 3,250 feet.
Number and types of lifts: 24—7 quad superchairs, 1 gondola, 2 quad chairs, 3 triple chairs, 6 double chairs, 5 surface lifts
Acreage: 3,992 skiable acres Percent of snowmaking: 8.3 percent
Uphill capacity: 35,820 skiers per hour Bed base: 41,305 within 10 miles

Beaver Creek Resort Facts
Base elevation: 8,100'; Summit elevation: 11,440'; Vertical drop: 3,340 feet
Number and types of lifts: 10—2 quad superchairs, 4 triple chairs, 4 doubles
Acreage: 1,050 skiable acres Percent of snowmaking: 23.1 percent.
Uphill capacity: 19,075 skiers per hour Bed base: 4,700 at resort, 4,000 in Avon

other entire section to ski or bowl to explore. While Vail thus does not have the ultra-steep and deep of some of its Utah cousins, what it does have is a whole front face of long, twisting, turning cruisers with plenty of good vertical grade, and a whole back bowl experience of wide-open adventure that is unlike anything this side of the Atlantic.

Vail's network of seven quad superchairs is also the largest in the world. Combined, this mountain and that lift system mean that you can do more skiing and less back-tracking in a day at Vail than at almost any other resort you can name.

And Vail is growing again this season. A new triple chair and three new surface lifts will new areas of the back bowls and the Golden Peak area.

But skiing only constitutes part of the total ski experience. A true world-class resort has to have an authentic atmosphere. Some skiers complain that Vail does not have the authenticity of the mining towns turned ski resorts, such as Aspen, Crested Butte or Telluride.

One need only walk down the narrow streets of the main village, with its small squares, myriad boutiques and steepled chalets, and continue down toward nearby Lionshead with its larger block hotels and mall-like feel, to understand just how perishable and worthy the effect of Vail Village truly is. The challenge for the resort in the years of expansion to come will be to preserve that precious *Gemütlichkeit* (*Gemütlichkeit* is to village atmosphere what *Fahrvergnügen* is to driving). The challenge for the visitor will be to pay the price for that special combination of atmosphere and skiing, which seems to cost more here than just about anywhere.

Beaver Creek Resort

Don't make the mistake of visiting Vail for anything more than a weekend without spending a day at Beaver Creek Resort, Vail's sister resort 10 miles down I-70. Beaver Creek Resort is a purpose-built complex of condominiums, hotels, a small shopping mall and excellent base facilities. Its purpose, quite simply, is to plop those with a taste for pampering squarely in the lap of luxury. What it lacks in atmosphere Beaver Creek Resort largely makes up for in elegance. While there's a family atmosphere and live music in the main lodge in the base area just after skiing, at night most of the skiers disappear into expensive condos or retire to the multi-million dollar homes that dot the golf course on the way up to the resort. The emphasis is on laid-back and mellow.

To get a fix on Beaver Creek Resort, drive up the mountain and pay to park in the underground parking (shuttlebuses to Vail also depart on the half hour for a cost of $2, or you can park free at the base of the mountain and take a free shuttle up). As you spill from the parking garage directly into the main base-lodge area, stop and take a load off at the roaring outdoor fire pit outside the Hyatt Regency. Order a hot toddy from the waiter and wave to the guests in the outdoor heated swimming pool or boiling Jacuzzis. Wonder what the poor slobs back at the office are doing. Now you're in a Beaver Creek state of mind.

Where to ski

Vail Mountain is both marvelous and expansive—you could never cover it all in a day. But fortunately, although it is one of the biggest single ski mountains in North America, it is also segmented: skiers can concentrate on separate bowls and faces for a morning or afternoon, skiing repeatedly and always having the choice of a new path down the mountain. And none of these runs seems intimidating, although there is plenty of challenge for every level of skier.

Beginners have areas at Golden Peak and Lionshead. A series of crisscrossing catwalks aptly named Cub's Way, Gitalong and so on, allow even beginners to work their way down the mountain, shifting from trail to trail.

Intermediates will be in heaven. There are few other mountains (perhaps Heavenly in California or Park City in Utah), and certainly none in Colorado, that offer an intermediate the same expansive terrain and seemingly countless trails. Especially worthy cruising areas include the long ride down the mountain under and to the right of the Lionshead gondola; almost any of the runs bordering the Avanti express chair; the Northwoods run; and the relatively short but sweet trio down to Game Creek Bowl — The Woods, Baccarat and Dealer's Choice. Our vote for best run on the mountain, and one available to advanced intermediates (though parts are rated black), is the top-to-bottom, miles long autobahn named Riva Ridge.

Vail's Back Bowls

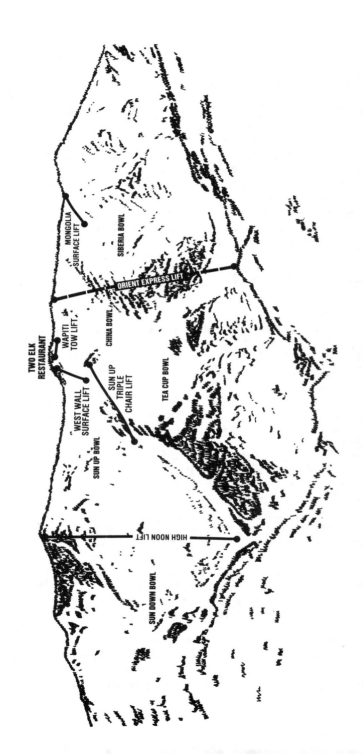

Much of the intermediate skiing on Vail Mountain is of good enough grade that experts won't even notice they're not being stretched to their limits. Those that want to be so challenged, however, should head to the far left of the mountain face and a trio of double-black diamonds named Blue Ox, Highline and Rogers Run. The straight-down-the-lift, waist-high mogul masher Highline is the stiffest test of the three. Nearby Prima is almost equally challenging, and the short drop of Pronto down to the Northwoods chair lets you strut your mogul-mauling stuff in front of the lift lines. The only authentic gut-suckers on the front face are the tops of South and North Rim off the Northwoods lift, leading to a tight but nice Gandy Dancer.

Experts can drop down the Northeast Bowl or come off Prima Ridge through tight trees on Gandy Dancer, Prima Cornice or Pronto to the Northwoods area.

Experts, of course, will also want to explore Vail's famous Back Bowls. They adds up to more than 2,600 acres of choose-your-own-path, wide-open skiing. On a beautiful day, these back bowls are about as good as skiing gets.

Beaver Creek Resort

Somehow in its enthusiasm to sell itself as a resort to pamper the well-off, Beaver Creek Resort acquired a reputation as strictly a beginner and intermediate cruiser mountain. Not so. Advanced skiers and experts visiting the Vail area should spend at least a day here and maybe more. Our advice is to choose a Saturday or Sunday, when the lines at Vail can climb over the 15-20 minute barrier, yet prove nonexistent at Beaver Creek Resort.

Strangely enough, the mountain is laid out almost upside down, with the easiest skiing at the top down the Stump Park Lift. It's doubtful that there's an intermediate or advanced skier in the world who won't get a thrill out of turning his skis loose down the cruisers under the Centennial express lift, which covers the first half of the mountain. Like Riva Ridge at Vail, this is one of those intermediate runs that instantly make our classic list.

What's most surprising about Beaver Creek Resort is the amount of truly tough stuff there is for a fairly small resort. The three Birds of Prey rival just about anything at Vail, and are all long, steep and mogul-studded. While somewhat shorter, Ripsaw and Cataract in Rose Bowl, and

Loco over in Larkspur Bowl, are equally challenging. Grouse Mountain, opened last season and serviced by a high-speed quad chair, provides even more great expert terrain and it now being outfitted with snowmaking. This skiing at Grouse Mountain is a challenge and is the steepest you will find. It is for advanced intermdiates and above, but there is enough width to allow uncertain intermediates to traverse their way down.

Mountain rating

Vail is the most complete mountain in North America for handling the needs of all levels of skiers and one of the best overall ski mountains in the world. Only super experts will feel that perhaps the extreme skiing of Snowbird or Squaw Valley is missing. Experts have the massive Back Bowls, with some of the best powder skiing in America. Advanced and intermediate skiers have long cruises and beginners have good initial terrain.

Beaver Creek is coming into its own with the addition of Grouse Mountain and its great expert pitch. Lower intermediates will also be happy at Beaver Creek Resort with its long runs and virtually no lift lines. In fact, anyone who does not want to see anything resembling a line should take a trip to Beaver Creek Resort. And experts who have strong legs will love the Birds of Prey and Grouse Mountain. Vail doesn't have anything to compare with the sustained steep trails found here.

Cross-country

Cross-country facilities have recently received more attention at Vail and Beaver Creek Resort. Although the resort is renowned for its downhill skiing, Beaver Creek Resort has created a 30-kilometer track system at McCoy Park at the top of Chair 12. This area is considered 20 percent advanced, 60 percent intermediate and 20 percent beginner. Because it's at the top of the mountain the track system has beautiful views in every direction. It is open from 9 a.m. to 3 p.m. daily. Adult track fees are $14 for an all-day pass, $10 for a half day beginning at noon; children pay $7 for an all-day pass, $5 for a half day.

There are also a series of backcountry opportunities from Golden Peak base. All-day tours cost $46; afternoon tours are $30; Gourmet Tours, including lunch, cost $60.

Check with the ski school for more information on cross-country, because tours and classes take place on selected days rather than daily. One day on a multiday lift ticket may be exchanged for a half-day cross-country lesson or a half-day cross-country tour and rental equipment at either Vail or Beaver Creek Resort. Rentals are available at Golden Peak or the Beaver Creek Cross-Country Center located at the base of Chair 12. Call 476-3239.

Snowboarding

Shredders are welcome both at Vail and Beaver Creek. At Vail, snowboarders will want to head for the halfpipe on Golden Peak. There is also a halfpipe in Rose Bowl at Beaver Creek Resort called Border Beach. Both resorts also offer snowboarding lessons.

Ski school (90/91 prices)

The Vail/Beaver Creek Ski School offers a wide range of private and group lessons for adults and children. Instructors concentrate not only on getting skiers past skiing milestones and perfecting their techniques, but also on giving them a balanced and graceful style. The ski school also makes every effort to create a learning environment where improvements are reached through enjoyment, where perfecting a turn is secondary to enjoying the skiing experience.

In Vail, the ski school has offices and meeting places at Vail Village, where private lessons meet, near the base of the Vista Bahn Express; at Lionshead next to the gondola; at Golden Peak next to Chairs 6 and 12; at Mid-Vail next to Chairs 3 and 4; at the Eagle's Nest at the top of the gondola; at Cascade Village, near the Westin; and at the Two Elk Restaurant, near China Bowl.

In Beaver Creek Resort, the school locations are in Village Hall next to Chair 1 and at Spruce Saddle atop the Centennial Express lift. Call the Vail Ski School at 476-3239; for Beaver Creek Resort Ski School, call 949-5750.

The ski school has a video that demonstrates the nine levels of skiing skills the school uses to form classes. Skiers watch the video and then place themselves in classes ranging from never-evers to advanced skiing.

A free Ski Tips program meets at 11 a.m. daily at Mid-Vail, Eagles Nest or Spruce Saddle. The session gives you a chance to ski down a gentle slope alongside an instructor who will provide a critique and suggestions on the next step to becoming a better skier. The instructor will also suggest which program provides the best benefits.

Private lessons are the ultimate learning session, custom-designed for your abilities and needs. You may make reservations, which are suggested, at least 24 hours in advance. One hour costs $85 for one to five students; two hours cost $170 for one to five; half day (three and a half hours) costs $230 for one to five skiers; full day (8:30 a.m. to 3:30 p.m.) costs $340 for one to five people.

Group lessons let you receive coaching in a class environment and meet other skiers. These lessons cost $48 for a full day (10 a.m. to 3:30 p.m.), $150 for three days.

Never-evers can sign up for the three-day learn-to-ski program, which includes lift tickets, for $270, or they can pay a flat $48 a day without lifts. The half-day program for never-evers costs $52 for lifts and lessons.

There is a style clinic every day from 12:30 p.m. to 3:45 p.m. for $42; a race class from 9 a.m. until noon for $42; bump and powder workshops from 12:30 p.m. to 3:45 p.m. for $42; a Super Class, with fast-paced skiing, for $60 a day; and a SyberVision™ Workshop concentrating on ski imaging for $75 a day. For teenagers there is a daily all-day class designed for skiers between 13 and 18 years. Teen classes cost the same as adult lessons.

Pepi's Wedel Weeks were created in the European tradition: they allow skiers to start off the ski season with an inexpensive lesson package. These classes are held for three weeks only, starting November 23 and 30 and December 7. They include a full seven-day program with breakfast, lessons every morning and afternoon, races, a welcome reception, an evening party, a fashion show and a farewell dinner. For reservations, call (800) 445-8245 or (800) 433-8735 in Colorado.

The Children's Ski School is anchored by Sport Goofy, the Ambassador of Children's Skiing. The real adventure for kids, however, starts outside the high walls of Fort Whippersnapper atop the Golden Peak lift. Here, children enter a magical land and follow in the tracks of the little Indians Gitche and Gumee, as they accompany Jackrabbit Joe and Sourdough Pete on a quest to find the treasure of the Lost Silver Mine. This adventure is just part of the program offered by the new Golden Peak Children's Ski Center, which has the most extensive facilities at Vail for children of all ages. There are also special Kids Nights Out featuring dinner, theater and special games.

In all, however, Vail has three children's centers: Golden Peak (479-2040), Lionshead (479-2042) and Small World Playschool at Beaver Creek Resort (949-2304). Fort Whippersnapper above Golden Peak features Indian Camps, adventures through mines, creative ski courses and snow terrain designed for fun. Registration is from 8 to 9:15 a.m., or preregister the day before.

Children between three and a half and six years have a supervised playroom and programs when not skiing, and the prices include lunch and snacks. Beginners pay $60 for a full day, including lessons, lunch and equipment, or $33 for a half day, plus $8 for equipment. Other ability levels pay $60 a day for lifts, lessons and lunch, but children must bring their own equipment.

Children between six and a half and 12 years can spend their day on the mountain, be entertained with videos and have supervised meeting rooms. Lunch is also supervised but not included in the price ($7 is suggested as adequate lunch money).

All other normal group lessons are $60 a day for lessons and lifts.

There are children's NASTAR race classes on Fridays and Saturdays for $60 with lifts, plus a $5 NASTAR fee.

Lift tickets (91/92 prices)
Full day, $40 adults/$27 children (12 and under); half day from noon, $35/$22; two days, $80/$54; three days, $120/$81; four of five days, $156/$108; five of six days, $195/$135. Senior citizens 65 to 69 years pay only $30 a day and those 70 and over ski free.

Accommodations
Vail Village and Lionshead
Vail's premier properties are clustered in Vail Village at the base of the Vista Bahn Express. Selecting the best place in town is a virtual tossup between four hotels.

The Lodge at Vail (800-237-1236 or 476-5011) is the original, around which the rest of the resort was built. It is only steps away from the lifts, ski school and the main street action. **Gasthof Gramshammer** (476-5626) is located at the crossroads of Vail Village. Our favorite and the most economical within this group of hotels is the **Christiania** (476-5641). **The Sonnenalp Hotel** (800-654-8312 or 303-476-5656) is a group of buildings that exude Alpine warmth and charm. All are expensive. Regular season sevennight/six-day ground packages cost around $1,700.

At the Lionshead end of town the **Marriott's Mark** (476-4444) is the top of the line and has an excellent location only three minutes' walk from the gondola. The seven-night/six-day package will cost about $1,300.

The Westin Hotel (476-7111) in Cascade Village is also at the top of the luxury line. The Cascade Athletic Club is across the parking lot from the hotel and is available without extra charge to Westin guests. The hotel has a dedicated ski lift, which makes getting to the slopes a pleasure and the hotel shuttle does make regular rounds. The seven-night/six-day package will cost $1,500-$1,800.

Condominiums are plentiful in the Vail region and the prices are sky-high. The most reasonable for those who want to be on the shuttlebus route are found in Lionshead, clustered around the gondola. Village studio units go for about $200 a night; two-bedroom units for about $500; three-bedroom units for about $700 a night with lifts.

For relatively more affordable rates try **Days Inn** (476-3890) in West Vail; **Antlers** (476-2471), **Vailglo Lodge** (476-5506), and **L'Ostello** (476-5506) in Lionshead; **Manor Vail** (476-5651) in Gold Peak; and the **Holiday Inn at Vail** (476-5631) and **Vail Village Inn** (476-5622) in Vail Village.

Beaver Creek Resort

In Beaver Creek Resort most properties are clustered around the base area and the Beaver Creek Resort village.

Hyatt Regency Beaver Creek has rates ranging from as low as $205 for a standard room to $225-$325 for a mountain view room. The hotel also features an unusual program which matches up singles who want to take advantage of the double occupancy rates. Call (800) 233-1234 for information about Single Share or reservations. The Hyatt also has organized a fascinating storytelling program which started out for kids but has gained widespread interest. Frank Doll, 69, whose family settled over 100 years ago spins yarns around the lobby fireplace.

The Centennial Lodge (800-845-7060) and **Creekside Lodge** (949-7071) are just over 300 yards from the base of the Centennial Lift. The seven-night/six-day hotel/lifts package will cost about $1,500 based on double occupancy.

The Charter Lodge (949-6660) is a bit more expensive and exclusive. **The Poste Montane** (845-7500) is located directly in Beaver Creek Resort Village as is **The Inn at Beaver Creek. Camberley Club Hotel, B.C. Lodge** and **St. James Place**.

The absolute bargain condominiums are in Avon at the beginning of the Beaver Creek Resort access road, about a 20-minute drive from Vail's slopes and as close as you can get in a private car to Beaver Creek Resort without staying on the mountain. The Avon condominiums are served by a shuttlebus system. Prices in Avon will be about $170-$220 for a one-bedroom unit.

The **Comfort Inn** (949-5511) has five-night packages with four days of lifts for $448 per person during value season and seven-night packages with six days of lifts for $746 per person, double occupancy, regular season. Or try the **Christie Lodge** (949-7700).

Dining
Vail Village and Lionshead

Vail has a collection of acceptable restaurants, but has not developed the gourmet reputation of Aspen, Deer Valley or even Steamboat. After speaking with scores of locals and tourists, we have these recommendations for the area's best in dining.

If you have deep pockets, this first group of restaurants is worth testing. **L'Ostello** at the The Lodge in Vail serves wonderful Italian food that tastes like it was prepared in Italy (take it from someone who lived there over a decade). **The Tyrolean Inn** (476-2204) has fine game and is a favorite among visiting Europeans. **Ambrosia's** (476-1964) and **La Tour** (476-4403) also receive consistent and excellent ratings. **Sweet Basil** (476-0125) was recommended by both upscale and blue-collar folk as a great place for lunch and dinner. **Lancelot** (476-5828) has the best prime rib in town, with prices from expensive to moderate. **Alfredo's** (476-7111) in the Westin has perhaps the best Northern Italian fare. **Windows Restaurant** (476-

4444) in Marriott's Mark carries on the Marriott tradition of great dining with a spectacular view.

In Beaver Creek try dining one night at **Saddle Ridge** owned by American Express and first built as a corporate retreat for executives. The price is steep, but the food is wonderful. The setting, depending on your point of view, is either an example of what wonderful architecture corporate financing can create or an example of flagrant corporate waste and excess.

For more moderate prices, stop at the **Ore House** (476-5100) in the village and the **Chart House** (476-1525) in Lionshead for steaks. **Blu's** (476-3113) can be moderate if you choose carefully, and **Bully Pub** (476-5656) in the Sonnenalp's **Bavaria Haus** keeps prices traditionally low.

Those on a budget should try **Pazzo's** (476-9026) across from Crossroads, which offers spaghetti or soup and pizza for less than $4, or head to the **Lionshead Bar and Grill** (476-3060) in Lionshead. **Bart and Yetti's** (476-2754) in Lionshead is a good place to head for lunch or light dinner.

The Jackalope (476-4314) in West Vail is a great spot for inexpensive, basic good eats, and a local atmosphere.

In Beaver Creek Resort, try the **Golden Eagle Inn** on the mall, a restaurant run by Pepi Langegger of the Tyrolean Inn. **Legends** (949-5540) in the Poste Montane has the best fish in the area. **Mirabelle** (949-7728) at the bottom of the Beaver Creek Resort access road serves well-prepared nouvelle cuisine. **Covered Bridge Cafe** in the Park Plaza is the most moderately priced of the resort area restaurants. In Avon try the **The Brass Parrot** and **Cassidy's**.

Visitors who are looking for something special and have a car or are willing to take a taxi, head to nearby Minturn. Here, you'll find the **Minturn Country Club** where you choose your own T-bone, filet or swordfish steak, and then cook it yourself over open grills. Just across the street, the area's best Mexican food is dished out at the **Saloon** or **Chili Willy's**. Casual to the nth degree, they offer pitchers of margaritas and Mexican food so authentic that both will bring tears to your eyes.

Up on the mountain make it a point to have lunch at the beautiful **Two Elk Restaurant** which is being expanded this season. This is what every on-mountain cafeteria dining experience should be.

A memorable Vail dining experience is a night at **Beano's Cabin** at Beaver Creek Resort. Groups meet at the base of the mountain and are served a hot chocolate or coffee. They are bundled onto a 40-person sleigh and pulled up the mountain under under the stars by a snowcat. Unfortunately the ride up isn't the romantic experience it might be. The sled is steel, garnished with plastic evergreens. You'll be forced to listen to loud and bad singing, stories of marauding black bears, and depending on the wind you have to suffer through diesel exhaust fumes. All in all, the ride is appropriate for spring break in Lauderdale than romance. Once you get there, Beano's Cabin, itself, is beautiful, modern and rustic completed by a roaring stone-hearth fire, log beams, an 11-point buck head, and exciting well-prepared cuisine. The cost is $69 per person. Reservations, 949-5750.

Après-ski/nightlife

Après-ski in Vail is centered in the Village or in Lionshead. In the Village, try **Cyrano's**; **Sarah's** in the Christiania for squeezebox music with Helmut Fricker on Tuesdays, Wednesdays and Fridays; **Pepi's** for Austrian music; and **Vendetta's**, which normally has live music. **Mickey's** at the Lodge at Vail is the top piano bar après-ski spot. In Lionshead, **Sundance Saloon** fills up with locals and probably has the best drink prices in town, especially during happy hour in the late afternoon. There are pool tables, a locals' keg party on Thursdays and live music on the weekends. **The Hong Kong Café** is also a hot locals' bar.

For later nightlife with live music, dancing and such, try **Nick's**, which has rock'n'roll with a disk jockey. **The Club** normally offers acoustic guitar music. **Cyrano's** has a disco in Vail Village. On weekends the **Sundance Saloon** and **Jackalope** have live music. **Bogies** in Marriot's Mark is the class act in Lionshead.

Child care

The child care facility is run by the ski school. Reservations are advised, especially during the holidays. A nursery facility, Small World Play School, is in Beaver Creek Resort (949-2306), with another in the Golden Peak base area (479-2044). Infants, two to 18 months, toddlers 18 to 30 months and preschool children two and a half to six years may be enrolled in the program. Costs are $48 a day for infants, or toddlers and preschool children. Half-day programs are available but only for preschoolers on a space-available basis for $30, either in the morning or afternoon. For babysitters call 479-2292 or 476-7400.

Other activities

Vail has a number of athletic clubs. The Cascade Club across from the Westin has indoor tennis courts, squash courts, racquetball courts, Nautilus and free weights, indoor track, outdoor heated pool and thermal spa.

The Vail Athletic Club (476-0700) also has fitness facilities in Vail Village. The Vail Racquet Club (476-3267) in East Vail has indoor tennis, squash and racquetball courts, swimming pool, Nautilus and weight room.

Beano's Sleigh Ride Dinners can be booked by calling 949-9090; they include a ride up to the cabin and a hearty meal. Steve Jones Sleigh Rides on the Vail Golf Course can be booked by calling 476-8057.

Getting there

Vail/Beaver Creek Resort are on I-70, 100 miles west of Denver and 140 miles east of Grand Junction.

There are flights to Vail/Eagle County airport, about 35 miles west of Vail, and Denver's Stapleton International Airport 110 miles east of Vail. The Eagle County airport is served by American with nonstop flights from Chicago, Miami and Dallas; by America West with nonstops from Phoenix, Los Angeles and San Francisco; by Delta with nonstops from Salt Lake City; and by Taesa Airlines from Mexico City.

There is frequent ground shuttle service between Denver and Vail. The trip to Vail takes about two and a half hours. Contact Colorado Mountain Express at (800) 424-6363; or Vans to Vail at (800) 222-2112.

Information/reservations

Vail/Beaver Creek Reservations at (800) 525-2257 or (800) 824-5737 handles air tickets, transfers and lodging.

Winter Park Colorado

Winter Park doesn't have the glamor and glitz of Aspen or Vail, nor the quaint Victorian charm of Telluride, Breckenridge or Crested Butte. What Winter Park does have is a great mountain with a phenomenal variety of terrain and some of the most affordable big mountain skiing in the United States.

With the completion, early in the century, of the Moffat Tunnel through the Rockies, Denverites began to ride the train to the area. The shacks first built for the tunnel construction crews made perfect warming huts for hardy skiers who climbed the mountains and schussed down on seven-foot boards. Today Winter Park ranks as one of the largest ski areas in Colorado, with 112 trails, 20 lifts and more than 1,300 acres of skiable terrain.

Winter Park has no massive condo complexes lining the roads, no brightly lit stores, no real built-up center of town. A traveler might well ride through Winter Park and miss the ski area, never realizing that the region has more than 13,200 beds in more than 100 properties.

That's part of the charm: the ski area is off the main highway, and the condos have been tucked into the forests for the most part. Lodging is affordable—designed with families in mind, the ski school is one of Colorado's most respected and the children's center is the biggest and most advanced of any ski resort in the world.

Winter Park Facts

Base elevation: *9,000'*; **Summit elevation:** *11,220'*; **Vertical drop:** *2,220 feet*
Number of lifts: *20—4 super quad chairs; 4 triple chairs, 12 double chairs*
Percent snowmaking: *50% of Winter Park mountain only*
Total acreage by trails: *1,301 acres skiable terrain*
Uphill capacity: *30,551 per hour* **Bed Base:** *13,200 in Fraser Valley*

Although Winter Park has maintained a great family reputation, it is also one of the best destinations for singles. The Mary Jane section of the resort has tough skiing as difficult as any in Colorado; the town benefits from having only a few, but very good, nightlife centers, meaning that you get to meet most of the other skiers in town if that's what you desire; and the Mountain Inn lodging offers singles a great opportunity to meet other vacationers over dinner and drinks, or while enjoying the hot tubs. If you are looking for a solidly good time without the fanfare, Winter Park presents you with some of the best.

The skiing

This season Winter Park in opening a new bowl to skiers—the Parsenn Bowl on the backside of Mary Jane mountain. This expansion will mean an additional 200 acres of tree skiing and bowl skiing reached by a double chair. All in all the new terrain will mean more space for intermediates and advanced intermediates, but only one of the new trails will be groomed to keep the mountain in a more natural condition and to add to the difficulty.

Visitors who have read most reports about Winter Park arrive expecting a good intermediate resort with plenty of lower intermediate skiing and beginner trails. Yes, that's all here—what is surprising is the amount of expert terrain. There are two base areas: The Mary Jane Base and the Winter Park Base. Both have parking, but the spaces fill up, especially on weekends, with heavy traffic from Denver. When staying in Winter Park, the efficient shuttlebus makes it easy to get around without a car

The Winter Park base area serves most of the beginner and intermediate trails, with a handful of advanced trails dropping down the left side as you look up. Beginners can ride to the top of the mountain to Sunspot and then ski down Allan Phipps, March Hare and Mad Tea Party, or they can ski all the way back to the base using the Cranmer Cutoff or drop down to the Turnpike. Intermediates starting from the same mountaintop can play down Jabberwocky, White Rabbit and Cheshire Cat.

The Vasquez Ridge area also has an excellent collection of intermediate cruising runs and is served by a quad superchair. (The only drawback to the Vasquez Ridge area is a long runout down the Big Valley trail. The Buckaroo

Town Map
Winter Park

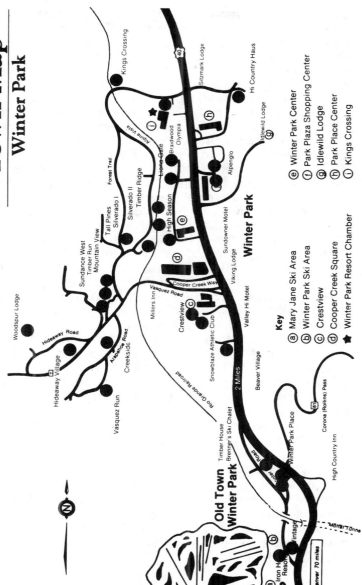

trail lets you avoid the runout.) If you find yourself on the other side of the ridge, keep up your speed and tuck for the run back to the Pioneer Express lift. Gambler and Aces and Eights are two short, steep mogul runs that take you to the Olympia Lift. To change mountains, Gunbarrel takes skiers to the High Lonesome Express superchair for a drop into the Mary Jane area.

For advanced skiers, the most popular lift on the Winter Park side will probably be the Zephyr Express Superchair: it skirts the far left boundary of the area and allows drops down Bradley's Bash, Balch, Mulligan's Mile and Hughes—all good advanced terrain. From the top of Zephyr, bump fanatics can dance down Outhouse, one of the most sustained pitched bump runs in Colorado, and end up at the base area of Mary Jane.

Now on to the Mary Jane side of the resort: a blast for any solid intermediate or advanced skier, with some chutes that will make the hair stand up on the expert's neck. The Mary Jane section has a long superchair lift and five other chair lifts—basically, the trails to the right of the Summit Express Superchair lift are slightly easier than the trails to the left, which in turn are easier than the trails on the backside. Suffice it to say that no advanced skier will be bored with Mary Jane.

For experts who believe in super-steeps try the chutes accessible only through controlled gates: Hole in the Wall, Awe Chute, Baldy's Chute, Jeff's Chute and Runaway will challenge any skier and should be heavenly after a good powder dump. The other backside runs are served by a triple chair, Sunnyside Lift, running up Mary Jane's dimpled backside. These are intermediate playgrounds—Columbine, Roundhouse, Edelweiss and Bluebell.

Snowboarding

Snowboarding is allowed on the entire mountain. Many of the rental shops in the area have boards for hire. Lessons include a 4 1/2 hr. first time lesson free with the purchase or a full-day lift ticket. There is a series of three-hour workshops for $40. Private lessons are $80 for an hour and a half.

Cross-country

There are three major ski touring centers near Winter Park. Tour Ski Idlewild (726-5564) has 30 kilometers of machine-maintained trails for all levels of skier.

Trail fees are $9 a day for adults and $6 for children and seniors; half days cost $6 adult, and $4 for children; children 6 and under ski free. Private lessons are $20 an hour. A learn-to-ski package costs $25 for a full day including equipment. Children and seniors: $20 a full day.

Devil's Thumb Ranch (726-8231), near Tabernash, connects with Idlewild to form an 85 km. network. The rates for both areas are identical.

Snow Mountain Ranch (726-4628) offers 85 km. of maintained trails for all levels. There is also a lighted 3-km. loop for night cross-country skiing. The trail fee is $7 a day and children under 12 pay $3. Group lessons are available for $12 and private lessons are $20 an hour.

Ski school (92/93 prices)

Regularly rated by experts one of the best in the country, Winter Park ski school offers something for everyone from never-evers to hot skiers and shredders.

The Winter Park side is the focus of most group lessons. Beginners can get a free four and a half hour lesson with the purchase fo their first lift ticket; lessons for the second day on skis cost $25; and for the third day on skis the price will be $35.

Other group lessons have four and a half hours of lessons per day for $45 and a three day clinic for $135. Advanced skiers can choose from a series of three-hour workshops, including Parallel Breakthrough for $45 or, Bumps and Style and Technique, which cost $40. Women's Only Workshops are held Tuesday, Wednesday and Saturday for $40. "Prime Timers' Workshop" is offered Tuesday, Wednesday and Saturday. Racing Workshops run gates on Tuesday, Thursday and Saturday.

On the Mary Jane side shorter programs, taught in one-and-a-half-hour segments, cost $25.

Private lessons are $80 an hour and a half for 1-4 persons. A full day of private lessons costs $320; a half day, $160.

National Sports Center for the Disabled

Winter Park operates the leading disabled skiing program in the world. It also has a full-time race training program for disabled skiers. The programs are designed to help such skiers reach their potential for full mountain enjoyment. Basic instruction is available for all levels, and the race program is open to physically disabled skiers of advanced intermediate level or above.

Lift tickets (92/93 prices)

All day, $36 for adults and $15 for children 6-13 (also seniors 62-69 and disabled skiers); half day, $24; consecutive-day tickets for 2-6 days will cost $30 a day for adults and $15 for children.

The resort has also introduced limited-lift tickets. The beginner-only lift at Mary Jane costs $3 a day. For $15 a day skiers will have access to five lifts (Galloping Goose and Pony Express at Mary Jane, and Arrow, Gemini and Discovery at Winter Park) servicing 200 acres of terrain on both sides of the resort with up to 1,000 feet of vertical. These lift tickets should be perfect for parents skiing with children who don't need access to all the terrain.

Accommodations

Winter Park has a group of mountain inns unique in Colorado: they are like small bed-and-breakfasts but with dinner thrown in as well. They all serve meals family style, so that guests get a chance to meet one another easily. Most inns have transportation to and from the slopes, making a car unnecessary. The food is usually fantastic and plentiful, and the inn owners go out of their way to please their guests.

There are eight such mountain inns in Winter Park. Perhaps the most upscale is the **Gasthaus Eichler** (726-5133). This inn is very European and the rooms are well decorated with down comforters on the beds. Each bathroom is equipped with a Jacuzzi tub. It's perfect for those wanting quiet, elegant accommodations right in the center of town within walking distance of restaurants and nightlife. Rates based on double occupancy are approximately $65 per person during regular season for bed, breakfast and a massive dinner. This is a quality bargain that is hard to beat.

Arapahoe Ski Lodge (726-8222 or 800-338-2698) also located downtown, is one of the more luxurious of the mountain inns. It features a large spa and indoor swimming pool. Prices based on double occupancy are $69 per night with dinner, breakfast and transport to the slopes.

The Woodspur Lodge (726-8417 or 800-626-6562) The lodge living room is massive with a fireplace, soaring roof and plenty of space. This central area makes a perfect meeting place for the guests. The rooms here are of two types—newly restored and old style. Ask for one of the updated rooms if you are staying as a couple and one of the older rooms for larger groups. The lodge is served by local buses as well as lodge vans that shuttle skiers to the area and the town. Rates based on double occupancy are $65 including breakfast and dinner. The food is great.

The Timber House Ski Lodge (726-5477 or 800-843-3502) is tucked into the woods at the edge of the ski area. A private trail lets you ski directly back to the lodge. The emphasis is on a chance to meet fellow guests either in the giant living room with stone fireplace, sitting at long tables with food served family style, or soaking in the outdoor hot tub. Rates based on double occupancy are $57-$88 per night including breakfast and dinner.

The remaining mountain inns are outside of town toward Tabernash. **The Outpost Inn** (726-5346) is the most comfortable and homey. Here Jerry and Susie Frye serve nonstop hospitality and homecooked meals. Vans shuttle skiers to the ski area each morning and collect guests again when the lifts close. There is a spa attached to the building which becomes a social center in the evenings. A maximum of 20 guests at a time stay at the inn. Rates are $42 per person per night, double occupancy, with breakfast only or $62 with dinner as well.

High Mountain Lodge at Tally Ho Ranch (726-5958) is a rambling lodge more akin to a motel in its room arrangements, but with a cozy group living room and dining area that are the signature of the mountain inns. The inn overlooks a frozen lake and gives you splendid isolation. Transportation back and forth to the ski area is provided. Rates are about $67 per day with breakfast and dinner.

The next lodges are not part of the Mountain Inn Association, but offer similar accommodations.

Chalet Z (726-5416) is a tiny B&B just around the corner from the Timber House with a personality of its own. It is accessible from the ski area by the Billy Woods Trail, which also ends at the Timber House. Rates based on double occupancy are $50 per night including breakfast.

Beau West B&B (726-5145 or 800-473-5145) is only 500 yards from Winter Park base and features gourmet breakfasts. It has a hot tub and great views. Rates are $48-$65 per person based on double occupancy.

The next two inns are located in cross-country areas. **Idlewild Lodge** (726-5562), at the area of the same name, and the **Devil's Thumb Ranch** (726-5632). Both charge about $55 per person for two sharing a room and include breakfast and dinner.

The condos of Winter Park are the mainstay accommodations for most skiers. The most luxurious is the **Iron Horse Resort** (726-8851), the closest that Winter Park has to a true ski-in/ski-out complex, though that stretches the definition a bit. There is a swimming pool and fitness center. The condos range from studios to two-bedroom suites. One-bedroom units cost $160-$295 a night, and two bedrooms $215-$285. Iron Horse is located a bit outside of the town center, but there is excellent shuttle service for those who want to strike out for nightlife.

The Vintage (726-8801) is also slightly out of the center of town but right next to the ski areas. It features a restaurant, fitness room, swimming pool and good shuttle service into the town. One of the finest properties in Winter Park, the Vintage has studios for $150 a night; two-room suites for $310; three-room suites for $370.

For some of the best condominiums in the center of town, try either the **Snowblaze** or **Crestview Place**. Both are virtually across the street from Cooper Creek Square. Snowblaze (726-5701) also features a full athletic club with racquetball court, swimming pool and fitness center, which are included in the price of the condominiums. The units are all equipped with color TVs. Studio units normally come with a Murphy bed, and two- and three-bedroom units have baths for each bedroom, private saunas and fireplaces. Approximate costs: two-bedroom units cost $180-$198; and three-bedroom units, which sleep up to eight, $240-$264.

The Crestview (726-9421), just remodeled, does not have an athletic club or private saunas, but has fireplaces and full kitchens. Costs: two-bedroom units, $132-$294 a night; three-bedroom units, $176-$392.

One of the most popularly priced condominiums is the **Hi Country Haus** (726-9421). These condos are spread out in a dozen buildings and share a recreation center with four hot tubs, sauna and heated swimming pool. They are within walking distance of town and are on the shuttlebus routes. Costs: studio units, $76-$150 a night; two-bedroom units, $96-$186; and three-bedroom units, $128-$248.

Dining

Winter Park isn't packed with high-priced restaurants because the emphasis is on good, solid cooking for hungry skiers and families.

The **Gasthaus Eichler** (726-5133) in the center of Winter Park has an Austrian/German-influenced menu. A more formal restaurant with an excellent bar and lounge, best enjoyed with a sparkling blond in front of the flickering fireplace is **Soufflés**, located in the Park Place Shopping Center across from Silver Screen Cinema (726-9404). The food is reputed to be some of the best in town.

Locals all raved about **The Last Waltz** (726-4877), which is in the King's Crossing Shopping Center on Highway 40. One resident claims the Last Waltz has the best breakfast in town and the others give unanimous thumbs up to the solid American and Mexican menu.

For venison and fondue, head to the **Chalet Lucerne** (726-5402). **Fizzy Rats** (726-9912) has southwestern cuisine and specializes in flaming fajitas. **The Divide Grill** in the Cooper Creek Square serves up acceptable Northern Italian dishes. And surprisingly, both the **Panhandler** in the Stampede (726-9433) and **Expectations** at The Slope (726-5727) get good marks for excellent fare in the town's top nightlife spots. Of the two Expectations is fancier and serves more elegant meals.

For family fare try the **Crooked Creek Saloon** in Fraser, a couple of miles away, for basic steaks and down-home cooking. **Lani's Place** is the spot for basic Mexican food at great prices.

For the best breakfast in town head straight to **The Kitchen** and ask Rosie to rustle up some eggs. You probably won't find Rosie doing much cooking but if she's around she'll liven up the breakfast crowd.

On the slopes, the best lunch is found in the **Club Car** restaurant at the Mary Jane base area. Plus there is a unique pizza service where you can phone from the top of the Winter Park section of the mountain, **Sunspot**, down to the **Mama Mia's Pizzeria** in Snoasis and have your pizza waiting when you arrive.

For something different, try the sleigh ride to the **Lodge at Sunspot**, the new mountain restaurant at Winter Park. There are sleighride dinners several days a week. Call 726-5514 for information and reservations.

Après-ski/nightlife

For après-ski, the **Derailer Bar** in the West Portal of the Winter Park Base area is the place to be. **The Slope** also gets a good crowd with happy hour, 4-6 p.m. If there are any sports events on tap, the place to go is **Deno's Mountain Bistro**, which has a half-dozen TV sets, plus more than a 100 types of beer and 200 wines. **Lani's Place** in Cooper Creek Square serves up excellent happy-hour 99¢ margaritas and tacos.

The later nightlife centers in two main dancing places. **The Slope** has live music every night, and **The Stampede** in the Cooper Creek Square has disco and infrequent live bands. For a quiet drink after dinner without the loud music and dancers head down to **Soufflés**. The **Iron Horse** often has a guitar player in the bar and a Comedy Club.

The Crooked Creek Saloon in downtown Fraser also has food and music . . . the only problem is transportation.

Child care

Here, Winter Park clearly stands far above the rest of the skiing world. Winter Park has the absolute best children's programs and children's center in American skidom, and its commitment is evident in the multistory center built expressly for the purpose. On some days the program handles more than 600 children—anyone who has organized anything for a group that size (of whatever age) knows what an undertaking this is. The center is open from 8 a.m. to 4 p.m.

Child care for ages two months to five years, including lunch, will cost $45 a day; $30 half day. Utes, Cheyenne and Navajo are ski programs designed for skiers three to seven years, and include all-day supervision, morning and afternoon ski programs, lunch and lift tickets. One day is $50, with rentals, $60.

The Arapahoes program offers lessons for children eight to 12, including lifts and lunch. Prices are the same as Utes and Navajo programs.

A teen program for those from 13 to 16 is organized during holiday periods (Thanksgiving, Christmas, Presidents' Weekend and the month of March). This allows a teen to be in a less structured environment, but with the supervision of a qualified instructor. Costs are $45 a day for lifts, lessons and lunch.

Reservations are required for all child care. Reservation forms may be obtained from Winter Park Central Reservations, or write to: Children's Center, Winter Park Resort, Box 36, Winter Park, CO 80482.

Other activities

Jim's sleigh rides leave each evening at 7 p.m. and 8:30 p.m. You'll ride along a two-and-a-half-mile trail, pass log cabins and make a brief stop for hot refreshments around a roaring campfire. Adults pay $12 and children under 12 pay $9. For reservations, call 726-5527.

Dashing Through the Snow offers trips at 7 p.m. and 8:45 p.m. and can be contacted at 726-5376.

Snowmobile tours are available with Trailblazer (726-8452) or Sporting Country Guide Services (726-9247). Snowmobile tours run $33 for one hour, $48 for two hours and $95 for four hours. For dog sled rides call 726-5527.

One special activity rarely seen in an organized manner at ski resorts is tubing—where you get to slide down a hill upon an inflated innertube. The Fraser Valley Tubing Hill has everything you'll need for a night of tubing. There is one hill and two rope tows to pull you back to the top. The operators have also figured that most people don't carry innertubes with them to ski resorts, so they will rent you one for tubing fun. It's a blast. Call 726-5954.

Getting there

Winter Park is 67 miles northwest of Denver on U.S. Highway 40. Take I-70 West to Exit 232, then head toward Granby on Highway 40. There is scheduled bus and van service to and from Stapleton International Airport. Home James and Vanex vans leave from Door 6 of Stapleton arrivals. The one-way fare is $24 from the airport to Winter Park; $46 round trip. Reserve through central reservations, or contact the van lines directly. Home James: 726-5060 in Colorado; or (800) 525-3304.

Amtrak's California Zephyr, which races between Chicago and Los Angeles, also makes a stop in Fraser, only a few miles down the road, twice daily. This means skiers from Chicago or the West Coast can board the train in the afternoon and arrive in Winter Park the next morning. There are packages from $355 for a round trip, three nights' accommodations and three days of lift tickets. Call central reservations for details.

Call Amtrak for information and train-only reservations: (800) USA-RAIL.

Denver to Winter Park Rio Grande Ski Train

The Rio Grande Ski Train is a unique institution in the United States. This special skiers' train leaves Denver on weekends 19 December 1992 to 4 April 1993.

The ski train, operating for more than 50 years, brings 800 skiers from Denver directly to the Winter Park base area, chuffing along 56 miles and climbing 4,000 feet. The 14-car train snakes through the spectacular Rocky Mountains, burrowing through 28 tunnels and crossing canyons, ravines, and ice-crusted rivers. The scenery is as gripping as any I have seen in years of train travel through the Swiss and Austrian Alps. The train leaves Denver at 7:15 a.m. and departs Winter Park at 4:15 p.m.

Two classes of service—first and coach—are available; first class includes a continental breakfast. Through February 6, 1993 first class ticket costs $40; coach seats are $25. Rated then jump to $45, first class and $30, second class. For information and reservations, call 296-I SKI.

Information/reservations
Winter Park Central Reservations, Box 36, Winter Park CO 80482; (800) 453-2525 (nationwide); or (303) 726-5587.

Utah skiing

and staying in Salt Lake City

Snow is the most important ingredient for any ski vacation. Utah is blessed with some of the best—dry, light, fluffy and lots of it. It makes lousy snowballs and snowmen, but provides some of the best ski conditions on the planet. It billows over your head, temporarily blinds you as you sense your way down a steep incline, and occasionally chokes you as you howl and laugh at the wonderful sensation.

But it takes more than snow to make a perfect ski vacation. The mountains form the structure, the lifts open the experience and the towns provide the soul. Utah's ski areas are perhaps the most varied of any state. Within an

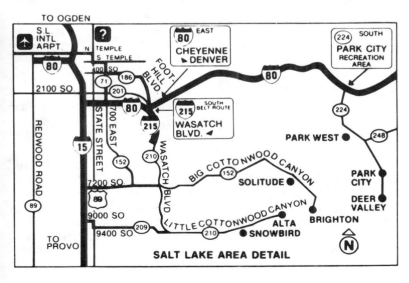

SALT LAKE AREA DETAIL

hour's drive of Salt Lake City, you can find one ski resort that pampers guests like no other (Deer Valley); others that leave you alone (Alta, ParkWest); still others with a bustling, urban feel (Snowbird, Park City); and the ones that have an isolated, backcountry atmosphere (Snowbasin, Sundance). Some of Utah's ski towns resound with the deep bass of live rock bands and the raucous whooping of rowdy skiers; in others, the loudest night noises are the snores of exhausted weekend athletes. Utah has ski areas with frightening precipices, others with gently undulating meadows.

Utah's biggest blessing is its accessibility. No other region has so many major ski areas so close to a major airport (Lake Tahoe comes close, but Reno doesn't have nearly the flights Salt Lake City does). Seven major ski areas are within a 45-minute drive; two others are 90 minutes off. Transportation is well-organized and efficient, so you don't even need a car.

Utah's biggest detriment is its lingering reputation for being a stick-in-the-mud. Utah's liquor laws have changed radically in the last decade, but many skiers still believe that finding a palm tree in Maine is easier than buying a drink in Utah. Not any more. And as far as entertainment goes, Utah is unsurpassed in variety. You can watch a professional basketball or hockey game; see a ballet, symphony or theater performance; laugh 'til your sides ache at a comedy club; and even dance the night away in a crowded, pulsating night club.

Salt Lake City

Salt Lake City pushes itself as a perfect spot for enjoying the pleasures of Utah skiing. For those who want to sample more than one of the major ski areas in the vicinity, it makes sense to stay here.

The Utah Transit Authority (UTA) has a very efficient ski bus system serving Brighton and Solitude in Big Cottonwood Canyon and Snowbird and Alta in Little Cottonwood Canyon. The buses are clean, pleasant, inexpensive and go directly from downtown to the ski areas. UTA has a free fare zone downtown, convenient for sightseeing and evening activities. Unlike many other urban areas, downtown Salt Lake City is safe for groups to walk at night. Lewis Brothers Stages (800-826-5844 or 801-359-8677) runs vans and motorcoaches to the areas.

Accommodations

Although rates a little higher in the downtown area than in outlying parts of the city, it is worth the extra few bucks to be close to Salt Lake City's major attractions. The convention and visitors bureau has complete lodging lists. Here are some recommendations (all rates are per night, double occupancy; 801 is the area code):

Salt Lake Marriott (800-345-4754 or 531-0800) is across from the Salt Palace, home of the Utah Jazz basketball team and Salt Lake Golden Eagles hockey team. The hotel also is connected to the Crossroads Plaza shopping mall. Rates are $69-$149.

Howard Johnson Hotel (800-366-3684 or 521-0130) also has a great location close to the Marriott. Temple Square is across the street. Rates are $48-$150.

Red Lion Hotel (328-2000) is a few blocks farther south on West Temple, but it's within stumbling distance of the Zephyr nightclub (see Après-ski/nightlife). Rates are $89-$120. A less expensive choice in this area is the **Peery Hotel** (521-4300; $59-$99). A restored building, its main drawback is street noise.

In the vicinity of West Temple and 500 South are several good hotels. **Little America Hotel and Towers** (363-6781) has some of the largest rooms we've ever seen in a hotel—great for spreading out all the junk that skiers bring on a trip. The views are nice—try to get a northeast corner room for vistas of the Wasatch Mountains to the east and downtown to the north. Rates are $65-$108.

Also recommended are **Embassy Suites Hotel** (359-7800; $89-$99) and the **Salt Lake Hilton** (532-3344; $92-$127).

For budget downtown accommodations, try the **Travelodge Salt Palace** (532-1000), **Travelodge Temple Square** (533-8200), **Travelodge City Center** (531-7100), **Deseret Inn** (532-2900), **Emerald Inn** (533-9300) or **Best Western Olympus Motel** (521-7373). All have rooms between $32 and $50.

For more hotel and Bed & Breakfast listings, contact the **Salt Lake City Convention and Visitors Bureau**, 800-541-4955 or 521-2822.

Dining

Downtown Salt Lake City has more than 60 restaurants, some chains such as Benihana of Tokyo, but many locally owned. They vary in decor and menu, and while you will feel comfortable in most of them with casual après-ski wear, you may want to dress up a bit for the finer establishments.

For a commanding night view of the state capitol and downtown, try **Nino's** (136 E. South Temple, 359-0506) at the top of the University Club Building for elegant Italian dining. More casual Italian dining can be found at **Baci's Trattoria** (134 W. Pierpont Ave., 328-1500), **Club Cabana** (31 E. 400 South, 359-6271), **Ferrantelli Ristorante Italiano** (300 Trolley Square, 531-8228) with its New York atmosphere, and **Ristorante Della Fontana** (336 S. 400 East, 328-4243), which is in a converted church with stained-glass windows and a waterfall cascading from the ceiling.

Three Chinese restaurants are downtown. **Charlie Chow** (277 Trolley Square, 575-6700) has the most interesting atmosphere and **On's Chinese** (Crossroads Plaza, 50 S. Main, 328-0888) reputedly has the best food. **Pagoda** (26 E St., 355-8155) has been around the longest, since 1946. **Mikado** (67 W. 100 South, 328-0929) has private Japanese zashiki rooms and **Asakusa Sushi** (321 S. Main, 364-7142) has a karaoke bar.

Cafe Pierpont (122 W. Pierpont Ave., 364-1222) and **Rio Grande Cafe** (270 S. Rio Grande, at the Amtrak Station, 364-3302) are downtown's best bets for Mexican food.

American and steak and seafood restaurants abound. **New Yorker** (60 Post Office Place, 363-0166) has an elegant atmosphere in the dining room. Its more casual neighbors, **Market Street Grill** (322-4668) and **Oyster Bar** (531-6044) emphasize seafood, but also serve steaks and chicken. **Lamb's** (169 S. Main, 364-7166) is Utah's oldest restaurant, dating back to 1919 and still packed today. **The Green Parrot** (155 W. 200 South, 363-3201) plays rock-jazz-blues while serving the renowned cuisine of Chef Glen Austin. Another spectacular night view awaits diners at **Room at the Top** (150 W. 500 South, 532-3344), the Salt Lake Hilton's fine restaurant. **Shenanigan's** (274 S. West Temple, 364-3663) has a fun atmosphere.

Après-ski/nightlife
Utah's liquor laws

For many skiers, apres-ski just isn't the same without a cold brew or hot toddy. There was a time, not very long ago, when getting a simple glass of wine here was a major effort, requiring a trip to the state liquor store before going to a restaurant, then paying corkage or a set-up fee before you could consume your own brown-bagged bottle. As noted, the liquor laws have changed drastically in the past decade, but there are still a couple of rules you should know:

The establishments we know as bars are called private clubs in Utah. You can't get in unless you're a member, but it's easy to become one. Utah residents buy an annual membership card costing $25-$35 for each club. Visitors pay $5 for a temporary, two-week membership. The more daring visitors can ask a local to sponsor them into the club, because members may bring up to five guests. Private clubs may serve liquor throughout the day. Restaurants may serve liquor without requiring a club card, but only after 1 p.m. That said, here are some recommendations:

For a unique happy hour after a day on the slopes, stop by the hole-in-the-wall **Cotton Bottom Inn**, at the base of Big and Little Cottonwood Canyons. This is a raucous, sawdust-on-the-floor tavern with the best garlicburgers in Utah (okay . . . but they are good) and an earthy crowd. The address is 2320 E. 6200 South, but it's a little hard to find. Ask a local to direct you.

For lively après-ski downtown, try the **Dead Goat Saloon** (Arrow Press Square, 165 S. West Temple). A quieter, pleasant location is **D.B. Cooper's** (19 E. 200 South), which Salt Lake City's career crowd seems to favor. Another excellent choice is **Squatter's Pub Brewery** (147 W. Broadway), where they brew several kinds of fresh beer right on the premises (yes, Virginia, in Utah).

When the Convention and Visitors Bureau puts a visit to rehearsals of the Mormon Tabernacle Choir high on its list of recommendations for Salt Lake City after dark, you know you're not in Vegas or even Elko (no nudges, please).

A nightlife tour might go like this—after choir rehersals head to **Club Baci**, the private club attached to the Baci Restaurant, then moved on to dinner at **Allie's Pantry**, a charming country-style restaurant at the Salt Lake Marriott. From there, head to **Bella Vista**, the private club next to Nino's Restaurant for a great view, looking to the south and a coffee-and-Kahlua drink. Your final stop is **Zephyr** (301 S. West Temple), which lives up to its billing as "Salt Lake City's premier showcase for local and national entertainment." A rock-jazz band called Crazy 8s was playing, and the dance floor was jammed.

Other rowdy night spots include **Studebakers** (175 E. 400 South) for '50s and '60s dance music, **Club Max** at the Red Lion Hotel, and for those with a car, **Nickelodeon Club**, at the University Park Hotel, 480 Wakara Way, near the University of Utah for dancing to DJ music.

The Interconnect Adventure Tour

Utah has a unique trek for experienced skiers; it takes them to five different resorts in a single day via backcountry routes. The tours are led by experienced mountain guides. You meet early in the morning and the guides take you on a few practice runs just to be sure you can handle the terrain. You are issued a beeper and off you go. The backcountry routes require traversing and walking—you need to be a confident skier in condition.

The five-area tour begins in Park City and goes to Solitude, Brighton, Alta and Snowbird, and is offered Monday, Wednesday, Friday and Sunday. The four-area tour starts at Snowbird and includes all the areas except Park City. It operates Tuesday, Thursday and Saturday. Each tour lasts about eight hours and costs $95, including a private lunch and transportation back to the point of origin. (And an exclusive ski pin that shows you did it.)

Groups range from six to 14 skiers. Reservations are necessary. Call 801-534-1907 and have a credit card.

Park City Area

Park City, Deer Valley ParkWest

About a hundred years ago, soldiers were sent out West to discourage Brigham Young from seceding from the Union. While the blue coats accomplished their mission, perhaps their most enduring legacy was the creation of a rambunctious and slightly quirky town in Utah's Rockies that has the true credentials of a world-class ski resort.

Along the way, of course, there was the small matter of a silver rush that drew 10,000 miners and sundry fortune seekers to Park City. It is those mining camp roots—going back to a time when Main Street boasted 30 saloons and numerous bordellos and gambling houses, and everyone assumed a boom-or-bust mentality much at odds with the Mormon Church—that give Park City its feisty and fiercely independent character.

Today, most of those century-old buildings on Main Street have been carefully restored (64 buildings in the townare listed on the National Register of Historic Places), there is no lack of saloons, and the streets teem with the comings and goings of prospectors of an altogether different ilk. If you haven't heard, there's a motherlode of 24 karat powder in them thar hills.

Actually, Park City is home to three ski resorts. Just up from the old, rustic Park City proper is new, opulent Deer Valley, with its wood-glass-and-brass veneer burnished to a fine sheen. Two valleys away, toward Salt Lake City, is unpretentious and slightly creaky Park West. All three areas generally share many of the same accommodations, restaurants and nightlife, and together they form a ski resort that can hold its own with just about anyone.

Where Park City excels over almost all its major league competition, however, is accessibility. Lying just 27 miles outside of Salt Lake City by six-lane I-80 and Utah 224, this resort is literally only a 45-minute trip from the airport. That's 45 minutes *door-to-door*. For those avid skiers on the East Coast who carefully chart days of actual skiing per vacation days taken, that can mean one and a half extra days of board time per trip because you do not have to devote an entire day to getting there and back.

Park City Ski Area—The skiing

Most reviews of Park City characterize this area as a cruising paradise for intermediates, which is true enough. While it may not have the steep and "gulp!" of Snowbird or Alta, it has some bowl skiing that has to be considered serious even on the expert scale, and plenty of open and gentle terrain for beginners and lower intermediates.

Beginners, even those just getting into their snowplow turns, can take the gondola—the longest four-passenger gondola ride in the Western United States—to the Summit House, with a very long run back. This trail starts with Claimjumper, shifts to Bonanza, then finishes at the base area on Sidewinder. Here at the base area, the Three Kings and First Time lifts service excellent learning terrain. And for an adventure and a chance to see a different part of the mountain, take the Webster Run down to the Pioneer Lift—you can have lunch at the mid-mountain restaurant and watch experts bouncing down the steep face of Blue Slip.

For intermediates the choices are mind-boggling. If you want to start with a worthy cruiser to get your blood flowing and your ski legs on, take Pay Day from the top of the lift by the same name. The views are spectacular on this autobahn run, and at night it becomes the longest lighted run in the Rockies. Probably the most popular runs for intermediates are the wide-open trails served by the King Consolidated chair lift. Both intermediates and

---

Park City Ski Area Facts

Base elevation: 6,900'; **Summit elevation:** 10,000'; **Vertical drop:** 3,100 feet
Number of lifts: 13—1 gondola, 2 quad chairs, 5 triple chairs, 5 double chairs
Snowmaking as percent of area: 17 percent **Total acreage:** 2,200
Uphill capacity: 19,700 per hour **Bed base:** 12,000

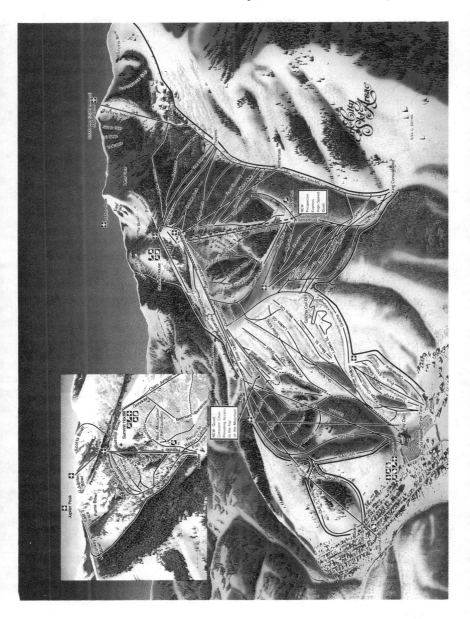

experts will enjoy the runs that snake under and around the new Prospector quad superchair, which opened last year. The new express lift has cut riding time to the ridge from 12 to 6 minutes.

Experts looking for a solid challenge will find Park City most accommodating. Take a trip to the top of Blue Slip Bowl. Reportedly, when this was the boundary of the ski area, resort workers regularly slipped under the ropes, made tracks down the bowl and then skied back into the resort; the management regularly passed out blue (you're fired) slips to anyone caught floating through this powder bowl. If you can ski Blue Slip then you can probably ski Jupiter Bowl, but if looking over the edge of Blue Slip puts your heart in your throat you had better stay out of Jupiter Bowl, McConkey's and Puma Bowl—from Blue Slip, you can choose easier descents, but from Jupiter it's all just as steep, and has two or three times as much vertical to contend with.

Jupiter Bowl has every type of steep expert terrain. The only way to access the Jupiter lift is by taking the Jupiter access road from the top the Pioneer or Thaynes lifts. To the left as you get off the Jupiter lift there are wide-open faces, especially on the West Face, which is the easiest way down (for those interested). There are narrow gullies and chutes dropping between tightly packed evergreens, such as Silver Cliff, 6 Bells and Indicator. Or head to the right as you get off the chair and try Portuguese Gap, a run more akin to the floor opening below you, or traverse to Scott's Bowl, which is just as steep as Portuguese Gap. For the adventuresome and those with parachutes there are definite thrills in the McConkey Bowl and Puma Bowl areas. When open, these are reached by a relatively long traverse across the West Face ridge and some climbing and hiking over the Pioneer Ridge. We asked Park City officials why they don't put a lift in to access these bowls, but they prefer to keep them the wild and untamed reward for those willing to make the hike. We're of two minds on that philosophy, but it certainly makes sense for those who want to make virgin tracks in a powder bowl. The cornice at the top of both bowls deposits skiers into steep faces and chutes, which empty out into the Pioneer lift area.

Getting to the slopes at Park City is simple. A shuttle-bus, running every 20 minutes connects all lodging with the resort center. For those staying in town, there is the town lift, which brings skiers from the lower part of Main Street up to the mid-station of the gondola.

Snowboarding
There is no snowboarding allowed at Park City, but shredders are welcomed at nearby Park West.

Park City—Lift tickets (92/93 prices)
One day, $40 for adults, $18 for children under 12; three of four days, $114 and $54; four of five days, $148 and $71; five of six days, $180 and $88; six of seven days, $216 and $104.

Multi-area books (coupons good for a day of skiing at Park City, ParkWest, Deer Valley, Alta, Snowbird, Brighton, Solitude or Sundance): five of six days, $190 for adults, $90 for children; six of seven days $228 and $108.

Deer Valley—The skiing

Deer Valley Facts
Base elevation: 7,200'; Summit elevation: 9,400'; Vertical drop: 2,200 feet
Number of lifts: 11—1 quad superchair, 9 triple chairs, 1 double chair
Snowmaking as percent of area: 25 percent Total acreage: 1,000 acres
Uphill capacity: 19,200 per hour Bed base: 12,000

Deer Valley isrenowned for pampering its guests with the best gourmet meals and palatial accommodations, but the pampering extends to the slopes themselves. We're not talking only about the guest service attendants who help get skis off ski racks, the toque-wearing slopeside cafeteria help, or the ski corral where you can safely leave the best equipment—the grooming crews at Deer Valley virtually comb the snow to ensure that it is so pool-table smooth that it will make any beginner into an instant intermediate. Although some experts may sneer at the dialy slope manicure, for cruising and collecting lots of vertical this place is a dreamland.

Deer Valley really is a fantasy world of sorts: there are phones on the slopes, perfect for a quick call to your broker or agent; there are restaurants to make a gourmet salivate; and the people here are as well groomed as the slopes and as perfectly outfitted as the wooden chalets. This is the place for mixing with the upper crust. Its competition

Park City, ParkWest, Deer Valley - Utah

Bald Mt. - 9400 ft.

Perseverance Bowl

Mayflower Bowl

Elev. - 7440 ft.

ILL. C. BROWN

in that department might be Sun Valley, Aspen and Vail, but for ski run manicure, it has no competition.

Last year saw the opening of the new lift up Flagstaff Mountain, an area formerly accessed only by snowcat. As is abundantly clear on the ride up, mogul monkeys will want to head left off the lift, and cruisers to the right. For experts, a short traverse to the left off the top of this lift will open up an entire mountain face of wide-open bowl, Ontario Bowl, and tree skiing. Don't miss this experience.

If you want to be seen, and have plenty of company and beautiful scenery, the best runs are Sunset, Birds-eye and Success. But if you head for Mayflower Bowl or Perseverance Bowl you'll have the trails virtually to yourself. Even the Wasatch lift tends to be empty, and run after run down Legal Tender, Wizard, Keno and Nabob are a blast. The Mayflower and Perseverance expert sections are not all groomed, but with so little traffic the bumps never grow monstrous. Morning Star, Fortune Teller, and Paradise start off steep and Deer-Valley-bumpy, but mellow in the lower half where they get groomed. Orient Express is a perfect cruiser with good advanced pitch, and Perseverance, coupled with the initial steeper sections of Thunderer, Blue Ledge and Grizzly makes an advanced intermediate paradise.

For the super experts looking for thrills or the bumpers looking for new moguls to conquer, Deer Valley is the wrong place to ski. This is the land of the smooth cruiser, where a skier can play like a bird on wing, swooping to the right or left, bouncing over a bump and settling back into flight. These slopes are perfect for playing with balance and testing edges, for leaning into turns and letting your skis arc you through their curve. Some poor jaded souls find it boring. Others, blessed with an appreciation of beauty, find it ethereal.

Daily complimentary tours of the mountain are available beginning at 10 a.m. The hosts are found at the base of the Carpenter Express lift, Snow Park Lodge.

From outside Deer Valley the best way to the slopes is the Park City Shuttle. A Main Street bus runs between Deer Valley's Snow Park Lodge and the Park City Resort Center every 20 minutes. Buses to Silver Lake and Stein Eriksen Lodge leave from Snow Park Lodge at quarter to and quarter past the hour from 7:45 a.m. to 4:15 p.m.

Deer Valley—Lift tickets (92/93 prices)

Full day, $43 for adults, $28 for seniors 65 and over and children four to 12; Half day (1-4 p.m.) $32 and $20; two of seven days, $84 and $54; three of seven days, $123 and $78; four of seven days, $164 and $104.

Over Christmas (Dec. 25 to Jan. 1) there's a special nine-day pass for $414 and $279 for children and seniors. Full-day passes jump to $46 for adults, $31 for children and seniors. Half-day passes are not available.

Ticket sales are limited to 5,000 skiers, so on holidays the extra buck or so to ski Deer Valley is worth it.

There are special prices for tots three and under: $18 a day and $13 a half day.

Multi-area books (coupons good for a day of skiing at Park City, ParkWest, Deer Valley, Alta, Snowbird, Brighton, Solitude or Sundance): five of six days, $190 for adults, $90 for children; six of seven days $228 and $108.

ParkWest-The skiing

ParkWest Facts

Base elevation: 6,800'; Summit elevation: 9,000'; Vertical drop: 2,200 feet
Number of lifts: 7 double chairs
Snowmaking as percent of area: 7 percent; Total acreage: 850 skiable acres
Uphill capacity: 6,700 per hour Bed base: 12,000

ParkWest's runs aren't manicured like Deer Valley's nor does it enjoy the wide-open bowls of Park City. It's not home to affluent crowds like Deer Valley, nor is it nestled up to an old town as is Park City. With no fluff and no façade, it's a people's ski resort. Every level of skier can enjoy the mountains from almost any point. ParkWest entices skiers to "ski the hidden peaks." From the base area only a tiny part of the skiable terrain is visible. Behind the first lifts and the mild terrain of Arrowhead, two massive ridges allow access to upwards of 50 runs.

Super experts will find plenty to keep them busy on the south face of Ironhorse Peak. The chutes and gullies here are as extreme (in fact, impossible to ski without deep powder) as any in Utah. Bumpers who feel cheated by the chic grooming at Deer Valley will find Massacre the most relentless bump run in Utah, and will have a field day comparing Renegade, Bad Hombre, Double Barrel, Grizzly and Bear Claw. ParkWest has upgraded its grooming fleet and now regularly mows down at least a bump run a week.

For skiers unwilling to be limited by lift-served terrain, ParkWest has opened a bowl section; if you're willing to hike the last 600 feet up to Murdock Bowl, you can enjoy the trail less traveled: a three-quarter-mile wide bowl with 120 acres of skiable terrain with views as far as the Great Salt Lake and into the Cottonwood Canyons.

Lookout Peak has a spread of black and blue runs, including the steep Badlands and Slaughterhouse, which occasionally get groomed. The Shortswing Lift serves Ricochet and Haystack, two of the widest and more consistent cruisers.

Beginners and lower intermediates have the Arrowhead section with two dedicated beginner lifts. From the deck of the base lodge parents can watch their children progress from uncertain wedge turns to smooth stem christies.

ParkWest buses connect the Park City Resort Center and ParkWest every half hour at a minimum. If there are more skiers, the buses will leave more frequently. If your hotel is off the normal route, any group of three or more skiers may call the shuttle service for a special pickup. Call: 649-5400. From Deer Valley, take the Park City bus into Park City and then transfer to the ParkWest bus.

Snowboarding

ParkWest prides itself as Utah's snowboarding headquarters, with more certified instructors than any other Utah ski area. Shredders are encouraged to explore off-trail boarding, and there are two designated halfpipes.

ParkWest—Lift tickets (91/92 prices)

Full day, $25 for adults, $15 for children under 12; half day, $15 adults, $8 for kids; three of seven days, $60 and $23; four of seven days, $76 and $30; five of seven days, $90 and $36.

Senior citizens 65+ pay $8. With the purchase of an adult full-day lift ticket, one child (8 and younger) from the immediate family may ski free. With the purchase of two adult full-day tickets, $50, up to four children from the immediate family ski free. Half-day refunds are given if you return your ticket before 12:30 p.m. Half-day refunds are not available with the kids-ski-free program.

Ski school
Park City Ski Area ski school (92/93 prices)

Park City uses the graduated length method (GLM) for beginners. There are five different packages for all ranges of ski schoolers.

Private lessons cost $67 per one-hour lesson for one student, $113 for a two-hour lesson, $160 for a half day (three hours), and $320 for a full day (six hours). If you get a small private group together the prices for a group of three will be only $87 for one hour, $133 for two hours, $190 for the half day and $370 for the full day. It makes more sense, based on price, to take a two-hour lesson than the half day.

Group lessons cost $38 for a full day and $31 for a half-day program. Three consecutive days cost $108 and five consecutive days are $170. For children enrolled in the group lessons there is a supervised lunch for $23.

Race clinics (3 hours) cost $35 with two timed runs.

Park City Mountain Experience classes are designed for high intermediates and advanced skiers. The classes explore Jupiter Bowl, off-trail skiing and deep powder. These are four-hour classes with an instructor/guide who will comment on your technique and suggest improvements in your skiing. Classes run from 10 a.m. to 2 p.m. and cost $37 a day.

The Kinderschule ski lessons, for children three to six years, can be combined with a day care option. The combined day care/ski lessons are $42 for a half day, either morning or afternoon, including a snack and an hour and a half lesson; a full day, including lunch and lessons in the morning and afternoon, costs $58; and a three-day course is $160. There is a modest increase during holiday seasons. For lessons only (one and half hours in the morning and afternoon), the cost is $29 for a half day and $35 for a full day. Private lessons are also available for $50 an hour with one child; $55 an hour with two children; $60 an hour for three children.

Deer Valley ski school (92/93 prices)

Instructors here pamper the psyche of the skier, working to develop good interaction with the student.

Private lessons for one or two cost: $70 for one hour, $128 for two hours, $200 for a full morning or afternoon and $375 for a full day of instruction.

Group all-day lessons for adults 13 and over cost $55.

Children's (six to 12 years) group lessons are $60 for the full day, including lunch. There is a Kinderschule program for three to five year olds for $80 with lunch.

There is also a black diamond workshop for advanced skiers 13 years and older. This all-day class runs from 11 a.m. to 4 p.m. and costs $55. Beginner lessons for three days cost $219 including lessons and lifts.

ParkWest ski school

Here classes are small and the attention is almost personal for each of the students. There is also race training on Tuesdays, Wednesdays and Thursdays, which includes timed runs through gates. ParkWest also has snowboarding lessons. "Kids Central" is for children between the ages of four and nine. All-day programs with lessons, lifts, day care and supervised lunch are available.

Cross-country

White Pine Touring (649-8701 or 649-8710) offers track skiing, lessons and tours at the Park City golf course. Rates are $3 daily, and those 12 and under and 70+ ski free. There are 10 km. of set tracks, plus mountain tours and overnight cabins. The Norwegian School of Nature Life (649-5322) offers cross-country lessons and guided backcountry tours.

The Homestead Resort (649-2060) is also developing a cross-country network. Currently there is a 10-km. course. Day fees are $4.

Accommodations

In and around the Park City Area there are bed-and-breakfasts, country inns, hotels and condominiums. At Deer Valley the accommodations have a decidedly upscale flavor and tariffs to match.

Park City's accommodations are roughly grouped either in the old town surrounding the Resort Center Complex or in the Prospector Square area. All are served by the shuttlebus systems.

In old Park City the best is the **Washington School Inn**, 543 Park Ave.; (800) 824-1672 or 649-3800. This is classified as a bed-and-breakfast but is really a very elegant country inn built in a former schoolhouse. Each room's name honors a former Park City teacher and everything is definitely first class, from the service to the furnishings to the hearty American breakfasts. A Jacuzzi and steambath offer relaxation after a day on the slopes, and the inn is only a few steps away from the center of the old town with its restaurants, shops and taverns. Prices normally dictate the clientele of these hotels so expect the upscale, quiet and conservative. If you are on your honeymoon, ask for the Miss Urie Room. It is bright and beautiful. Rates during normal ski season: deluxe suite with fireplace, $190 a night; deluxe suite, $175 a night; guestroom, $145 a night. No children under 12 or pets.

The Blue Church Lodge & Townhouses at 424 Park Ave.; 649-8009. This is a unique property, constructed around an old church. It is only a block from Main Street and is a grouping of seven condominiums ranging from one to four bedrooms in the church, with four additional townhouses across the street. Again, this is rated as a B&B because breakfast is provided in a common area each morning. It doesn't fit the category of B&B in the classic sense or a country inn either, but it's comfortable and well done. There are both indoor and outdoor spas. Rates during regular season: single room (lock off), $95 a night; two-bedroom, two-bath condo, $230 a night; four bedroom, three-bath condo, $315.

If the three keys to lodging, as in real estate, are location, location, and location, then **Treasure Mountain Inn** (800-344-2460) at the top of Main Street is a sure hit in our book. These are basically studio and one and two bedroom condos with full kitchens and maid service. Each of the three buildings has a coin-operated laundry, and there is a Jacuzzi in the courtyard. Cost for a studio units is $100 per night, one-bedroom units run $130 per night, and $185 per night for the two-bedroom units.

The bargain basement accommodations are dormitory digs and some rooms in the **Chateau Après Lodge**, which has room rates of $48 for one or two persons, $53 for three and $54 for four. Dormitory rates are $15 per person.

Near the Resort Center you'll find another cluster of hotels and condos. The best is the **Silver King Hotel**, 1485 Empire Ave; (800) 331-8652 or 649-5500. This condominium hotel is only a hundred yards from the lifts and at the hub of the transportation system for the entire area. There is an indoor/outdoor swimming pool and each condo has all amenities and underground parking. Some units even have private hot tubs next to the king-sized bed. Rates: studio, $200; penthouse suite, to $440; two-bedroom condos, $370.

The Resort Center is the second choice for luxury. It literally surrounds the base area lifts. Call (800) 824-5331 or 649-0800. These condos feature swimming pool, saunas and spas. Rates: studio, $185; one-bedroom, $285; two-bedroom, $315; three-bedroom, $595; four-bedroom, $730.

Shadow Ridge is the other top property near the lifts; (800) 451-3031 or 649-4300. There is a sauna, Jacuzzi and parking. Rates in regular season: hotel room, $90-$120; one-bedroom, $180-$280; two-bedroom, $215-$360.

The Snow Flower, a ski-in/ski-out hotel at the base of the lifts, is only a 100 feet from the base of the beginner's area. Call (800) 852-3101 or 649-6400. Studios during regular season are $145; one-bedroom condo, $237; two-bedroom, two-bath condo, $303; three-bedroom, three-bath loft condo, $358.

For more economical condos, try the rennovated **Edelweiss Haus** directly across the street from the lifts and the Silver King Hotel. Address: 1482 Empire Ave.; (800) 438-3855 for reservations only or 649-9342 to contact anyone in the hotel. Hotel rooms cost between $85 and $90. Two-bedroom condos run from $140-$165. The hotel has a heated outdoor pool and Jacuzzi.

The final main cluster of hotels serving Park City is just outside town. Here try the **Prospector Square Hotel** down Kearns Blvd. on the way to Heber City; (800) 453-3812 or 649-7100. This group of condos includes use of its athletic club in the rates. **The Yarrow Hotel** (800) 327-2332 or 649-7000, on Park Avenue, is considered a good family accommodation. Children under 12 stay free and the hotel sits in the middle of plenty of shopping, movies and restaurants. It is on the shuttlebus route, only about a five-minute ride from Park City's Main Street. The 200-room **Olympia Hotel** at 1895 Sidewinder Road, with excellent accommodations, swimming pool and exercise room, is also in this same area. Call (800)234-9003 or 649-2900.

A bit farther out of town you'll find the **Best Western Landmark Inn**; (800) 548-8824 or 649-7300. It's just off the interstate. You'll need a car. The **Radisson Inn**, (800) 345-5076 or 649-5000, is not quite as far away and on the ParkWest bus route, but for access to downtown Park City plan on having a car.

The Homestead is a rambling country inn located 25 minutes from Park City. This retreat offers excellent activities including cross-country and snowmobiling in a perfect setting. This is one of the Great Inns of the Rockies, rated Four Diamond by AAA. 1992/93 ski packages including breakfast and dinner, seven nights lodging, skierized rental car, five days of downhill skiing at any Utah area listed in this book, two hours of snowmobiling or cross-country skiing with pass and rentals, cost $849 per person and $449 per child based on double occupancy. Call (800) 327-7220 or 654-1102 for reservations and information. The Park City number is 649-2060.

For luxury condos and houses at affordable prices as well as a chance to get some last-minute/off-peak bargains in the entire Park City area, call **Affordable Luxury Lodging**, (800) 321-4754; fax (801) 649-1128. The staff is helpful and will offer suggestions for all aspects of your Utah vacation from skiing to après-ski.

Accommodations—Deer Valley

Top dog is the **Stein Eriksen Lodge**; (800) 453-1302 or 649-3700. Think of any luxury or service and you will probably find it—heated sidewalks between buildings, fireplaces in the rooms, maids twice a day, fresh terrycloth robes, floor-to-ceiling windows. Don't worry, you won't have to rub shoulders with the proletariat in these digs. Room rates during winter season start at $300 a night, one-bedroom suites start at $640. Two-bedroom suites range from $940; three-bedroom suites are $1,240 and four-bedroom suites $1,540.

The **Goldener Hirsch** (800) 252-3373 or 649-7770, offers the elegance and service of a top Austrian hotel at midmountain in Deer Valley.

Other accommodations are run by **Deer Valley Lodging**; (800) 453-3833 or 649-4040. Almost all have private spas and all are right on the mountain. Although not all are ski-in/ski-out, they all feature daily maid service, color TV, fireplaces, bell and concierge service. After Stein's the place to stay on the mountain is the **Stag Lodge**.

The **Pinnacle Condominiums** with three- and four-story living rooms are as spectacular on the inside as they appear when you drive by. Closer to the lifts—actually ski-in/ski-out properties—are the **Pine Inn** and **La Maconnerie**. All units have private spas.

The most economical Deer Valley properties are the **Lakeside** units, which do not have private spas but do have public Jacuzzis, and Deer Valley lodging's only outdoor heated pool. At Lakeside you slum it, Deer Valley-style.

Deer Valley condominium reservations can be made with Deer Valley Lodging noted above or with Deer Valley Connection at (800) 458-8612 or 645-7700.

Dining—Deer Valley

The best dining is in Deer Valley, but it is difficult to reach in the evenings from Park City unless you have a car or are willing to pay $10+ taxi fare each way. If you want to make advance dinner reservations from anywhere in the United States, call (800) 424-DEER. Shuttlebus only runs until 10 p.m. to Snow Park Lodge.

Café Mariposa at Silver Lake Lodge is the gourmets' top choice. Reservations are a must 649-1005.

The Glitretind Restaurant in Stein Eriksen Lodge offers meals with a Norwegian flair. This is not the place to come if pinching pennies. Entrées range from $22 to $27, with pasta weighing in at $17. Don't expect to leave for less than $100 for two. Reservations required: 649-3700.

The Seafood Buffet at **Snow Park Lodge**, spread out Mondays through Saturdays, gets rave reviews from everyone who has had the chance to sample the fare. Adults pay $34 and children pay $17 and it's all you can eat. Reservations: 649-1007.

McHenry's Grill in the Silver Lake Lodge serves moderately priced lunches and dinners.

For breakfast, head to the buffet at the **Huggery** in Snow Park Lodge and for lunch it's the **Snuggery** at Silver Lake Lodge. The food is laid out like a magazine illustration, a spectacular presentation. These cafeteria-style restaurants glisten with shiny brass and sparkling glass, and the cooks decked out in kitchen whites complete with toques add another touch of class.

Dining—Park City

There are almost 70 restaurants in the Park City. After speaking with scores of locals, here's our verdict.

The best two restaurants in town are **Alex's** on Main Street, 649-6644, for French fare, and **Adolph's** just outside town on the golf course, 649-7177, for German and American cuisine. Alex's offers a fixed-price meal for $21.95, with other entrées ranging between $13 and $20. Adolph's is a bit pricier, with entrée prices hovering around $20. A bit outside the mainstream is the **Snowed Inn**, which has gourmet food in an elegant old Victorian setting. There are two seatings each night: a four-course meal for $22 at 6:30 p.m. and a seven-course dinner for $35 at 8:30 p.m. You'll need your own transportation. Reservations required; call 649-6368.

Mileti's on Main Street, 649-8211, serves the town's best Italian food. **Ichiban Sushi** on Main Street, 649-2865, is perhaps unique in the United States, with a Japanese-trained, female sushi chef. Even Japanese visitors eat here . . . 'nuff said. Then there's **Scrooge's** on Main Street; 649-XMAS. Here Christmas is celebrated year round, and cantankerous Scrooge even comes through the restaurant on occasion. It's great fun for kids of all ages. Expect to spend between $10 and $15 per person. Scrooge also offers the only Dinosaur Steak we've heard of, but this requires a party of 500 or more and depends on the availability of fresh dinosaur at the market. **Cisero's** on Main Street serves great continental Italian food.

More recommendations are: **Baja Cantina** at the Resort Center and the **Irish Camel** on Main Street for good drinks and acceptable Tex-Mex food. **The Eating Establishment** is a locals' "cheap eats" favorite. **Texas Red's Pit Barbeque** is one of the deals of the century, with 16-ounce T-bone steaks topping off the menu at only $10.95. **The Yarrow** offers a family bonanza with all-you-can-eat

prime rib buffets every Friday and Saturday for only
$9.95. **The Grub Steak** also gets high marks from families.
And the **Riverhorse Café** and **Barking Frog** on Main Street
got excellent compliments from locals and tourists alike.

We only do lunch alerts for eating on the mountain
when there something special to experience. In the case of
Park City, **Mid-Mountain Restaurant** qualifies for its setting. Reached on Webster Run near the bottom of Pioneer
lift, this beautiful building nestled in the trees was
formerly a lodge for miners. It was moved from the Angel
Station on the gondola and fully restored. The proprietor
plays classical music on the expansive deck, which blends
beautifully with the surroundings.

Après-ski/nightlife

Despite rumors of the Utah party blahs, Park City has
some of the best nightlife of any ski town.

Immediate après-ski centers are **Steeps** and the **Baja
Cantina**, both located in the Resort Center, and downtown
at **Cisero's** where the happy hour can get very lively. **The
Columbine** in the Resort Center attracts a quieter crowd.
All seem to wind down between 5 p.m. and 6 p.m., but after
dinner the night crowds begin to stream in.

If you're thirsting for something a little different, try
the **Wasatch Brew Pub** at the top of Main Street, where you
can watch the brewing process even as you reap its yeasty
rewards. The owner grew up in Milwaukee, and he makes
beer just the way his grandfather taught him.

The Club caters to a fairly young crowd and is a good
place for singles. The dance floor upstairs, where the motif
is velvet bordello, is a place to see and be seen. **The Alamo**
next door is your basic saloon, with pool, loud music and
louder conversation. The only thing missing is sawdust on
the floor. Anyone with a serious case of dancing feet
should check out **Z Place**, which inside boasts a ballroom
dance floor and very modern music. Z Place often features
national bands and on Saturdays everything kicks off
with local comedians. If you're older than 21, **Cisero's** on
Main Street is one of the best downtown spots to meet
other singles and dance a bit with a mixed crowd ranging
from 20s to 40s. **Steeps** in the Resort Center is another
main dancing hub of Park City. Here bands often play and
there is plenty of room to dance and a great good-time

crowd. The age group is similar to Cisero's. **The Down Under** normally has acoustic guitar. A favorite is **Mileti's,** which occasionally features jazz groups. It offers a nice, relatively quiet atmosphere. **Adolph's,** with piano music, has been recommended for quieter evenings.

When the 60-year-old **Egyptian Vaudeville Theater** has shows, it makes a nice evening's entertainment.

Child care (92/93 prices)

Child care—Deer Valley

Deer Valley has a licensed facility that handles children between two and 12 years. It's never reached capacity but has come close during the holiday season. Call the ski school for reservations. Full-day child care, including lunch, costs $42. Half-day programs, morning or afternoon, cost $30.

Deer Valley also has limited infant care for children as young as six months. During slow periods the nursery will often take infants as young as two months. Make sure to call for reservations. Full-day infant care, including lunch, is $57, and half-day without lunch, either morning or afternoon, is $34.

Designed for 3 and 4 year old beginners, the Bambi Special program runs from 9 a.m. to 4 p.m. Cost is $80 including lift tickets, a private lesson and children's activities.

The child care phone number is 649-1000, Ext. 1682.

Child care—Park City

With the Kinderschule programs outlined in the ski school section, there are other child care programs.

The Children's Chalet is located west of Jeremy Ranch on South Frontage Road of I-80. It is a fully licensed preschool and child care facility that also accepts infants. Call 649-5959.

Creative Beginnings Preschool and Child Care and Nightowls baby sitting service with professional baby sitters are also available in town. The Park City Chamber can get you information about these and other licensed child care facilities in the area as well.

Child care—ParkWest

Miss Billie's Kid's Campus has been welcoming infants and children through nine years for the past 12 years. This fully licensed facility is located directly across from the ParkWest ski resort. Call 649-9502 or 649-KIDS.

Getting there

Park City is only 27 miles east of Salt Lake City, by I-80 and Utah 224. The drive from the airport to Park City is not arduous and takes only 45 minutes. Two transfer services provide regular transportation between Park City hotels and the airport.

The Lewis Brothers Stages, (800) 826-5844 or 649-2256 in Park City, 359-8677 in Salt Lake City, run buses that leave the airport for Park City every hour on the half hour 9:30 a.m. to 11:30 p.m. The fare is $14 per person each way, children half price. Make reservations at least 48 hours in advance for pickup in Park City and for guaranteed seating.

Park City Transportation, (800) 637-3803 or 649-8567, has a series of van runs to Park City. Call ahead to make sure that a van will be waiting. If you arrive without reservations, just go to the transportation counter at the Salt Lake City airport and a representative will put you on the next available van. Cost is $15 from airport to hotel. Call 48 hours in advance for return reservations.

Key Transportation, (800) 678-2360 or (649-6955), runs vans between the airport and Park City every 30 minutes. Cost is $15 one way or $30 round trip.

Both Lewis Bros. and Park City Transportation have buses that connect with Snowbird and Alta. The Lewis Bros. Stage leaves Park City at 8 a.m. and arrives in Alta/Snowbird at 9:30 a.m. The return trip leaves Alta at 4:30 p.m., leaves Snowbird at 4:45 p.m. and arrives in Park City at 6 p.m. Rate is $17 round trip per person. Other transportation services are provided by All Resort Express and Summit Transportation.

Other activities

Park City's calendar has some unique opportunities during the ski year. The Senators' Ski Cup normally takes place in mid-January and the Sundance Film Festival immediately follows, showcasing new films from around the world. In February the Coca-Cola snow-sculpture/Winterfest contest takes place.

Old fashioned, horse-drawn sleigh rides to cozy dinners are available through the Park City Sleigh Company.

Several companies give balloon trips. Call Balloon Biz, Park city reat Balloon Escape, Sunrise Fantasy Balloon, and Balloon Affaire.

Snowmobile tours are available. Both High Country Tours (645-7533) and Snowwest Snowmobiles (645-7669) have dinner tours.

There are indoor tennis courts at Park City Racquet Club (649-8080), as well as volleyball and aerobic workouts. The Prospector Square Athletic Club has complete health club facilities; 649-6670.

Utah's only brewery, the Schirf Brewing Company, maker of Wasatch Ale, provides tours of its Park City brewery; 645-9500. They also have a pub on Main Street where you can test the local product.

Park City Visitor's Information Center and Museum is open Monday through Saturday, 10 a.m. to 7 p.m., Sundays from noon to 6 p.m. It is packed with history of the Old West and has a self-guided city tour, with background on historical buildings in town.

Information/reservations

There is no single central reservations number for Park City, but these reservation agencies can book everything from airline reservations to hotels, ski rentals, lessons and insurance. Each of these organizations offers special packages for ParkWest, Park City and Deer Valley.

Park City Ski Holidays; (800) 222-PARK; 649-0493; telex 453143; fax 649-0532. **Advance Reservations**, (800) 453-4565; 649-7700. You can also try A-Vermeer's Reservations, Budget Reservations, Central Resort Reservations and Tuft Ski Tours.

Deer Valley Central Reservations 800-424-3337 801-649-1000. Can make reservations for air, transfers, lifts, rentals,and lodging (Deer Valley, Park City area and some properties in Salt Lake City).

Information: Park City Area Chamber of Commerce/Convention and Visitors Bureau, 1910 Prospector Avenue, P.O. Box 1630, Park City UT 84060; tel: (800) 453-1360 or 649-6100.

Alta, Utah

Just as much as a snow story, Alta is a people's story. While no one can discount the importance of its natural endowments—the 500-plus inches of light-and-fluffy falling in this canyon snow trap—Alta has people at its heart.

Alta has a dichotomous character that makes it appealing but puzzling. There is absolutely nothing in, about, or emanating from Alta that makes it highbrow or brochure-slick. (You sometimes get the impression that Little Cottonwood denizens, operators included, rather wish the fuss about its powder would cease so fewer people would arrive up-canyon.) The dichotomy lies in what happens after the people arrive. Once they're here, ruddy-faced, smiling and shouldering skis, visitors get such a hearty dose of friendliness and hospitality that keen observers shake their heads, not sure what Altans want.

The history is no less a mixture of opposites. In half a century of mining, Alta went from obscurity to boom, followed by outrageous scandal when the mines suddenly collapsed in the early 1900s. At a time when glamorous international figures were being courted by the new Sun Valley, Alta was born from the unpretentious desire of Salt Lake residents to have a place where they could ski without having to climb uphill. Beginning in 1939 using its old ore tram, it's been cranking skiers up to its ridges well nigh into their third generation. It still bears the original name, Alta Ski Lifts, without the word "resort" being mentioned.

Alta Facts
Base elevation: 8,590'; **Summit elevation:** 10,550'; **Vertical drop:** 2,000 feet
Number of lifts: 12—1 triple chair, 7 double chairs, 4 rope tows
Snowmaking as percent of area: none **Snowmaking as total acreage:** none
Total acreage: 2,200
Uphill capacity: 8,900 per hour **Bed base:** 1,136

In Little Cottonwood Canyon, just a mile up the road from its neighbor Snowbird, Alta provides a fine contrast. Where Snowbird with its massive high-speed tram is high-tech, Alta is homey. Where Snowbird is huge, Alta is manageable. While first-time visitors may need a guide at Snowbird, they'll catch the lay of the land quickly at Alta.

The ski area has a front and backside, with the first base station you reach, Wildcat Base, serving the entire front side and the second, Albion Base, housing the Children's Center, Ski School and retail and rental operations. Beginner slopes are served from Albion, but it has expert terrain at higher elevations. Between Albion and Wildcat base centers, the terrain is so gradual that there's a two-way transfer rope tow connecting them. It's either a slow bore or more fun than a carnival ride, depending on your friends and your frame of mind. This link between the two centers is all there is at the bottom. There's no town, just a smattering of quiet hotels and condominiums. Skiing is the focus, not nightlife, and it doesn't matter if your ski clothes match. Flannel shirts and boots work as well as play here.

The Skiing

Powder is what Alta is all about, not just because it gets a lot, but because, with its terrain of tree skiing and sheltered, hidden gullies, it tends to keep it longer. While most skiers are swishing down groomed runs a couple ofdays after a storm, the Alta cognoscenti are secretly diving into snow pockets in side canyons and upper elevations.

Alta, like Snowbird, is a what-you-see, you-can-ski resort, with many "ways down" which aren't actually named routes but simply that, ways down. Be individual. Be creative. That's the spirit of Alta.

Uphill from the Main Ticket Office, Wildcat and Collins lifts serve advanced runs on the right side—narrow trails, bump runs, and many glades—with intermediate as well as, yes, more advanced runs on the left. Those to the left are wider, the main intermediate route down being Meadow.

From the left of these two lifts, skiers can access an entirely different ridge, West Rustler, by taking the Germania lift. That means more steep and deep at Eagle's Nest and High Rustler for experts, and intermediate slopes as well, with less intimidating names like Ballroom and Mambo. The line at Germania lift may appear daunting on powder days but rarely averages more than ten minutes, although if there's powder on weekends, it can crank up to twenty. Last season the chair was upgraded from a double to a triple to cut down on the wait.

From the top of Germania Pass the runs down the front side return you to Wildcat base area; runs down the back return you to Albion. Skiers wishing to cross back into the Germania area must do the dreaded Germania Shuffle, an extensive traverse around the rim of a huge bowl (reportedly much improved for this season). It has a wonderful view, and at that elevation, you'll stop amid your huffing to admire it a few times. The only other Albion-to-Wildcat route is all the way down at the base on the transfer tow. Alta owners recognize a need for more upper mountain linkage and are planning to improve it. In the meantime, it's work.

From the Albion base station, Sunnyside and Albion lifts are slow riders across gentle terrain, a wide, rolling beginner's playground, but at the top, experts can take Supreme lift to Point Supreme, the 10,550-foot summit, and from there have plenty of steep tree skiing to the left in an area near the boundary called Spiney Ridge. Some sections are known as Piney Glades and White Squaw. It's all known as steep, and tremendously popular with knowing Salt Lake skiers. Up here you can ski all day without ever going the same way twice.

Also accessible midmountain on the Albion side is Sugarloaf lift, which serves expert bowls as far as the eye can see. Swooping down into a gully to the left of the lift as you descend usually gives you powder pockets. A day or two after a storm, try Devils' Castle, the steeps under the rocks accessible from Sugarloaf.

To follow the sun, start the morning on Sugarloaf, then move to Germania on the front side at midday, and finish on Supreme.

Alta's A-Race course is on Sunnyside run and is open Friday and Saturday. The $3 race fee is payable at the race arena. Snowboarding is not permitted at Alta.

Mountain Rating

With an ideal breakdown of 25 percent beginner, 40 percent intermediate and 35 percent advanced terrain, Alta is a great place for any level of skier. There is an expansive beginner area, wide-open intermediate trails and super expert steeps. The major difference for the expert between Alta and its larger neighbor is size, vertical to be precise. The difference is the Snowbird tram that opens almost 3,000 feet of continuous expert vertical versus the maximum expert drop of 1,000 at Alta.

For intermediates the nod would have to go to Alta because it has at least twice the usable intermediate terrain of Snowbird. Most of it is served from Wildcat and Collins lifts from the base area and Germania for higher terrain.

And beginners . . .? Go to Alta for the less intimidating homeyness if for no other reason. Besides, Snowbird doesn't have any place to train upper beginners and lower intermediates. A mile-long beginner run serviced by the Albion lift can make a beginner feel like a real skier—and that's what the sport is all about. Once mastering that, careful beginners or lower intermediates can take Sugarloaf to reach a peak that gives any beginner a heady feeling of being on top of the mountain.

Ski school (91/92 prices)

Bearing the name of Alf Engen, Norwegian ski jumper who came to Utah in 1930, the ski school is bound to have Old World flavor and expertise. More than 100 instructors are quite a sizable squad for a resort this size. Private lessons are $45 for an hour, $135 for a morning and $110 for an afternoon, with $225 for all day. Two-hour group lessons and race classes are $19. Afternoon workshops focusing on specific skills are called Bumps Bumps Bumps, Conditions du Jour, and Diamond Challenge, and are $28 for two and a half hours; meet at the blue and white signs below the base of Germania lift. Mountain Masters classes ($50 all day, $40 half day), designed for the better skier in good physical condition, explore all of Alta including hiking to places inaccessible by lift; meet on Wildcat Ticket Office deck at 10 a.m. All other lessons begin at the base of Albion lift.

Lift Tickets (91/92 prices)

Alta's low prices combined with its legendary powder make it one of Utah's great deals. That's why they need little promotion. Constant efforts to keep the prices down are genuine, which keeps its laid-back atmosphere as a necessary side effect. There is one price for everyone because, according to management, children, seniors, and adults all occupy the same space.

Full day (all lifts), $21; half day, $16; three days, $63; five days, $105; seven days, $147. Beginner lifts only: full day, $15; half day, $10.

Good news: Alta *does* take credit cards now.

Accommodations

Most ski packages include lodging, breakfast and dinner. If you book a package, be aware that most hotels will require you to purchase lunch as well. If your package is at a condominium, meal requirements do not apply.

Another irritation is that, as a general rule the lodges do not accept credit cards, though they do accept approved checks. Hotels will automatically add a 15percent service charge, as well as local taxes. Always ask if your room has a private bath; some of them do not. Rates from 1990/91.

Rustler Lodge (tel. 801-742-2200) thought by many to be Alta's most luxurious, is midway between the Albion and Rustler/Wildcat base areas. It has an outdoor pool, saunas and Jacuzzis. Low season is mid-December, then again after New Year's weekend for the rest of January and the second week of April. Prices include breakfast and dinner, per person, double occupancy. Small room with twins or queen is $89 without private bath, $119 with; large is $139. Low season rates are 10-15 percent less.

Alta Peruvian (tel. 801-453-8488 or 801-742-3000 reservations only) is the other option for those who seek fine accommodations. It has similar amenities, features movies each night, and is a short walk from the Wildcat base. The rates include breakfast, lunch, dinner and lift ticket. Double room with private bath range from $126 to $138 (per person, double occupancy).

Goldminer's Daughter (tel. 801-742-2300 or 800-453-4573 for reservations only), named after a huge mining claim, is closest to the Wildcat lift. That translates to step out your door into the lift line, and drop by to your room in between runs for a hat or neck gaiter. Recently expanded with a lofty atrium dining area, all rooms have private bath. Per-person double occupancy rates with breakfast and dinner are $79 to $85 during regular season. Dorm rooms are $69. Additional children are charged $35.

Two large condominiums, **Hellgate** (tel. 801-742-2020) and **Blackjack** (tel. 801-343-0347) are located between Alta and Snowbird, with Blackjack better situated for skiing between the two resorts and therefore slightly higher, although Hellgate has van service to the ski areas. Studios range from $132 to $140; one-bedrooms sleeping four, $165 to $220; two-bedrooms sleeping six, $216 to $295; three-bedrooms, $275 to $365. There is no service charge.

There are several RV parks open all winter surrounding Salt Lake, the closest of which is Mineral Springs in Draper; (801) 571-4024.

Dining

At Alta you eat in your condo or your hotel, and if you're headed for a condo, stop in Salt Lake for groceries.

On the slopes, **Chic's Place** is a fine if unpretentious restaurant serving homey cooking for moderate prices.

Après-ski/nightlife

Bring your own. There's nothing going on but what visitors cook up—either in their condominium living rooms or the hotel bar. Try Snowbird, except on Sunday and Monday nights, when the action there matches Alta. The most night action you'll get in Little Cottonwood are the chipmunks. Salt Lake City is only 45 minutes away.

Child care

Alta's child care center is in the Albion Day Lodge (tel. 801-742-3042) with programs for children three months to 12 years which include lunch and appropriate types of on-snow activities, including ski lessons if desired.

All-day infant care by reservation only is $50; $200 for a five-day package. All-day child care with lunch is $35; $135 for a five-day package.

Other activities

Heliskiing is available in Little Cottonwood Canyon from Wasatch Powder Birds, (801) 742-2800.

Getting there

Alta is 25 miles southeast of Salt Lake City in Little Cottonwood Canyon on State Highway 210. Driving time from the city or the airport is one hour, with the most direct route from the airport east on I-80, south on I-215, Exit 6 to Wasatch Blvd., then follow the signs to Alta.

You can get here from the airport by limousine, taxi, rental car, bus and helicopter. Canyon Transportation vans and Utah Transit Authority buses to Little Cottonwood Canyon can be secured at the Transportation Desk, or make advance reservations at Central Reservations or with Canyon Transportation at (801) 942-1108 or (800) 255-1841. UTA buses leave the airport almost every hour. Fare is $6 each way.

From downtown hotels, UTA buses leave every 10 or 15 minutes between 8 a.m. and 9 a.m., with a similar schedule returning in the afternoon. Call 262-5626 to find its nearest stop to your lodging. Fare is $3 each way but it's time consuming because there are many stops. Lewis Brothers Stage Line (800-826-5844; 801-359-8347) picks up at hotels each morning, returns in the afternoon and is more direct. Bus service links Alta and Snowbird for $1.

Salt Lake is a major Amtrak and bus depot, and Salt Lake International Airport has facilities for private planes.

Tourist Information

The Alta Reservations Service is the central reservations agent for Alta; call (801) 942-0404. The agency can also arrange rental cars and rooms in Salt Lake City. Alta Lifts is at (801) 742-3333. Recorded snow report is (801) 572-3939.

Snowbird, Utah

Big-time skiing, deep powder and fast ascents are the hallmarks of Snowbird skiing. The descents are up to you, but if you're a powder skier, Snowbird is the Promised land. An eight-minute tram ride to the summit is all it takes to taste what has earned Snowbird's legend as the supreme powder skier's domain. In a discussion on heli-skiing, Canadian powder guides said they measured their powder by Snowbird standards. "Ayuh, it's good, but it's not quite Snowbird powder," they said. It's hard to imagine a more flattering comparison, and Little Cottonwood Canyon, where Snowbird is located, gets an average of 500 inches of it a year.

So what's its difference from Alta, just over the ridge? Snowbird has 1,000 more feet of vertical—and it's all skiable in one long run from the top of the tram right back down to the Cliff Lodge. An intermediate would find Snowbird a heady experience, not just manageable, but loads of fun. Don't let the "Banzai" photo intimidate—in all the years we've been checking out Snowbird, none of us has ever seen anyone coming out of the trams on the fly; it's probably illegal. The closest we've come is to see Santa being lowered from the tram just after the Christmas Eve parade of lights, throwing candy to children.

Another difference from Alta: Snowbird is sleek, high-tech. Its tram carries 125 skiers 3,100 feet to the summit in eight minutes; its lifts have footrests; its Resort Center is modern. Snowbird celebrates its twentieth anniversary in 1992; Alta is over fifty.

Snowbird Facts
Base elevation: 7,900'; **Summit elevation:** 11,000'; **Vertical drop:** 3,100 feet
Number of lifts: 8—1 aerial tram, 7 double chairs
Snowmaking as percent of area: none **Total acreage:** 2,000
Uphill capacity: 9,000 per hour **Bed base:** 900+

While the blue and red tram has become Snowbird's trade image, and the powder has long been its mystique, the stark and monstrous Cliff Lodge has become its man-made hallmark. Set against soaring, craggy mountains, the gray concrete-and-glass hotel, spa and conference center exudes total functionality. Its blocklike form dominating the valley. Walking from your room to the bar, or from a restaurant to a club, may seem to some like taking a stroll through a bomb shelter (this might be a perfect location to film James Bond infiltrating a secret military facility). Nevertheless, inside, the views are spectacular, the restaurants and clubs tastefully decorated, the food wonderfully prepared, the service extraordinary, the rooms comfortable—and sooo accessible to the slopes.

There is no town. Other than a clustering of restaurants, shops and skier services in another large modern resort center at the base of the tram, and three huge condominium complexes, that's all there is at Snowbird. Except, ah yes, the snow.

The Skiing

To get the lay of the land at Snowbird, understand first the function of the tram. Mounting one lower peak, hanging across a cirque and rising to the 11,000 foot summit, it brings 125 skiers at a time to Hidden Peak, unseen from the base lodge. On powder days, when the first tram arrives, there's a dash for the slopes. Skiers hurl their equipment and then themselves over the railings in order to make the "first tracks." After the thrill of doing this, things calm down a bit. Now decisions can be made whether to get equipment on quickly and be the first of the 125-person group down the cirque or wait a bit, let others dash, and then go where they don't.

The choices are to drop under the tram into Peruvian Gulch, with intermediate, advanced and expert routes down, or to head left into the Little Cloud area.

Most tram riders opt for Peruvian. Intermediates peel off the upper ridge at Chip's Run, often marked with large orange balls as "Easiest Way Down," but offering a few expert options en route. Experts tackle The Cirque, a plunge beginning the route that drops into almost 3,000 vertical feet of expert slopes. You can choose a run about as steep as you want, some with chutes that hold only powder enough to slow your virtual freefall. Anyone who has dropped down upper Silver fox, Great Scott or Upper Cirque (marked with yellow warning stripes on the trail map) deserves to be treated with reverence—they're using up the extra lives they were blessed with.

From the tram ridge, Primrose Path is an unrelenting black diamond, normally the choice of those who think twice about tiptoeing around The Cirque. The lower section of the Peruvian side of the ridge offers five trails marked expert, but here at Snowbird, what you can see you can normally ski. So pick your own way.

Should you decide to drop over to the Little Cloud side of Hidden Peak from the tram terminal, the skiing is somewhat tamer. That's tamer by Snowbird standards. It's a wide, wide scoop carved out of the side of the mountain, with cliffs above and swoops below. Here, Little Cloud, the highest black run, skirts along the top of the bowl and then drops down a third of the resort's distance to Little Cloud lift for a quick ride up the bowl again, or halfway down to the Mid Gad Restaurant. Entering the bowl a bit lower than Little Cloud run, Regulator Johnson charts a more direct, steeper route to either destination.

There are five lifts stretching out of Gad Valley. Wilbere is short and serves beginners and intermediates. Mid Gad and Gad I lifts rise higher and primarily serve wide intermediate slopes. Mid Gad serves a run called Big Emma, which gives beginners the feel of covering ground. You get more vertical for your ride on Gad I and can access some mid-mountain expert runs. A good starter for upper intermediates is Bassackwards. When that's as smooth as silk, they can stretch themselves on a black run called Carbonate, where they'll get the feel of a steeper, but not terrifying, pitch. The expert terrain is up higher at Gad II lift, which opens narrower trails through the trees and over megabumps. Two trail names tell the story—Gadzooks and Tiger Tail, but Black Forest and Organ Grinder are equal challenges.

Real beginners shouldn't tackle the Wilbere lift until they've learned a modicum of control on Chickadee, purely a first-timer's short slope.

The resort sells day passes that do not include the tram, for a saving of 20 percent.

A coin-operated mechanical race course is set up between Wilbere lift and Mid Gad lift, accessible from either.

Note: A good way for first-time visitors to explore Snowbird's mountain is the Snowbird Host and Hostess Program. It provides free introductory tours of the mountain, taking skiers to the part best suited to their abilities. Tours meet at the "Free Guided Tour" sign, plaza level of the Snowbird Center. They leave daily at 9 a.m., 10 a.m. and 1 p.m. This is not the normal meet-the-mountain tour some resorts offer, often sticking to intermediate and beginner terrain and seeming to move at a snail's pace: the hosts sort out the groups skillfully and then move off to appropriate terrain. It's a great way to meet people.

Every day the mountain operations staff designs a Fun Run marked by large orange balls that show the easiest way down from the tram. The route changes slightly based on conditions and grooming, although Snowbird feels a major commitment to groom every possible part of the mountain every night.

If you want to avoid crowds, start at 9 and ski Gad II and Little Cloud until 11. Then for the next hour and a half, work the Gad Valley chairs. Between 12:30 and 1:30 the lines lighten up and you can go back to the top. Remember, however, that even a 20-minute wait for the tram is equivalent to two lifts; you get more skiing for your wait. If you want to ski in the sun, the Gad Valley lifts are more protected and get morning sun. In the afternoon, head up to Little Cloud.

Mountain Rating

Experts, you have arrived in Mecca. A healthy half of Snowbird terrain is for you.

Intermediates, expect to be pushed. Owner Dick Bass, who has climbed the highest mountain on every continent, affirms, "What we gain too easily we esteem too lightly." Let that be your rallying cry. You will improve more here than at most other areas, a phenomenon you may not recognize until you go back to ski those "home slopes" you thought were a challenge. Intermediates will be comfortable on half the mountain: 30 percent of the terrain is designated intermediate, 20 percent beginner. If Snowbird exhausts you or you're here for a week and know by heart all the routes in your comfort zone, go up the valley to Alta which has more mellow intermediate trails.

Beginner, yes, you can learn here, but the pickings are slim. It might be better to go to Alta or Brighton for your baptism on skis.

Snowboarding

Snowboarding is permitted on all of the mountain, although there are no special facilities. Instruction is $25 for a one-and-a-half-hour class.

Ski School (91/92 prices)

The instructional menu is varied. There are racing clinics, adult learn-to-ski clinics, and a Super Clinic which includes videotaping. The Mountain Experience is a Snowbird marque, letting a skier of advanced or expert class join a member of the Snowbird ski family and launch an assault on the entire mountain. Silver Wings presents skiers over 50 with the opportunity to ski with people of the same ability and age group. Mountain Experience, Super Clinic, and Silver Wings are $65 for one day (five hours), $180 for three days, $275 for five days. Learn-to-Ski Clinics are $40 for a full day, $25 for half day. Adult Skiing Enhancement Clinics are $40 for a three-hour group lesson, $105 for three days, $155 for five days.

For children, a Chickadee one-and-a-half-hour lesson is $35, including lift ticket. A lesson and full-day supervision with lunch is $59. A full-day Mountain Adventure, Kinderbird or Children's Classic is $50; half day is $35. Three days is $135; five days is $200.

Private lessons are $55 per hour, with $20 for each additional person. A 3-hour, half-day lesson is $140, with $35 for each additional person. A all-day (6-hour) lesson is $250, with $50 for each additional person.

Ski School offices are in Cliff Lodge and Snowbird Center. Morning classes meet on the plaza level near the skiers' bridge; afternoon classes meet on Big Emma.

Lift tickets (91/92 prices)

Full day (with tram) is $36 for adults; $21 for children (12 and under) and seniors over 62. Full day, chairs only, is $29/$16. Half day with tram, a.m. or p.m., is $29/$16. Half day chairs only, a.m. or p.m., is $23/$14. Three to seven consecutive-day lift tickets are available for $31/$20 per day.

Children under 12 who are staying at Snowbird ski free when an accompanying adult purchases a lift ticket. Seniors 70 and over also ski free.

Accommodations

Lodgings at Snowbird consist of the ultra-modern Cliff Lodge and three additional condominium lodges, all built within walking distance of the base lifts. Additional accommodations, accessible by shuttlebus, are plentiful in Salt Lake City (see "Getting There"). For reservations at the four Snowbird lodges call (800) 453-3000 or (801) 742-2222. Snowbird has four pricing seasons: Peak season is basically Christmas, February and March; early season is early December; value season is January after New Year's Day; and late season is April through June. The multiday rates include vouchers that are redeemable for lift tickets at Snowbird, Alta or at the Park City area resorts for an additional charge. These vouchers can also be used for selected spa treatments at the rate of $30 a voucher.

The Cliff Lodge spreads like eagle's wings in flight at the base of Snowbird. In summer, climbers have been known to scale its sides and curved overhang. In fact, if you look hard at Chickadee lift you can see the pitons. Inside, there's an 11-story atrium with glassed-in rooftop and snow-level dining. Rooms with picture windows opening from the shower into the sleeping area add a touch of whimsy as well as a view. The pool, fitness center and spa on top of the hotel offer every variety of body rejuvenation, active and passive. The Cliff Lodge has six restaurants, a children's center, in-room babysitting, full-service beauty salon, aerobics classes, ski check and just about anything else the staff can arrange. Rates based on double occupancy are $87-$97 per person a night during peak season, and $69-$79 during value season. One-bedroom deluxe suites start at $237 per person a night during peak season or $119 during value season. Two-bedroom deluxe suites start from $379 per person a night during peak season or $312 during value season. Children under 12 stay free with adults.

The Lodge at Snowbird, The Inn, and **The Iron Blosam** are three condominium complexes with similar layouts.

They're suitable for friendly groups or families. There's no valet parking or room service, and the surrounding are not as elegant as the Cliff Lodge, but the condos are well maintained, roomy and comfortable. Amenities include outdoor swimming pools, indoor hot tubs, saunas. Iron Blosam requires a bit of an uphill walk to the tram and base facility, but is just across the street from the short Wilbere Lift. Rates during peak season are $179 a night for an efficiency or studio; $336 for a one-bedroom unit; and $493 for one-bedroom with loft. During value season, the rates are $145, $270 and $395 respectively.

Dormitory space is available for $25-$40 a night at the Cliff Lodge.

There are several RV parks open all winter surrounding Salt Lake although there are none in Little Cottonwood Canyon. The closest is Mineral Springs in Draper; 571-4024.

Dining

The Aerie on top of the Cliff Lodge is Snowbird's most elegant for exquisite dining and dancing. The **Atrium** at lobby level serves cocktails and wonderful hefty buffet breakfasts. **The Mexican Keyhole**, also in the Cliff Lodge, offers adequate Mexican fare.

Other restaurants are in the base facility, Snowbird Center. **The Steak Pit** is a generic Chart House which serves hefty portions for hungry skiers. There's normally a wait to get in, but it's worth it. Across from the entrance to the tram on the plaza level is **The Forklift**, a great lunch spot with easy access back up the slopes yet with a carpeted, clothed restaurant atmosphere rather than a burger and chili cafeteria. For that need go downstairs; the cafeteria is one of the "carry your tray to different stations" variety, with a well-stocked salad island in the center.

For the best breakfast in the canyon, most locals vote for The Forklift.

The Lodge Club in the Lodge at Snowbird has a good light dinner, and the **Wildflower** in the Iron Blosam serves up good pasta.

Après-ski/nightlife

Unless you're staying at Alta, you'll find Snowbird's nightlife on the quiet side. When the area's brochure highlights the video arcade as a spot for nightlife, you know you're in trouble if you're a reveler at heart.

For immediate après-ski, The **Forklift** and the **Wildflower Lodge** are your best bets. In the evening, **The Aerie** has a bar with quiet piano music and the Atrium might have an acoustic guitar or small jazz group, or a Christmas ensemble during the holidays. There is also a comedy circuit which takes place in Snowbird Wednesday through Saturday. The show costs $10.75.

Child care

Year-round, Snowbird offers its lodge guests licensed day care at the Cliff Lodge Children's Center for toilet-trained children three years and older. Charges for the 1991/92 season were $33 a day and $23 for a half day, which includes lunch. The hourly rate is $5.50, with a one-hour minimum. Daytime babysitting is provided, with a two-week advance reservation required, for $8 an hour. Evening sitter service is $7 an hour, with one-day advance reservation required. The front desk at your lodge will have more information, or call the Children's Center at 742-2222, Ext. 5026. The Children's Center services are also open to day-skiers not staying in Snowbird, on a space-available basis.

The Ski School handles programs that combine ski instruction with day care.

Other Activities

There is no cross country skiing or snowmobiling in Little Cottonwood Canyon, but spectacular helicopter skiing is available from Wasatch Powderbird Guides operating out of the Cliff Lodge, Box 57, Snowbird UT 84092; 742-2222, ext. 4190 or 4191.

Perhaps the major activity other than skiing is the Cliff Spa Program. Treatments range from shiatzu massage to being wrapped in volcanic ash and paraffin mold.

The spa is open from 6 a.m. until 11 p.m. daily, and the salon is open from 9 a.m. until 9 p.m. A half-day and full day packages are available. Call 742-2222, Ext. 5900 for spa services, Ext. 5960 for the salon.

Getting There

Snowbird is located 25 miles southeast of Salt Lake City in Little Cottonwood Canyon on State Highway 210. Driving time from the city or Salt Lake International Airport is 35-45 minutes. Most direct route from the airport is east on I-80, south on I-215, exit on Wasatch Blvd. (Exit 6), then follow signs to Alta.

From the airport, limousines, taxis, rental cars, buses and helicopters are available. Canyon Transportation vans and Utah Transit Authority buses heading into the canyon can be secured at the Transportation Desk. UTA buses leave the airport every 45 minutes from 9:30 to 11 a.m., then every hour and a quarter from 12:15 p.m. to 3:45 p.m. Fare is $6 each way.

From downtown hotels, UTA buses leave every 10 or 15 minutes between 8 a.m. and 9 a.m., with a similar schedule returning in the afternoon. Call 262-5626 to find its nearest stop to your lodging. Fare is $3 each way but it's time-consuming because there are many stops. Lewis Brothers Stage Line (800-826-5844; 801-359-8347) picks up at hotels in the morning, too, and delivers in the afternoon and is more direct. UTA operates a shuttle service between Alta and Snowbird for $1.

Salt Lake is a major Amtrak and Trailways bus depot, and Salt Lake International Airport has an airstrip for use by private planes.

Information/reservations

Central reservations number is (800) 453-3000. The resort address is Snowbird Ski and Summer Resort, PO Box 929000, Snowbird UT 84092-9000; 521-6040, or 742-2222, which is also the snow report number.

Telephone area code is 801.

Big Cottonwood Canyon

Solitude Ski Resort and Brighton Ski Resort

Of any 10 skiers waiting at a bus stop in downtown Salt Lake City for the ski express, it's a sure bet that seven will board the Snowbird/Alta bu to Little Cottonwood Canyon. The other three will board the Brighton/Solitude bus to Big Cottonwood Canyon.

If you're one of the three, be prepared for a silent judgment of your skiing ability by the Snowbird/Alta seven.

One will start the waiting-for-the-bus small talk. "Where are you headed?" he'll ask with a jaunty smile, perhaps with the thought that his group may invite you along on their search for the Steep and Deep.

"Brighton," you answer with an equally jaunty smile.

Your questioner's smile fades as his eyes take in your clothing, how far above your head your skis extend, and whether there is a tell-tale rental-shop sticker at the binding. He's too polite to ask, "If you can't handle Snowbird or Alta, then what are you doing on *those* skis?"

Big Cottonwood Canyon's reputation as the place where the locals learn to ski has more to do with prices than terrain. Snowbird charges $36 a day to use its lifts; Solitude's ticket is $26 and Brighton's is a mere $21.

Neither area is as vast as its neighbors in the next canyon. But to dismiss these two areas as a playground where beginners whet their appetites for the real thing is to woefully underestimate the terrain. Solitude's Honeycomb Canyon has slopes that will bring out the adrenalin in the best of skiers. While Brighton's expert offerings are fewer, they're present.

Solitude Ski Resort

Solitude Facts
Base elevation: 8,000'; **Summit elevation:** 10,030'; **Vertical drop:** 2,040 feet
Number of lifts: 7—1 quad superchair, 2 triple chairs, 4 double chairs
Snowmaking as percent of area: none **Total acreage:** 1,100 plus 540 acres in Honeycomb Canyon
Uphill capacity: 10,750 per hour **Bed base:** 12,000 in Salt Lake City

Solitude has been making changes that will bring it into the Utah big leagues very soon. A redesign of its runs and lift system brought it the 1990 *Snow Country* magazine award for slope and trail design. It restored a 33-year-old building, the Roundhouse, into an elegant on-mountain restaurant. The resort also plans a new base village with an Alpine design, including a much-needed 60-room hotel.

There is now a logical progression from beginner to expert areas. Beginners start on the Link chair, a slow-moving lift that accesses a nearly flat, very wide, completely isolated run, Easy Street. Never-evers can learn here unintimidated.

Those with a bit of time under their slats move on to the Moonbeam II chair, where Little Dollie, Pokey Pine and Same Street will take them back down for another run. The next step is either the Apex or Sunrise chairs, where one green trail is surrounded by lots of blue.

The next level is the Powderhorn or Eagle Express chairs, where there are no green runs, just blue with a few black. If you can handle that, then you're ready for the Summit chair. From the top of the Summit chair, you can go one of three ways.

The first takes you back down to the Summit chair on some upper intermediate runs like Dynamite and Liberty. Eventually you'll meet the runs off the Sunrise chair, which will take you back to the base.

Way Number Two heads toward Brighton on the SolBright trail. You could go all the way over to Brighton, or you could head down Courageous, a cleared but steep black-diamond run clearly visible from the Summit chair. You also could head down Headwall Forest, where you pick your own line through the trees. Or you could jump into a couple of long, steep, narrow chutes you can see from the ridge.

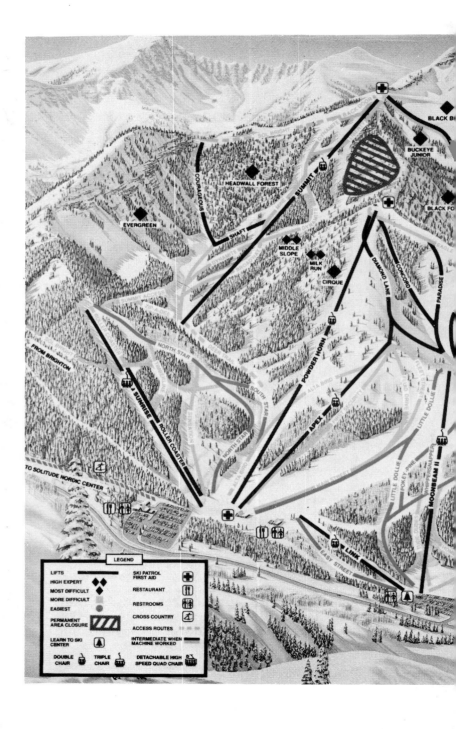

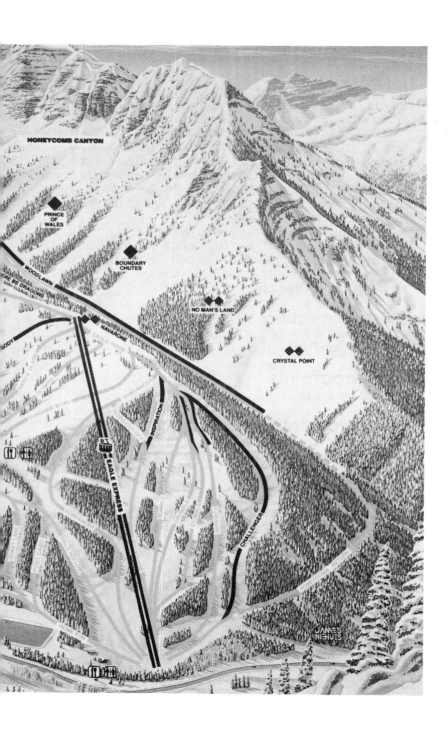

The third option will take you into Honeycomb Canyon, a wonderful playground for advanced intermediates and experts. Woodlawn is a marked run that follows the canyon floor. On the map it's a blue line, a black line overlapping it. Solitude should skip the blue line on the next printing: Woodlawn has some surprises that only a confident skier can handle. Chief among them are a couple of gigantic mogul fields and an extremely steep section that looks like it might be a small waterfall in the summer. Though covered with snow, not ice, it was a huge, sudden dropoff.

The canyon sides are an expert skier's delight. From the top, traverse until you find a line you like, then go for it. Honeycomb Canyon also can be reached from the Eagle Ridge run in the main part of the ski area, but this entry is strictly double-diamond through trees.

Mountain rating

Solitude is one of the few ski areas in the United States that has excellent terrain for all skier levels.

Snowboarding

Not permitted.

Cross-country (91/92 prices)

Right at the base of the mountain is the Solitude Nordic Center with 18 kilometers (11 miles) of machine-set track. A recent feature is an intermediate trail to Silver Lake, which starts at the top of the Sunrise lift (your Nordic pass will get you on).

Trail passes are $7 for those 13 and older, $4 for ages 8-12 and free for children younger than 8 and adults 65 and older. A half-day pass is $6.

A very popular new addition is yurt dining. You ski to a yurt, a round tent-like building popular with the nomads of Central Asia. There they have a gourmet meal and ski back. Reservations are a must for this, and don't be too disappointed if you can't get in. Salt Lake City residents really enjoy it and hog many of the available spaces. The cost is $45 per person, but no children younger than 8 are allowed. Call 272-7613 for reservations.

Lift tickets (91/92 prices)

Adult day ticket, $26. An afternoon ticket is $20. Children 12 and younger pay $16; seniors 65-74 pay $14. 75 and older ski free. The Link beginner lift is free, and a Moonbeam II-only is is $16. Multi-day discounts are available. A Big Cottonwood Pass, for both areas, is $36.

Ski School (91/92 prices)

A beginner package including rentals, lift ticket and a lesson is $34. Group lessons are $20. Private instruction is $40 per hour, with each additional person $20.

Child care

SKIwee is for children 4 to 7 years old. Quad Squad is for kids 8 to 12. A full-day lesson with lunch is $50; $30 for half-day without lunch. Solitude has no child care.

Brighton Ski Resort

> ## Brighton Ski Resort Facts
> **Base elevation:** 8,755'; **Summit elevation:** 10,200'; **Vertical drop:** 1,445 feet
> **Number of lifts:** 6—1 quad superchair; 1 triple chair, 3 double chairs, 1 rope tow
> **Snowmaking as percent of area:** 25 percent **Total acreage:** 575 trail acres
> **Uphill capacity:** 6,000 per hour **Ski area bed base:** 12,000 in Salt Lake City

Most of the cabins you'll see in Big Cottonwood Canyon have been in Utah families for generations. Families came here to rough it on winter holidays. Brighton retains a lot of that hardy log-cabin feeling.

Brighton has made some improvements, notably a high-speed detachable quad chair and a fairly new base lodge, but mostly it has a pioneer atmosphere.

Good beginner runs descend from the Majestic chair, and from the Snake Creek chair, which goes to the top of the mountain. Beginners ought to keep an eye out so they don't get off onto an intermediate trail: green and blue runs do a lot of intertwining here.

Intermediates have the run of practically the whole area. The Snake Creek chair is a little less crowded than the new Crest Express high-speed quad and the Majestic chairs. On this side of the area you'll find heavily wooded, fairly narrow runs. On the other side of the parking lot is the Millicent Chair and its wide-open terrain underneath. It's a little steeper over here, but with fewer trees.

Experts should try a short but heart-stopping run called Hard Coin off the Snake Creek chair. The trees are so thick that you can hardly pick a line, but it's a marked trail. Advanced skiers will enjoy the Millicent side of the ski area more, because of its steepness.

Mountain rating
Good for beginners and intermediates, and not bad advanced and expert skiing, although this pales next to the neighboring resorts..

Snowboarding
Allowed on the entire mountain. There is a halfpipe and rentals are available. Lessons cost $16.

Lift tickets (91/92 prices)
Adult day ticket, $21. An afternoon ticket is $18; one that extends to 9 p.m. is $26. Night skiing is $8. Children's prices are half-price, but two children 10 and younger can ski free with a paying adult. Seniors 70 and older ski free. A Big Cottonwood pass, good at both ski areas, is $36.

Ski School (91-92 prices)
Brighton is proud of its learn-to-ski programs. A beginners package including rentals, lift ticket and a lesson is $25. Group lessons are $16.

Private instruction is $40 per hour, with each additional person $20.

Kinderski is for children 3 to 6 years old. Lessons are one hour and 45 minutes, and cost $20 without equipment, $28 with. Classes are limited to five.

Child care
Brighton has no child care.

Accommodations
Most skiers stay in Salt Lake City (see pg. 218-222). The Brighton Lodge is a small, cozy lodge at the base of the lifts with heated outdoor pool, Jacuzzi and bar. Rates are

$75 per night for a room; $99 for a suite and $45 for an "economy hostel." Call (800) 873-5512 or (801) 532-4731.

Getting there

The Utah Transit Authority has excellent bus service from downtown Salt Lake City hotels.

Information

Solitude, Big Cottonwood Canyon, Box 17557, Salt Lake City, UT 84117 (801-534-1400)

Brighton Ski Resort, Brighton, UT 84121 (800-873-5512 outside Utah, 801-532-4731 in the state).

Sun Valley, Idaho

Sun Valley is an aging beauty who hasn't lost step with the times. America's first ski resort, built in 1936 by Union Pacific tycoon Averell Harriman, has put $8.1 million into an automated and computerized snowmaking system that covers half of Mount Baldy's groomed terrain, assuring Thanksgiving and Christmas skiing. The area that put up the world's first chair lift, designed by railroad engineers to take skiers up Dollar Mountain one at a time, now has North America's largest vertical lift.

However vast and varied the skiing, it's the Sawtooth Mountain shapes and the towns nestled below in a meandering valley that make the greatest impression. Nostaglia would be the one word to describe Sun Valley. It has a European accent mixed with the Wild West. It is isolated, yet comfortable; rough in texture, but also refined; Austrian in tone, cowboy in spirit.

This is Hemingway country, where the author wrote *For Whom The Bell Tolls* in Room 206 of the Sun Valley Lodge. Black-and-white lodge photos show Darryl Zanuck and the other Hollywood celebrities who first made the place famous. Sun Valley has developed or trained many famous athletes—also pictured: Gretchen Fraser, who was the first American Winter Olympic medalist in 1948, through Christin Cooper, a 1984 champion; ice skaters Peggy Fleming, Dorothy Hamill and Scott Hamilton.

The lodge is the heart of Sun Valley, a place to relax on terrace overlooks and in grand sitting rooms beneath cop-

---

Sun Valley Facts

BALDY: *Base: 5,740'; Summit elevation: 9,140'; Vertical drop: 3,400 feet*
DOLLAR: *Base: 6,010'; Summit elevation: 6638'; Vertical drop: 628 feet*
Number of lifts: 11—3 super quad chairs, 7 triple chairs, 5 doubles
Percent snowmaking: 33 percent **Total acreage:** *1,275 skiable acres*
Uphill capacity: 23,580 per hour **Bed Base:** *3,500*

pery chandeliers. Gleaming outside is a skating rink once ruled by ice queen Sonja Henie. *Sun Valley Serenade*, the 40s movie romance starring Henie and John Payne, and featuring music by Glenn Miller, is still shown in the village Opera House. The village is a 3,000-acre Alpine enclave of archways, wall paintings, snow sculptures, and spruce foliage set in a larger western retreat.

At last count, 42 coaches and participants in Olympic Games from 1936 to 1984 lived in the Wood River Valley. That tells you something of the pleasures of the outdoors here. The low-key magnificence attracts celebrities like Brooke Shields, Clint Eastwood, Janet Leigh, the original Batman Adam West, and Bruce Willis and Demi Moore, who have houses here.

Ketchum, about a mile west of Sun Valley, is a flash of red brick. It is a cut of prime rib at the Pioneer Saloon, Saltwater Grill chowder and oysters. The compact shopping and lodging district lies beneath the broad-shouldered, evergreen rise of Bald Mountain, which is draped with snow ribbons.

The town elevation of 5,740 feet rises to 9,140 feet on Baldy. On the River Run side of the mountain, closest to Ketchum, there is a large parking lot; limited parking around the mountain on the Warm Springs side, with two of the three high-speed quads, makes buses the way to go.

The ski terrain is best known for its consistency. Skiing Baldy is concentrating on turns from top to bottom, rather than snoozing off on a flat, or bailing out on a cliff or wall. Mile-long ridge runs lead to a clutch of advanced and intermediate bowls. There are short and long black-diamond challenges, and plenty of cruising territory. Twelve lifts serve the wraparound geography of the face and long Warm Springs trails.

Some magazine surveys have placed Sun Valley ahead of Aspen and Vail, with high marks given for short lift lines, romantic atmosphere, and intermediate descents.

Places like Elkhorn have seen considerable growth through condo projects, but the community as a whole has maintained its dreamy, hilly, tucked-away atmosphere as gateway to the immense, appropriately named Sawtooth Mountains.

The skiing

Sun Valley is a paradise for the intermediate and advanced skier. Trails are apt to be wide and long. Limelight is a long, excellent bump run for skiers with strong knees and elastic spinal columns. Of the other black descents, the Exhibition plunge is one of the best known. Fire Trail, on the ski area boundary, is a darting, tree-covered descent for those who can make quick, flowing turns. Above the bowls, on a clear day, the Seattle Ridge trail seems to go forever, with hypnotic views. The bowl area has something for every level of skier. The Warm Springs side has some marvelous cruisers. Beginners have a whole mountain across the valley, Dollar/Elkhorn.

Cross-country (91/92 prices)

There are 25 miles of cross-country ski trails, groomed and marked for difficulty, near the Sun Valley Lodge. They range from easy to isolated forest escapes. There is a half-track width for children as well as a terrain garden. The Sawtooth National Recreation Area, just north of Ketchum, has many trails and meadows. At Sun Valley the daily trail maintenance fee is $10.50, or $8.50 a half day after 1 p.m. Children 6-12 years old pay $6. A group lesson costs $12, a private lesson $43. Ski rentals cost $13, or $11 a half day after 1 p.m.; $8 for a child, $5 a half day.

Snowboarding

Dollar Mountain has a halfpipe and snowboarding events. Private lessons for all abilities are available on Dollar and Baldy Mountains, with reservations required.

Ski school (91/92 prices)

The Sun Valley Ski School has, in addition to private instruction, adult and children's clinics, a master's race clinic and ladies' clinic. Adult group lesson prices are $37 for one day (3 hours), $70 for two days, $100 for three days and $150 for five days (15 hours). Children's lessons include a supervised ski break and run four hours each day. They cost $47 for one day, $90 for two days, $130 for three days, and $195 for five days. Private lessons cost $58 per person for one hour to $130 for three hours. An all-day private lesson costs $270.

Lift tickets (91/92 prices)

One-day adult, $40; half-day adult, $29; three-day adult $110; five-day adult $180; one-day child (11 and under) $21; half-day child $15; three-day child $55; five-day child $90.

Accommodations (91/92 prices)

Standard rooms at the **Sun Valley Lodge** begin at $125 per night, $1,050 for seven days, and go up to $275 and $2,100 for parlor suites.

The Sun Valley Inn runs $100 for a standard room to $190 for a family suite. Packages are available. Condos run $100 to $280; condo suites $115 to $390. For information call (800) SUN VALY.

Elkhorn Resort, near the base of Dollar Mountain, has rooms ranging from $80 to $140, and condos from $120 to $265. Call (800) 635-9356. **The Tyrolean Lodge,** a Best Western, has rooms for about $75. Call (800) 333-7912.

Dining

Baldy Mountain has four restaurants. The nicest is the **Roundhouse,** with a huge stone fireplace and an outdoor deck that looks 2,000 feet below to the valley.

The **Sun Valley Lodge** dining room has old-time elegance and is the only spot in the community with live music and dancing with meals. Specialties include Steak Diane, $22.50, Chauteaubriand Béarnaise Bouquetière (for two), $49, and fresh Idaho trout or poached salmon, $22.

The Pioneer Saloon, a local hangout going back into Ketchum history, is known for its prime rib, priced $12.50 to $18.50. For French cuisine, **Chez Michel's** in Trail Creek Village is recommended. Meals run $40-$50.

A favorite Italian spot, **Louie's,** in an old church, is a family place with a wide-ranging menu, and super pizza.

If you like fish, try the **Saltwater Grill.** Red Snapper Cartagena costs $13.95, Salmon En Croute $16.95, Coquilles St. Jacques, $14.95.

The lunch and après-ski spot that draws well is **Baldy Base Camp.** It's where the stars are seen.

Après-ski/nightlife

Sun Valley's historic landmark, the **Ram Bar**, has comedy shows and music. **Elkhorn Village Saloon** has comedy and music. The Fabulous Varnettes, an all-female cabaret-type show, plays Tuesday, Friday and Saturday nights. **The Creekside Bar and Grill** at Warm Springs has half a dozen concerts a year featuring groups like Kilimanjaro and Bonnie Raitt. **Whiskey Jacque's** in Ketchum has live music and attracts a young crowd. **The Opera House** at Sun Valley has Warren Miller movies, Sonja Henie's *Sun Valley Serenade*, and recent releases.

Child care

Youngsters 17 and under, staying with a parent in a Sun Valley Company hotel or condo, can ski and stay for free for nearly 75 percent of the season.

Just-for-children ski school classes include a supervised lunch and a "ski break." These group classes are taught by a specially trained school staff.

Sun Valley's Playschool, located on the Sun Valley Mall, offers supervised activities, hot lunches and ice skating. Reservations are required 622-2288.

Getting there

Friedman Memorial airport, 12 miles south of the resort in Hailey, is served by Horizon Air and Delta's SkyWest Airlines. Sun Valley Company guests receive complimentary transportation.

Charter bus service is available to Sun Valley from Boise, Idaho Falls, Twin Falls, and Salt Lake City.

Get around the town and the ski areas with the free shuttlebus linking Sun Valley, Ketchum and Baldy.

Information/reservations

For reservations and information call (800) SUN VALY. For the snow report call (800) 635-4150. The address is Sun Valley Company, Sun Valley, Idaho 83353.

Local telephone area code is 208.

Other Idaho ski areas

Bogus Basin Boise ID (800) 367-4397;
6 lifts, 45 trails, 1,790 vertical feet

Bogus Basin, where counterfeit gold was manufactured in the Western gold rush days, has no counterfeit ski slopes. Sixteen miles north of Boise and 168 miles west of Sun Valley, it is an area known to skiers who go beyond the big-name resorts in search of excellent sleepers. Bogus has first-rate glade skiing and its night skiing is up there with any in the country. Several black runs as well as intermediates and beginners are lighted, twelve in all. They take a skier through enchanted forests to the backside and flanks of a low but wide mountain crown (7,590 feet at Shafer Butte, the summit), offering scintillating city, valley and mountain views. Bogus Basin is open 13 hours on Saturdays and Sundays, 12 hours weekdays, so that a skier hot for vertical feet can find true exhaustion. An impressive 2,600 skiable acres (Sun Valley has 1,275) offers a great variety of terrain. The ski school, with 130 instructors, is one of the largest in the Northwest. The mountain has two restaurants and the 70-unit Pioneer Inn halfway up the slopes; lift lines are rare.

Schweitzer Mountain Resort Sandpoint ID (208) 263-9555;
6 lifts with superchair, 48 trails, 2,400 vertical feet

This is Idaho's second largest ski area, and first when it comes to snow. With a drought afflicting many Western areas the last few years, Schweitzer has fallen from its normal 120-130 inches of snowpack at the summit to 110 inches on top and 72 at the base. The mountain presents challenges, with almost a third of its slopes advanced to expert, and has two large bowls and trails cut through old cedar forests. Terrain is handsome and far-flung. The new 82-room Green Gables Lodge at the base is Idaho's No. 1 ski hotel, a smaller version of Canada's chateau-style Canadian Pacific hotels. Schweitzer, in fact, is by design becoming a smaller version of Canada's Whistler/

Blackcomb, with hotels above commercial shops, brick paved plazas, and underground parking.

Eight miles down the road is the pretty lakeside village of Sandpoint, frequented in summer by residents of Spokane, 72 miles southwest. Pend Oreille, Idaho's largest lake, is a marvelous water picture beneath the slopes.

Silver Mountain

Kellogg ID (70 miles east of Spokane), (800) 678-8633, (208) 783-1111; 4 chair lifts, 43 trails, 2,200 vertical feet

Kellogg is trying to go the route of Crested Butte, Telluride, Park City and other boom-to-bust Western mining towns that came back with skiing. As the silver mining plays out here, the skiing plays in. The world's longest single-stage gondola offers a 16-minute ride above part of the old town to the ski area, rising from 2,300 feet to 5,700 feet. Three forested, north-facing bowls present intermediate trails and challenging walls and glades. If you took all the trails you'd ski 15 miles and enjoy many handsome views. There is a feeling of seclusion, of getting away from it all, on this mountain. Kellogg has only 150 beds, but the Coeur d'Alene resort, situated on one of the West's most beautiful lakes, has packages including lodging, lifts and transportation to and from the slopes. Far-off ski clubs have booked very good deals—one from New Jersey, for instance, had a 7-night, 5-day package with air, for $699. "A deal I couldn't refuse," said a member used to paying much more for trips to Colorado.

Brundage Ski Mountain

McCall, Idaho (800) 888-7544, (208) 634-4151
3 chair lifts, 3 surface lifts, 32 trails, 1,800 foot vertical

Payette Lake, which Brundage overlooks, is an unknown Lake Tahoe. It is beautiful and unpopulated, with many outdoor activities including good intermediate downhill skiing. Numerous local skiers have been in the Winter Olympics, and every February the town has a Winter Carnival. From the top of the mountain, the Salmon River Mountains, Payette Lakes, Oregon's Eagle Cap Wilderness and the Seven Devils towering over Hells Canyon, America's deepest river gorge, can be seen. The skiing on 1,300 acres is pleasant and uncrowded, with occasional challenging drops, but mostly cruisers.

The Big Mountain
Whitefish, Montana

This big mountain tucked into the far northwest corner of Montana is a spectacular surprise for dedicated skiers who have not yet discovered it. The resort and the community are working hard to break out of the undiscovered category. PR and advertising efforts aside, the people of Whitefish and The Big Mountain, quick to greet you with a smile and friendly "howdy," are turning visitors into believers. Their genuine hospitality and the splendor of unspoiled nature, where hoarfrost-crusted trees frame the rugged peaks of Glacier National Park are the ingredients that make for destination greatness.

The best way in and out of the area is still by train and the most popular nightlife event in Whitefish seems to be the mouse races. But if you love to ski and that's the real reason you plan a ski vacation, this really is a big mountain in no uncertain terms—the skiing is fabulous.

The ski area is eight miles from the town of Whitefish, up a long and winding access road that can be treacherous in bad weather. At the ski area base there is a cluster of five hotels and a circle of condos with a few restaurants and bars. Don't expect anything too ritzy. This is a down-home comfortable place where a fur coat would look out of place except on a grizzly-bearded mountain man. Folk who choose to stay on the mountain come here to ski and

---

Big Mountain Facts
Base elevation: 4,800'; **Summit elevation:** 7,000'; **Vertical drop:** 2,300 feet.
Number and types of lifts: 9, including 1 superchair, 1 quad, 4 triples, 1 double and 2 surface lifts **Acreage:** 3,000 skiable acres, 50 marked trails
Percent of snowmaking: 1 percent Three trails, top to bottom
Uphill capacity: 11,270 skiers per hour **Bed base:** 1,500 on mountain

take it seriously. Après-ski is basic beer and burger variety followed by a well-deserved hot tub and discussions about the day's skiing in front of the lodge fireplace. For dinner, carbo loading is *de rigueur* rather than picking at a sparse nouvelle creation.

Down the mountain in Whitefish you'll find more hotels, the best restaurants in the area, shopping and virtually all the nightlife. If you're planning on focusing on more than simply skiing during your stay here, set up camp in town. Whitefish is a town where one can slow down, relax and enjoy life. The most excitement may be generated by the arrival of the train or the passage through town of one of the movie or football stars who seem to be making this one of their favorite getaways. Mind you, the excitement is stirred mainly in the tourist population—locals seem barely to notice.

The weather here is a mix of the Rockies and Pacific Northwest maritime. They call it "inland maritime." The climate creates spectacular snow monsters which frost up around the trees at the summit, and also means plenty of snow. Somehow it produces fantastic light powder but without the sunshine you'll find in the southern Rockies. If you forget your sunscreen you'll probably survive, but don't forget your goggles.

The Skiing

Ski anywhere on the mountain you dare. This is not a resort limited to cut trails and in-bounds bowls. Within the sprawling 4,000 acres of mountain everything is in bounds. The Big Mountain has a mountain host program with free tours of the mountain daily.

The main access to The Big Mountain is the high-speed superchair, The Glacier Chaser, which moves skiers up over 2000 feet of vertical to the summit, surrounded by snow ghosts, and serves almost all The Big Mountain's terrain. If you want to ski the front side of the mountain, all is accessible from The Glacier Chaser. If you ski straight ahead when you get off the superchair you'll drop down the north slope, a mostly intermediate series of runs alternating with tree-studded steeps. The return to the summit is by Chair 7.

If you make a U-turn when when you get off the Glacier Chaser you'll reach wide and well-groomed intermediate trails that drop from the summit. Toni Matt, The Big Ravine or North Bowl are all perfect for power cruising with wide GS turns. Both Toni Matt and the Big Ravine provide top-to-bottom cruising with 2,000 feet of vertical. On the backside of the mountain, the North Slope has another collection of long intermediate trails.

All of these groomed runs are surrounded by fields of powder and thousands of trees beckoning to advanced and expert skiers. Good Medicine defines The Big Mountain experience. This is more an area of the mountain than a defined run through the trees. Through the entire Good Medicine area skiers can choose how tight they want their trees, and they have plenty of opportunities to bail out onto the groomed trails. Locals also can direct you to Movie Land, which starts with dense trees and then opens for great steep tree skiing before ending on Easy Street.

For those who insist on getting air, The Big Mountain has a cornice next to the Summit House. Runs from this cornice and almost all skiing to the left of the superchair ends up on Easy Street.

Advanced beginners will spend most of their time on Chairs 2 and 3 and the T-bar until they make the leap up to the summit on The Glacier Chaser. This advanced beginner area is also the part lighted for night skiing. Trails from the new Chair 6 are new beginner options.

Mountain Rating

A friend described Big Mountain as an intermediate Jackson Hole. This is a wide-open, ski-anywhere-you-can mountain with consistent pitch and the added intrigue of nature's own slalom course through acres of frosty pines. Experts can find their share of thrills and extreme skiing, but it is the tree skiing that makes this a delight ifor good skiers. Advanced skiers can dance between wide cut trails and the trees, testing their ability. Intermediates have long runs they'll dream about for days. Chair 6 now serves a good beginner area.

Cross-country

The Big Mountain offers excellent cross-country for all levels of skinny-ski skiers. Next to the ski area, The Big Mountain Nordic Center has 8 km. of trails just

The Big Mountain - Montana

BACKSIDE

Montana - The Big Mountain

below Chair 4. Lessons and rentals are available (862-3511). Trail fees are $5 for adults, $2 for juniors (13-18), $1 for children (7-12) and free for anyone younger when accompanied by an adult. Downhill ski pass holders can use the cross-country trails for $2 a day.

Grouse Moutain Lodge (862-3000) offers 15 km. of groomed cross-country trails and the town's only night skiing with 5 km. lighted .

The Izaak Walton Inn (888-5700), 62 miles east on Highway 2 has 30 km. of groomed trails as well as guides who take skiers into the Glacier National Park wilderness. Guides for groups of two to three cost $75 per person and $60 each for groups of four or more (90/91 prices).

Glacier National Park provides a natural cross-country skier's paradise. Here the unplowed park roads and trails provide kilometer after kilometer of ungroomed passages into the heart of the mountains. Check with the local rangers or the communications center (888-5441) for current weather and snow conditions.

Snowboarding

The entire mountain is open for snowboarding. The rental shop has rentals and the ski school offers lessons costing $20 for a two-hour group lesson, or $35 for a two-hour private lesson. There is a natural halfpipe under Chair 7 on the north side of the mountain.

Ski school (92/93 prices)

Group lessons for a half day cost $20 and for a full day $32. Lesson packages for three half-day lessons are $54. Five half-day lessons are $90. Snowboarding and cross-country lessons are also available. For children's programs see the Child Care section. Senior citizens receive a 50 percent discount on group lessons.

Workshops for bumps, steeps and powder are given from 1:30 to 3:30 p.m. for $20. Special beginner lessons including lifts and lessons cost $18 for a two-hour session.

Private lessons require reservations (862-3511). Rates are $45 for an hour, $65 for one and a half hours, $105 for a half day (two and a half hours), and $225 for a full six-hour day.

Lift tickets (92/93 prices)

Since The Big Mountain has night skiing the lift ticket rates include a day rate from 9 a.m. to 4:30 p.m., and what the resort calls a swing shift rate from 1 to 10 p.m., good Wednesday to Sunday. This rate is $30 for adults; $23 for juniors 13-18, college students and seniors 62+; $15 for children 7-12; and free for those six and under.

Late arrival tickets (half-day tickets in normal skier language) cost $23 for adults, $19 for juniors and seniors, and $12 for children seven to 12. Night skiing costs $10 for adults; $8 for juniors and seniors, and $7 for children seven to 12.

Accommodations

The properties located at The Big Mountain village may all be reserved by calling (406) 862-3511 or (800) 858-5439. Regular season is January 4 through April 3. Value season is November 25 - December 17 and April 4-13. Holiday season is December 18 - January 3.

The Kandahar Lodge (862-6095) at The Big Mountain ski area looks like a mountain lodge should—wooden beams, spacious public areas and a soaring stone fireplace. The rooms are large, the food good and the loacation right on the slopes. A shuttle takes guests to the base area and at the end of the day skiers can glide right to the door. Regular season doubles cost $112 per night.

In the center of the ski area village is the **Alpinglow Inn** (862-6966). This lodging has beautiful views from the restaurant and perhaps the most convenient location for

A Chalet (Administration, Hellroaring Saloon)
B Big Mountain Ski Shop
C Alpinglow Inn
D Lodge (Moguls, Moose's on the Mountain, Ticket Office)
E Alpinsnack Cafeteria, Kiddie Korner Day Care
F Bierstube
G Edelweiss Condominiums
H Anapurna Alpine Homes Office, convenience store
I Kandahar Lodge
J Hibernation House, Big Mountain Alpine Homes Check-in
K Ticket Office
L Anapurna Alpine Homes and Big Mountain Alpine Village Homes

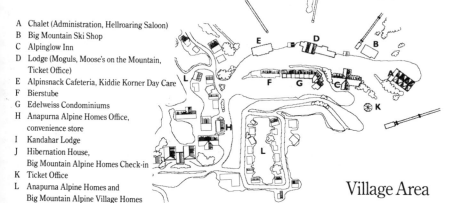

Village Area

skiers. Several of the rooms are packed with beds and most sport simple paneling . . . but you can't beat the location. Two persons pay $98 per night in regular season.

The Hibernation House (862-3511) is the economy bed-and-breakfast. Here rooms will house as many as five guests and there is also an indoor hot tub. Rooms for two during regular season are $70 per night.

Anapurna Properties and **The Big Mountain Village Homes** are the two main condominium management companies. Anapurna guests have access to the only indoor pool on the mountain.

The **Edelweiss Condominiums**, in the center of the village (862-5252) are part of the RCI organization, which offers timeshare swaps.

Down in Whitefish the **Grouse Mountain Lodge** (800-321-8822 or 406-862-3000) is the most comfortable and convenient hotel. Its rooms are spacious and a shuttlebus takes guests to the mountain every morning. There is cross-country skiing out the back door and downtown is only a short walk or ride away. Regular season double rooms rates are $65-$90.

The Duck Inn (862-3825; 800-344-2377) is set along the Whitefish River. Rooms feature brass or white iron beds, pine furniture and gas fireplaces. There is a Jacuzzi room with views of Big Mountain, 8 miles away, and of the river where geese provide entertainment. It is only one block from the WART shuttle. Rates are $60 a night per double room with breakfast.

The Garden Wall (862-3440) is an antique-filled B&B only a block from the city shuttle. This home is perfect for couples. Rates are $87 per night per double with breakfast.

The Castle Bed and Breakfast (862-1257), now in the National Register of Historic Places, is one of Montana's most unusual buildings. The living room is massive with a great fireplace. This house has three guest rooms, one with private bath, two with shared bath. Double rooms with breakfast are $52 to $78 per night.

Dining

This is a town where you find good honest American cooking, and that includes American-Italian, American-Chinese and Tex-Mex.

The **Summit House** serves dinners with a Glacier Park peak view on Wednesday and Saturday nights from 5:30 to 9 p.m. The Glacier Chaser chairs are replaced by gondola cars to whisk diners up the mountain for this special experience. Call 862-3511 for reservations.

At the base of the ski area the best food can be found at the **Hellroaring, Moose's** or **Mogul's Bar and Grill**. They are all casual eateries with relatively basic menus. Of the group, Mogul's Bar and Grill makes the most effort to be upscale. Other base area restaurants include the **Café Kandahar, Alpinglow Restaurant** with a great view, and the **Bierstube** for Back Door Burgers and such.

The bulk of restaurants are found down in Whitefish. The finest dining in the area is at **Logan's Bar and Grill** in the Grouse Mountain Lodge (862-3000) or across the street in the **Whitefish Lake Restaurant** (862-5285) at the golf course. **The Bistro** (862-8922) serves fine cajun meals in a tiny dining room packed with art. **The Glacier Grande** (862-9400) combines nightlife with Southwest dinners.

Dos Amigos (862-9994) is a basic Tex-Mex spot with a good selection of imported beers. At **Rocco's** (756-5834) you'll find good Italian seafood dishes as well as traditional Italian pastas and chicken, steak and veal Florentined and pizziola-ed. **The Coyote Roadhouse** (837-4250) is the spot to head for Cajun cooking and super-fresh fish. **Stumptown Station** (862-4979) grills up great steaks. **Jimmy Lee's** (862-5303) is the recommended Chinese restaurant if you have a craving for a stir-fry, straw mushrooms or Szechwan duck.

A bit out of Whitefish, in Kalispell, try **Diamond Lil's** and **Pancho Magoo's** if you're good and hungry.

For breakfast, the place to see and be seen is **The Buffalo Café** (862-BUFF) in Whitefish. If you can get a seat and listen a bit you'll hear about everything happening in town. Try the Buffalo Pie, layers of hashbrowns, ham, cheese and poached eggs, or order the Cinnamon Swirl French Toast; get a side order of chorizo if you decide to stick with basic eggs. It's open for lunch as well.

Après-ski/nightlife

As far as serious beer and nacho après-ski goes, head to the **Bierstube, Moose's on the Mountain,** or **Hellroaring Saloon** at the base of the lifts. These bars continue with nightlife and occasional live bands (five times a week at the Bierstube), but the action really depends on the crowd one finds staying up on the mountain. For something quieter try your hotel lounge and fireplace or hot tub.

Nightlife, for the most part, is centered downtown along Central Avenue in Whitefish. Having all the bars lined up makes it easy to check out the scene and decide where you want to set up camp. Choose from The **Great Northern, Glacier Grande Café, The Palace, Remington's, Bulldog Saloon, Casey's** or **Stumptown**. Each is notable in its own way. On Saturday nights the internationally famous mouse races are held at the Palace Bar—beyond that unique competition, the nightlife is relatively normal and a good time for those cruising for rock or country music and drinks. The only drag is getting back up the mountain if your lodgings are at the resort.

For quieter evenings try drinks at **Logans Bar at the Grouse Mountain Lodge** which features a band playing music with, as they call it, a "quieter accent."

For a real rowdy cowboy evening, complete with live foot-stomping music and longneck beer bottles, you can slip in your back pockets, head to the **Blue Moon Nite Club** in Columbia Falls at the intersection of Highways 2 and 40. It has live music Wednesday through Saturday. Ladies Night, on Wednesday, features free champagne. Beer flows for only 75¢ from 4 to 9 p.m. on Fridays.

Child care

The main day care facility on the mountain is the Kiddie Korner Child Care Center (862-3511, Ext. 455). Rates are all hourly and based on the age of the children. Care for those under 12 months or for any nonwalking infant costs $4.25 an hour. All other children are charged $3.25 per hour of child care. Reservations are recommended for all children and required for infants under 12 months and non-walkers. Lunches are provided for a nominal fee, or parents provide them or take their children out to lunch. Child care hours are 9 a.m. to 5 p.m.

The ski school has a variety of programs for kids starting at 3-4 years of age. For those 4-6 there are one- or two-hour Platter Lift Lessons costing $10 per hour. The program for younger children are in conjunction with the Kidie Korner Day Care Center. Ski school instructors will accompany children from the day care center for basic skiing lessons and snow fun. The full-day ski school program for older children includes five-hour lessons for $32 and half day lessons for $16. Lunch is optional and will cost an additional $6.

Other activities

Life at The Big Mountain and in Kalispell is not limited to only skiing during the winter. In the evenings there are sleigh ride dinners and sing-alongs. Near the ski area Old West Adventures has sleigh rides through the forests to an Old West roadhouse where hot drinks are served. On Saturday night the sleigh ride includes dinner and singing as well as a historical narrative about opening the West. Call 862-0606 for reservations.

Downtown in Whitefish sleigh rides leave the Grouse Mountain Lodge and slip twenty minutes to a camp near Lost Coon Lake. Call 862-3000 for reservations.

Snowmobiling is well organized in this part of the country. Groomed trails are maintained and a guide is available by calling the Flathead Convention and Visitors Association at (800) 543-3105. Several of the trails climb to the summit of The Big Mountain.

Snowcat powder skiing is also offered in areas of the mountain which will soon be developed for lift-served skiing. Snowcats cost $35 for four hours of skiing.

Dog sledding adventures provide a unique 12-mile tour of the wilderness. Call 881-2275 for more information.

Getting there

This resort, tucked in the far northwest corner of Montana, is a bit out of the way for skiers from most of the United States.

The nearest airport, Glacier Park International in Kalispell, is only 19 miles south of the resort. However, service in and out of this airport is limited to twice-a-day service on Delta from Salt Lake City and to several Horizon Air commuter flights from nearby Northwest area airports. Glacier Park International is also the nearest airport for private pilots.

Train transportation via Amtrak's Streamliners is the most important form of destination skier travel.

Trains stop twice daily eastward from Seattle and Portland and westward from Chicago and Minneapolis.

Driving to The Big Mountain is along some of North America's most scenic highways. Access south from Banff, Canada or north from Missoula is Highway 93. Highway 2 runs east and west through Kalispell on a northern tier, and I-90 takes a more southern route through Missoula, where travelers will turn north on Highway 93 to Kalispell.

Whitefish Area Rapid Transit (WART) links the greater Whitefish and Big Mountain areas on a limited basis approximately four times a day.

Nearest RV site is Whitefish RV Park on Highway 93 south.

Information/reservations

The Big Mountain maintains a central reservations system for all lodging on the mountain. Call (406) 862-3511 or (800) 858-5439 in U.S.; (800) 637-7547 in Canada.

For more information about the Flathead Valley and activities in Kalispell and Whitefish contact the Flathead Convention and Visitors Association at (800) 543-3105 or (406) 756-9091. The Whitefish Chamber of Commerce also provides information at (406) 862-3501.

Local telephone area code is 406.

Big Sky, Montana

Lone Mountain's glacial horn juts up there by itself at 11,166 feet, cutting the heavens above Big Sky Resort, north of Yellowstone.

Beneath the Big Sky horn is the new seven-floor Shoshone Condominum Hotel, and beside that a shopping mall. Wide-open beginner's and intermediate terrain create a 360-degree scenic wrap for a village that has both traditional European and ultra-modern architecture.

The resort has the feel of a mountain enclave plugged into big-city convenience. Sixty percent of the visitors fly in from Alabama and New Jersey and Minnesota. Everything is available in the considerable space of a village that changes in appearance and attitude, from rowdy and crowded in one section to stately and reserved in another. The resort is cavernous, modern and variable.

Big Sky opened in 1973, founded by TV announcer Chet Huntley and other investors. Everett Kircher, owner of Boyne Mountain in Michigan, bought Big Sky in 1976. John Kircher, Everett's son, has transformed the place in the last five years with new equipment, lifts and runs. In 1992, 230,000 skier days were recorded, up from 116,000 six years ago. However, they are all swallowed by the 1,500-acre terrain. A big daily turnout is 3,000, meaning short lines for the gondolas.

There is a European accent to the place. Ski school director Robert Kirchschlager is from Salzburg, Austria, and each year brings in English-speaking Europeans to teach. And each skier feeds a ski pass into machines

Big Sky Facts
Base elevation: 6,970'; **Summit elevation:** 10,000'; **Vertical drop:** 3,030 feet.
Number and types of lifts: 9, including 1 superchair, 1 gondola, 2 triples, 3 doubles and 2 surface lifts
Acreage: 1,500 skiable acres, 50 marked trails **Snowmaking:** 20 percent of trails
Uphill capacity: 11,100 skiers per hour **Bed base:** 1,500 on mountain

that open gates for lift rides, like the computer systems found in the Alps.

Nearly everyone who visits spends at least a day in Yellowstone, only an hour away. Snowmobiling and wildlife viewing there are spectacular.

The skiing

Two gondolas carry skiers up Lone Mountain, which has beginner, cruiser, mildly challenging and hair-raising descents. The Challenger lift provides 400 to 450 acres of bowl, glade and tree skiing on steep inclines and endless seas of bumps that grizzlies as far away as Yellowstone may see. Country Club surface tows serve the A-Z chutes, The Pinnacles and Parachute, which speak for themselves.

The resort averages more than 33 feet of snow a year, and most of this falls on gentle walls extending east to Andesite Mountain. Open Alpine meadows, groomed widths, occasional mogul fields, a challenging cornice and long sweeping descents are featured on Andesite.

In addition to the two high-speed gondolas, the area has six chair lifts and two rope tows. Fifty-five miles of skiing stretch over 50 slopes. The curve of the mountains gives each portion direct sunshine at different times of day. The longest run is 3 miles and average daytime temperature is 20 degrees. The vertical rise from the Mad Wolf base is 3,030 feet and from the village base, 2,530.

Mountain rating

The mountain is rated 20 percent beginner, 50 percent intermediate, 30 percent advanced.

Cross-Country

Nationally renowned Lone Mountain Guest Ranch offers more than 45 miles of groomed trails. Five miles from Mountain Village, the terrain is set in gently rolling hills. Scenic trails wind through forested areas, wide-open meadows and high Alpine terrain. Nordic ski lessons, rental equipment and guided tours are available. A favorite trip is a guided cross-country tour into Yellowstone National Park. Call (406) 995-4644.

Ski School

Ski School Director Robert Kirchschlager has more than 30 years of professional experience, 14 of them at Big Sky. His ski instructors come from the U.S. and Europe.

Group lessons cost $20 for half-day, $64 for 4 half-day sessions, $70 for 5 half-day sessions.

Seven different kinds of clinics cost $20 each.

The Learn to Ski package costs $30.

Private lessons cost $45 for an hour, $220 for full day lesson, with additional skiers paying extra.

For information call (406) 995-4211, Ext. 2189.

Lift Tickets

Half day: adult $28; children 12 and under, seniors 70 and older, $12; full day: $34 and $17.

Twilight: adult $34, child $17.

Night: adult $15 ; child $8 .

Multi-day rates: 2 days adult $68, child $34; 3 days adult $99, child $51; 4 days adult $128, child $68; 5 days adult $160, child $85; 6 days adult $186, child $102.

Accommodations

Big Sky is divided into three areas—the Mountain Village, the Meadow Village and the Canyon. Each area features vacation retreats ranging from lodge rooms to suites and one-to-five-bedroom condos.

In Mountain Village, **Hill**, **Stillwater**, **Arrowhead**, **Skycrest** and **Beaverhead** offer a full range of condos. Beaverhead and Arrowhead are ski-in, ski-out. Hill condos are Big Sky's most economical units, with studios at $85 and $95, and one bedroom with loft $130.

In Meadow Village, **Yellowstone** and **Glacier** feature indoor swimming pools. **Golden Eagle Lodge** is newly renovated and offers suites, a restaurant and bar.

For convenience and luxury at the Mountain Village, the 204-room **Huntley Lodge** and Shoshone Condominium Hotel has its own indoor pool and Jacuzzis, two restaurants, a cocktail lounge, gift shop and game room. The lodge runs $106-$164 for a single to $142-$203 for four people. It also includes the new Yellowstone Conference Center with a ballroom, amphitheater and breakout rooms. Call (800) 548-4486 or (406) 995-4211.

Dining

Huntley Lodge is known for its fine dining and one of Montana's largest wine selections. In the Mountain Mall, **Whiskey Jack** and **M.R. Hummers** are known for their house specialties. If you like Italian, try **Andiamo** in Arrowhead Mall.

In the Meadow Village, **First Place** is known for fresh seafood. **Cafe Edelweiss** has excellent Austrian and German food.

In the Gallatin Canyon, **Buck's T-4** is the Big Sky traditional spot for Montana beef, seafood specialties and wild game.

The **Lone Mountain Guest Ranch** features a gourmet dining room and a sleigh-ride dinner served in a log cabin where your meal is prepared on a 100-year-old wood stove to the melodic accompaniment of local folk singers.

Après-ski/nightlife

First check Big Sky's local newspaper, *The Lone Peak Lookout*, which has current entertainment listings.

The **Whiskey Jack** frequently features recording artisits such as The Guess and Nicolette Larson, as well as well-known local bands include Sgt. Rock, Sawmill Creek and Final Exam.

Montana Rose has a country following, Loose Tubes rocks with rhythm and blues on Blue Monday at the **Mountain Lounge**.

Local talent also performs at the **Corral, Chet's Bar** and **Scissorbills**.

Happy Hour at Chet's Bar often features live entertainment. Warren Miller ski movies and films are shown in the amphitheatre.

Poker, which is legal in Montana, is available, as are quarter electronic keno machines. Video games are offered in the lodge's recreation room.

"Theatre in the Mountains," organized by the Big Sky Association for the Arts, presents muscials and comic dramas.

Other activities

Snowmobiles are available at Big Sky and West Yellowstone, giving access to Yellowstone National Park. In the park, one can travel to Old Faithful in two or three hours. Wildlife includes buffalo, bald eagles, geese and moose. Bus service is provided between Big Sky and West Yellowstone snowmobile rental shops. For information, Rendezvous Snowmobile Rentals, 800-426-7669 or (406) 646-9564; Snowmobile Yellowstone, 800-221-1151; Yellowstone Adventures, 800-231-5991 or (406) 646-7735; West Yellowstone, 800-541-7354 or (406) 646-9695.

Getting there

Northwest, Continental and Delta fly into Bozeman Gallatin Field Airport. Horizon Air and SkyWest also have service there. Big Sky shuttles run daily and meet most major flights in winter. It takes about an hour to reach the resort from the airport.

The easiest transit is the Karst Stage 42-passenger skier shuttle that runs between the airport, Big Sky and West Yellowstone.

Rental cars are available at the Bozeman Airport through Avis, National, Budget, Hertz, Payless and several local agencies.

City Taxi of Bozeman has a 5-passenger taxi and 15-passenger van.

The resort is 43 miles south of I-90—the turn-off is just west of Bozeman, Montana. It is 50 miles north of West Yellowstone on U.S. 191.

Information/reservations

Big Sky Ski & Summer Resort, 800-548-4486 nation-wide; 800-824-7767 toll-free in Montana, (406) 995-4211 in Montana.

Taos, New Mexico

Primitive yet sophisticated, Taos is a place of three identities. For skiers, it is the sequestered, legendary resort known for its challenging steeps set in a European-style ski village. For lovers of the Southwest, it is a town of artists and craftspeople, a center of Southwestern cuisine and the heart of a vast, silent landscape. For the Indians of Taos Pueblo, it is a homeland striking deep into the past, pulsing with the rhythms of dances and fiestas that punctuate their lives. Of Taos, Zane Grey wrote, "You must see, feel, hear and taste this wonderful country, and, once having done so, you will never be the same again."

The mystique carries over to the ski resort, Taos Ski Valley, 18 miles north of the town and more than 2,000 feet higher. At the border of Carson National Forest, where the terrain changes from sage and piñon to tall evergreen, the building style changes from Southwestern pueblo to European alpine. The effect is magical.

Because of its high altitude (a summit of 11,819 feet), its location in the sunbelt and the protection offered by a treeline twice as high as in the Alps, Taos possesses the perfect contradiction—fresh snow and sunshine. Those were the elements that attracted the late Ernie Blake, Taos' German-Swiss developer.

Founder Ernie's spirit of fun, his respect for the mountains and his love for human beings are still present at Taos Ski Valley. Taos is operated by Ernie's sons, daughter, wife, grandchildren and loyal employees, some of whose grandchildren now work the mountain.

Taos Facts

Base elevation: 9,207; **Summit elevation:** 11,819; **Vertical drop:** 2,612 feet
Number of lifts: 11—3 quad chairs, 1 triple chair, 7 double chairs, 1 surface lift
Percent snowmaking: 34 percent
Total acreage: 1,096 acres terrain, 687 acres of trails
Uphill capacity: 9,700 per hour   **Bed Base:** 3,705 in Ski Valley and town

Although cautioned against developing Taos because of its steep terrain, Blake pursued anyway. "I thought the skill of the American skier was advancing so fast that they'd want challenging terrain," he once said. "In part that was an error, because they also want flats where they can look like heroes."

So after developing the gut-churning plunges, Blake carved out intermediate and beginner trails and bowls. To counteract the intimidation felt by many first-time Taos skiers ready to hightail it home without so much as buckling their bindings, he put up a sign at the base of the lifts: "Don't panic. You're looking at only 1/30th of Taos Ski Valley. We have many easy runs, too!"

Eighteen miles down-valley from the ski area the artistically rich town of Taos spreads across the high desert with its squares of adobe buildings. The land grips with a tenacious hold the artists who have immortalized it. Nearly 70 galleries and craft shops keep alive ancient artistic traditions while in the forefront of contemporary American art. Southwestern cuisine, that blend of Spanish, Mexican and Indian dishes, adds to Taos culture.

Many choose to stay at the resort, Taos Ski Valley, distinguished from the town below by its unofficial label, the Village. It does resemble an alpine hamlet, and its inns reflect Blake's European origins. What may appear odd at first is to witness, in one of those Swiss chalets, an evening entertainment of Tiwa Indian dances executed with full costume and pounding rhythms. To the local, however, the contrast is natural—the land is big enough to accommodate all human diversity.

In the 36 years since Taos has opened, certain traditions have developed. One is the quest for hidden porrons, hand-blown Mexican glass flasks filled with martinis and buried in the snow under trees for classes to discover. "They're made with gin," Blake once said, "because gin gives you courage." Another tradition is that Blake's grandchildren serve free hot chocolate in winter or lemonade in spring in lift lines if they get too long. Such personal care for guests epitomizes the Taos experience, where skiers feel the family atmosphere and adopt a proprietary interest.

Perhaps it's the mystique of the ancient land that encourages such traditions and love, just as it has fired the spirit of skiers and artists for years. Of the Sangre de Cristo peaks surrounding Taos and the layered New Mexican mesa, master photographer Ansel Adams wrote, "The skies and the land are so enormous and detail so precise and exquisite, that wherever you are, you are isolated in a glowing world . . . where clocks stopped long ago."

Where to ski

The gigantic topography of Taos Ski Valley is made comfortable for the skier by two factors: a caring staff eager to help the newcomer and an outstanding instruction program. Every morning, a crew of red-jacketed hosts is stationed at ticket area, base, and tops of all lifts to answer questions about lift lines and newly groomed runs, and help skiers choose appropriate trails.

An intermediate run like Lower Stauffenberg or Porcupine might be considered advanced at smaller resorts. Here, it is no disgrace for a newcomer to warm up on a green run—it's a good idea.

Smooth intermediate bowls can be found off new Kachina quad chair, the widest being Shalako. The least crowded is Hunziker, named after a Swiss lift engineer, kept isolated by a short climb to its entrance. The Hunziker Bowl entices you with a mild concave slope, but just when you feel confident and relaxed, it drops off with the steepness of a waterfall and narrows down to force you into precision skiing in short turns.

Taos is never crowded: ticket sales are cut off at 4,800 and the mountain can accommodate much more, but if you're looking for no people at all, the farthest run west, Lower Stauffenberg running into Don't Tell, both now covered by snowmaking, will probably be empty.

For tree skiers, Taos has a special challenge, the twin runs Castor and Pollux. They hardly look like runs, just steep, wooded parts of the mountain, unskiable, where some joker put a sign that looks just like a trail marker. Then you realize those markers are real. The trees are from two to 15 feet apart.

Powder skiing lasts on Highline Ridge and Kachina Peak. These are not for the faint of heart for two reasons: they are double black diamonds and Kachina Peak is reachable only after an hour-and-fifteen-minute hike from the top chair at 11,800 feet to the ridge at 12,500 feet.

You can, however, ski off Highline Ridge and West Basin Ridge after only a 15-minute hike. Skiers are advised to go with an instructor or a patrolman; at the very least, they must check in with the patrol at the top of Chair 6. The ski patrol will give you a rough screening to see if you can handle the double-diamond terrain. In any case you must ski the ridge with a partner.

Taos' skiing is on two sides of a ridge marked by green-circle Bambi at the top and black-diamond Al's Run at the bottom. To the left of the ridge, as you look at the mountain, are wider, gentler runs such as Shalako Bowl, Honeysuckle, and Upper and Lower Totemoff. To the right of the ridge are narrower, steeper runs like dense, tree-filled Castor and Pollux, and the beginner trails-cum-catwalks Camino Sinuoso, Whitefeather and Bambi.

While experts will adore Taos for its challenge, intermediates and below may be frustrated. Most of the green-circle trails are no more than narrow, high-traffic access runs to more challenging terrain. Skiers getting off Chairs 2 and 6 who want to ski the right side have only two ways to go: down green-circle Bambi or black-diamond Reforma and Blitz, so probably 80 percent of them take Bambi, zipping past wedgers who are already scared enough as it is. At the end of the day, those not up for the black stuff must use two green-circle catwalk runs: Whitefeather on the right and Rubezahl on the left. Despite the slow-down efforts of ski hosts stationed every 20 feet or so, both runs resemble the Ventura Freeway at rush hour, the slower skiers gingerly wedging their way and the more proficient sailing in and out of the traffic. On busy days it's a mess.

Mountain rating

The name Taos Ski Valley is almost too genteel. It implies a softness to the slopes. Less appealing but more accurate would be Taos Ski Gorge. No one seeing the terrain would doubt its classification as a challenging mountain. The terrain statistics are somewhat misleading. A whopping 51 percent of the runs are rated expert, but that doesn't mention that 19 of those 36 runs are double black diamonds. At Taos they're marked with dotted black lines on trail maps, and many of them hang precipitously from a narrow traverse that itself is labeled as a double black.

Most experts would be satisfied enough with single-black-diamond runs like Al's, directly under the chair lift, a long, straight highway to heaven composed of bumps as steep as angels' steps and guarded by walls of overhanging evergreens like brooding mourners. Longhorn, to the left off Chair 5, is 37 degrees at the upper part, and Upper Stauffenberg is even steeper, but that's a double-black-diamond run.

On the front of the mountain, intermediates should look for Powderhorn, a long cruising swath with occasional steeper pitches and moguls at the entry. Skiers just beginning to work on moguls will find challenge on the north part of Kachina basin—Hunziker Bowl, Patton and Baby Bear are all intermediate runs available from the Kachina lift. Skiers wanting to explore beyond beginner level, but not wanting to encounter moguls, will find Porcupine on the front part of the mountain a well-manicured intermediate run.

Beginners and lower intermediates will do well to take a lesson—not only to improve their skills but also to find the best part of the mountain for them. Also, it's nearly impossible to avoid moguls entirely here—if you go into panic mode at the sight of a snow pimple, take a lesson. Last suggestion: take a trail map and use it.

Cross-country

While Taos Ski Valley has no Nordic center, there is cross-country skiing nearby. New Mexico's only exclusively Nordic area is Enchanted Forest Cross-Country Ski Area, 40 miles northeast of Taos by Highways 522 and 38. Just below the summit of Bobcat Pass, 3 miles east of Red River, it has 30 km. of groomed trails and a peak elevation of 10,300 feet. Rates are $7 for adults, $4 for teenagers and seniors, and $2 kids under 12. Call 754-2374.

Other possibilities for Nordic skiing include day and moonlight tours with these operators: Los Rios Anglers, 223B Paseo del Pueblo Norte, Taos, NM 87571; 758-2798. Brian Shields, former coach of the Taos Junior Cross-Country Racing Team, Rte. 1, Box 71, Taos NM 87571; 758-3209. The Southwest Nordic Center, Box 3212, Taos NM 87517; (800) 99X-CSKI.

Snowboarding

No snowboarding is permitted. Taos has always been a resort dedicated to Alpine skiing and feels that snowboards don't mix well with skiing. This is a mountain that takes full concentration. Monoskis and telemarking are allowed.

Ski school (92/93 prices)

Some say the exceptional instruction at Taos is necessarily so—the terrain demands it. But the reason goes deeper. Blake often said, "The art of skiing is a question of turning, not of becoming fearless and crashing down the slopes. Many advanced skiers are willing to take lessons here at Taos that they'd refuse with a sneer anywhere else. It's not just the mountain. We blackmail them into it because it's a social thing."

Ski Weeks, are the core of the Taos ski experience, developed by former French junior Alpine champion and ski school technical director Jean Mayer: six mornings of intensive, fast-moving lessons. Participants are carefully matched, and they ski with same instructor all week, usually making tremendous progress. In fact, 65 percent of the pupils are intermediate level or higher.

"Oh, it's possible to learn to ski, or learn to ski Taos, without instruction," Blake used to say with a gentle, knowing smile. "The Wright brothers learned to fly without instruction. The thing to consider is that the survival rate is low."

The Ski Week program makes Taos more enjoyable for beginners and intermediates. The resort claims that it can take someone who is in reasonably good physical shape, but has never skied before, and by the end of the week, make them a solid intermediate skier.

Ski Week costs $312, lifts and lessons, for adults and teens. Juniors 6 to 12 can enroll for $294, and further discounts are available to children and those over 65. Many lodging properties offer this program as a package with meals and accommodations; indeed you can't stay at Jean Mayer's hotel St. Bernard unless you're signed up for the ski week. Examples of lessons-lifts-lodgings-meals packages are $845 at the Salsa del Salto bed-and-breakfast 9 miles from the ski area, $1,200 at the on-slope Hotel Edelweiss, $1,300 at the St. Bernard; and $455 at the

Abominable Snow Mansion Skiers' Hostel, about 10 miles from the area.

Single group lessons (two hours, morning or afternoon) cost $24; three or more days cost $21.

Private lessons are $50 a person for the first hour; $35 each additional person or hour. An all-day private lesson is $325, with a maximum of three skiers; half-day private lesson is $200.

The Yellowbird Special for never-ever skiers includes Novice lift ticket, morning and afternoon lessons for $39; $45 includes equipment rental.

The Junior Elite program for children seven to 12 includes all-day lift ticket, morning ski lesson, lunch, afternoon supervised skiing, free NASTAR race, video and awards, for $50. Teenagers are grouped together by skill level and attitude in the Learn-to-Ski-Better program.

Super Ski Week is a special program that combines the classic Ski Better Week with the Taos Race Camp. The program covers race training, moguls, powder skiing, style improvements, and turning exercises. It's offered at selected times and costs an additional $100 to $113 over the cost of the Ski Week packages.

The Ski School also has three-day programs in mogul introduction, mountain cruising, Steep and Deep, telemark introduction, and exploration with a guide. The three-day programs cost $52 per day, including lift ticket.

All morning classes begin at 9:45 a.m.; afternoon classes begin at 1:45 p.m.

Lift tickets (91/92 prices)

Adult, all-day lift ticket is $35. For children 12 years or younger, the all-day ticket is $20.

Multiday tickets (three or more consecutive days) are $32 for adults, $18 for children.

There are reductions during January value season.

Seniors 65-69 ski for $10; 70 years and older ski free.

Accommodations

What gives Taos its European atmosphere is the emphasis on the complete week-long experience of lessons and an extended period of time in the walking village. Therefore, the **Learn-to-Ski-Better Week** packages include up to seven nights lodging (Saturday to Saturday), 20

meals, six lift tickets and six morning lessons. Prices
listed here reflect 1991/92 rates and vary according to accommodation. At the Village they range from $1,300 per
person, double occupancy, at **Hotel St. Bernard** with three
meals a day, to about $520 without meals at **Alpine
Village**. Between these prices are 8 other establishments.

The **Hotel St. Bernard Condos** managed by Jean Mayer,
Taos ski school technical director, offer the flavor of a
European retreat. Dinner is in the famed Hotel St.
Bernard, circa 1957, where the cuisine and ambiance are
both legendary—and French. Breakfast is buffet.

Kandahar Condominiums on the slopes (776-2226) has
prices ranging from $136 for a hotel room to $295 for a
two-bedroom condo. With the seven-day Ski Week
program, but no meals, the rate $745 based on four or six
people per condo unit.

The least expensive is the skiers' hostel, **The
Abominable Snowmansion** in Arroyo Seco, nine miles
from the Village, where the rates are an astonishing
$12.50-$20 for a dorm bed. Contact: Box 3271, Taos NM
87571; 776-8298.

Everything in Taos Ski Valley can be booked through
Taos Valley Resort Association, (800) 776-1111.

Midway between the ski area and town is a bed-and-
breakfast inn, the **Salsa del Salto**. Formerly the residence
of Hotel St. Bernard owner Jean Mayer, it's now run by
Jean's brother Dadou, a French-trained chef who cooks
Salsa del Salto's gourmet breakfasts. Prices range from
$95 to $160 per room per night. It's perfect for those who
want to spend part of their time skiing and part exploring
the art galleries and historic attractions. B&Bs can be
booked through the Taos B&B Association, (800) 876-7857.

The town of Taos offers a wide range of accommodations, many of them including the "Learn-to-Ski-Better"
lift/lesson package, and most of them less expensive than
staying at Taos Ski Valley. At the northern edge of town,
Quail Ridge Inn is a fully appointed condominium complex of 110 units at a tennis ranch, including indoor and
outdoor courts. Looking much like a pueblo, it exudes the
Southwestern atmosphere. Rates range from $60 to $300 a
night. More information from Box 707, Taos NM 87571;
776-2211 or (800) 624-4448. Rooms at **El Pueblo Lodge** (Box

92, Taos 87571; 800-433-9612) run $60-$70. **Indian Hills Inn** (Box 1229; 800-444-2346) tops that at $35-$47.

The historic **Taos Inn** is the cultural center of Taos. The lobby, built around the old town well, is a gathering place for artists, and the Adobe Bar, serving shrimp and oysters, has a gentle après-ski atmosphere that spills over into the lobby library. Rooms featuring adobe fireplaces, antiques, Taos-style natural furniture built by local artisans, and handloomed Indian bedspreads range from $80 to $195. Call (800) TAOS-INN.

The **Sagebrush Inn** is an historic inn with a lobby full of a priceless collection of Southwestern art and the best nightlife in town. Room rates range from $60 to $100. Call (800) 428-3626 or 758-2254.

Taos Valley Resort Association, (800) 992-7669, in NM (505) 776-2233, organizes all-inclusive 3- to 7-day packages including air, transfers to Taos, lodging, lifts and lessons. Rates average about $1200 for a full week from New York and Chicago to about $950 from L.A. Four-day/three-night packages from Chicago run about $575 and from L.A. about $445.

Dining

Because so many properties at Taos Ski Valley offer the Ski Better Week packages, which include meals, most restaurants have been operated by the lodges for the needs of their guests. It's still that way at the Hotel St. Bernard and Thunderbird Lodge, two of the top restaurants. Lately more establishments have opened in the Taos Ski Valley. The best are **Rhoda's Restaurant** and **Tim's Stray Dog Cantina.** Rhoda's, named for Ernie Blake's wife, has many New Mexican specialties, and prices are $8.50 to $15.50. At Tim's Stray Dog (an inevitable name: owner Tim Harter used to work at the Hotel St. Bernard, a.k.a. "The Dog"), try the Tequila Shrimp.

For breakfast and lunch, the Hotel Edelweiss' **La Croissanterie** is excellent, along with those noted.

On the road into the valley, the **Casa Cordova** specializes in European cuisine (entrées are $14-$20). Its Chef's Secret is a pasta with meat or seafood sauce baked in capers ($25 for two). Call 776-2500 for reservations. Also on the road between Taos and the Ski Valley, the **Chile Connection** (776-8787) is known for its chicken chimichanga and pollo boracho (half chicken marinated in wine). Entrées run $7-$11. **The Brett House**, at the junction of Highways 64 and 150, serves continental cuisine in the $10-$18 range. Call: 776-8545. **Carl's French Quarter** at the Quail Ridge Inn (776-8319) specializes in Cajun cuisine—gumbo and shrimp artichoke bisque.

However you get there, the town has a lot to offer in ambiance, culture and cuisine. Southwestern specialties are green chile (a stew made from green chile, beef or pork, onions, garlic and spices), blue corn tortillas, sopaipillas (deep-fried dough pillows served with honey to neutralize "picante" or hot entrées) and posole (hominy-style corn spiced with chile and meat). Very popular are fajitas, or skirt steak strips marinated in lime juice, red chile, vinegar and salt, served with a tortilla.

The menu at the intimate **Apple Tree Restaurant** lists Southwestern dishes and continental cuisine, which is helpful for groups that can't decide what kind of food they want. Unusual and elegant desserts are also featured. Reservations are taken, but sometimes not necessary; call 758-1900. Right on the historic plaza, **The Garden Restaurant** is moderately priced and offers New Mexican as well as American, Italian and French entrées; call 758-9483. **Doc Martin's** in the Taos Inn, has creative Southwestern cuisine—or breakfast, sopaipilla stuffed with scrambled eggs and chile; for lunch New Mexican cassoulet, a hearty stew of lamb, duck, vegetables and green chile; and for dinner, buffalo steak or turkey enchiladas with blue corn tortillas. **Michael's Kitchen**, 304C Paseo de Pueblo Norte, (the main drag) gets raves from locals for its breakfasts. Another restaurant that gets high marks for dinner is Roberto's, which serves exceptional New Mexican dishes. Slight problem: owner Bobby Garcia is an avid skier, so the restaurant may close unexpectedly during the season. Call ahead: 758-2434. Or try another of Taos' fine restaurants. There are lots.

Après-ski/nightlife

Yawn. That is the sound of Taos' bone-tired skiers headed off to dreamland soon after dinner. The nightlife will never make any Top 10 lists in the ski magazines.

After the lifts close, skiers will be found on the deck of the **Hotel St. Bernard**, the **Martini Tree Bar** at the Resort

Center, or the **Twining Tavern** at the Thunderbird Lodge, sometimes with live music. The St. Bernard has live music every night—an eclectic mix of reggae, country, jazz, and acoustic guitar. **The Thunderbird Lodge** has live music in spurts. Each January, the Thunderbird stages its Jazz Legends concerts; The Martini Tree has live music daily.

Things are a little more lively in town. **The Sagebrush Inn**, at the south end, has Country & Western dances every Friday and Saturday night, plus C & W music the rest of the week. The Kachina Lodge's **Cabaret Room** has the largest dance floor in town and often attracts name singers and bands who are passing through. **Ogelvie's Bar and Grill** in Taos Plaza is also lively.

A gentle après-ski environment where skiers and local artists mix is the **Adobe Bar** of the Taos Inn, its been called the living room for artsy locals.

Dinner theater on weekends is staged at Carl's French Quarter at the Quail Ridge Inn, 14 miles down the valley toward Taos; 776-8319.

The TAOS NEWS has a weekly entertainment guide.

Child care

Taos Ski Valley has these programs for children:

The Junior Elite program, ages 6 to 12, includes a two-hour morning lesson, lunch and afternoon ski session for $50 a day, $245 for five days, and $294 for six days.

Kinderkäfig is a learning child care program for potty-trained children ages three to five. The three to four year olds are in an all-day program, which includes at least one hour of skiing in the morning and afternoon, supervised snowplay and games, crafts, puppets and storytelling, as well as lunch, for $40 per day. The five and six year olds have two hours of ski lessons in the morning and two hours of supervised skiing with an instructor in the afternoon, plus lunch. Price is $40 per child. Reservations are strongly recommended during busy holidays. Parents must rent skis first before delivering their children to Kinderkäfig located in the A-frame building on the far side of Strawberry Hill at the top of the surface lift.

Kinderkare is a new service for little ones (between 1 and 2 years) who are not yet skiing. These toddlers enjoy directed play, lunch and naps. Rates including lunch and snacks are $40 a day. Six days cost $240. The program operates daily from 8:30 a.m. to 4 p.m.

Bebekare started last season. Infants—even newborns—receive care while parents ski. Parents must bring diapers and formula. Rates: $8 per hour, $25 a half day, $40 a full day, $240 for six days; 8:30 a.m. to 4 p.m.

A pickup service is available from the Ski Valley lodges; however, prior arrangements must be made through the lodge. Down parkas and warmup pants may be rented from the Taos Ski Valley Sportswear Shop located on the second floor of the Day Skier's Lodge.

Other activities

Although Georgia O'Keeffe and R.C. Gorman have made Taos legendary among art lovers, countless other artists have extended the reputation of Taos as an art center. Nearly 70 galleries and studios are tucked in Taos side streets. A descriptive list is available from Taos Chamber of Commerce, Drawer 1, Taos NM 87571; 758-3873 or (800) 732-TAOS. On Tuesday and Thursday evenings through mid-December, Taos Inn hosts its Meet-the-Artists series of informal discussions, music, slides, videos and readings. Taos Ski Valley Resort Center hosts Taos History and Art Talks.

It is between the town of Taos and Taos Ski Village, in Taos Pueblo at an elevation of 7,000 feet, where the roots of Southwestern culture dig deep. For here, in adobe dwellings whose style is emulated throughout New Mexico, the Tiwa Indians have lived for 700 years. The mission church of St. Francis of Assisi remains from the Spanish colonial era and two massive Pueblo structures. In 1680, when the Indians launched a revolt against the Spanish, the settlement looked much as it does now.

In no other ski area in the nation can visiting skiers be treated to such long-standing cultural riches. The Tiwa Indians welcome visitors to their pueblo, their workshops, their ceremonies and sacred dances. The pueblo is open from 9 a.m. to 4:30 p.m. in winter. Entrance fee is $5 per vehicle; a fee of $5 per still camera, $10 for a video or movie camera, is also requested.

Four miles north of Taos, the Millicent Rogers Museum houses an extensive collection of native American and Hispanic art. Admission is $3 for adults, $1 for children. The museum is open Monday and Tuesday, 12-8 p.m.; Wednesday through Sunday, 10 a.m. to 4 p.m.

Getting there

Taos Ski Valley is 135 miles—about two and a half hours—north of Albuquerque, the nearest major airport. Renting a car is highly recommended for a couple of reasons: the drive is extremely scenic and public transportation for the 18 miles between Taos and the ski area is spotty, especially since the free evening shuttle was discontinued. The usual rental agencies are at the Albuquerque airport. Payless Rental Cars does not have a desk there, but manager George Vaughn is very helpful to skiers. He'll take collect calls at 247-9255, or call (800) 541-1566. Their van will pick you up at the airport.

Faust's Transportation operates bus service from Albuquerque twice daily, (morning and early afternoon), once on Sunday and three times on Saturday. Fare is $45 round trip, $25 one way. The number is 758-3410. Pride of Taos shuttle also provides service. Call 758-8340 in NM or (800) 821-2437 elsewhere.

AMTRAK service rolls from Chicago and Los Angeles. Chicago service stops in Raton, NM and the Los Angeles train stops in Albuquerque.

Overnight RV parking, without hookups, is permitted in the Taos Ski Valley parking lot. Two other RV parks: Taos Motel and RV Park (800) 323-6009 or 758-1667, and Kit Carson Campgrounds and RV Park 758-3660.

Information/reservations

The 1991/92 season begins November 28 and ends April 5. For information, write Box BB, Taos Ski Valley NM 87525 or call 776-2291. Lodging reservations in the town of Taos, and in the Village, are available from Taos Valley Resort Association, (800) 776-1111 or 776-2233.

Taos' elevation, one of the highest of ski areas in the United States, makes for dry light powder, with an average snowfall of 325 inches yearly. Yet thanks to the southerly location, it is never as severely cold as in the northern Rockies. Take plenty of sunscreen. March and April are normally windy. (The ancient Indian legend affirms that the winds are sent to awaken the trees for the new season.) The snow report number is 776-2916. Area code is 505.

Santa Fe Ski Basin New Mexico

Take the sunlight of the high desert and an unlimited supply of fresh powder days. Add pre-Columbian Indian Pueblos, Spanish architecture and about 170 art galleries. Mix well with spicy cuisine, a western frontier abandon and a skier-friendly mountain that will satisfy just about any taste, and you get Santa Fe.

It is a land of enchanting contradiction. It is old and new, high mountain and flat desert, cruising cool and hot, hot, hot skiing. Santa Fe skiing is unlike skiing anywhere else on the continent. U.S. skiers need a passport to get further away from the average ski experience.

While Taos (about 150 miles from Albuquerque) has won an international reputation among the head banging ski-til-you-drop crowd, just one hour north of Albuquerque, Santa Fe is the ski destination for ski families looking for more variety than vertical.

Santa Fe marks the end of the overland westward trail. Founded by Spanish conquistadors in 1610, 10 years before the pilgrims landed in Plymouth, Santa Fe is the oldest capital city in North America. Unlike many ski resorts, built on abandoned mines in isolated wilderness, Santa Fe is rich in history and culture.

When the Spanish arrived, the area was already populated with an estimated 100,000 Native Americans, who spoke nine languages and lived in some 70 multi-storied adobe pueblos, some still inhabited today. In 1680,

---

Santa Fe Facts

Base elevation: 10,350'; Summit elevation: 12,000'; Vertical drop: 1,650 feet.
Number and types of lifts: 7—1 quad chair, 1 triple chair, 2 double chairs and 3 surface lifts
Acreage: 700 skiable acres Snowmaking: 30 percent
Uphill capacity: 7,300 skiers per hour Bed base: 4,000 in Santa Fe

the Indians revolted against their Spanish conquerors, but in 1692, Don Diego de Vargas recaptured the region in a bloodless siege.

For the next 150 years, Santa Fe grew as a frontier military base and trading center, where Spanish regulars and missionaries, Anglo mountain men and Native Americans mixed. In 1846, during the Mexican-American War, New Mexico was ceded to the United States and Santa Fe, at the end of the Santa Fe Trail, became the quintessential frontier town, hosting the likes of Billy the Kid and Kit Carson.

In the early part of this century, Santa Fe took on a new persona. The Pueblo Indians have known the area as the "dancing ground of the sun" for centuries, and drawn by the ethereal desert light, the 7,000 elevation and the mild climate, Santa Fe became a magnet for men and women of arts and letters. D.H. Lawrence, Ezra Pound, Willa Cather, Jack London and H.L. Mencken either lived or vacationed here. Artists Edward Hopper and Marsden Hartley spent time here and Santa Fe was home to Robert Henri, George Bellows and Randall Davey. Composer Aaron Copland lived in Santa Fe. Today the town of just 60,000 is home of one of the world's premier art colonies. Santa Fe also boasts an renowned opera company.

Santa Fe is a ski destination for skiers who know après-ski is more than cheese fondue, European flavored architecture and a disco.

Where to ski

Santa Fe Ski Basin sits 18 miles outside Santa Fe proper. While the mountain is known as a day-area destination for Santa Fe and Albuquerque skiers, out of town visitors will find there is more than enough terrain here for everyone.

A good intermediate mountain, if there is fresh snow, most experts will find it takes two to three days to exhaust all the possibilities.

All the mountain amenities, restaurants, ski rentals, child care, ski school and ticket sales are located at the base of the mountain, just a few steps from the parking lot.

Beginners will be happiest on the lower part of the mountain, learning the basics on the wide boulevard of Easy Street. Lower intermediates will find more challenges and a slightly steeper pitch on Open Slope and Upper and Lower Midland.

On a fresh powder day (average once a week last season) local intermediates head straight for the Tesuque Peak triple chair, to 12,000 feet and the top of the mountain. To the right (facing the mountain) of the lift is Gayway, a glorious groomed pitch with several spicy turns, that gives new meaning to the term spectacular scenery. On a clear day, skiers can see for 150 miles from this intermediate's delight. Parachute, which parallels Gayway, is a groomed black diamond alternative to Gayway, with a somewhat steeper pitch. Both trails are perfect for arching turns and ego-inflating skiing.

For the most part, the mountain's expert terrain is to the left of the Tesuque Peak chair. With fresh snow, locals go first to Columbine, Big Rocks and Wizard. One thing to note is that because of its exposure, Columbine can hold snow for up to two weeks after a dump. These runs all check in as very steep, for advanced skiers only.

Roadrunner is the expert bump run directly under the Tesuque chair. Tequila Sunrise has the best glade skiing.

On the far side of the mountain, reached by the Santa Fe Super Chief quad, Muerte and Defasio offer narrow, isolated tree skiing for the intermediate.

While there are hopes to overcome some environmental objections and put in a lift in the Big Tesuque Bowl, for the moment the intrepid ski into this area via Cornice (itself a taste of the bowl). Big Tesuque skiers find natural powder, bowl skiing and trees. The bowls dumps out on the area's entrance road. Skiers then hitch-hike back up to the base area. First timers in this area should go with a local who knows the area: it's genuine wilderness, it's big and people occasionally get lost.

Cross-country

There are maintained backcountry trails in the surrounding Santa Fe National Forest. Maps and specific information are available from the National Forest Service: (505) 988-6940. For trail and snow conditions in the Santa Fe National Forest call (505) 984-0606.

Snowboarding

Unlike at Taos, shredding is allowed. Depending on conditions, Santa Fe opens its half-pipe.

Ski school (92-93 prices)

Adult group (all day) $30; adult group (half day) $22; one hour private $45, additional person $20; two hour private $80, additional person $40; half-day private $120.

Children's ski school—(ages 3-4) all day supervision, including lunch, rental and two hour lesson $50; (ages 5-6) all day supervision, lunch and fours of lessons, $44; (rentals $8 extra) 1/2 day, $31; (ages 7-9) all day supervision, lunch and four hours of lessons, $50; 1/2 day, $35. (rentals are $10 extra)

Lift tickets

All day adult $30; half-day adult, $20; beginner chair lift, $15; child and senior (12 and under/62-71 years), $18; super seniors, free; Children (under 46 inches tall), free; 3-day adult, $84; 4-day adult, $110; 5-day adult, $135. Child/senior multi-day: 3-day $48; 4-day $62; 5-day $75.

Accommodations

There is no lodging at the Santa Fe Ski Basin, and even if there were, you'd want to drive back to Santa Fe for dining, shopping and the museums. There are more than 70 hotels, motels, inns, condominiums and B&B's serving Santa Fe visitors. Winter is low season in Santa Fe, so bargains abound. Expect to pay about $40 a night for a hotel located on the Cerrillos Road strip.

A downtown hotel located on the Plaza will run about $100 a night. These prices can be cut considerably if bought as a package incl uding lift tickets.

La Fonda Hotel is the historic place to stay in Santa Fe. An inn of one sort or another has been on this site for 300 years. Billy the Kid worked in the kitchen here washing dishes. The current La Fonda incarnation was built in the 1920s. This local landmark is an elegant old-style reminder of what Santa Fe once was. Rooms are about $100 a night. Even if you don't stay here, go inside and take a look. They don't make them like this anymore.

The way they make them now is across the Plaza from La Fonda. **The Inn of the Anasazi** is the politically correct place to stay in Santa Fe. Just completed last year, the Anasazi is chi-chi '90s Santa Fe. Much brighter than the older Spanish style found at La Fonda, the Anasazi is all muted pastels and desert hues. Before building, the owner consulted with Native American holy men and received their blessings. The wrought iron, Navajo weavings, and wood carvings that decorate the Anasazi were all done by local artisans. Even the vegetables served in the Anasazi restaurants were grown by local Native Americans. Leftovers are given to a homeless shelter and everything is recycled. In case you fear being overwhelmed by all this, note that the Anasazi has become the address of choice by celebrities staying in Santa Fe.

For information on any of the accommodations and ski packages available in Santa Fe call 800-982-SNOW or the Santa Fe Visitors Bureau at 800-777 984-CITY.

Dining

On the mountain, skiers have two choices. La Casa Cafeteria in the base lodge called La Casa Mall, and Totemoff's Bar and Grill at the base of the Tesuque Peak Chair. La Casa offers standard ski fare—chili, burgers, fries and so forth, as well as some lighter selections. Totemoff's grill features burgers, and cocktails.

While ski cuisine may be fine on the mountain, back in the city, Santa Fe cooks. If you include fast food, Santa Fe has nearly 200 places to throw on the feed bag. From traditional New Mexican cuisine (move over Tex-Mex) to steaks and seafood , Santa Fe has it all.

The Pink Adobe, 406 Old Santa Fe Trail (983-7712) is a local favorite dining spot and is therefore sometimes difficult to get in. They specialize in New Mexican and Creole foods, reservations are necessary. Prices are moderate to expensive.

Tomasita's Cafe, 500 S. Guadalupe (983-5721) is fast food with a twist. It's good. Portions are large. The service is friendly. It is a favorite of Santa Fe families, so there can be a wait. It is inexpensive, and features some of the best New Mexican fare in town .

If you are in town at lunch time, do what locals do and go stand in line at **Josie's Casa de Comida**, 225 E. Marcy

(983-5311). The regional dishes, created by a real Josie, are excellent. Despite its linoleum tables and homey appearance, you'll find yourself seated next to backpackers, artists, politicians and wealthy Santa Fe matrons. The homemade desserts are legendary in Santa Fe. Josie's is very inexpensive, but closed on weekends.

Après-ski/nightlife

If it is night life you are looking for, don't bother with Santa Fe. However, there are a zillion things to do away from the slopes.

One of the more wonderful ways to work out the kinks of a fresh powder day is to stop at **Ten Thousand Waves** (988-1047, 982-9304) for a relaxing hot tub under the stars. Between Santa Fe and the ski basin, (about three miles from the Plaza) Ten Thousand Waves is a Japanese-style hot tub resort. Featuring kimonos, sandals, massage and sexually segregated dressing rooms, a soak under the brilliant New Mexican sky is heavenly. There are seven private tubs and one communal tub.

For a completely different hot tub experience, locals like to drive out to **Ojo Caliente** (583-2233). About an hour out of Santa Fe there is a funky old (read somewhat run-down) soaking pool built over a natural hot spring. It is not open in the evening.

In Santa Fe, a wonderful place to mix dinner with entertainment is at **La Casa Sena** (988-9232) in the historic Sena Plaza. The stately adobe casa was built as a family home in the 1860's. Today, the traditional style retreat is the home to offices and shops. La Casa Sena restaurant features a full menu of New Mexican specialties—and singing waiters and waitresses. Most of these very talented Hollywood and Broadway wannabes are just testing their acts before taking them on the road. For about $20, you can eat, drink and hear what amounts to an exceptional dinner theater show, belted out between courses. Children are welcome, reservations a must.

If you are going to ski Santa Fe, it is strongly recommended that you take at least one day to shop, visit the museums and visit a Native American pueblo.

There are more than 100 galleries featuring everything from Native American jewelry, blankets and fine art to cutting edge sculpture, pottery and paintings, normally seen only in places like New York, Florence or Paris. For lazy, romantic, artistic meandering, there is no place on earth like the old adobe galleries on Canyon Road. There are entire guidebooks devoted to this area.

The museums in Santa Fe are first rate. The Museum of International Folk Art (strong in area Spanish art) and the Museum of Indian Arts and Culture should be considered must-sees. Skiers with an interest in art should take time to visit the Museum of Fine Arts (with several Georgia O'Keeffe paintings) and the more contemporary Center for Contemporary Arts.

After having done the museums, galleries and shops, one particularly nice place to visit is the Shidoni Forge in Tesuque. It features five acres of bronze sculpture and a working forge. Saturdays, visitors can watch while workman pour molten bronze—an unforgettable experience.

Every Indian pueblo holds a festival dance each year to honor its patron saint. Most are held in the summer, but skiers in Santa Fe in late January can attend the festival at San Ildefonso. This celebration, where the Indians wear traditional clothing and dance traditional dances, is not unlike any religious ceremony held in a church or temple. Visitors are welcome, but the moving, sacred rituals would be performed whether any tourist showed up or not.

Call the Santa Fe Visitors Bureau (505-984-6760) for up-to-date information on Pueblo festivals.

Getting there

Getting to and from Santa Fe and the ski area is difficult without a car. There is a shuttle, called Shuttle Jack, but it costs $10 per person, each way. The sensible thing to do is fly into Albuquerque and rent a car.

Information/reservations

The first place to call for information on skiing Santa Fe is Ski New Mexico (505) 982-5300. They have more ski-specific informationand package deals (lifts and lodging). Second, call Ski Santa Fe at (800) 982-SNOW, this is the agency run by Santa Fe Ski Basin. Their information is current. Finally, call the Santa Fe Convention and Visitors Bureau at (505) 984-6760 or (800) 777-CITY. They will send you information on visiting Santa Fe, even if skiing is the furthest thing from your mind.

Other New Mexico
ski areas

Taos Ski Valley gets the most publicity, but New Mexico
has other downhill ski areas. Most are smaller than Taos,
but many have gentler terrain. We cover Santa Fe Ski
Basin in detail. Others are:

Angel Fire, a four-season resort 22 miles east of Taos,
is well suited for beginner and intermediate skiers. With a
peak elevation of 10,680 feet and a vertical drop of 2,180
this is definitely a destination resort. Its relatively gentle
terrain attracts many multi-generations of families, who
cruise down the three-and-a-half mile, green, Headin'
Home from the summit to the base as if they had been
skiing all their lives. Angel Fire has challenging runs too,
but this area will make lower level skiers feel like skiing
champs. Angel Fire Chamber of Commerce: 377-6661;
Angel Fire Resort: 377-6401.

Pajarito Mountain is a day area near Los Alamos,
about 90 minutes south of Taos and an hour north of
Santa Fe. Privately owned by the Los Alamos Ski Club,
Pajarito has 1,200 vertical feet of mostly intermediate to
expert terrain—especially bumps. It's a little hard to find,
partly because New Mexicans guard their "private"
enclave and partly because the club's nonprofit status
doesn't permit it to market itself, or even to put up
directional signs—but the mountain is open to the public,
Ask your hotelier for directions or call (505) 662-5725.

Red River is another family-oriented area, 37 miles
northeast of Taos. Its terrain leans toward beginner and
intermediate levels. Lodging is within a mile of the slopes
and ranges from rustic cabins to luxurious condos. Red
River Chamber of Commerce, (505) 754-2366; Red River
Ski Area, (505) 754-2382.

Sandia Peak Ski Area is Albuquerque's playground.
Just east of New Mexico's largest city, it has 25 miles of
runs for all levels. Take the Sandia Peak Aerial Tramway,
a tourist attraction the year round. For information call
(505) 242-9052.

Sipapu Ski Area was the first New Mexico area to welcome snowboards and has since added a halfpipe. About 30 miles southeast of Taos, Sipapu has lodging close to the lifts and terrain for all levels.

Ski Apache, located near Ruidoso in south-central New Mexico, 200 miles from Albuquerque, is owned and operated by the Mescalero Apache Indian tribe. It has no lodging at the ski area, but there is plenty in Ruidoso, 16 miles away. Ski Apache's terrain is 45 percent advanced, but the beginner and intermediate trails have a good reputation for being well groomed. The view from the 11,500-foot peak is reportedly spectacular. Ski Apache also has the state's largest and oldest program for disabled skiers. Snowboarding is not allowed here; it is the only New Mexico area besides Taos that doesn't allow it. For information call (505) 336-4357.

Arizona Resorts

Apache Sunrise, McNary AZ 85930, 800-772-SNOW; 800-55-HOTEL; (602) 735-7600; 2 quads, 4 double chairs, 3 surface lifts, 60 trails, 800 skiable acres, 1,800-foot vertical

The drive east of Phoenix takes you into Zane Grey country, where he wrote his Western novels in a cabin. Farther on is a town called Show Low, where early settlers decided on a ranch ownership with a card game won with a deuce of clubs, the low draw. In Whiteriver, U.S. troops and Apache scouts subdued rebellious Apaches a little more than a century ago.

Today the White Mountain Apache Tribe owns and operates Apache Sunrise, by far the state's largest ski area. It is located 215 miles east of Phoenix, about a five-hour drive. Three ski mountains feature wide-open runs and lifts than can take 15,000 skiers per hour. The base area at 9,200 feet rises to an 11,000-foot summit. Much of the terrain is intermediate, with a few challenging, advanced drops. Weather this far south is often good, and snowfall averages 250 inches a year. Last winter Apache Sunrise had some of the best snow in the West.

Fairfield Snowbowl, Flagstaff AZ 86002; (602) 779-4577.

2 triple chairs, 2 double chairs, 32 trails, 2,300-foot vertical

The San Francisco Peaks rise abruptly above Flagstaff, 140 miles north of Phoenix. They provide the most challenging skiing in Arizona and some of the best views anywhere. Ridge Run, more than a mile long, as well as Casino and Tiger bump runs, could be at top Colorado or Utah resorts. Terrain is rated 30 percent beginner, 40 percent intermediate, 30 percent advanced. The altitude here is surprising for a state known for its deserts and canyons—the base area is 9,000 feet and climbs to 11,500 feet. From the top of Mount Agassiz the view includes the Grand Canyon slash, red rocks of Sedona, and mountains outside Kingman. The Earth's curvature is visible from this lofty perch. Snowbowl has 196 skiable acres, with 65 of those acres at Hart Prairie, a beginner's slope just down the road from lifts. Hart Prairie has a modern lodge with room for 500 people; the Agassiz Lodge, at the base of the higher lifts, is 33 years old and tight on space. Motels: lodging/ski lift packages run $30 to $60 per person, double occupancy.

For general Arizona information, write or call the **Arizona Office of Tourism**, 1480 E. Bethany Home #180, Phoenix AZ 85014, (602) 542-8687. **The Phoenix and Valley of the Sun Convention and Visitors' Bureau** is at 505 N. 2nd Street, Suite 300, Phoenix AZ 85004, (602) 254-6500.

Mount Bachelor Oregon

The Cascades are a different kind of mountain range from most, composed entirely of stately volcanic cones separated by high desert and range land, but stretching from Mount St. Helens in the north to Shasta in the south.

On the eastern side of the Cascade Range, where snow is lighter and drier than other northwestern resorts, Mount Bachelor has become an eligible destination for western skiers. Like the extinct volcano, the ski area has also been considered a sleeper—a resort without resort flavor, where no one notices or cares whether your ski clothes match, where there is no lodging on the mountain and certainly no hot nightlife, but where there is a dependable 16-foot snowpack, clear, dry air, an average daytime winter temperature of 26 degrees and some fine skiing from early November to July. Few skiers outside Oregon knew this, and because air transportation into Bend was not convenient, the mountain served contented Oregon skiers who had their winter playground to themselves for more than 25 years.

Suddenly, it exploded into the limelight: air transportation was facilitated, year-round resort grew 18 miles away and Mount Bachelor completed one-third of an ambitious 10-year expansion plan. For most of those early years, skiers threaded their way through evergreen trails and intermediate slopes on the lower mountain and could only drool at the massive, snow-crowned summit

---

Mt. Bachelor Facts
Base elevation: 6,000'; **Summit elevation:** 9,065'; **Vertical drop:** 3,100 feet
Number of lifts: 3 super quad chairs, 1 super triple chair, 4 triple chairs, 1 double chair, 2 surface lifts **Snowmaking as percent of area:** none
Total acreage: 3,200 acres skiable terrain accessed by lifts
Uphill capacity: 19,720 per hour **Bed base:** 7,500

above the tree line. However, nine years ago, Summit Chair, a high-speed triple superchair was installed all the way to the top making 360-degree skiing possible—down the front via wide bowls and tree-bordered serpentine swatches, or around the back where open snowfields, often untouched. With the opening of the high-speed quad Outback lift, the whole cone of the mountain is now lift-served. This area now boasts four quad superchairs.

The summit at 9,060 feet commands a panorama of the Cascades with the Three Sisters and jagged Broken Top mountains closest—all inactive volcanos bursting above sage, piñon and the town of Bend, 21 miles away and just 2,000 feet lower in altitude. The view across to the other peaks is heady, but so is the view below.

Mount Bachelor is well suited to family skiing, with lots of variety. There's a choice of trails for different ability levels available from each lift, so families can ride the same chair, ski on runs suited to each member, and meet at the bottom.

There's another appeal, particularly to families. It's the genuineness of central Oregon, the attitude that helping a lost or fallen skier is the natural thing to do. People talk with sincere friendliness, and one has the undeniable feeling that the locals enjoy getting to know visitors.

Six lodges serve the mountain, each with a different flavor, and together they represent the multifaceted character of Mount Bachelor. The West Village Lodge, modern and with full service, including bar, attracts tourists and singles. Locals tend to congregate at the other large lodge, Sunrise, where they know there's parking closer to the lifts and where the chef specializes in Mexican food. Blue Lodge is small and spartan, with a concrete floor and not much character. Because it's close to race courses, racers congregate there, including lots of kids from the Mighty Mites racing program. Tiny Egan Lodge is the original, built in 1958, homey and unpretentious. Directly up the mountain from the Main Lodge near the Orange Chair, it looks more like a service building than a lodge. But it has a spectacular view of Three Sisters and Broken Top, and is the home of the Mountain Masters children ski program.

Where to ski

The steepest descent is through The Pinnacles, a jagged rock formation reached by a 150-foot hike from the top of the Summit lift, then across the broad, ungroomed expanse of Cirque Bowl. Next might well be Cow's Face, far to the left of Summit Chair, steep but smooth. Because it's unknown to many skiers, it doesn't get carved into moguls, but wind often packs it down hard. When other slopes are in late afternoon shade, Cow's Face still has sun.

To the far right of the mountain is the Outback, 125 acres added in 1987, less trafficked than the center of the mountain. That light traffic sometimes means powder when other parts of the mountain have been tracked out. Most of the runs on the Outback are sinuous intermediate, but one called Down Under is a steady mogul run, often left ungroomed so its moguls grow.

The longest vertical (3,100 feet) can be had by taking the Summit chair off the backside, occasionally traversing right and ending up at bottom of the Outback chair.

Between the Outback chair and the Red chair is an unusual geologic feature, a lone cinder cone. It's not served by a lift, so powder lasts there until it becomes wind-packed, and tracks remain sharply defined between snowfalls. By getting up a head of steam from Last Chance, skiers can swoop up nearly two-thirds of the way and climb the rest. Cinder Cone is practically the only part of the mountain that offers tree skiing.

Most of the lower mountain is sheltered by trees, but some runs, such as Flying Dutchman and Tippytoe, give the exuberance of upper mountain skiing. You can usually find moguls on Grotto, Canyon and Coffee Run, all served by the Pine Marten Super Express quad chair that whisks you up the mountain in five and a half minutes. Guaranteed to bring squeals is Dilly Dally Alley, a gentle but narrow chute filled with loops, bumps and surprises. Once you're in it, there's no way out, yet once it's over you'll want to do it again. At the top of Sunrise lift, go right and then halfway down a run called Marshmallow. It's the swooping gully on the right.

If ever there's a swarm of skiers waiting to get on a lift, it's at the West Village Lodge at the beginning of ski school sessions (10 a.m. and 2 p.m.).

Mountain rating

Most of the terrain is best suited, as noted, for intermediates. Expert skiers seeking a challenge will feel restless after a weekend—they'll have to discover the pleasures of the backside and Cinder Cone. One of Mount Bachelor's advantages is that intermediates can experience the heady sensation of being on the summit and still get down safely using the broad Healy Heights and Beverly Hills, which are always groomed. In fact, intermediates can't actually get into trouble at Mount Bachelor: anything beyond their skill requires a knowledgeable decision before entering— for example, the hike up to The Pinnacles.

Lower intermediates will be comfortable using the Skyliner superchair. A surface lift for never-evers takes off from the Lodge at West Village with only a 15-foot vertical rise. The Orange and Yellow chairs in the same area are the lift-served slopes beginners should tackle.

Cross-country (91/92 rates)

The Mount Bachelor Rossignol Cross-Country Center gives you 60 kilometers of machine-set trails designed for both touring and skating. There are nine loops—from the easy, one-kilometer First Time Around to the challenging, 12-kilometer Oli's Alley. The six-kilometer intermediate trail, called Zigzag, leads to an enclosed shelter, a heated building that affords a good view of the Cascades and where many stop to eat brown-bag lunches. The Cross-Country Center, a traditional log lodge, includes equipment rental, repairs, trail and lesson information, lunch service and a roaring fire.

All-day trail passes are $9 for adults, $4.50 for children seven to 12. Half-day rates starting at noon are $6.50 for adults, $3 for children.

Ski school (91/92 prices)

Lessons are offered at West Village Lodge and Sunrise Lodge. Adult and children's (ages seven to 12) classes are 10 a.m.-12:30 p.m. and 2 p.m.-3:30 p.m. All classes receive lift line privileges, but students must purchase lift tickets.

Tiny Tracks ski school is a specially designed program for children ages four to six, during the same hours.

Split-session (morning and afternoon), three-hour lessons are $28 for adults, children and Tiny Tracks. Afternoon-only sessions are $24.

Guaranteed Learn-to-Ski is a one- or two-day discount package, including a Midway lift ticket, complete rental package and split-session, three-hour lesson for $38. (Not available to Tiny Tracks.)

Private lessons cost $38 per hour plus $14 for each additional person.

Mount Bachelor Ski School has an certified staff of 119 professional instructors using the American Teaching System. Call (503) 382-2442, Ext. 2112; or 800-829-2442.

There are NASTAR races, daily clinics and coin-operated races.

Lift tickets (91/92 prices)

Daily lift pass	All day	Half Day (12-4 p.m.)
Adult	$31	$25.50
Child (seven to 12)	$17.50	$13
Senior (over 65)	$15.50	$13
Student	$23.50	$18
Children six and under	free	

Multiple day passes	Adult	Child (7-12)
three of four days	$84	$40
five of six days	$134	$61.50
six of seven days	$160.50	$70.50

The Nordic Option lets you trade one Alpine day for a Nordic trail pass and rentals.

This season Mt. Bachelor is installing a SKIDATA computerized lift ticket system which eventually will allow them to sell lift tiecket bases on specific lifts, specific times, and a specific number of lift rides rather than simply full-day or half day. The resort will offer flextime tickets as well as the normal variety of full-day and half-day passes during the 92/93 season. The familiar beep of computers checking lift tickets will soon be heard here in the U.S. as it already is in Europe and Canada.

Accommodations

Mount Bachelor has no accommodations close to the lifts. Three-quarters of the visitors stay in Bend, 21 miles away, and the rest at lodgings in the foothills, primarily Sunriver and Inn of the Seventh Mountain.

The most extensive complex of lodgings is **Sunriver**, a 3,300-acre resort community in the pines, 18 miles from Mount Bachelor and 15 miles south of Bend. The complex has its own private airport, groomed Nordic trails, restaurants, grocery stores and shopping mall. Visitors can rent homes, lodge suites and condominiums amid wooded acres connected by winding roads and pathways.

Other activities include horseback riding, tennis on 29 courts, movies, teen dances, ice skating (2 p.m. to 9 p.m.), holiday sleigh rides, and scenic flights to Crater Lake and Mount St. Helens. For reservations, call 593-1221, Ext. 4420). There is also live entertainment and dancing at Owl's Nest Lounge.

Visitors without cars may feel somewhat isolated and stranded at Sunriver. Within Sunriver a shuttle takes visitors between the accommodations, restaurants and shopping. A shuttle leaves for Mount Bachelor morning and noon for $7 round trip (this fee is included in some packages). Among the half dozen restaurants, a popular one with a wide menu is **The Provisions** in the lodge. It serves sandwiches, salads, seafood, steak and pastas in a marketplace atmosphere. Rates run approximately $87 for a lodge bedroom, $141 for a lodge suite, and $158 to $306 for private resort homes and condominiums. Some packages include lift tickets. For more information, write: P.O. Box 3609, Sunriver OR 97707; or call (800) 547-3922; in Oregon, (800) 452-6874.

Inn of the Seventh Mountain Mount Bachelor's closest lodging, studios and condominiums. **El Crab Catcher** is the formal dining room, and the **Poppy Seed** is the cafe for lighter meals. In addition, there is a deli and grocery store. Economy rooms are $58 midweek and $64 weekends, and family two-bedroom condominiums are $226 midweek; $238 weekend, with many offerings in between. Skating rink, hot tub, snowmobile and sleigh rides, as well as a shuttle to the mountain, are available. Write Box 1207, Bend OR 97709; or call (800) 452-6810 in the U.S.; (800) 874-9402 from Canada.

The most deluxe accommodations in Bend are at **River House**, nestled along the banks of the Deschutes River only steps from of restaurants and entertainment centers. Pool, indoor and outdoor spas, Nautilus exercise room, saunas, and nine-hole golf course make this a mini-resort in the heart of town. Nightly rates range from $49 for a normal room to $89 for a river view suite with three queen beds, two rooms and kitchen. Write 3075 N. Highway 97, Bend OR 97701; (800) 547-3928; or (503) 381-3111.

Moderate lodgings in town are at **Best Western, Thunderbird** and **Red Lion**, where rates are $45-$60.

If staying in Bend, you may wish to use the very comfortable free shuttle to the mountain, which leaves five times in the morning and has staggered departures.

There are two area RV parks: Crooked River Ranch (923-1441); and Crown Villa RV Park (388-1131).

Dining

Although you'll pay more at the elegant **River House**, the best seafood in town is moderately priced at **McGrath's**, which has several interesting and unusual entrées nightly, especially those from Northwestern waters.

In Bend, **Player's Grill** has an interesting menu (dill pickle soup, anyone?) and an active bar with a young crowd. **De Nicola's**, a tiny place on Wall Street near Franklin, has large pocket pizzas, with pizza by the slice, and fast service. **Victorian Pantry** just off Century Drive on the way to the slopes has wonderful breakfasts and home cooking. **Beef & Brew** is the yuppie steak house. It also serves chicken and is known for good service. **Murrieta's** in Sunriver has quality Mexican food, is family-run and serves a family clientele. In fact, the grandchildren might wait on tables. More sophisticated, with a faster pace, a bar and live music, and about the same quality food, is **Roline's Cantina**.

Après-ski/nightlife

Mount Bachelor is not known for an exciting après-ski atmosphere, nor is Bend noted for its dynamic nightlife, though both can be found. The **Castle Keep Lounge** in the lower level of the Main Lodge, West Village, offers lively, near-slope après-ski. Also check **River House, E.L. Bender's** (197 N.E. Third) and **Roline's Cantina** in town.

After dinner there is dancing at **River House** and **Sunriver** and **Inn of the Seventh Mountain. Pine Tavern** has a mature adult atmosphere and a view of Mirror Pond. **McKensey's Ore House**, a steak restaurant and bar, rocks out on weekends.

Child care

A state-licensed day care center for children six weeks to seven years operates 8:30 a.m. to 4:30 p.m. daily at both West Village and Sunrise Lodges. Trained and nurturing care-givers offer planned activities. Parents must provide lunch. Reservations are recommended. Call (800) 829-2442, or write Mount Bachelor Day care Center, Box 1031, Bend OR 97709. Cost is $27 a day per child.

Other activities

Although skiing lasts through June, Mount Bachelor is a summer playground after Memorial Day, with mountain bike rentals and signtseeing rides. Even into the summer there are racing camps for all ages.

Sunriver and Inn of the Seventh Mountain have ice skating, horseback riding, sleigh rides and snowmobiling.

For ballooning, call Morning Glory Balloon Co. in Redmond, (503) 389-8739.

Getting there

Mount Bachelor is 21 miles southwest of Bend, Oregon, on the scenic Cascade Lakes Highway. From Portland, 162 miles away, take Route 26. State Highway 126 comes from Eugene (132 miles). Bus service operates daily from Bend .

United Express provides flights into Redmond/Bend Airport (16 miles from Bend) from San Francisco and Los Angeles. United Express and Horizon Air (800-547-9308) fly from Portland, Seattle and Eugene.

A car is helpful but not absolutely necessary if you take resort shuttles.

AMTRAK (800-835-8725) provides daily service from Los Angeles, Oakland/San Francisco and Redding northbound, and from Vancouver, Seattle, Portland and Eugene southbound to Chemult, 60 miles south of Bend. Arrange ahead for taxi pickup.

Tourist information

Central Reservations (800-800-8334) will assist with lodging, air and ground transportation and packages. In Oregon call (503) 382-8334, or write Central Oregon Reservations Center, P.O. Box 7587, Bend, OR 97708.

The ski report phone is (503) 382-7888.

Jackson Hole
Wyoming

Some ski areas dress up the models for their ads in cowboy hats and chaps so you think you'll be skiing smack in the middle of the Authentic Wild West. When you get there, you find that the cowpoke sashaying next to you on the saloon dance floor learned his two-step in a Manhattan Country & Western bar.

Some ski areas claim terrain steep enough to scare the fingernails off Freddie Krueger. But when you arrive, you discover nothing of the sort.

Some ski areas brag about their extra-friendly employees and townspeople. You arrive only to learn that friendly greetings seems proportional to the amount of money they think you'll spend.

Jackson Hole lives up to everything it claims.

It has real cowboys, lots of elk, moose and cows. If its herds could be counted in the U.S. Census, Congress would have a lot more representatives wearing big silver belt buckles and boots.

Oh, baby, does it ever have gnarly slopes. They don't sell "I Survived the Tram" ski pins here for nothing.

And it has friendly people.

Okay, Jackson Hole doesn't *quite* live up to its advertising. Its marketing brochure shows skiers in brand-new, colorful, matching outfits. If it wanted to be absolutely truthful, it would show some of them wearing mismatched

---

Jackson Hole Facts
Base elevation: 6,311'; **Summit elevation:** 10,450'; **Vertical drop:** 4,139 feet
Number and types of lifts: 10—1 aerial tram, 1 quad chair, 1 triple chair, 5 double chairs, and 2 surface lifts
Acreage: 2,500 acres of terrain **Percent of snowmaking:** 10 percent
Uphill capacity: 9,115 skiers per hour **Bed base:** 5,000

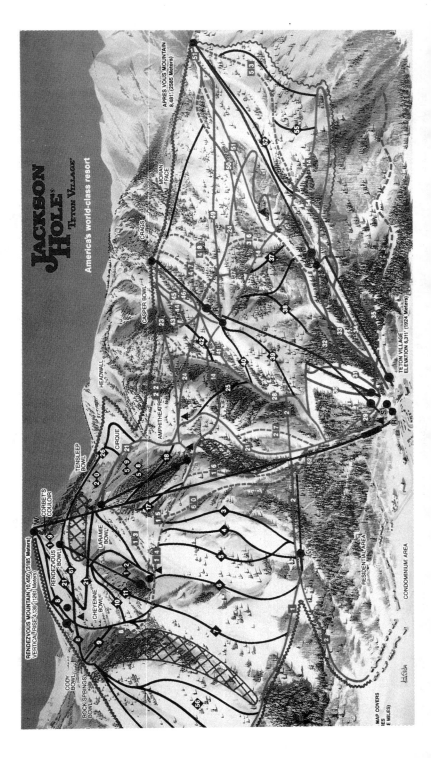

TRAIL DIFFICULTY SYMBOLS

● EASIEST

■ MODERATELY
DIFFICULT

▬ ▬ MORE DIFFICULT —
VARIED TERRAIN PLUS
SNOW CONDITIONS
FOR THE BETTER THAN
AVERAGE SKIER

◆ MOST DIFFICULT —
EXPERT

◆◆ MOST DIFFICULT —
EXPERT USE EXTRA
CAUTION

TRAIL NAMES

1. Union Pass Traverse
2. Way Home
3. North Colter Ridge
4. Buffalo Bowl
5. South Colter Ridge
6. Rawlins Bowl
7. Lower Sublette Ridge
8. Rendezvous Trail
9. Bivouac
10. Bird In The Hand
11. Pepi's Run
12. Alta Chutes
13. Grand
14. South Pass Traverse
15. Gannett
16. Lower Tram Line
17. Riverton Bowl
18. Thunder
19. East Ridge Traverse
20. Expert Chutes

21. Gros Ventre
22. Nez Perce Traverse
23. Amphitheatre Traverse
24. Solitude Traverse
25. Avalanche
26. Downhill
27. Slalom
28. Sundance Gully
29. Eagle's Rest Cutoff
30. Eagle's Rest
31. Pooh Bear
32. Antelope Flats
33. Lower Werner
34. Lower Teewinot
35. Cross Country Ski Trail
36. Solitude Cutoff
37. Ashley Ridge
38. Beaver Tooth
39. Jackson Face
40. Nez Perce
41. Blacktail

42. Sunrise
43. Camp Ground
44. Timbered Island
45. Easy Does It
46. Lift Line
47. Sleeping Indian
48. Wide Open
49. Togwotee Pass Traverse
50. Moran
51. Upper Werner
52. Upper Teewinot
53. St. Johns
54. Teewinot Gully
55. Secret Slope
56. North Hoback
57. South Hoback
58. Tower Three Chute
59. Paint Brush
60. Lander Bowl
61. Hanging Rock
62. U.P. Connection

LIFTS

AERIAL TRAM 2.4 Miles Long
12 Minutes 4,139' Vertical Rise
1. **EAGLE'S REST DOUBLE CHAIR** 2,260' Long
5 Minutes 330' Vertical Rise
2. **TEEWINOT DOUBLE CHAIR** 3,060' Long
7 Minutes 425' Vertical Rise
3. **APRES VOUS DOUBLE CHAIR** 5,000' Long
10 Minutes 1,745' Vertical Rise
4. **THUNDER DOUBLE CHAIR** 3,770' Long
8 Minutes 1,466' Vertical Rise
5. **CASPER BOWL TRIPLE CHAIR** 3,450' Long
8 Minutes 1,046' Vertical Rise
6. **CRYSTAL SPRINGS DOUBLE CHAIR** 4,113' Long
9 Minutes 1,196' Vertical Rise
7. **UPPER SUBLETTE RIDGE QUAD CHAIR** 4,108' Long
9 Minutes 1,630' Vertical Rise
*8. **RENDEZVOUS BOWL SURFACE LIFT** 2,714' Long
5 Minutes 824' Vertical Rise
9. **UNION PASS SURFACE LIFT** 1,360' Long
2 Minutes 150' Vertical Rise

* This lift does not operate during periods of adverse wind,
weather or snow conditions.

IMPORTANT NOTICE
FOR SKI PATROL ASSISTANCE,
DIAL 150 ON ANY SKI PATROL TELEPHONE,
OR CONTACT NEAREST LIFT OPERATOR.

This trail map is conceptual in nature and generally represents the location and difficulty of ski
trails. The classification of ski runs is based on
good weather and snow conditions. During
periods of low visibility or other inclement
weather and snow conditions, the degree of difficulty of the ski runs may change. For specific trail
conditions, ask ski patrol or ski host.

Be aware of changing conditions. Natural and
man-made obstacles exist. Grooming activities
are routinely in progress on slopes and trails. *Use
caution, ski in control, and ski only on designated
slopes or trails.*

Skiing closed areas is a misdemeanor and subject
to a fine of up to $100.00

THE JACKSON HOLE SKI RESORT
IS OPERATED IN COOPERATION
WITH THE BRIDGER-TETON
NATIONAL FOREST.

PRINTED IN USA 1990

well-worn ski clothes
patched here and there with
duct tape. At Jackson Hole,
skiers would rather make a
statement with their ability,
not their attire.

The skiing

Jackson Hole's 4,139-foot
vertical drop is the largest in
the United States. Fully half
of its 2,000 acres is marked
with a black diamond. With
stats like that, it's no wonder
the area has a reputation for
steep, exciting skiing.

But remember that fully half
of the 2,000 acres is *not*
black diamond. Even better,
most of the tough stuff is
completely separate from the
easier runs—intermediates
seldom have to worry about
getting over their heads.

Skiing is spread across three
areas. Rendezvous Mountain
is where you'll find Jackson
Hole's tram and a lot of
chutes, cliffs, bumps and
steep faces. Apres Vous
Mountain has 2,170 vertical
feet of beginner and intermediate terrain, and Casper
Bowl has wide-open
intermediate runs, sprinkled
with a few advanced runs.

One surprising feature of
Jackson Hole is its excellent
beginner terrain. The base of
Apres Vous mountain has
several long, wide, gentle
green runs, perfect for
learning and served by the

Teewinot and Eagle's Rest chairs. Think ahead: in later life, when you're comparing learn-to-ski stories, won't it be more impressive to say you learned to ski here rather than Powder Puff Valley Ski Area?

Jackson Hole is a marvelous place for beginners, but tough for advancing beginners and lower intermediates. It's a big step from those gently undulating green-circle slopes to Jackson Hole's blues. Although the upper parts of Apres Vous and all of Casper Bowl are wide and groomed, they have a much steeper pitch than blues at other resorts, enough to intimidate some lower-level skiers.

Solid intermediates will have a ball. In general, follow the solid blue lines for groomed terrain and the broken blue lines for ungroomed powder or bumps. You'll run out of gas before you run out of terrain. There are 22 miles of groomed intermediate trails alone.

Still too tame for you? Then board the big red tram for the 4,139-foot, 12-minute rise to the top of Rendezvous Mountain. This is where the big boys and girls go to play. Because area management charges an extra $2 for each tram ride, on top of your lift ticket, you really have to want to be here. And be forewarned: The "easiest" way down from the summit is Rendezvous Bowl, a huge, treeless face littered with gigantic moguls. Head the opposite direction and you'll face one of the most famous runs in North America, Corbet's Couloir. The most famous of Jackson Hole's many chutes, Corbet's is a narrow, rocky passage that requires a 10- to 20-foot airborne entry.

Further down the mountain are the Hobacks, a spacious area that offers some of the best lift-served powder skiing in America. Experts looking for a warmup should try Rendezvous' longest run, Gros Ventre, which starts out in Rendezvous Bowl, winds across the tops of Cheyenne and Laramie bowls, then mellows just enough the rest of the way down to earn a blue rating on the trail map It may be bright blue on the map, but navy blue under your skis.

Mountain rating

Color Rendezvous Mountain and the Hobacks jet black, with occasional splashes of navy-blue advanced intermediate. Casper Bowl is for intermediates up to experts, depending on the grooming. When groomed, Casper's runs can be a cruising delight. Ungroomed, they are just plain hard work, worthy of advanced skiers. Apres Vous is fantastic for advanced intermediates, so-so for advancing beginners and great for solid intermediates.

Snowboarding

Snowboarding is permitted on all areas of the mountain. A couple of natural halfpipes are Sundance Gully and Dick's Ditch. The ski school gives snowboard lessons and local shops rent boards.

Nearby skiing

The **Snow King Ski Area** is in downtown Jackson, about 12 miles from Jackson Hole. Sixty percent of its 400 acres is rated advanced, thanks to a north-facing slope that plunges sharply above the streets of the town. Its only green-rated terrain is a snaky catwalk that traverses the mountain from the summit to the base. Because it is so steep, always shaded and often icy, locals call it "Eastern skiing out West." Lift tickets are $25 for adults; kids 14 and younger and seniors 60 and older, $16. The hill is open for night skiing Tuesday through Saturday, and tickets are $12 after 5:30 p.m.

Grand Targhee is a 45-minute drive from Jackson. Known for superb powder runs, its 1,500 acres also has excellent groomed trails for intermediates and a separate learning area. If you like ungroomed powder, this is the place.

Cross country (92/93 prices)

Jackson Hole has some of the most beautiful natural surroundings in the United States. Nordic skiers can strike out for marked trails in Grand Teton or Yellowstone National Parks, or try one of the six touring centers in Jackson and Grand Targhee.

The **Jackson Hole Touring Center** (307-733-2292, Ext. 129) serves as the hub of the Nordic systems in Teton Village with 22 kilometers of groomed track. Because it is next to the downhill ski area, it has telemark lessons as an option. Full-day beginner group lessons, including rentals and trail fee, are $30 adult and $18 child. Half-day lessons for all levels are $25 and $12 respectively. Private instruction is $45 per hour for one student, with additional students paying $10 apiece.

The excursions into the back country are exciting. A tour of the Grand Teton National Park trails costs $40 each for four skiers in a group, or $65 each for a two-skier group. The half-day tour costs $40 per skier, based on a two-person minimum.

Rentals are $12 a day (boots, skis and poles), or $7 for children and seniors. Trail fees are $8 for adults and $5 for children; after 12:30 p.m., prices are $5 and $3.

Other touring centers are **Grand Targhee** (307-353-2304 or 800-443-8146), **Spring Creek** (307-733-8833), **Teton Pines** (307-733-1005) **Togwotee Mountain Lodge** (307-543-2847 or 800-543-2847) and **Trails End Ranch** (307-733-1616).

Ski school (92/93 prices)

Given Jackson Hole's extreme terrain, it's good that the ski school is headed by a three-time Olympic skiing medalist Pepe Stiegler, who has one medal of each metal. The school not only helps the skier make major improvements in his abilities, but is also the place to engage a knowledgeable mountain guide. Jackson Hole's nooks and crannies can best be enjoyed with someone who knows how to reach them.

Full-day and half-day adult group lessons are $40 and $30 respectively. Private lessons cost $45 per hour for a single skier and $10 for each additional skier (if you want Stiegler to teach you, it's $100 per 90 minutes; $25 for each additional person). Three-day group-lesson packages, a.m. or p.m., are $70, and the four-day Ski Meister course in moguls, powder and racing is $150.

The SKIwee program for children has full-day group lessons running $30 and half-day lessons for $22.

Lift tickets (92/93 prices)

Full day, $39; afternoon, $30; four days, $140; five days, $165. Multi-day purchases may be extended for $32 to $35 a day. Children 14 and younger and seniors 65 and older pay about half the adult price. As noted above, each tram ride is $2 additional.

Accommodations (92/93 prices)

You have three locations to choose from: Teton Village at the base of the slopes, with fewer restaurants and nightlife options; the town of Jackson, with lots of eating, shopping and partying, but 12 miles from skiing; or a few condo developments and a major butte-top resort in between the two. Bus transportation between town and ski area is readily available.

Teton Village: The following hotels are all within steps of the slopes and each other, so make your choice on facilities rather than location. The seven-day package is per person double occupancy, the daily rate is per room.

Alpenhof (800-732-3244; 307-733-3242) is the most luxurious of the hotels. Built in peaked-roof Alpine style with lots of exposed wood, it has an excellent restaurant and a large lounge that is a center of relaxed apres-ski activity. It has a heated outdoor pool, Jacuzzi, sauna and game room. Rooms generally are rented in a seven-day package that includes a five-day lift pass and round-trip transportation from the airport. Double occupancy cost ranges from $488 to $1,1188 based on time of year. Daily rates, when rooms are available, are $89-$289.

The Best Western Inn at Jackson Hole (800-842-7666; 307-733-2311) has the most spacious rooms available (short of condos). It has a heated outdoor pool and Jacuzzi. Rates for the seven-day package based on double occupancy in a standard room are $352 to $1,034. Daily rates are $50-$245.

Sojourner Inn (800-445-4655; 307-733-3657) started out as a European lodge but additions have turned it into a rambling hotel with pool, sauna and Jacuzzi. The Main Lodge has the cozier rooms; the one in the Mountain Lodge are larger and more modern. Seven-day package rate is $439 to $964; daily rate is $75 to $225.

Hostel (307-733-3415) has some of the most inexpensive slopeside lodging in the United States—$316 for the seven-day package and $41 per night per room with one or two skiers; $54 per room for three or four (that's $13 per night!)

Crystal Springs Inn (307-733-4423) is motel-like—clean and unluxurious. The seven-day package rate is $408-$471; daily rates are $66-$84 per double room.

Condominiums are available through Jackson Hole Vacation Rentals (800-443-6840, 307-733-4610) and Jackson Hole Realty Property Management (800-443-8613, 307-733-7945). A two-bedroom unit ranges from about $628 to $1,927 for the seven-day package; $129 to $500 per night.

Town of Jackson: Probably the best hotel in terms of facilities and location is the **Wort Hotel**, an 1880s-style, four-diamond AAA-rated hotel that is just off the main square. The seven-day package runs $525 to $893; single nights are $105-$210.

Snow King Resort is another popular vacationers' choice, although it has more of a Holiday Inn atmosphere. Also, it's a little further from downtown, but right next to the Snow King Ski Area, which has night skiing. Seven-day package is $473-$1,313; single nights, $90-$330.

The **Antler Motel** and the **Parkway Inn** have medium-priced lodging, about $48-$96 per night. The least expensive place in town is the **Western Motel** at $36-$52 per night and $299-$355 for the seven-day package. The Western even has a hot tub and cable TV.

Between town and the ski area: One of the most impressive sights in this area is the ragged peak of Grand Teton Mountain. Unfortunately, you can't see it from the ski area (too close) or from town (the East Gros Ventre Butte blocks the way). The solution? Stay on top of the offending butte at the **Spring Creek Resort**. The resort has luxurious hotel rooms, condominiums and a couple of homes for rent, a marvelous gourmet restaurant and unsurpassed views of the Jackson Valley, Grand Teton and the ski area. Rates start about $120-$500 per couple per night, and the package range is $578-$1,980. Shuttles to town and the ski area are provided.

Dining

Jackson has a lot of excellent eatin' places, most of which you'll find in town. But you won't starve in Teton Village either. At one end of the spectrum is the **Alpenhof Hotel Restaurant** (733-3462), a quiet, genteel place that serves German and Austrian specialties. At the other extreme is **The Mangy Moose** (733-4913), beloved for its salad bar, down-home steak-and-seafood menu, and lively atmosphere. Somewhere between is **The Sojourner Inn's Fondue Pot,** (733-3657) where cheese and seafood fondue warm a crisp winter night. Seems the proprietors of these Teton Village restaurants got together for a price-setting session—all are in the $7-$15 range for dinner.

In town, you have many choices. For casual, fun, inexpensive dining, it's **Bubba's** heaping plates of "bubbaqued" ribs, chicken, beef and pork. No sense in giving you the phone number, because Bubba's doesn't take reservations. Be prepared to wait, and don't expect any favors. Local legend says that Maria Shriver and Arnold Schwarzenegger wanted to be seated immediately upon arrival and Bubba's told them to wait, or walk. (Never did find out which they chose, but they should have waited.) And while you wait, send a member of your party across the street to the conveniently located liquor store—Bubba's is BYOB.

Other casual places are the **Calico Pizza Parlor** (733-2460), where actor Harrison Ford celebrates his birthday; and **Mountain High Pizza Pie** (733-3646).

For excellent dining, **the Granary** (733-8833) at Spring Creek Resort is hard to beat. Entrees range from $15 to $25 and include such local delicacies as medallions of elk. Other good choices are **The Blue Lion** (733-3912), known for its roast rack of lamb; **Gouloff's** (733-1886), with several interesting game bird dishes on its menu; and **Sweetwater Restaurant** (733-3553), with a variety of upscale beef, chicken and fish selections. **Cadillac** (733-3279) is trendy—sometimes fantastic, sometimes so-so. **Lame Duck** (733-4311) has the best reputation of the two Chinese restaurants in town. For Mexican food, go to **Vista Grande** (744-6964), and for pasta, head for **Nani's Genuine Pasta House** (733-3888).

For breakfast, try **Bubba's**, **The Bunnery** (733-5474), which has excellent omelets, whole-grain waffles and bakery items; or **Jedediah's** for great sourdough specialties.

Après ski/nightlife

In Teton Village the rowdiest spot by far is **The Mangy Moose**. In town, **The Million Dollar Cowboy Bar** attracts tourists who love the authentic saddle bar stools and the silver dollars encased in the bar's surface, and locals who like to two-step to the live Country & Western bands and watch the tourists take pictures of each other on the saddle stools. As corny as it sounds, you gotta go. Once. **The Silver Dollar Bar** is similar, but has more silver dollars in the bar and less kitsch. **The Shady Lady Saloon** at the Snow King Resort has live entertainment several nights a week.

Child care

Infant care (2-18 months) is $43 for a full day; $30 for half day. Child care (18 months to 14 years) is the same price, but includes lunch and a snack.

A four-hour ski lesson with lift ticket and child care the rest of the day runs $48 per day for ages 3-5 and $66 for ages 6-14, with multi-day discounts available. Lunch is $14 extra. Reservations required for all programs.

Other activities

One of the more unusual activities is a sleigh ride through Jackson's elk refuge. Thousands of elk winter in the valley, eating the hay provided by their human friends and going calmly about their business as the sleigh passes. The cost is about $15, including transportation from your hotel. Reservations required; call 733-3135 or 733-2888.

Another fun sleigh ride is along the East Gros Ventre Butte at night to see the sparkling lights of Jackson below. Rides leave from the Granary restaurant at Spring Creek Resort; ride and dinner cost $45. Call 733-8833 for reservations.

Other activities include dog-sled rides, snowmobile excursions to Granite Hot Springs, helicopter touring and skiing, and of course nearby Grand Teton and Yellowstone National Parks.

Jackson has many art galleries and excellent shopping.

Getting there

American, Delta, Continental, United and United Express serve the Jackson Hole airport. Rental cars are plentiful, but skiers can get along fine without one. Southern Teton Area Rapid Transit (START) buses run frequently between Jackson and Teton Village at a cost of $2 each way. Jackson Hole Transportation runs airport shuttles.

Information/reservations

Jackson Hole Central Reservations, 800-443-6931, for lodging, lifts and transfers.

Grand Targhee Wyoming

Grand Targhee never thinks about putting in snowmaking equipment. It boasts "Snow from the sky, not from a hose." Regulars get concerned when they have to share their 500 inches a year with visitors busing in from other less blessed areas. They're friendly at Targhee, which has a sweeping cowboy panorama like no other. It's just that they like to have their snow and ski it too. They fret at waiting a couple minutes in a lift line.

Grand comes from the backdrop of 13,700-foot Grand Teton Mountain, and Targhee from a local peacekeeping Indian in the mid-1800's. When Averell Harriman was scouting for his dream resort, he narrowed it down to Targhee and the site that became Sun Valley. Local ranchers and farmers opened Targhee as a ski resort more than 20 years ago.

The lift attendants are ranchers who have been at the area forever. Their working attire includes 10-gallon hats, and they'll lasso your skis if you edge ahead in the lift line. In fact, they chute waiting skiers like cattle, holding them back with ropes and sporting with them. A back rub for women is common. Gloria Steinem wouldn't like it.

Any kind of village would seem crowded on this far-flung terrain. The resort buildings are a hodge-podge of shape and color, quaint and modern at the same time. A fire destroyed the base lodge, retail building and adminis-

---

Grand Targhee Facts

Base: 8,000'; **Summit elevation:** 10,250'; **Vertical drop:** 2,200 feet
Number of lifts: 4—3 double chairs,1 surface lift
Snowmaking: none **Total acreage:** 1,500 skiable acres
Bed Base: 432 at the mountain

trative offices in March of 1990. Rebuilt in time for the winter season, the resort won a *Snow Country* award for the best day lodge design in North America.

Expansion is coming, with three lifts planned for Peaked Mountain to the south, where snowcat skiing is now offered. One of the existing three lifts is to be replaced with a high speed detachable quad in 1993, and a new hotel is planned for 1994.

The skiing

Three chair lifts open high, broad descents mostly above treeline. However, 1,500 acres are more than you expect from three chairs, and most of the terrain is skiable. The gentle, consistent fall lines are good for learning how to powder ski. Most of the skiing is for families and intermediates, with few narrow trails. The 2,200-foot vertical rises from an 8,000-foot-high base. Lifts can take up 3,600 skiers an hour, but on a big day at Targhee the crowd is 1,600.

Fred's Mountain, where most of the skiing is done, has excellent cruiser runs and good bump slopes. Tree skiing can be found here and there.

Peak Mountain, just south, has another 1,500 acres reserved for snowcat skiing. In 1991-92 1800 snowcat skier days were recorded. Almost half were intermediates who learned how to powder ski.

Snowboarding

The area has a gradual, groomed half-pipe that is safer than most. Snowboarding is allowed on all of Fred's Mountain.

Cross-country

The Targhee Nordic Center has ten kilometers of track groomed for touring and skating. The track courses through varied terrain, offering vistas of the Greater Yellowstone area as well as meadows and aspen glades.

The Nordic Education Center teaches telemarking as well as touring and skating techniques to both adults and children.

Group lessons are $18 and private lessons $40 an hour.

Guided tours are offered through meadows and along streams. Telemarkers are taken to the powder bowls of

Teton Pass. Full day per-person rates are $95 for one, $60 for two, $45 for three and $35 for four or more. Half day rates are $55 for one, $35 for two, $25 for three, and $20 for four or more.

Trail Pass Rates are $6 a day, $3 for a senior or child, $35 for a 10-day pass, $80 for a season pass, children under 5 free.

For information telephone (800) 443-8146, Ext. 1352, or write Targhee Nordic, Box Ski, Alta, WY 83422.

Ski school

Many instructors have stayed on at a ski school dating back to 1969. The school is noted for its teaching of children and advanced lessons with a coaching approach.

The Small Fry Ski Program offers group half-day lessons for $10 (ages 5-9) and private lessons for $20 (ages 2 and up).

The Targhee Tigers Ski Program offers special coaching and techniques to children 9 to 12 years old. The group half day lesson costs $12.

For adults, private lessons run $40 an hour and half-day group lessons $18.

Lift tickets

Full day is $27; half-day is $17 a.m. or p.m. Other discounts are available for seniors, children, and disabled skiers. Kids 5 years and under ski free.

Snowcat Skiing: 2800-foot vertical, 1,500 acres, gourmet lunch provided for full-day skiers. Full-day $125 for Targhee lodging guests, $145 everyone else, $90 half-day. For reservations call (800) 443-8146 or 353-2304.

Accommodations

The village sleeps 432 people at two lodges and three condos.

Nightly rates per room at the lodges run from $77 to $227, at the condos $145 to $382.

Packages that include ski tickets and one group lesson are offered for seven nights and six days, five nights and four days, and three nights and three days.

For the lodges, regular season packages per person for two people range from $210 to $249 for three days, $313 to

$370 for five nights and four days, $444 to $524 for seven nights and six days.

For the Sioux Lodge condo lofts, regular season packages per person for two people range from $371 to $395 for three days and three nights, $583 to $623 for five nights and four days, and $822 to $879 for seven nights and six days.

Call (800) 443-8146 for information.

Dining

In the village, Cicero's Bistro has homebaked croissants and pastries and many kinds of coffee.

Skadi's has Rocky Mountain Oysters for an appetizer, "The original bull fry fritter, horseradish, cocktail sauce," for $4.75. The restaurant has a woody, crackling atmosphere that features a huge stuffed grizzly bear. Entrées include Louisiana Jambalaya, $13.95, rack of spring lamb, $14.75, sauteed red trout fillet, $11.95, fillet of Norwegian salmon, $13.50.

Salsa de Border has shrimp fajitas for $10.25, taco salad Grand Targhee for $5.75, pork carnitas for $7.95.

Après ski/nightlife

Grandly isolated, this isn't Targhee's strength. However, there is music nightly at the **Trap Bar,** an outdoor heated swiming pool, and complimentary movies. Jackson is an hour away.

Getting there

Targhee is served by jetports in Jackson, Wyoming and Idaho Falls, Idaho. Resort shuttles pick up guests at both airports by reservation for $20. Children are free. Car rentals are available at the airports and at Grand Targhee.

Targhee is eight miles inside the Wyoming border on the west side of the Tetons, accessible only from Idaho. By car, it is 42 miles northwest of Jackson, Wyoming; 87 miles northeast of Idaho Falls; 290 miles north of Salt Lake City.

Information/reservations

Write Grand Targhee Ski & Summer Resort, Box Ski, Alta WY 83422. (800) 443-8146.

Sugarloaf/USA
Maine

Tucked far upcountry in Maine, Sugarloaf/USA is a condo-studded ski resort with the small town of Kingfield nearby. But the main focus is the resort and the skiing. This is a skiers' mountain—a major, *major* mountain, with 2,837 feet of skiable vertical. Sugarloaf's slogan is "Quality service and quality snow"—according to our researchers, they live up to it.

The first impression of Sugarloaf, as you wind along Route 27 and then round "Omigosh!" corner for your initial unobstructed look at the mountain, is that of a very big, very well *utilized* Berg. Runs snake down from the crown in every direction. This is pure northeast skiing zigzagging through cut evergreen forest. Because there are so many runs from the top, each with its own unique twists and turns, Sugarloaf offers a variety of skiing that goes beyond its already impressive size. As one guide put it, "Sugarloaf not only has good *uphill* capacity in its lifts, it has exceptional *downhill* capacity too."

Because of its situation facing north toward the nearby Canadian border, the one thing Sugarloaf does not have an overabundance of is sunshine on the slopes. Because of this, combined with its high latitude, Sugarloaf boasts snow that tends to come early and stay late.

Sugarloaf/USA Facts
Base elevation: 1,400'; **Summit elevation:** 4,237'; **Vertical drop:** 2,837 feet.
Number and types of lifts: 14—1 4-passenger gondola, 2 quad chairs, 1 triple chair, 8 double chairs, 2 surface lifts
Acreage: 400 skiable acres; **Percent of snowmaking:** 90 percent.
Uphill capacity: 19,400 skiers per hour **Bed base:** 6,000

The Skiing

This is a good all-round mountain for any level of skier, but what sets it apart from more run-of-the-mill areas is that it has enough steep and challenging runs to keep experts happily banging the boards all day. Except for the exposed snowfields (rarely open) just below the gondola at the top knoll of the mountain, the skiing is below the tree line.

Experts will need little assistance to figure out where to go on this mountain. Double-diamond on the trail map is the honest truth.

Steep black runs beckon from the summit on both sides of the main gondola, though the ones on the left are the more difficult grade. The blacks down to the new King Pine highspeed quad are all sweet and steep, if a little short. Bump monkeys should head for Choker on this side of the mountain, or to Skidder on the west side; groomers purposely leave them undisturbed for mogul skiing. The very-steep King Pine T-bar also accesses this area and is the only way up on windy days when the quad is closed. Another challenge for experts is to ski straight down gondola line—it's groomed, but steep.

Advanced intermediates will find that they can handle most of the single-diamond blacks on this mountain. The Narrow Gauge run from the Spillway East chair is particularly worthy, and because it is officially rated for Downhill, Super-G and Slalom racing, in early season you can find yourself skiing next to the U.S. Ski Team. This is also the closest an intermediate should get to the top. The entire section served by the Wiffletree highspeed quad is an intermediate skiers playground. On the other side of the mountain the Tote Road stretches from the top of the gondola and winds down three miles to the base lodge.

Beginners will find the broad and very gentle Boardwalk run and the base of the mountain to their liking. The West Mountain run, under the chair by that name, off to the right as you face the mountain is also excellent for beginners. Those looking for a little more challenge graduate to the paths leading back down to the base lodge from the top of Bucksaw chair.

Try skiing down the trails served by the Bucksaw chair for easy end-of-the-day cruising which is particularly enjoyable on sunny days when they catch the last rays.

Snowboarding

Allowed on the entire mountain. There is a halfpipe as well as lessons and rentals. Maine does not require leashes on snowboards.

Cross-country

Sugarloaf has over 80 km. (groomed, double-track) of cross-country trails. The Carrabassett Valley Ski Touring Center is the largest and most complete in Maine. The center is off Route 27, south of the entrance to the Sugarloaf/USA access road. Both rentals and lessons are offered. The center also has an Olympic-sized outdoor skating rink and spacious facilities for the skiers—giant fireplace, large, south-facing deck and both hot and cold food and drink.

Group lessons are $10 an hour. Private lessons are $20 an hour. The all-day trail fee is $8 for adults, $7 for junior/senior citizens. Equipment rentals are $10 a day for adults and $7 for juniors and seniors. Call (207) 237-2205.

Multiday Alpine ticket purchasers may exchange a day of skiing at Sugarloaf/USA for a day of cross-country including trail fee, lesson and equipment. Exchange tickets at the guest services desk in the base lodge.

Ski school (92/93 prices)

Sugarloaf has an extensive array of ski school programs. Group lessons are $20 per two-hour course for adults over 14 years. Private lessons are $40 an hour.

For kids between seven and 14 years there is a Mountain Adventure program for $55 a day, including lunch, or $40 for a half day. Younger children from four to six years are in Mountain Magic that costs $42 for a full day including lunch. Half days cost $27; a five-day, full-day package will add up to $190; and the five half-days program is $115. Registration is in the children's center.

Special weeks have been organized through the season. Ski Challenge Week runs 24-28 February and includes two cocktail receptions, a group dinner and timed races for $680 per person, double occupancy.

A women's ski week 24-28 February includes five days of lifts, coaching, fashion show, video sessions, races and

sugarloaf/usa

SUMMIT 4,237'

BE AWARE.
SKI WITH CARE.

SUGARLOAF GOLF CLUB

BIRCH HOOK
WINDROW EXT.
BUCKSAW X-CUT
BULLWINKLE'S

WEST MOUNTAIN

HORSESHOE

WEST MOUNTAIN CUT

U WINDROW

SCOOT

WINDROW

GLANCER

SPUR LINE

MAINTENANCE ROAD

VILLAGE

P

JAMES
NIEHUES

MOUNTAINSIDE ROAD

ARTREE
TH CLUB

W. BROOK

SUGARLOAF ACCESS ROAD

WEST MOUNTAIN ROAD

CHECK-IN
CENTER

EAST MOUNTAIN ROAD

P

LIFTS

GONDOLA: ⑤

HIGH CAPACITY QUADS:
① KING PINE ② WHIFFLETREE

TRIPLE CHAIR:
④ SNUBBER

DOUBLE CHAIRS:
⑥ SKIDWAY ⑦ SAWDUSTER ⑧ DOUBLE
CHAIR EAST ⑨ DOUBLE CHAIR WEST
⑩ SPILLWAY EAST ⑪ SPILLWAY WEST
⑬ BUCKSAW ⑭ WEST MOUNTAIN

T-BARS:
③ KING PINE ⑫ BATEAU

storage for $680 with lodging. $430 without lodging. A weekend women's clinic is held on December 14-15 for $450 with lodging per person double occupancy.

Lift tickets (92/93 prices)

Full day, $38 for adults; $31 for teens 13-18; and $21 children and seniors (six to 12 and 65+); half day (a.m. or p.m.), $30 and $17; two days, $68 adult, $54 teen, and $38 child; three days, $99 adults, $78 teens, and $51; five days, $150 adults, $120 teens, and $80 child; seven days, $210, $168 teens, and $112child.

Accommodations

Sugarloaf is basically a planned condominium community in the mold of a Keystone or Copper Mountain. That said, it is one of the more tasteful layouts we've seen, with the central village blending in well with the overall environment. The more luxurious of the two hotels, **The Sugarloaf Mountain Hotel**, is attached to the central village. Per unit rates are $80-$260. The slightly more modest **Sugarloaf Inn** has a quaint New England inn feel. Sugarloaf Inn offers packages that include use of the Sugar Tree Health Club, with pool and weight room.

The most luxurious condominiums in the area are the **Village on the Green**. While these are very high-end units, they are not convenient to the slopes. In summer they're perfect for the golf course, but to get to the lifts in the winter you need car or shuttlebus. (In good snow years it would be possible to ski back to the condos.)

In the ski village area the top property is the **Bigelow** unit. The **Sugartree** units are not as luxurious as the Bigelow but have the health club attached and are very popular and have chairlift access. The **Gondola Village** is the building that houses the nursery, making it extremely popular with families.

There is a special RV parking area at the resort serviced by lifts.

Dining

Sugarloaf is a compact resort, but there are no fewer than 14 restaurants and eateries in the village center alone. The **Truffle Hound** (237-2355; reservations suggested) has elegant, fine dining. Prize for the best piece of meat goes to **Gepetto's** for their teriyaki steak. Our favorite for fine dining and atmosphere was the **Seasons** at the Sugarloaf Inn (237-2000). For pizza or burgers in a homey, noisy atmosphere, try **The Bag and Kettle** (locals simply call it "The Bag."). The owner is deservedly famous for his homemade soups, and this is the best spot to hear the lore of Sugarloaf from the locals. **Galdstone's** is a major lunch spot and the place to mingle with the ski school. **Snow Peas** in the Sugarloaf Mountain Hotel serves Asian cuisine and features live enterainment on Friday and Saturday.

No trip to a northeast ski area is complete in our view without a visit to an authentic New England inn, and the **The Inn on Winter's Hill** in Kingfield is worth the 20-mile drive. The food and atmosphere in **Julia's** is excellent, and ask proprietors Richard and Carolyn Winnick for a tour of this fully renovated inn (265-5426). **One Stanley Avenue** and the **Herbert Hotel** in Kingfield are also worth a visit. **One Stanley Avenue** features a unique menu full of Maine-grown fare.

In Eustis, 20 minutes north of Sugarloaf, there are also two restaurants worth checking out: **The Trail's End** for steaks and the **Porter House Restaurant** for home cooking. **Tufulio's**, on Route 27 near Sugarloaf, offers Italian and American dishes in a casual atmosphere.

Après-ski/nightlife

The nightlife choices are few at Sugarloaf, though not far between. On sunny days, the après-ski crowd gathers on the decks of **Arabella's at the Gladstone's** or at **The Bag**. **Gringo's** with good Mexican munchies and the nearby **Widowmaker** at the base lodge are other good après-ski.

The hottest spot for live music (weekends only) and dancing at night is the aforementioned **Widowmaker**, and there's also music and dancing in a more subdued atmosphere at **The Sugarloaf Inn**.

On Route 27 in the valley, you'll find the locals at **Carrabassett Yacht Club** or **Judson's**.

Teenagers can head to **Rascals**, an alcohol-free teen spot with video games, music videos, snack bar, pool table and special dances. Thursdays, Sugarloaf Mountain Hotel holds Reggae Night.

Child care

There is a special section of the mountain called Moose Alley which offers kids the chance to do some controlled glade (tree) skiing.

There are children's activities almost every night in the Mountain Magic Room in the base lodge. On Mondays there is storytelling, Disney movies on Tuesdays, skating on Wednesdays at the touring center, and games on Thursday.

Other activities

Dog sled rides are available by calling Tim Diehl at (207) 246-4461.

Guest services at 237-2000 can arrange activities ranging from the dog sleds to skating and can help out with almost any question from automobile service to conferences and child care.

Getting there

Driving: Take I-95 north to Augusta, Route 27 through Farmington and Kingfield to Sugarloaf/USA. Or take the Maine Turnpike to the Auburn exit, follow Route 4 to Route 27N at Farmington, through Kingfield to Sugarloaf/USA. The resort is approximately two and a half hours from Portland.

By air: The closest major airport with nationwide service is Portland Jetport. Sugarloaf has a Mountain Express shuttle from Portland, with daily service in 13-passenger vans. There's a ground transportation desk at Portland Jetport, (800) 628-2821. The closest private airport is Sugarloaf Regional, 8 miles from the resort.

Information/reservations

For lodging reservations, call (800) THE-LOAF nationwide and Canada; or (207) 237-2000.

Snow report: (207) 737-2000.

Write: Sugarloaf/USA, Carrabassett Valley, ME 04947.

Another reservation number for accommodations only is the Sugarloaf Area Chamber Reservation Service, tel. (207) 235-2500).

Sunday River, Maine

Sunday River, just outside of Bethel and tucked against the New Hampshire border, is a surprising resort and a pleasant blend of old New England tradition with modern ski condominiums. Bethel is a typically picturesque New England town, complete with white-steepled church and ivy-covered prep school. The main street is lined with historic old buildings, and the village common is anchored by the 75-year-old Bethel Inn.

The Sunday River Ski Resort rises six miles to the north, an hour and a half drive from the Portland airport and three to three and a half hours from Boston. As you drive up the access road to the base area, you see condominium complexes right and left. But they don't assault you, they blend with the trees and hills.

The resort doesn't have a main center packed with restaurants, shops and bars. Three separate base lodges— South Ridge, Barker Mountain, and White Cap—provide basic cafeteria and sports shop facilities. South Ridge Lodge is the hub, housing the ski school, the corporate offices and a grocery store. The condominium complexes are small centers to themselves with most boasting an indoor or heated outdoor pool, Jacuzzis and saunas. A sense of quiet results: the bustle of people created by a town or central hub is dispersed into the condominiums.

Sunday River Facts

Base elevation: 782'; **Summit elevation:** 2,793'; **Vertical drop:** 2,011 feet
Number of lifts: 1 high-speed quad, 4 quad chairs, 4 triple chairs, 2 double chairs
Percent of snowmaking: 95 percent **Snowmaking (total acreage):** 453 acres
Total acreage: 480 skiable acres
Uphill capacity: 21,000 per hour **Bed base:** 4,720

The skiing

The original base area was Barker Mountain. With the addition of the South Ridge beginner area, which opened access for the surrounding condominiums, and with the development of the Aurora Peak area the resort offers skiing on six peaks. Each area of the mountain provides distinctive skiing.

Beginners start on Sundance and then have the entire South Ridge area to practice linking their turns. There are twelve beginner runs in the South Ridge area serviced by two doubles and a triple chair. Advanced beginners can also head to the White Cap quad and enjoy the relatively mellow Moonstruck, Starburst and Starlight runs.

Once a skier is past the basic snowplow and into stem christies, the rest of Sunday River beckons. The North Peak triple chair lift opens long mellow practice runs like Dreammaker and Escapade.

Other chairs open both intermediate and advanced terrain. Spruce Peak is a cruiser's delight along with Risky Business, American Express and Downdraft. Though one of these trails is rated black, a competent intermediate will have no trouble with it.

The Aurora area served by a fixed quad chair provides experts with plenty of challenge. Since the area is only reached by a black diamond run, the area remains, for the most part, the province of experts and advanced intermediates. On Vortex you can expect a long long plunge through big big bumps. Though Northern Lights is marked intermediate, the access is very narrow and during our visits scraped ice.

From the top of Barker Mountain there is a steep trio—Right Stuff, Top Gun and Agony which will provide advanced skiers long sustained pitches. Agony and Top Gun are premier bump runs, almost never smoothed. Right Stuff is a dreamlike cruiser early in the day after it's been groomed, but normally develops mellow moguls by the afternoon. After Agony, try Ecstasy for relaxed cruising.

From the top of Locke Mountain, T-2, plunging down the tracks of an old T-bar, provides a direct fall-line drop, and taking the turn around Bim's Whim provides a spectacular view of Bethel, the valley and Mt. Washington to the west. If you aren't looking for your skiing to be pushed, Sunday Punch is another mellow cruiser, or split off Upper Sunday Punch and take Cascades down to the Barker Base area. Halfway down Cascades, skiers can take a right turn onto Tempest (this trail is a steep intermediate in the morning, but bumped by afternoon), which together with Wildfire and the short Jibe, is served by the Little White Cap Quad (Lift 9). A halfpipe curls at the bottom of Tempest. Another trail to try for advanced intermediates is Monday Mourning which starts out steep and wide and mellows towards the end which is home of the NASTAR course.

In the morning the sun shines on advanced intermediate and advanced skiers heading up the White Heat quad. From the peak the White Heat run, a wide swath, cuts straight down the mountain from the peak of White Cap. When you put all the superlatives together, this run is the steepest, longest and widest lift-served expert trail in the East. Double-diamond Shockwave offers 975 vertical feet of big bumps and steep pitches. On the opposite side of White Hear, Obsession is a sweet regulation GS trail.

Mountain Rating

Sunday River is perfect for beginners, with one of the most extensive lift-served beginner areas in New England, outpaced perhaps only by Killington with its Snowshed area. The ski school here is oriented to getting beginners on skis and skiing fast. They guarantee that you learn to ski in a day, or your money back. And last year out of 9056 beginners only a handful failed.

For intermediates, a mountain full of terrain that a good intermediate can handle makes Sunday River just what the ski doctor ordered. For experts, you'll find super steeps and monster bumps on Aurora Peak, Barker Mountain and White Cap.

Come with the attitude for great sustained cruising and packing in vertical, using the detachable quad to power you up the mountain and setting your sights on any of Sunday River's great cruisers.

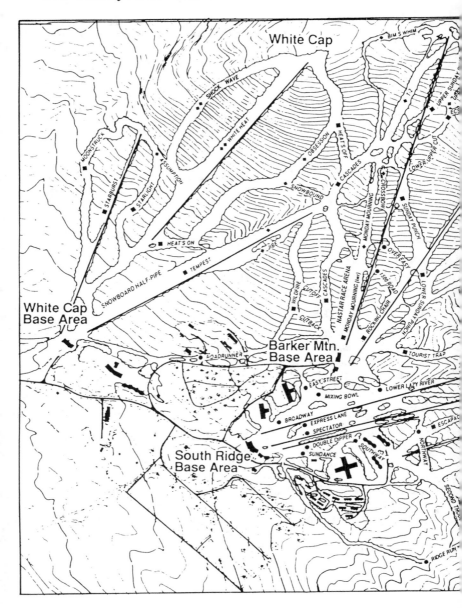

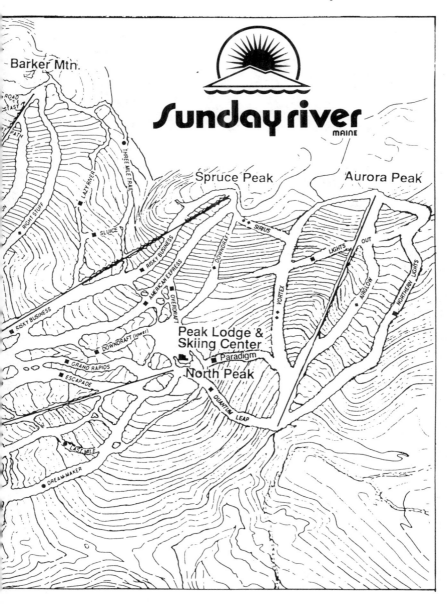

Cross-country

Though Sunday River does not have a dedicated cross-country center, this area of Maine is known for some of the best cross-country in New England. The Bethel Inn Cross-country Ski Center behind the hotel links up with 30 km. of marked and groomed trials. They have rentals, lessons and guided moonlight tours. The Bethel Inn also has facilities for instructing in telemark. Call: 824-2175.

Trail fees are $7 during the week and $10 on weekends. The fee during the week is also good for entrance to the recreation center, with outdoor heated pool, sauna and fitness center, until 2 p.m.

The Sunday River Ski Touring Center (824-2410) is run by the Sunday River Inn on the Sunday River access road. It has 40 km. of groomed and tracked trails.

Forty-five minutes from Bethel is the Jackson Ski Touring Center. See the Mt. Washington Valley chapter for full details of their ski touring programs.

Snowboarding

Snowboarders are allowed to shred anywhere at Sunday River. There are no leashes required in Maine. There is a halfpipe at the bottom of the Tempest Trail. The ski school offers Learn-to-Shred and Shred Better clinics which meet at the White Cap Lodge Shred Center. The Learn-to-Shred program, including board, boots and limited lifts, costs $45. The Shred Better clinic lasts one-and-a-half hours and costs $24.

Ski school

Prices in this section are, for the most part, from last season. The Sunday River Ski School has been revamped under the umbrella name Perfect Turn™ Skier Development Program. This program consists of a series of clinics normally lasting 75 minutes with a maximum of six skiers.

Levels 1, 2 and 3 of Perfect Turn make up Guaranteed Learn-to-Ski in One Day™. The program is open to beginners 13 years and over. Level 1 costs $35 per person covered lessons, equipment and lifts for the first day. If you are not satisfied and the instructor agrees, you either got your money back or got a chance to try again the next day or next weekend for free. Levels 2 and 3 cost $45. Followup days will cost $45 a day as you improved skiing skills.

Other Perfect Turn clinics, from level 4 to 10, train skiers to continue to improve their skiing. These clinics will be priced at $20 apiece. Lesson levels four through ten feature use of video to help you perfect your techinque. Lessons meet at the North Peak Lodge which means you are already up the mountain and ready to ski.

Private lesson prices are $45 an hour for one ($20 for each additional student). A special Early Bird private lesson is offered on weekends and holidays from 8:30 to 9:30 a.m. for $35 for one student and $18 for each additional skier. A half-day private lesson (three hours) $105, and a full day (six hours) is $195.

The Black Diamond Club, for advanced to expert skiers, lasts two hours and claims to allow skiers to get in as much as 10,000 vertical feet per session. They are offered Tuesday, Thursday, Saturday and Sunday.

A Woman's Program offers intermediate and advanced skiers a chance to perfect their turns.

Sunday River's learn to ski programs for children are organized into age groups and are designed to work with a game-like atmosphere. Tiny Turns program combines a half- or full-day session in day care with an hour of private instructions for children 3-4 years. SKIwee is for youngsters 4 to 6 years of age. Mogul Meisters is for those from 7 to 12 years of age. All-day lessons for both programs including lunch, lifts and equipment, cost $49. The morning or afternoon programs, without lunch, cost $45 with a full-day lift ticket and $35 for only a p.m. lift ticket.

Lift tickets (91/92 prices)

Weekend full day, $36 adults/$22 children (6-12); weekday full day, $32/$20; weekend half-day, $25/$12; weekday half-day, $22/$15; two-day weekend, $68/$40; three-day weekend, $99/$59; two-day weekday, $62/$40; three-day weekday, $90/$59; four-day weekday, $120/$78; five-day weekday, $160/$95.

Accommodations

The condominium accommodations are the most convenient to the slopes. But Bethel also has a group of excellent bed-and-breakfasts and old country inns. If you are planning a Sunday River vacation call the central reservations number which will handle everything from air travel to day care reservations.

The resort has built a ski dorm designed primarily for groups within walking distance of the slopes.

The **Summit Hotel** and conference center is being built as we go to press. It will be upscale and trailside.

Locke Mountain Townhouses are the most upscale, with the **Merrill Brook** condominiums not far behind. Condominium units are all convenient to the slopes and all have trolley service. If you can avoid the **North Peak** condos, do so. Otherwise the condominium units meet the same standards. Expect to pay $149-$164 midweek for one-bedroom units with a pullout couch. Two-bedroom units run $298 to $325. Additional beds in these units are available for $15 per person per night.

In Bethel the **Bethel Inn** (824-2175) has old stylish atmosphere and first-rate rooms. The rates include breakfast and dinner. Double rates run $75 to $125 per person.

The **Douglass Place** is Bethel's original bed-and-breakfast (824-2229). The proprietor has many tales to tell. **The Four Seasons** is in an old, elegant building with excellent French cuisine (824-2755 or 800-227-7458). **The Sudbury Inn** is one of the best restaurants in town and a favorite watering hole (824-2174). **The Holidae House** in Bethel has drawn praise for its beautiful decor (824-3400). These B&B's cost about $45 to $65 per person per night.

Less than a mile from the base of the mountain, the **Sunday River Inn** (824-2410 offers a relaxed setting reminiscent of the great ski lodges of the 60s. It also operates the closest cross-country center.

Additional lodging can be arranged through Sunday River's reservation line (800) 543-2SKI or the Bethel Area Chamber of Commerce, (207) 824-3585.

Dining

The **Peak Lodge and Skiing Center**, at the summit of North Peak, is a popular lunch spot with a giant deck and great views. **BUMPS! Pub**, also in the White Cap Lodge, serves a pub menu which should be avoided unless you're starving. In contrast **Saturday's**, in the South Ridge base is packed for lunch and dinners with good reason.

The **Fall Line** in the Fall Line Condominiums is convenient, consistent and serves good steaks and seafood. **Rosetto's Italian Restaurant** in the White Cap Lodge is open for dinner everyday and for lunch on weekends and holiday periods.

In Bethel try the **Sudbury Inn** and the **Bethel Inn** which are very popular. For French cuisine head to **The Four Seasons** or to **L'Auberge**. **Mother's** on Upper Main Street is a favorite of students from the Gould Academy as well as skiers. **Cisco and Poncho's** offers Mexican food. **The Backstage** is an odd mix of C&W saloon and Hollywood motif; it is popular with locals serving honest steak-house fare for a reasonable price. **Skidders**, tucked in a tiny storefront on Main Street, makes fantastic deli take-out. The best pizza is reportedly in West Bethel at **The Only Place**, and the best breakfasts in the **Red Top Truck Stop** which opens at 5 a.m. for local loggers.

Après-ski/nightlife

Don't plan on hot action during the week at Sunday River—to be kind . . . basically, Bethel and Sunday River are defunct as far as organized partying. (A last minute flash claims several new bars and a pub with its own micro-brewery are opening next season.)

Immediate après-ski, when found, is at the base of the slopes. Try the **Barker Mountain Base Area**, which has mellow acoustic guitar on weekends, or **BUMPS!** at the White Cap Lodge for libations. **Saturday's** is the liveliest of the mountain spots. In town head to **Sudbury's.**

At night, **BUMPS!** is the focus on the mountain with bands plucking out "top 40" tunes on weekends. Downtown, the **Backstage** usually has country and western or early rock and roll bands on weekends but no entertainment on weekdays. **Sudbury's** has bands ranging from blues to bluegrass on weekends. Crowds are mixed in all dance places but tends to be younger at BUMPS! You'll tend to find more locals at the Backstage and more tourists at Sudbury's.

Child care

The nursery and day-care facilities are located in the Merrill Brook Village Building II.

The nursery is for infants from six weeks to two and a half years. The hourly rate is $6, with additional children in the same family costing $3 per hour. Bring extra diapers, formula and food for infants. All-day programs cost $35 including lunch for older toddlers ($17.50 for additional toddlers from the same family). Call for reservations, especially on weekends (207-824-3000).

Other activities

Sunday River has swimming pools and saunas in virtually every condominium complex except Merrill Brook and the South Ridge Townhouses. Fall Line, Cascades and Sunrise have indoor pools. The Brookside, North Peak and White Cap Village have heated outdoor pools. Pools and saunas do not open before noon. Video games and pool tables can be found at the ski dorm.

Getting there

Sunday River is in western Maine an hour and a half from Portland and three and a half hours from Boston.

Driving: Coming by I-95, take Exit 11 to Route 26 North, continue to Bethel, then take Route 2 six miles north of Bethel to Sunday River Road.

RV parking is allowed in designated parking areas at the resort. No hookups are available. An RV park is also located at White Birch Camping, in Shelburne, on Route 2.

By air: The most convenient airport is Portland International Jetport, 75 miles from Sunday River and served by Continental, Delta, United and USAir. Private pilots can land in Bethel, five miles away. Guests arriving in Bethel may be picked up with advance arrangement.

Information/reservations

Sunday River Resort Reservations: (800) 543-2SKI .
Bethel Area Chamber of Commerce: (207) 824-3585
Ski Report and Information: (207) 824-6400
Address: Sunday River Ski Resort, PO Box 450, Bethel, ME 04217. Administration phone: (207) 824-3000.

Mt. Washington Valley New Hampshire

Wildcat, Cranmore, Attitash, Black Mountain,King Pine, Jackson Touring

These five relatively small ski areas, set into spectacular White Mountain terrain, with the Jackson Ski Touring Foundation (one of the world's best cross-country trail systems), the wild skiing on Mount Washington, and the year-round resort attractions of Mt. Washington Valley, combine to become a multifaceted destination resort.

This was a destination resort long before anyone came here to ski: a quarter century before the Civil War, fashionable northeasterners started coming here for the summer, first by stage line and then by railroad and carriage, to meet Hawthorne and Emerson, enjoy the scenery with Bierstadt, beat the heat, and find suitable husbands for their daughters. Many of the grand old hotels they visited have been brought up to date to add their charm to the mix of condos, motels, country inns, and B&Bs.

Legends of the early days of skiing—the late Thirties—surround you. Ride up the Wildcat gondola and look back at the fantastic bulk of Mt. Washington with its huge scooped-out ravines: this is hallowed ground, where Toni Matt on his wooden boards schussed over the Tuckerman headwall in one long arc to win the 1939 Inferno race, summit to base in six minutes and a half.

Most of all, what makes this area one of the pioneers of downhill skiing in America is the Eastern Slope Ski School, founded by Carroll Reed. This is where the Arlberg method of ski instruction was introduced to North Amer-

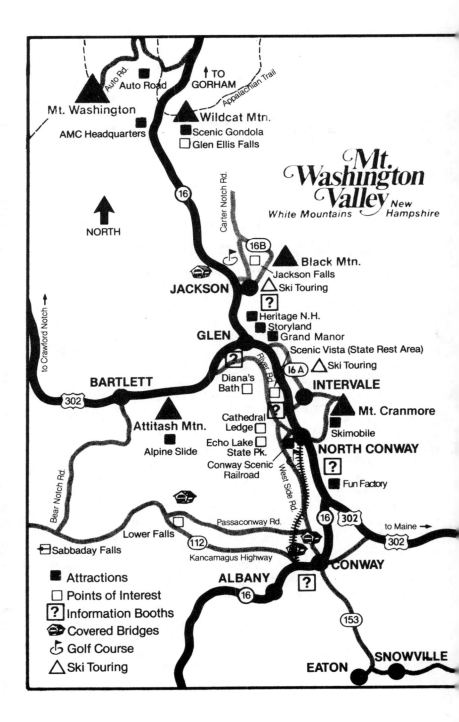

Auto Rd.

Auto Road

↑ TO GORHAM

Appalachian Trail

Mt. Washington

AMC Headquarters

Wildcat Mtn.

Scenic Gondola

Glen Ellis Falls

Mt. Washington Valley New Hampshire

White Mountains

Carter Notch Rd.

16

NORTH

16B

Black Mtn.

Jackson Falls

△ Ski Touring

JACKSON

?

Heritage N.H.

Storyland

Grand Manor

Scenic Vista (State Rest Area)

GLEN

△ Ski Touring

2

River Rd.

16 A

to Crawford Notch ↑

BARTLETT

302

Diana's Bath

INTERVALE

Attitash Mtn.

Cathedral Ledge

Mt. Cranmore

Alpine Slide

Echo Lake State Pk.

Skimobile

Conway Scenic Railroad

NORTH CONWAY

West Side Rd.

?

Fun Factory

Bear Notch Rd.

Passaconway Rd.

16   302

to Maine →

Lower Falls

112

302

Sabbaday Falls

Kancamagus Highway

CONWAY

Attractions

Points of Interest

? Information Booths

Covered Bridges

Golf Course

△ Ski Touring

ALBANY

?

16

153

EATON

SNOWVILLE

ica by Benno Rybizka, and by his Austrian teacher, the famous Hannes Schneider, who was released by the Nazis in return for banking concessions. His son Herbert Schneider is still active at Cranmore, one of many who were there at the beginning of the modern era.

If anyone wants a break from downhill skiing, this is the place: hiking, climbing, and camping out, always prime summer activities here, are pursued in the snow-and-ice season by local and visiting fanatics. And if you want to practice your rock-climbing skills on an indoor wall with chimneys and overhangs, you don't have to go any further.

Restaurants, many of them tucked into the tiny country inns or restored barns in the valley, are world class and have acknowledged gourmet reputations. In fact, this valley is home to one of the most famous cooking schools in the country.

Besides the skiing, picturesque inns and tempting restaurants, there are more tax-free factory outlet stores concentrated in Conway and North Conway than in any other area of the United States, making the region a top shopping destination the year round.

But above all, you're in the valley of Mt. Washington, which P. T. Barnum, an expert but no slave to false modesty, called "the second-greatest show on earth."

The skiing

Wildcat Facts

Base elevation: 1,950'; **Summit elevation:** 4,050'; **Vertical drop:** 2,100 feet.
Number and types of lifts: 6—1 gondola, 4 triple chairs, 1 double chair
Acreage: 120 acres, 15 miles of trails
Percent of snowmaking: 97 percent
Uphill capacity: 8,500 skiers per hour **Bed base:** 6,500+

For more than a decade, Wildcat has been voted the ski area with the most spectacular scenery in the Northeast, with beautiful views across Pinkham Notch to the towering Mt. Washington and Tuckerman's Ravine. Wildcat is known as an untamed resort. However, during the past three years Wildcat has been taming some of the bumpy runs, and a small fleet of grooming machines now smooth out all but two of the trails. The trails themselves have also been modified extensively, being widened and straightened. This resort is still cut out for strong advanced and expert skiers.

The skiing is tempered by three factors: the cold, the wind and the pitch of the slopes. The cold and wind are among the most extreme you'll find in North America and many of the slopes are among the steepest, most demanding and narrowest around, giving Wildcat its well-earned reputation for classic New England skiing. For the intermediate way down the slopes, head to the Polecat side of the gondola; for a descent where it is most prudent to pay attention to the details of skiing, loop to the opposite side. There are intermediate and beginner trails, but people who find themselves at Wildcat are probably there for the challenge. Call: 466-3326; for reservations (800) 255-6439.

Attitash Facts
Base elevation: 550'; Summit elevation: 2,300'; Vertical drop: 1,750 feet.
Number and types of lifts: 6—2 triple chairs, 4 double chairs
Acreage: 220 skiable acres **Percent of snowmaking:** *98 percent*
Uphill capacity: 5,500 skiers per hour **Bed base:** *6,500+*

Attitash, just west of Glen on Route 302 in Bartlett, is a great intermediate mountain, and over the past five years has increased beginner and expert terrain, the latter with Ptarmigan, Tim's Trauma and Idiot's Option; Attitash is one of five official U. S. Ski Team training sites nationwide. It's not too big and not too steep, and has great snowmaking, with 98 percent coverage. Attitash has also recently created the New England Learning Center for beginners, with its own protected learning slope and triple chair, and there are several beginner trails around the Borvig lifts. Ptarmigan is supposed to be one of the steepest trails in New England, but it is manageable for good intermediates because of the elbow room on the run. The rest of the mountain is enough to keep 80 percent of skiers perfectly satisfied, with Northwest Passage serving up great cruising. The grooming fleet smoothes out almost all the steep pitches nightly, but a couple of trails are allowed to bump up when temperatures and snow conditions allow.

Cranmore Facts
Base elevation: 497'; Summit elevation: 1,697'; Vertical drop: 1,200 feet.
Number and types of lifts: 5—1 triple chair, 4 double chairs
Acreage: 185 skiable acres **Percent of snowmaking:** *100 percent*
Uphill capacity: 3,500 skiers per hour **Bed base:** *6,500+*

Cranmore, which just celebrated its 51st anniversary, is one of the oldest resorts in America, one that features good, balanced terrain. If you arrive in North Conway in the evening, you can't miss it: the lights for night skiing, which lasts until 9 p.m., are visible from a long way off and add one more festive ingredient to the town. Because it's right in North Conway, it has the potential to attain a European-style relationship with the town. Cranmore's ambitious $10-million program of improvements lastr season, includes a triple chair lift, new beginner slopes, a fitness center and a 100 percent snowmaking system.

Black Mountain Facts

Base elevation: 1,300'; **Summit elevation:** 2,350'; **Vertical drop:** 1,050 feet.
Number and types of lifts: 4—1 triple chair, 1 double chair, 2 surface lifts.
Acreage: 65 trail acres, 8 miles of trails **Percent snowmaking:** 98 percent
Uphill capacity: 3,700 skiers per hour **Bed base:** 1,500+

Black Mountain, reached by heading up Rte. 16 north of Glen, taking Rte. 16A to Jackson, and following Rte. 16B 3 miles, may be the best place in the valley for beginning lessons and for family skiing. From the front side of the mountain, facing Whitneys' Inn, the area is reminiscent of a country club, but behind the ridge accessed by the double chair are 18 sunny and sheltered south-facing trails ranging from beginner to advanced intermediate skiing. Adjacent to the Jackson Ski Touring area, Black Mountain has also become a center for cross-country skiers interested in trying out telemark skiing. Finally, according to locals, Black Mountain with its southern exposure provides a place to ski when it's just plain too damn cold for anyone in his right mind to attempt Wildcat.

Snowboarding is limited on this mountain. Shredding is not allowed on Black Beauty or Lower Black Beauty trails. Black Mountain has a 350-foot halfpipe.

Mt. Washington—If you like to get to the top the old-fashioned way (you *climb* it) there is the famous spring skiing in Tuckerman's Ravine; all winter, there's the Sherburne Trail and several other areas. Start from Pinkham Notch Camp (see Other Activities). (Note: please check and heed all information, printed or posted, about weather and avalanche conditions. Mt. Washington, when it comes to vicious weather and quick changes, is another breed of cat.)

King Pine Facts

Base elevation: 500; **Summit elevation:** 850; **Vertical drop:** 350 feet.
Number and types of lifts: 4—1 triple chair, 1 double chairs; 2 J-bars
Acreage: 60 skiable acres **Percent of snowmaking:** 95 percent
Bed base: 6,500+

King pine is a small area which just joined the Mount Washington Valley group. It is tiny and has little vertical, but may be just the place for families just starting out to ski.

Snowboarding

New Hampshire law requires snowboarders to have some sort of leash or strap tethering the board to their leg.

Cross-country

Jackson Ski Touring Foundation, Box 216, Jackson, NH 03846, on Route 16A (383-9355) is a mecca for Nordic skiers. It has more than 156 kilometers of groomed trails, country inns are spaced throughout the region, Mt. Washington towers above.

Mt. Washington Valley Ski Touring Association, Box 646, Intervale NH 03845 has over 60 km. of trails. For ski school, rentals, or snow conditions, call (800) 282-5220.

The Appalachian Mountain Club maintains a network of ski touring trails radiating from the AMC Camp at Pinkham Notch; about 7 km. are Easiest (moderately flat) or More Difficult (requiring a strong snowplow and step turn), and about 40 km. are Most Difficult, with long, challenging hills and narrow trails. Call: 466-2721.

The Nestlenook Inn (383-9443), also in Jackson, offers an additional 35 km. of touring winding through its 65-acre farm.

Purity Spring Resort has a 8 km. of Nordic trails near Madison. Call (800) 367-8897 or (603) 367-8896.

Ski school

All the areas have extensive ski schools. Lessons are naturally slanted to the terrain available at each resort.

Group lessons are $20 per session at Wildcat and $16 at Attitash, $17 at Cranmore, and $15 at Black.

Private lessons are $40 an hour for one student at Wildcat; $35 an hour at Attitash, Cranmore and Black.

Lift tickets (92/93 prices)

Attitash's daily weekend ticket is $34 for adults and $19 for children (12 and under); midweek daily tickets, $27/$17. On Sunday, children 12 and younger pay their age to ski. Attitash prices are 91/92.

Wildcat Saturday tickets are $35 for adults, $19 for children 15 and under; Sunday tickets cost $29 for adults and $17 for children. Wildcat weekday tickets cost $27 for adults and $17 for children. On Wednesdays two can ski for the price of one.

Cranmore weekend tickets are $33 for adults and $18 for children 14 and under. Cranmore weekday tickets cost $23 for adults and $15 for children. Cranmore also offers, Friday and Saturday a Twilight Tickets (noon to 9 p.m.) for $33 adults, $18 children; Night Skiing (4 p.m.-9 p.m.) for $15 adults, $12 children.

Black Mountain charges $29 for adults on weekends and $12 midweek. They have a special family passport for $59 which includes two adults and two juniors.]

King Pine lift rates are $23 for adults on weekends, $15 weekdays. Kids ski for $10 a day midweek.

Three-out-of-four-day midweek tickets are interchangeable between Wildcat, Attitash, Cranmore and Black, and cost $78 for adults, $45 for children. The interchangeable four-out-of-five-day midweek pass for the Mt. Washington Valley costs $112 for adults and $64 for children 12 and under.

The Ski the White Mountains five-day, mid-week tickets are $130 for adults; no charge for one child, 6 to 12 years of age, accompanied by a parent purchasing a five-day pass. The five-day pass is also interchangeable at the four Mt. Washington resorts, plus Waterville Valley, Loon Mountain, Bretton Woods, Cannon and The Balsams.

Accommodations

Accommodations in the Mt. Washington Valley are among the best in skidom if you like rustic, romantic and tiny country inns and bed-and-breakfast establishments. You won't find high-rises. A Sheraton has opened and there are condominium projects springing up, but for the most part, these are concentrated at a few base areas. For information about lodging, call the Mt. Washington Valley Chamber of Commerce Central Reservation System; the same number is good for reservations: (800) 367-3364.

For the most luxurious in the area, stay at the Stonehurst Manor, Christmas Farm Inn, Hale's White Mountain Hotel and Resort or The Wentworth.

Stonehurst Manor, North Conway NH; 356-3271 or (800) 525-9100, is created from a turn-of-the-century mansion that belonged to the Bigelow family of carpet fame. It is still manorial. The setting, rooms and restaurant are absolute elegance. A room is $95; master bedroom with balcony or the suite is $135. Make sure you are staying in the manor; there is also a motel nearby with some lodging. Ask about the winter packages.

Sheraton White Mountain Inn at Settlers' Green in downtown North Conway, with 200 rooms and suites, is handy to all the best outlet stores as well as the rest of North Conway. It has its own fitness facility, swimming pool, fitness center and ice skating. Children stay and eat free. Call for details: (800) 648-4397; in NH 356-9300.

Hale's White Mountain Hotel and Resort, brand new, at the foot of Cathedral Ledges (the enormous sculptured slabs you see from everywhere in North Conway) is reached by taking River Road off Rte. 16, then West Side Road to Hale's Location. The views back across the valley toward Cranmore are unmatched. Call: (800) 533-6301, 356-7100.

The Eastern Slope Inn Resort in the heart of North Conway is a palatial New England Inn. This establishment has a bit of everything needed in a hotel. Rooms, suites and townhouses in winter range from $86 to $200 a night per room. Call (800) 258-4708 or (603) 356-6321.

The Eagle Mountain Resort, Jackson; 383-9111; for reservations, (800) 777-1700, is one of those lovingly restored classic 19th-century resort hotels; rates per room are Standard or Deluxe according to the view. Guest room Standard $90, Deluxe $105; Suites $120 Standard, $135 Deluxe. Children 17 and under free, sleeping in existing beds; additional adults, $15 per person daily. Modified American Plan available.

The Wentworth Resort Hotel, Jackson Village; 383-9700 or (800) 637-0013, is a grand old hotel in the elegant tradition. Rooms are spacious, furnished with antiques and equipped with period baths. Room rates in the hotel range between $65 and $119 a night. There are three- and five-day midweek cross-country packages that include lodging, breakfast and dinner, based on double occupancy, for $168 and $228 respectively.

The Christmas Farm Inn, Jackson Village; 383-4313, is a cluster of buildings around the main inn, each as quaint as the next. The main inn has 10 rooms, and the other buildings house larger rooms and small apartments. This is as convenient an inn as one can find for the Jackson Ski Touring Foundation trails. All rates include breakfast and dinner. A 15 percent service charge and taxes will be added to your bill. Daily rates in the main inn are $65-$75 a day; in the surrounding buildings they are between $78 and $90 a day. The inn offers three- and five-day packages, with savings of about $7 a day.

The Wildcat Inn and Tavern, Jackson Village NH: 383-4245, was built a hundred years ago, was once the original Carroll Reed Ski Shop, is now old-shoe comfortable and delightful. Right across the street from the Jackson Touring Foundation and Jack Frost Ski Shop. Rates per person, double occupancy: weekends bed-and-breakfast (a country breakfast), hall bath $35, private bath $40, Suite $45. Modified American Plan (same with dinner), hall bath $60, private bath $65, Suite $70. Numerous multi-day packages available.

Eastern Inns, North Conway, (800) 628-3750, 356-5447 is a very handy family-oriented motel at the northern end of North Conway Village with an enormous parking lot, fireplace in the lobby, heated swimming pool, video game room, and sauna. Midweek/weekend rates for a room with one king-size bed $59/$79; with two queen beds, $68/$90; children under 12 stay free. Two-room units with living room, dinette area, two queen beds and a fold-out chair, the rates are $85/$120, based on a family of four.

For smaller, cozier bed-and-breakfast establishments, **The Buttonwood Inn**, North Conway; 356-2625, is tucked in the woods with cross-country skiing from the back door, or any door for that matter. Rates, per person double occupancy, are from $85 for two weekend days, two breakfasts and a dinner; from $25 midweek for bed & breakfast.

The Eastman Inn, just south of the North Conway village on the main road, is a B&B with 14 rooms in one of the oldest houses in town, newly restored with antique charm. Rates per room are $55-$65 midweek, $65-$75 weekend. Breakfast is superb. Call (603) 356-6707 or (800) 626-5855.

The Scottish Lion is on the main drag in North Conway; 356-6381. Bed-and-breakfast rates: $49 to $75 per couple per room Cross-country is right out the back door.

Ellis River House in Jackson, 383-9339, overlooks the Ellis River, has only five rooms and also has some of Jackson's most popular touring outside the door. Rates: $25-$50 per person.

Riverside has been called the most romantic of the country inns. It's located on Rte. 16A in Intervale; 356-9060. Rates: $45-$95.

For larger resort lodges, try the **Best Western Fox Ridge** in North Conway; (603) 356-3151 or (800) 343-1804. This hotel is a giant, rambling, low motel-like building in a spectacular setting overlooking the town and the White Mountains. It has a giant pool. The rooms are great for children, with lofts and separate bunk rooms available. Rates: $79-$109 per room.

Red Jacket, (800) R-JACKET or (603) 356-5411, seems to be almost identical to Fox Ridge, except for the room locations. Rates: $88-$148 .

For slopeside condos, **Mt. Cranmore Condominiums** is right at the base and room rental includes guest privileges at the Cranmore Recreation Center (see Other Activities). Representative winter rates are: two bedrooms and loft $175 weekday, $225 weekend, $1,025 per week (based on four people per unit) ; three bedrooms, three and a half baths and loft $255 weekday, $350 weekend, $1,675 weekly (based on eight). Call: (800) 543-9206, (603) 356-6851; in New England, (800) SUN N SKI.

Attitash Mountain Village is equally close its lifts. A generous mix of amenities, including an indoor pool, hot tubs, sauna, a pond for skating, restaurant and lounge. Sample rates from a wide selection: one-bedroom unit sleeping 6-8, $129 midweek, $179 weekend; three-bedroom unit sleeping 10-14, $229 midweek, $309 weekend. Call: (800) 862-1600, (603) 374-6500.

To be really close to Mt. Washington, and for a head start if you're climbing, skiing, or using its cross-country trails, there's the **Joe Dodge Lodge** at Pinkham Notch, run by the Appalachian Mountain Club, with room for 106.

The 2- 3- and 4- bunk rooms are simple but useful, and rates include either one or two meals: lodging and breakfast on a weekend, for example, $31.25 for nonmembers, $6 less for AMC members. The public room has a fireplace, board games, and a well-used piano. Write: Reservations, Pinkham Notch Camp, Box 298-FG, Gorham NH 03581.

Dining

Mt. Washington valley is home to some of the best restaurants in the nation. Competition between restaurants is so intense that locals refer to this maneuvering as the "War of the Chefs."

The Bernerhof, 383-4414, has its own nationally famous cooking school and serves some of the best gourmet meals in the country, let alone the valley.

In Jackson, **The Christmas Farm Inn** (383-4313), **The Inn at Thorn Hill** (383-4242), **Wentworth Resort Hotel** (383-9700), and **Wildcat Inn and Tavern** (383-4245), as well as **Stonehurst** (356-3271) and **The 1785 Inn** in North Conway (356-9025) are all major "War of the Chefs" combatants.

For more down-to-earth meals, try the **Scottish Lion** or the **Red Parka** for great barbecued spare ribs (no reservations, expect up to a two-hour wait on Saturday nights). **Bellini's** and **Merlino's** are best for Italian food, **Jackson Square** for Cajun, **Horsefeathers** in North Conway for basic American, the **Shannon Door Pub** for Irish entertainment and pizzas, **Horsefeathers** at Attitash for a great buffet and the **Yankee Smokehouse** for all-you-can-eat ribs.

The best pizza is probably found at **Elvio's** on Main Street. **Peaches** on Main Street has a good breakfast. **The Big Pickle** in North Conway is another good breakfast spot.

Après-ski/nightlife

One of the best ski bars in the country is the **Red Parka**, which offers lively immediate après-ski and then until the wee hours of the night. Something is happening every night, and its informality is clearly evident by the beers served in Mason jars and the signs, license plates, and vintage skis plastered over the walls. On nights when there is no live music, live comedy or a movie is featured.

(Live comedy may be Bucky Lewis, a piece of live ammunition with guitar or microphone.) **Barnaby's** at the other edge of town has live music daily until 1 a.m. and is normally packed with a just-over-21 crowd and loud rock music. **Crawdad's** in the Eastern Slope Inn has more of the same. The place to be in Jackson is the **Wildcat Tavern** where folk rock is served up on weekends. On Friday and Saturday nights, **Horsefeathers** at Attitash hops, and the **Up Country Saloon** has live dance music. Locals hang out in **Hooligans, Fandangle's** and **Horsefeathers** in North Conway.

Child care

Attitash has the Attitots nursery that accepts children from one to six years. Cost is $3.75 an hour, $26.50 a day with lunch. Reservations recommended: 374-2368.

Wildcat's nursery, called the Kitten Club, offers creative toys, games and storytime. Children (18 months to seven years) are accepted at $25 a day, $15 a half day.

Cranmore has a nursery for children walking age or older, with lunch and snacks for $25 a day; $15 a half day.

Black Mountain also has nursery facilities for infants six months or older. Facilities are limited, so reservations are suggested. Rates: half day, $6; full day, $10. Lunch, lessons and rentals are available for an extra charge.

Other activities

The Mt. Cranmore Recreation Center, at Cranmore base, is a huge and very complete all-season facility, with four indoor tennis courts, pool, aerobics classes, steamroom, sauna, and outdoor skating rink; (800) SUN-N-SKI. It is also home to the largest (30 X 40 feet) indoor climbing wall in the Northeast, with several types of overhangs and an infinite variety of hand and foothold arrangements; fee for wall use is $10 weekdays, $12 weekends—this includes use of the other center facilities. Classes available through International Mountain Climbing School (356-6316) which also conducts ice-climbing and mountaineering classes: IMCS, Box 1666, North Conway NH 03860.

Eastern Mountain Sports in The Eastern Slope Inn also has a range of winter climbing and hiking programs, including ice-climbing instruction, ascents of Mt. Washington, and traverses of the Presidential Range; 356-5543.

The Appalachian Mountain Club has a very active, wide-ranging winter schedule of courses and workshops on ski touring, snowshoeing, avalanches, and much more. Their maps and guidebooks to these mountains are an unrivaled gold mine of indispensable information. Headquarters in the area is at Pinkham Notch, almost across the road from Wildcat. Write: AMC Pinkham Notch Camp, Box 289, Gorham NH 03581 (466-2721).

Take a sleigh ride in the valley. Try Nestlenook's horse-drawn sleigh (383-0845).

Getting there

The Mt. Washington valley is tucked in the heart of New Hampshire about 130 miles north of Boston. The closest airport is Portland, Maine, with major airline service from all over the country; it's about one and a half hours' drive from North Conway. Manchester Airport, further south in New Hampshire, is also served by US Air, United, Business Express and Northwest Airlink, and is about a two-hour drive from the valley.

North Conway is notorious for its weekend traffic jams going through town. Most visitors approach from the southern side of town, and most of the ski areas are on the northern side. It can take an hour to get through town. Try to drive during minimal traffic—at night or midday.

The best routes from Boston are up I-95 to Rte. 16, then north on 302. An alternate route is to come north on I-93 and take Rte. 104 to Rte. 25 to Rte. 16, and on to North Conway. From Portland, follow 302.

Information/reservations

The Mt. Washington Valley Chamber of Commerce can make reservations at all local hotels and inns. Call: (800) DO SEE NH or (800) 367-3364.

Attitash Travel and Lodging Bureau: (800) 223-SNOW or 374-2368.

Wildcat reservations: (800) 334-7378 or 466-3326.

Cranmore Ski and Stay: (800) 334-7378 or 356-5543.

Black Mountain information: (800) 367-8897.

King Pine and Purity Spring Resort: (800) 367-8897

Jackson Lodging Bureau: (800) 866-3334.

Local telephone area code is 603.

Ski 93
New Hampshire

Waterville Valley, Loon, Cannon, Bretton Woods

Waterville Valley, Loon Mountain, Cannon Mountain and Bretton Woods are all within 30 to 45 minutes of one another, on or just off I-93. Waterville is the most self contained of the resorts, while Loon has almost too much condo development. Cannon is the most natural and untamed area; and Bretton Woods is tame.

Waterville Valley
Waterville Valley is the best known mountain in New Hampshire. This resort has hosted more World Cup ski races than any other resort in North America. Though the area is perfect for racing, it isn't what we would want for an entire week of skiing; however, the five-day lift ticket is interchangeable at the Mt. Washington Valley resorts as well. This system, which allows skiing at nine resorts, guarantees that a skier will never have to ski the same trail twice in one week or even two weeks. Waterville Valley itself is self-contained enough to treat as a separate area; most visitors, once they enter the serene valley, do not venture farther than the slopes, which are just a short

---

Waterville Valley Facts
Base elevation: 1,815; Summit elevation: 3,835'; Vertical drop: 2,020 feet.
Number and types of lifts: 12—1 quad superchair, 3 triple chairs
4 double chairs, 4 surface lifts
Acreage: 255 skiable acres Percent snowmaking: 98 percent
Uphill capacity: 8,000 skiers per hour Bed base: 6,500

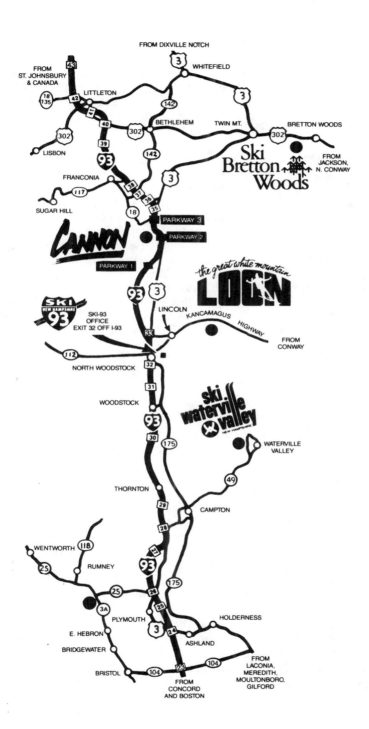

shuttlebus ride away, or the cross-country trails outside their front doors. It has snowmaking coverage for 96 percent of its terrain and one of the largest sports complexes for the non-skier, with indoor/outdoor swimming pools, tennis, squash and racquetball courts, and indoor track.

The skiing

Skiing is solid intermediate. These trails were cut more recently than the Front Four at Stowe or the trails down Cannon. They are not New England's typical steep and narrow: there's elbow room and a chance to check out the slope before committing to the fall line again.

The Valley Run is a beginner/lower intermediate heaven with enough width to allow skiing for a couple of days down different sections. Beginners have a small area with a separate chair lift. The toughest runs, Ciao, Gema and True Grit, develop major moguls and drop down the Sunnyside face. The trails such as White Caps, Sel's Choice, Old Tecumseh and Tippecanoe are intermediate and advanced playthings.

Snowboarders have a halfpipe on Snow's Mountain and Mount Tecumseh. Snowboarders are restricted from several trails.

Snowboarding

New Hampshire law requires snowboarders to have some sort of leash or strap tethering the board to their leg.

Cross-country

Waterville has 100 km. of trails, 70 of which are groomed and tracked for skating as well as traditional skiing through the White Mountain National Forest.

Rentals and lessons are available. Trail fees: weekends, $11 for adults, $8 for children 12 and under; midweek, $8 and $5. Reduced prices are in effect for multiday fees. A one-day beginner package, including pass, lessons and equipment, costs $28 for adults, $21 for children.

Ski school (91/92 prices)

Regular one-and-a-half-hour group lessons cost $20 per session. Private instruction will cost $49 an hour for one skier, $75 for two to five skiers. Vacation option packages, including three full days of lessons (two sessions per midweek day), cost $54; five full days (two sessions per midweek day) of lessons cost $75.

For children, the SKIwee program, costs $50 a day for ages three to five, including lunch and $55 a day for Mountain Scouts and Mountain Cadets, including lunch.

Lift tickets (91/92 prices)

Full-day weekend costs $37 for adults, $24 for children 6-12; full-day midweek, $30 and $20; two-day weekend, $69 and $44; three-day weekend, $95 and $67; three-day midweek, $85 and $54; six-day, $160 and $104.

The Kids Ski Free program lets kids 12 and under ski free during midweek for each parent buying a three-day or more ticket. Kids five and under ski free anytime.

Child care (91/92 prices)

A nursery is available for children from six weeks to two years. Rates are $38 a day on weekends and $32 a day midweek. Two days cost $72 weekends and $60 weekdays; three days cost $103 on weekends and $86 midweek; five days, $152 weekends and $128 midweek.

A day-care facility is available for toddlers two years and over, with rates about $5 a day less than the nursery.

Space is guaranteed only with a reservation. Call 236-8330, Ext. 3133.

Loon Mountain

A resort that seemingly grew out of nowhere in the late 1970s has become a behemoth—at least in terms of lodging. This is one of the few resorts where the bed base is almost double the lift capacity. Fortunately, bed base growth has slowed with the economy, and in the meantime the resort has ski terrain growth plans in a holding pattern while fighting environmental issues.

What has been created at Loon is a wonderful ski area and some of the best accommodations to be found in New Hampshire. It does get crowded, but the area limits lift ticket sales to keep the mountain experience positive. With the addition of the new gondola several seasons back, the occasions when the resort had to hang the sold-out sign dropped from every weekend to about ten days per season, with perhaps ten near-sellout days.

Loon Mountain Facts

Base elevation: 950'; Summit elevation: 3,050'; Vertical drop: 2,100 feet.
Number and types of lifts: 9—1 gondola, 2 triple chairs, 5 double chairs,
1 surface lift
Acreage: 234 trail acres Percent snowmaking: 85 percent
Uphill capacity: 10,200 skiers per hour Bed base: 13,000

The skiing

The intermediate runs are good and solid, with no expert surprises around the next clump of trees. Advanced North Peak runs are challenging and well removed from lower intermediate traffic. The steeps are there, but half the bumps are groomed out.

The upper trails are a bit twisted, narrow and seemingly undirected at the summit, but they open onto a series of wide intermediate pistes. A favorite is Flying Fox, a delightful cruise. Depending on snow conditions, skiers can link up with the West Basin via Upper Speakeasy, or they can drop down to the parking lot and take the 100-yard-long steam train ride to the adjacent base area. The West Basin area has another collection of intermediate trails.

The central portion of the mountain, serviced by the Seven Brothers triple chair, offers good intermediate-marked trails that advanced beginners can handle.

Beginners have their own area to the right of the West Basin served by the Kissin' Cousin double chair.

There isn't enough to keep a good skier busy for more than three days. However, the proximity of skiing at Bretton Woods, Cannon, Loon and Waterville Valley, solves this problem.

Snowboarding

Snowboarding is allowed on the entire mountain. Lessons and rentals are also available. New Hampshire law requires snowboarders to have some sort of leash or strap tethering the board to their leg.

Cross-country

The Loon Mountain Cross Country Center will be home to Rossignol Demo Center featuring all new demo equipment. It has 35 km. of groomed and tracked trails 745-8111, Ext. 5568.

Loon will also offer a Ladies Day once each week with a morning ski with an instructor, lunch, and an afternoon trail pass for one low price. Children five and under and seniors over 70 ski free on Loon's cross-country trails.

Ski school (92/93 prices)

Loon's Ski School offers group lessons in one-and-a-half-hour chunks for $20. Five sessions, $90.

Children three to eight are enrolled in the SKIwee program. There is also a Mountain Explorers class for ages six to 12, which includes lunch. This program groups children by ability level. Price is $40 a day.

A beginner special for both skiers and snowboarders that includes equipment, one lesson and a limited lift ticket costs $35 per day. Enroll at either rental shop.

The Black Diamond Ski Week program runs Monday through Friday and gives advanced skiers who pass a skiing test a program including racing lessons and video analysis designed by U.S. and Olympic Team member Pam Fletcher. This five-day program is $175.

Private lessons are $47 an hour; $70 for one-and-a-half hours.

Lift tickets (92/93 prices)

Ticket sales are cut off after approximately 5,500 have been sold. If you are serious about weekend tickets, call for reservations by 9 p.m. on Friday; call Teletron (800) 382-8080 or Telecharge (617) 720-3450.

All-day all lifts, including gondola, on a weekend costs $38 for adults, $32 for children 12 and under; all-day weekdays (all lifts) cost $31 for adults and $21 for children. Children five and under ski free.

Child care (92/93 prices)

The new Honeybear Nursery is located in the Mountain Club and welcomes kids from six weeks to six years from 8 a.m. to 4:30 p.m. Reservations are required (745-8111). For children from six weeks to two years, Monday through Friday rates are as follows: half day, $25; one day, $35; two days, $65; three days, $95; four days, $125; five days, $155. Older children are slightly less expensive.

Cannon Mountain

Cannon Mountain is state-owned and has long been known by experts as one of the most challenging mountains in the East. It has a 2,146-foot vertical served by a 70-passenger tram. When skiing here you see no signs of civilization except for the ski lodge and lifts. Although once known as a mountain where grooming consisted of shoveling some snow under the lifts, Cannon now takes mountain preparation to heart. Of Cannon's 100 acres, 85 percent are covered by snowmaking. The trails are narrower in legend than they are in reality and the mountain can actually be skied by most intermediate skiers. Chalk this one up as a place for advanced skiers to play and for intermediates to push themselves a bit.

A new fixed-grip quad has been installed to service the summit and exposes the skier to beautiful scenic vistas of the White Mountain National Forest. The new Profile Trail presents the advanced intermediate with a well-groomed, 2,400-foot thrill. The Upper Cannon, Tramway and Vista Way are all intermediate trails that are challenging, but certainly negotiable, the steepest being Upper Cannon which offers narrow New England style steeps. Once down any of those trails, long wide cruisers take you to the base.

The Front Five, as known to locals, are the intimidating trails seen from the highway. Three of them, Avalanche, Paulie's Folly and Zoomer, are marked black diamond and rightfully so, especially for their bumps. The other two, Rocket and Gary's, have the same vertical without the bumps.

Cannon Mountain Facts

Base elevation: 2,000'; **Summit elevation:** 4,146'; **Vertical drop:** 2,146 feet
Number and types of lifts: 6—1 aerial tram, 1 quad chair, 1 triple chair,
2 double chairs, 1 surface lift
Acreage: 140 trail acres **Percent snowmaking:** 85 percent
Uphill capacity: 6,000 skiers per hour **Bed base:** 13,000

Bretton Woods

Bretton Woods has been linked with the grand old Mt. Washington Hotel and international monetary meetings more than skiing, which is relatively new at the resort.

The skiing is mild and good for cruising. The resort also has a halfpipe for snowboarders.

Downhill variety is mixed with one of the best cross-country networks, outside of Jackson and Stowe, in New England, boasting more than 100 km. of prepared trails past dozens of country inns.

The touring area has been improved with the Clinton Trail being widened, and the replacement of six bridges in the area. A beginner special costs $29 for adults, $20 for children including trail pass, lessons and equipment; three-day midweek pass will be $17 for adults and $13 for juniors; children 5 and under and seniors 70+ ski free.

The Bretton Arms, just reopened as a winter resort, is a national historic landmark and has been called one of the most elegant and romantic inns in the state.

Ski 93 area accommodations

Waterville Valley: The **Golden Eagle Lodge** with 139 condominium suites features a distinctive design reminiscent of the turn-of-the-century grand hotels at the White Mountain resorts.

Additionally, Waterville has three hotel properties and a group of condominiums all located in the valley. **The Snowy Owl** is perhaps the most spectacular and something of a modern country inn with breakfast. The **Black Bear Lodge** is slightly larger and more hotel-like, and the **Valley Inn and Tavern** operates as a country inn with rates including breakfast and dinner. All are in the same price range with prices from $109 for a double on Friday and Saturday, $79 during midweek. Prices include entrance to the sports center. The Valley Inn prices include breakfast and dinner, but has no sports center. **Condominiums** are available and include access to the sports center.

Loon Mountain: The **Mountain Club on Loon**; (800) 229-STAY or (603) 745-8111. This ski-in/ski-out property has been so beautifully built that it seems like a piece of a western resort. Unique in New England, everything is under one roof—from parking to swimming pool, fitness club to restaurants. Rates: $132 for a double on weekends; $100 for a double midweek. Prices vary based on luxury.

There are also condominiums at Loon. Slopeside two-bedroom units go for $240 on weekends; $160 midweek.

Base area condo four-bedroom units run $265 on weekends; $205 midweek. Make reservations through the same numbers as the Mountain Club.

Away from the individual resorts, **Indian Head** off I-93, Exit 33 on Route 3 in Lincoln; 745-8181. This is one of the most reasonable and enjoyable places to stay, and a center of action. Rates per person, double occupancy: weekends, $38-$53; midweek, $45, includes lift ticket.

The Beacon Motel Swim and Tennis Club, on the same road as Indian Head, also offers good, reasonable lodging. Rates per person, double occupancy: $49, which includes lifts midweek and $49 per night with a two-night minimum and no lift ticket on weekends.

The Woodstock Inn B&B is typical quaint New England lodge. Rates: $35-$48 on weekends and $28-$45 midweek.

Dining

At Loon, try **Rachael's** (tel. 745-8111) at the Mountain Club or **Govoni's** at the base. The **Common Man** (745-DINE) offers great American dining with a roaring fireplace and rustic surroundings. The **Woodstock Inn** (745-3951) has excellent dinners and great breakfasts. **Gordi's Fish and Steak House** (745-6635) is family-oriented and features Maine lobster and steaks. The **Tavern at the Mill** (745-3603) is located in a spectacular building, which is also one of the nightlife centers just outside Loon. **Truant's Tavern** (tel. 745-2239) serves clever dinner entrées in a mock schoolhouse atmosphere. Drinking beer in class was never so much fun. The bar hops on weekends. **Woodstock Station**, built in an old train station on Main Street, offers an unbelievably huge menu selection of reasonable meals ranging from meatloaf to Mexican. **The Tavern Sports Bar** in the Millfront Marketplace is the spot for pizza (Pizzeria Uno), large-screen TV, pool tables and beer. **The Eagle Cliff Restaurant** in Lincoln (745-8742) serves great pizza or Italian food for sit-down or take-out.

In Waterville Valley head to **Chile Peppers** which has the area's best Mexican food. At Bretton Woods try **Darby's Tavern** for hearty family dining only a quarter-mile from the slopes. **Fabian's Station** is also a good eatery in an old railway station. In Franconia try a locals' favorite, **The Village House**, or head to **Hillwinds**.

For breakfast head to **Jasmann's Pastry Café and Bistrot** in the Millfront Marketplace which serves authentic NY bagels—with and without eggs—and gourmet coffee. **The Country Mile** serves a hearty family breakfast.

Après-ski/nightlife

For immediate after-skiing head across the parking lot to **Govani's** packed with skiers finishing off their day. **Gordi's Fish and Steak** in Lincoln serves up great après-ski munchies. The locals set up après-ski camp at **Truant's Tavern** and **Woodstock Station**.

At Loon the **Granite Bar in the Mountain Club** has good weekend entertainment and is a decent quieter après-ski spot. **Indian Head Resort** in Lincoln offers good après-ski. From Wednesday through Sunday, live bands rock the joint. The **Tavern Sports Bar** is a low-keyed darts, video game and pool hall. Downstairs, the **Tavern at the Mill**, has the area's best singles action with bands on weekends.

Getting there

Boston's Logan Airport is 130 miles away from the Ski 93 area, served by major airlines. Manchester Airport, 70 miles south, is serviced by Delta's Business Express, USAir, United and Northwest AirLink. It's a two-hour drive from Logan and an hour from Manchester airport.

Driving, the Ski 93 area is 325 miles from New York City. Waterville resort is just off at I-93 at Exit 28, about an hour north of Manchester. Loon Mountain is on the Kancamagus Highway just off I-93 at Exit 32 in Lincoln. Cannon is a stone's throw from I-93 and Bretton Woods is on Rte. 302, take exit 35 off I-93.

Information/reservations

Ski 93 Central Reservations handles 80 properties in the region and can arrange airline tickets, car rental, lift tickets and ski rentals with one call to (800) WE-SKI-93; in NH call (603) 745-2409.

Waterville Valley Lodging Bureau handles information and reservations: (800) GO-VALLEY or (800) 468-2553. Resort offices: 236-8311; ski reports: 236-4144.

Loon Mountain Lodging Bureau at (800) 433-3413 for slopeside lodging or (800) 227-4191 for area accommodation. Resort offices: 745-8111; snow phone: 745-8100.

Twin Mountain Lodging Bureau: (800) 245-TWIN.

NH telephone area code is 603.

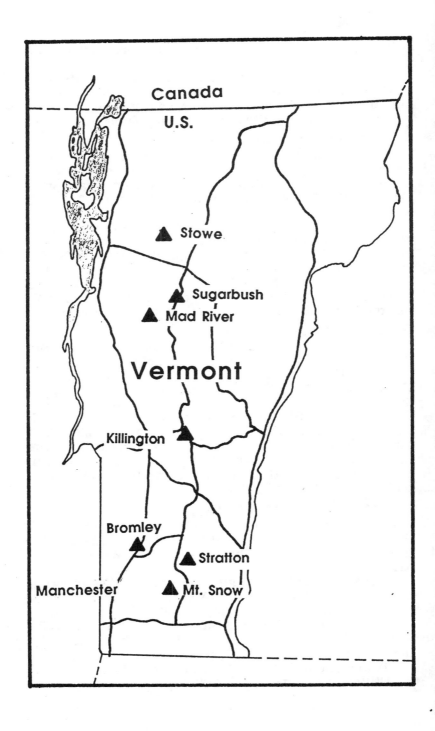

Killington, Vermont

The largest of the New England resorts is also one of the biggest in the United States. Killington stretches for miles and its trails cover six mountain peaks. One such trail, in fact, meanders for 10 miles (granted, it's mostly suited to beginners and cross-country skiers). Another mainly intermediate run, called the Four-Mile Trail, drops from the top of the gondola at Killington Peak to the base, down 3,000 feet of mellow vertical.

More important than sheer size, however, is that Killington is one of the best when it comes to snowmaking. This means that the season usually extends from mid-October into early June.

Killington has no quaint village anchoring the resort. An access road lined with hotels, restaurants, ski shops and discos winds up the mountain from Route 4 to the main condominium complexes. None of the accommodations on the road are particularly glitzy—some are just the opposite. Killington is essentially a major cluster of condos surrounding the main parking lots at the base of the lift system.

By organizing the skiing experience into packages, Killington has created some of the lowest-priced skiing packages in the country. These numerous packages offer substantial savings over buying the components individually. Killington additionally has developed one of the best central reservations systems, allowing you to book everything from air transportation to car rentals, lodging, child care and ski rentals with one call: (800) 372-2007.

Killington Facts

Base elevation: 1,045'; **Summit elevation:** 4,220'; **Vertical drop:** 3,175 feet
Number and types of lifts: 19—1 gondola, 2 quad superchairs, 5 quad chairs, 4 triple chairs, 5 double chairs, 2 surface lifts
Acreage: 721 trail acres **Percent of snowmaking:** 75 percent
Uphill capacity: 35,427 skiers per hour **Bed base:** 4,800 (base), 19,000 (region)

The skiing

The terrain is almost too sprawling to describe and make any sense of it. We'd suggest that you take the Meet the Mountains Tour, which leaves at 9:45 a.m. from the tour sign in front of the Snowshed Base Lodge. The guides will familiarize you with the area, and you'll pick up historical tidbits as you ski across the mountains. The groups are assembled as much as possible by ability levels, but small groups may require some mixing, so hot shots should be ready to cool it a bit for the learners.

There are five separate base areas. Three of them are clustered within striking distance of the end of the access road. Snowshed Base Lodge and Rams Head Base Lodge are across the street from one another, and Killington Base Lodge is just a little way up the access road. The other two base areas are Bear Mountain, with expert terrain, and Northeast Passage, which is right on Route 4. The Rams Head double-chair services mainly beginner and intermediate terrain. The runs alongside the chair lift are pleasant enough cruises. Vagabond, off to the left of Rams Head chair, is an advanced run connecting with the Snowdon area. The Snowdon area is another cruiser's delight, and is served by two chairs from the base area and a Poma lift serving Bunny Buster, often used by the ski school. Highline and Conclusion are good advanced cruising runs with excellent pitch. Bunny Buster and Chute are more of the same but with a more mellow pitch.

Between Snowdon Mountain and Killington Peak is some of Killington's most challenging terrain. This season a new quad chair will serve this expert paradise making access easier to Cascade, Downdraft, Double Dipper and Big Dipper.

Skye Peak, where Killington developed a group of new runs, has proved to be one of the most popular sections of the mountain. Experts and advanced intermediates can play repeatedly on Ovation, Superstar and Skye Lark.

From the top of Skye Peak advanced skiers can drop down Skye Burst, by following the Skye Peak quad. This connection is not recommended for lower intermediates because it leads you to the Bear Mountain quad, which services good advanced and expert terrain. From the top of the Bear Mountain quad, skiers can descend Devil's Fiddle or loop in the opposite direction down Wildfire. But for bumpers the real thrill is to drop directly under the chair lift and challenge Outer Limits, considered one of the best and most consistent steep bump runs in America.

Upon returning from Bear Mountain over to Skye Peak intermediates may want to try the Needle's Eye, which drops beneath the second section of the gondola. A trip back up the Needle's Eye will put skiers back on Skye Lark or Bittersweet for a smooth cruise back to the Killington Base Lodge or down to Snowshed.

Beginner trails lead from all six peaks, which allows starting skiers the panoramic vistas and thrill of skiing from the summit, not possible at most areas where the upper-mountain trails are reserved for seasoned skiers.

Snowboarding

Shredding is allowed on all sections of Killington. There are special lessons, and rentals are available at Snowshed and Killington Base Lodges. Killington hosts a snowboard mogul competition on Outer Limits in the spring.

Mountain rating

Overall, Killington rates as the perfect mountain for beginner and intermediate. There is no extreme skiing, but the experts can find trails that will test them. For beginners this is a perfect place to start. The Snowshed slope is served by four lifts, all reaching excellent beginner trails. Killington is designed so that after a day or two at the lower levels of the mountain, beginners can go right to the top and experience the beauty of skiing.

Ski school (91/92 prices)

The Killington Ski School has several innovative systems: Mountain Training Stations each have specially contoured snow and a ski drill set up to improve certain skills, such as weight distribution and short radius turns. Soon, these let you progress from station to station and actually teach yourself technique based on the changing character of the snow. An instructor is available to coach students over the terrain. These stations are an integral part of the Killington learning method.

There are many alternatives for learners. There are ski weeks, daily classes, individual lessons, advanced workshops, racing clinics and video workshops.

For the ski week packages, ask a representative at central reservations to send a brochure.

Group lessons cost $20 per person. Private lessons cost $49 an hour and each additional person is $25. A half day, or three hours, of private instruction will cost $130 for one and $225 for two to five students. The full day costs $240 for one and $395 for two to five students.

For children, Superstars programs provide a full day of instruction complete with lunch for kids between six and 12 years. The cost is $66 a day with lunch and $71 with rentals. The two-day program is $123, $134 with rentals. A five-day program costs $256, $283 with rentals.

Call the Killington Lodging Bureau at (802) 773-1330 to make reservations.

Lift tickets (91/92 prices)

Lift ticket prices are normally packaged with lodging and lessons. Killington guards prices vigilantly, even to the extent that daily rates are not listed in the travel planner it sends you in the mail. Prices with slash are weekday/weekend .

Full day $39/$40 for adults, $22/$22 children 12 years and younger; half day $31/$32 and $16/17; two-day $70/78 and $36/39; five-day $160/185 and $80-93; seven-day $226/259 and $113/130.

Junior and senior package prices are half those of adults. Children five and under ski free on Snowshed slope with a paying adult. These free tickets are available at the ski vacation center.

Cross-country

Mountain Top Inn has an extensive cross-country trail system. There are over 110 km. of trails; 40 km. worth are groomed daily. Snowmaking here ensures season-long skiing to match the trails at Killington. Mountain Top Inn also has sleigh rides, a great restaurant and its own sugarhouse where they make maple syrup. Call (800) 445-2100 or 483-2311 for more information. **Mountain Meadows Ski Touring Center** (775-7077) has 56 km. of trails, 32 km. groomed and 32 kilometers tracked.

Trailhead Ski Touring Center in Stockbridge (746-8038) offers 60 km. of trails, with 35 km. groomed and 35 km. tracked. In Woodstock, the **Ski Touring Center** (457-2114) has 75 km. of trails, with 58 km. of groomed trails and 50 km. of tracked.

Accommodations (92/93 rates)

Killington could never lay claim to being Vermont's best or most luxurious in this department. The hotels lining the Killington road are mostly average except for the new Inn of Six Mountains. If you want a bargain, call the Killington Lodging Bureau and describe exactly what you want. The tradeoff is normally between price and distance to the lifts. You may make reservations for all these properties by calling (800) 372-2007.

The top-of-the-line hotel in Killington is **The Inn of the Six Mountains** located on Killington Road (800-228-4676 or 802-422-4302). There is a 65-foot indoor lap pool, exercise room and frequent shuttles to the slopes. Rates for the five-day, five night plan are only $268 per person based on double occupancy which includes room, use of facilities and shuttles to the slopes.

There are good values in the midst of Killington Village and it may have the best location, with nearby athletic club facilities, some limited nightlife and an excellent shuttlebus system. Of the Killington Village condominiums, the **High Ridge** units are by far the most desirable. The **Sunrise** condos at the base of Bear Mountain are also at the top end of the Killington condo scale. At the far end of the Killington road is **The Woods at Killington Resort and Spa**, which boasts private Jacuzzis and saunas, and a shuttle to the Snowshed Base.

Both the **Mountain Inn** and the **Cascades Lodge** are very convenient, located in Killington Village, but they are also basic. It would be preferable to opt for a condo with friends rather than face a hotel room each night. The Cascades does have a nice indoor pool and the Mountain Inn has some of the best nightlife when the bar is hopping.

The Vermont Inn (800-541-7795 or 775-0708), with only 16 rooms and fireside dining, everything homemade, is a charming New England country inn. Breakfast and dinner are included at both these inns. Costs, based on double occupancy for two days and nights, range from

$150 to $160 per person; five nights of lodging and meals run from $275 to $300 per person.

Killington lists a category of lodges and resorts, ranging from rustic, rambling inns to sparkling hotels. A favorite is **The Summit Lodge**. Where else are you greeted at the door by two young St. Bernards? The food is excellent, the casual and friendly atmosphere is infectious and the staff is among the most helpful in the area. Rates, based on double occupancy, with breakfast only, two nights, $141; three nights, $197; five nights, $278.

The Cortina Inn (773-3331) on Route 4 is considered by many to be just as good as the Summit, but without the same rustic atmosphere. The Cortina Inn is more of a quality hotel property. Rates, per person, based on double occupancy with breakfast: three nights, $177; five nights, $295.

Of the other properties on Killington Road, you can rate **The Red Rob, Killington Village Inn** and **Chalet Killington** in that order. The food is reportedly best at the Red Rob, and both the Killington Village Inn and the Chalet offer a casual atmosphere. Rate per person, based on double occupancy with breakfast, for the Red Rob is $231 for a three-night stay. The Chalet for three nights is $195.

Near the base of the Killington Road is the **Northstar Lodge** (422-4040), which offers excellent modern accommodations. It has a pool and shuttle service, and is surrounded by good restaurants. Rates, double occupancy, are three nights, $173 per person; five nights, $216 per person.

The Grey Bonnet (775-2537) on Route 100 north has received numerous recommendations. There is a nice indoor pool, sauna and pub. Room with breakfast and dinner costs $215 per person for three nights and $269 per person for five nights. You will need your car to get back and forth to the ski area.

The Hawk Inn and Mountain Resort, Route 100, Plymouth, VT 05056 (800-685-HAWK) is a bit out of the way but has wonderful facilities with secluded condominiums. It is also close to Okemo Mountain as well.

Dining

The Killington area has over 60 restaurants. The best restaurant in the area—claimed by some to be the best in New England—is **Hemingway's** (422-3886).

Our favorites are **The Summit** (422-3535, reservations suggested), an award-winning restaurant with a menu that changes nightly and great wine list; **Jason's** (422-3303, reservations suggested) in the Red Rob for excellent Northern Italian food; the **Cortina** (773-3331) has excellent New England fare; and **The Vermont Inn** (800-541-7795 or 775-0708) has won awards the past two years for its fine formal dining. **Churchill's House of Beef and Seafood** on Rte. 4 between Killington and Rutland is worth the drive for great food and an extensive wine list.

Claude's and **Choices** (422-4030) on the Killington Road were recommended by more than a half-dozen locals. They are both in the same building and owned by the same chef. Claude's is the more elegant with entrées that include escargots, scallops and beef Wellington. Choices serves a menu of steak, shrimp and chicken.

There are some restaurants a bit kinder to the budget. The **Wobbly Barn** is the place for steaks and a great salad bar (no reservations); **Mrs. Brady's** and **The Grist Mill** are consistent; **Charity's** has specials every night for those hanging out after happy hour; and **The Back Behind Saloon** is inexpensive and getting more popular every year. All these restaurants except the Back Behind Saloon are on the Killington Road . . . you'll find the saloon located at the junction of Routes 4 and 100 at the foot of the Northeast Passage.

Après-ski/nightlife

Immediate après-ski action can be found in **Charity's**, where there is a happy hour from 4 p.m. to 6 p.m. The **Nightspot** features a happy hour as well. It is a favorite locals hangout on weekdays with entertainment and dancing tourists packed in on weekends. At the mountain, the Killington **Base Lodge** and the Snowshed **Pogonips** have some action immediately after skiing, or head to the lounge of the **Mountain Inn** or the **Cascades Lounge**. **The Pickle Barrel** has a lively happy hour with dancing later in the evening and is frequented by a young college crowd. Après-ski keeps going strong at **The Grist Mill** with karaoke music and more dancing tourists, this time singing as well. **Casey's Caboose** is a favorite locals haunt with killer spicy buffalo wings. An older, quieter set meets at the **Summit** for happy hour.

For rowdy après-ski and then dancing to loud music, head to the **Wobbly Barn**. When the bar at the **Mountain Inn** has live entertainment, it's great fun. **The Nightspot,** on Killington Road, has good dancing when it's cranking, and it's less expensive than the Wobbly Barn.

Child care (91/92 prices)

The Children's Center is located in the Snowshed Lodge. Killington takes children from six weeks to twelve years in the day-care program. The center is fully licensed.

Day-care for kids between six weeks and twelve years costs $39 per day and $22 for half day. Two-day rates: $42 for half days with no lunch, $70 for the full days with lunch. $99 for five half-days, $165 for five full days.

First Tracks is an introduction to skiing program for children between the ages of three and eight, which consists of two one-hour lessons in the terrain garden, rental equipment and snacks. This introduction program costs $52 for a full day and $28 for a half day. Two-day weekend rates are $52 for half days with no lunch and $99 for full days with lunch. The five-day program is $120 for half days and $240 for full days.

Reservations are required for children's center. Call 422-4255. All-day programs run from 8 a.m. to 4 p.m. Add $4.50 for lunch to half-day programs. Parents must supply food and beverage for children 23 months old and younger.

Other activities

Excursions to nearby Vermont towns, such as Woodstock, can be made. Woodstock is considered one of the most beautiful villages in Vermont and is packed with small art galleries and shops.

Nearby Bridgewater has a 60-outlet mall at the Marketplace at Bridgewater.

The Killington Village Health Spa has a complete fitness center, pool, racquetball courts, steam rooms and Jacuzzis. Call 422-9370.

There is an outdoor skating rink below the Summit Lodge on the Killington Road.

Snowmobiling is available in Rutland or in Killington; call the Cortina Inn, 773-4735.

Sleigh rides and horseback riding are available in Chittendon, 483-6089.

Getting there

Killington is at the intersection of Routes 4 and 100 in central Vermont near the city of Rutland.

Getting to Killington is easy if you have a car. It is about three hours from Boston and about an hour and a half south of Burlington. Green Mountain Limousine Service runs transfers between Burlington and Killington for $50 per person round trip, and normally meets each flight.

Airline transportation is available into Rutland by Mountain Aviation (775-5591). Thrifty Rental Cars has an office small offices at the Inn of the Six Mountains. Hertz and Avis have small offices at the Rutland airport.

Information/reservations

For all information, reservations, and ski packages call (800) 372-2007 from 8 a.m. to 9 p.m. daily.

Snow phone: 422-3261.

Address: Killington Ski Area, Killington VT 05751; 422-3333.

Local telephone area code is 802.

The Manchester Area Vermont

Stratton and Bromley

Manchester is the quintessential Vermont town gone chic. A Vermont farmer arriving here would think he was in some Disney caricature of what Vermont *should* be. Tourists love it—shopper's heaven, outlets everywhere, gift shops, craft shops, quaint shops, antique shops, Orvis fly fishing on the Battenkill River, steepled churches, manorial hotels, charming country inns, gourmet dining. And it's all upscale, very upscale for the most part. If you have young children, finding a place for your family to stay can be problematic; you'll be relegated for the most part to motelish accommodations or condominiums—forget the quaint inns. Weekend traffic is atrocious.

The skiing is not convenient to the town. You will have to drive at least 20 minutes to Bromley and perhaps 45 minutes or more, depending on traffic, to Stratton. But you'll see it promoted as The Manchester Area.

None of the mountains in this region can be considered a true destination resort. They just don't have the expanse and variety or terrain and trails to sustain demand-

---

Bromley Facts

Base elevation: 1,950; **Summit elevation:** 3,284; **Vertical drop:** 1,334 feet
Number and types of lifts: 9—1 quad chair, 6 double chairs, 2 surface lifts
Acreage: 161 skiable acres **Percent of snowmaking:** 84 percent
Uphill capacity: 9,045 skiers per hour **Bed base:** 8,000

Stratton Facts

Base elevation: 1,872; **Summit elevation:** 3,875; **Vertical drop:** 2,003 feet
Number and types of lifts: 12—1 twelve-passenger gondola, 4 quad chairs
1 triple chair,6 double chairs
Acreage: 480 skiable acres **Percent of snowmaking:** 65 percent
Uphill capacity: 20,020 skiers per hour **Bed base:** 8,000

ing skiers for more than two or three days. But together this duo of mountains is hard to beat, and offers something for everyone from the expert to the family to the dressed-to-the-teeth master of the universe.

Bromley is the real family mountain in the region. Call it laid-back and friendly. The staff has time to talk to you and is helpful. Here you can be yourself: wear the latest in ski fashion or descend the slopes in blue jeans; there is no one to impress.

Stratton is an Alpinesque condo village at the base of the lifts. After three years of construction American Tyrol East is open for business. Stratton is, village-wise, to Vermont what Vail is to Colorado. In the evenings activity centers around a few of bars, three hotels, and strolling in your fur coat through the upscale shopping arcades.

The skiing

Bromley: Bromley has an excellent mix of trails for a medium-sized area. This, make no mistake, is an intermediate mountain. The wide, smooth cruisers, Upper Thruway, West Meadow, and Spring Trail will pump up everyone's ego. Blue trails are wide enough for any beginner to handle. The expert-marked stuff is fun with lots of twists and turns for both intermediate and advanced skiers where you can frolic on Stargazer, Havoc, and Pabst Peril. The lift system leaves a bit to be desired—the Sun chair is slow, slow, slow.

Stratton: The skiing at Stratton has always been known as the best of the cruising variety. The upper mountain can provide some steeps for advanced intermediates. Upper Lift Line to Lower Lift Line is a nice cruiser made for big GS turns. Black Bear, Polar Bear, Grizzly Bear and Upper Tamarack all served by the Grizzly double chair are narrow runs in good New England tradition with good vertical. Upper Kidderbrook to Freefall provide another good advanced.cruise. Upper Standard starts with good steeps and is a wide cruiser at the bottom.

The double diamond trails are steep with big bumps which short skiers may have a hard time seeing over. Two of the newest trails are Freefall and Bear Down which continue this tradition. Upper Spruce is the easiest of the double-diamond trails.

The lower mountain and Sun Bowl are strictly for those who want to look good—very good. Stratton does its best to ensure that if a skier forgets to uplift during a turn he will still have a chance to get around.

Beginners have an entire side of the mountain to their left as they stand at the top of the gondola and look down toward the village. Intermediates can head out virtually anywhere on this hill and make it down.

Mountain rating

Bromley is an overall intermediate cruising mountain, and together with Stratton is perhaps one of America's best ego-inflating dual mountains. Perfect for beginner and intermediate, the excellent grooming makes it even easier. Experts can find some good challenges if they look, but don't expect to be pushed.

Cross-country

The Manchester area offers an excellent series of trails through the surrounding hills.

Hildene (362-1788) is in Manchester Village with 15 kilometers of trails winding through the pines across the estate of Robert Todd Lincoln.

Nordic Inn, (824-6444) just east of Peru has trails that wander into the Green Mountain National Forest.

The Stratton Ski Touring Center (297-1880) is located in the Stratton Mountain Country Club and offers 20 km. of tracked cross-country trails and 50 km. of backcountry skiing in the Sun Bowl area. There are excellent wilderness trails into the National Forest. Lessons and guided tours (including a moonlight trek) are available.

Viking Ski Touring Center (824-3933) in Londonderry provides 40 km. of groomed trails for cross-country skiers of all abilities through woodlands and open fields.

Porc Trails (824-3933) are a series of ungroomed trails maintained by the West River Outing Club of Londonderry. If you intend to use them, make sure somone knows where you are and when you intend to return: the trails are not patrolled daily. Call for directions and parking locations.

Ski school

Bromley's Ski School group lessons cost $20 for a two-hour lesson, $70 for a four-lesson book, and $130 for an eight-lesson book. Private lessons cost $40 per hour with additional skiers costing $20; two hours costs $65; half day $95; and a full day of private lessons, $160.

The Stratton ski school offers group lessons that cost $20 for each session, which lasts an hour and 45 minutes. Ten sessions cost $180 and twenty sessions cost $300. The multi-lesson books are transferable, making them perfect for families. Children between six and 12 pay the same as adults. Private lessons cost $45 an hour for one, with additional skiers paying $20. A half day of private instruction will cost $130 and a full day will run $230.

NASTAR races cost $4 for adults and $3 for children under 19. A self-timed race course costs $1 a run or $8 for ten runs.

Lift tickets

Bromley (91/92 prices)

	adults	children
one day, weekend/holiday	$36	$23
one day, midweek	$24	$13
two day, weekend/holiday	$59	$43
two day, midweek	$32	$26
three day, weekend/holiday	$89	$61
three day, midweek	$48	$39
five day, weekend/holiday	$139	$99
five day, midweek	$80	$65

Stratton (91/92 prices)

	adults	children
one day, weekend/holiday	$39	$23
one day, midweek	$32	$22
two day, weekend	$64	$40
two day, holiday	$70	$43
three of four days	$95	$50
five of six days	$145	$75

Accommodations

Manchester/Manchester Center

Manchester is filled with Vermont's many tiny bed-and-breakfast establishments and New England hotels in the Currier and Ives tradition. Most discourage children, but if you had children in these antique-filled homes, you would be a wreck before the trip was over.

Some of the best properties in the region are the **Wilberton Inn** (800-648-4944, 802-362-2500) which is a classic, fashionable address; the **Equinox** (800-362-4747, 802-362-4700) grand, impressive and expensive (but surprisingly reasonable if you get a package deal); **The Inn at Manchester** (362-1793) provides a quaint, smaller country inn with 21 rooms. **The Palmer House** (362-3600) is an unpretentious hotel in Manchester Center with comfortable, spacious, warm country decor, four-poster beds, hot tub and sauna, built around a courtyard.

For families, try the **Aspen Motel** (362-2450), **Johnny Seesaws** in Peru (824-5533), and **The Red Sled** on Rte. 11/30 (362-2161). All are motelish and basic, but you won't have worry about breaking anything.

For area central reservations, call (802) 824-6915.

Each of the ski areas has accommodations which are more convenient to their base areas than Manchester.

Bromley Mountain Ski Area has a collection of mountainside condominiums. For reservations: (802) 824-5522.

For **Stratton Reservations** call (800) 843-6867. This toll-free number also handles several properties off the mountain and in Manchester as well.

The **Village Lodge** is smack in the middle of Stratton and is the premier property for location—walk out your door and you are a hundred yards from the gondola. The Village Lodge, with rooms decorated in subdued hotel colors, has no amenities such as pool, dining room, or lounge; for those, take the shuttle to its sister hotel, the **Stratton Mountain Inn,** which is larger with a spa, dining areas and lounges. It has a variety of rooms in the center of the village. My personal favorite is **The Birkenhaus**, a Stratton tradition, which still has its old-world flavor with excellent service and European-style attention to making you comfortable. This is a small hostelry with the best food on the mountain. The **Liftline Lodge** provides Stratton's most economical lodging on the mountain and sprawls over several wings and buildings.

The **Mountain Villas** is a collection of condos suitable for families. Stratton Reservations has plenty of condos all within easy reach of the slopes. NOTE: The prices on these properties are significantly lower when you buy a Stratton Mountain package. Children under six stay and ski free anytime. Children 12 and under stay free in the same room with their parents.

The closest RV Park is in Dorset on Route 30.

Dining

In Manchester try these less formal, chef-owned eateries—**The Black Swan** (362-3807) which gets two thumbs up from everyone; **The Chantecleer** (362-1616) which is tableside gourmet dining; **Dina's Restaurant** (362-4982) which presents American cuisine in an 18th century farmhouse.

For family fare in Manchester strike out for the **Sirloin Saloon** (362-2600) with a rustic steakhouse atmosphere and a salad bar to write home to mom about and where children are readily welcomed. It is popular and mobbed on the weekends. **Laney's Restaurant** (362-4456) has an open kitchen where you can see grilled items being prepared. **Gurry's Restaurant** (362-9878) is burgers and pizza but with specials that are kind to the wallet.

For Mexican and Cajun head into Manchester and try the **Park Bench Cafe** (362-2557). For popular Italian/American meals and pasta try **Garlic John's** (362-9843) which attracts massive crowds. **Pam Pam's** is for pizza.

The best food on Stratton mountain is found in the **Birkenhaus**, which receives rave reviews from virtually everyone. The other on-mountain property that has attained a well-deserved niche in the hearts of the locals and repeat tourists is the **Liftline Lodge** with their special buffets. When lift line attendants say it's a deal, check it out.

A small restaurant not mentioned in any literature, which I came across in Stratton is **Brush Hill** (896-6100) located in West Wardsboro on Rte. 100, only eight miles away from Stratton Mountain Village. Ask a local how to find the back road to Mt. Snow and take it. When you hit Rte. 100, turn right and it's only a couple of hundred yards on your right. Chef Michael Sylva and his wife Lee have retreated to the woods from big-city restaurants to create his own Green Mountain cuisine. Dining here is by reservation only. Closed Mondays and Tuesdays.

The other top gourmet spots in the vicinity are **The Three O'Clock Inn** (824-6327) in an old restored farmhouse in South Londonderry; **Mistral's at Old Toll Gate** (362-1779) in the center of Manchester; and **The Dorset Inn** (867-5500) in Dorset on Rte. 30 which is the oldest continuously operating inn in Vermont. Jackets are preferred in these three. Most entrées will run from $15 to $20. The Dorset Inn is a half-hour drive from Manchester in the opposite direction from the ski areas.

For more down-to-earth, out-of-Manchester fare try the **River Cafe** (297-1010) in Bondville with the best ribs in the area. Upstairs at **The Red Fox** (297-2488) in Bondville was recommended by just about every local and regular. **Jamaica House** (874-4400) in Jamaica has great Italian food and a homey bar. Across the street in Jamaica you find the **Brookside Steak House** (874-4271) with a great spot on the river and giant salad bar.

For good simple sit-down food try **Jake's Marketplace Cafe** (824-3811) in Londonderry. **Johnny Seesaw's** (824-5533) in Peru has real Yankee cuisine.

Après-ski/nightlife

Once you finish skiing head to one of the lodges at the base of the slopes. Later when you get into Manchester the hottest meat market is **Park Bench Café** with pitchers of margaritas, or try **Mulligans Bar** in Manchester Village. Once you get started just wander through town bar to bar until you find the spot with the evening's action. Try **Alfie's**, but you need a car to get there.

At Stratton, when you get off the slopes, après-ski is on the packed deck of the **Bear's Den** with umm-pah-pah bands, or in **Mulligans** serving 50 different types of beer, or **Cafe Applause** in the Stratton Mountain Inn. In the evenings the action continues in Mulligans (with live entertainment on weekends) and the Cafe Applause (great 50s and 60s jukebox if there's no live music) if you are staying on the mountain. Off the mountain try the **Red Fox** down in Bondville for occasional music and dancing, or to the **Jamaica House** for simple bar with TV action.

Child care

Bromley: This is the home of Vermont's first ski area nursery accredited by the Vermont Department of Human Services. Lorraine Harrington has been the director for over 21 years. Children from one month to six years of age are accepted. Lunch is provided. Open 9 a.m. to 4 p.m. daily. Midweek rates are $30 for full day and $15 for half day. Weekend rates are $35 for full day and $18, half day.

The Mighty Moose Club is a nursery/ski program for children three to five years of age. Open 9 a.m. to 4 p.m..

For older skiers from six to twelve years, the All-Day Discoverski School runs from 10 a.m. to 3 p.m. with classes divided according to ability.

Stratton: The Baby Cub program takes children from six weeks through five years. It is located in the Base Lodge and is open from 8:30 a.m. to 4:30 p.m.

For children, there are the Big Cub and the Little Cub programs. Big Cub, for children six to 12 years provides supervision from 8:30 a.m. to 3:45 p.m., with lunch. Lift tickets are required for Big Cub children over seven. All-day, including lunch and two lessons, costs $45.

The Little Cub program for children (three to six years) all-day with two lessons and lunch, costs $45.

Other activities

The Sport Center has facilities for indoor tennis, racquetball, indoor pool, hot tubs, saunas, fitness center, tanning salons, and masagges.

Getting there

Manchester is not close to any major airport. It really requires a car for access. Driving mileage/time from New York City is 235 mi./four hours; from Boston, 139 mi./three hours; from Washington, D.C., 470 mi./nine hours. The resort is just off Route 30 outside the town of Bondville. From I-91 take Exit 2 at Brattleboro, follow signs to Route 30, then drive 38 miles north to Bondville. From Albany and points west, take New York Route 7 (which becomes Vermont Route 9) east to Bennington, then head north on Vermont Route 7.

Information/reservations

The main number for information on Stratton Mountain resort and for mountain lodging reservations is (800) 843-6867; for Bromley call 824-5522. If you want to make lodging arrangements in the Manchester area, 824-6915.

Telephone area code is 802.

Resort addresses: Bromley Mountain, Route 11, Peru VT 05152; (802) 824-5522.

The Stratton Corp., Stratton Mountain VT 05155; (802) 297-2200.

Mount Snow/Haystack Vermont

Mount Snow has the snowmaking efficiency of Killington, and is closer to major cities than Stratton, and has just as careful grooming, but somehow this resort has remained about as down-home and folksy and unpretentious as all Vermont resorts should be. This mountain certainly has the makings to flirt with getting giltzy or overcrowding the access roads, but thank heaven someone has kept a New England feel to the entire area. West Dover and Wilmington are true Vermont villages, without boutique-filled commercialism.

With the additional of Haystack Mountain last season, Mt. Snow now has 127 trails and 25 lifts—more than any area in the East. The two mountains are not interconnected by lifts, however a shuttlebus regularly plys the route between the two bases.

Mount Snow is a big New England area that works about as perfectly as any area in the country at making snow and moving skiers around on the mountain. It also has 84 trails, and quite uncharacteristic of New England, they are about 100 yards wide. As you look up at the mountain, the terrain is almost perfectly divided from right to left into expert, intermediate and beginner sections. Trails crisscross, forming a web of runs as dense as any in the country. Snowmaking blankets more than 80 percent

---

Mount Snow Facts

Base elevation: 1,900'; Summit elevation: 3,600'; Vertical drop: 1,700 feet
Number of lifts: 25—1 super quad chair, 1 quad-chair, 9 triple chairs,
10 double chairs, 3 surface lifts
Percent snowmaking: 82 percent Total acreage by trails: 410 acres
Uphill capacity: 35,690 per hour Bed Base: 8,000-9,000

of the mountain, providing snow from November through early May. Haystack has 1400 vertical feet with 43 trails and six lifts.

Mount Snow has about 4,000 beds clustered in condos and lodges at the base of the mountain. There are another 3,000 within 10 miles of the resort. While there isnot a village complex at the mountain base, West Dover (3 miles away) and Wilmington (9 miles away) are quaint, traditional Vermont towns with shops, white-steepled churches, etc.

Where to ski

Just about any level of skier can ski Mt. Snow anywhere. Solid intermediates can head to the North Face area, which is a grouping of isolated steeper runs, some of which are left to bump up. All the runs covering the face of the mountain dropping to the village area are great cruisers. The names give you an idea of what to expect—Ego Alley, Sundance and Snowdance. This is the perfect place to dance on the snow.

The Sunbrook area, which catches the sun, is an ideal spot for lower intermediates. The one expert trail in Sunbrook, Beartrap, with its south-facing exposure and snowmaking is a haven for bump skiers.

To the far south of the resort is the Carinthia, which offers long mellow runs for advanced beginners and lower intermediates and anyone who want to have a playful cruise. There are enough zigs and zags and small drops to keep a skier awake.

Haystack's upper mountain offers terrain for intermediates and the recently developed Witches area for experts. The lower mountain, segregated from the upper trails, is perfect for beginners.

Mountain Rating

The emphasis is definitely on the intermediate; experts can try some of relatively tough runs on the North Face of the resort, but if you are an expert don't plan on coming out of your way to ski these runs . . . they're not that tough. For beginners and novices, get ready for cruising—this mountain has it all.

HAYSTACK

MOUNT SNOW

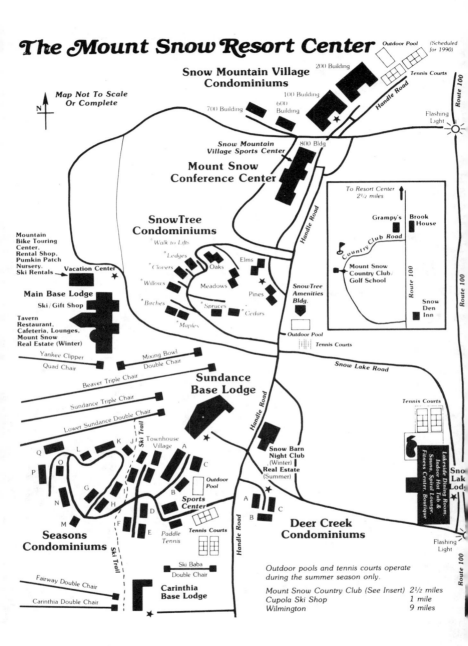

The Mount Snow Resort Center

Outdoor Pool (Scheduled for 1990)

Tennis Courts

Route 100

Snow Mountain Village Condominiums

200 Building

100 Building

600 Building

700 Building

800 Bldg

Flashing Light

Map Not To Scale Or Complete

N

Handle Road

Snow Mountain Village Sports Center

Mount Snow Conference Center

To Resort Center 2½ miles

Grampy's   Brook House

Country Club Road

SnowTree Condominiums

Walk to Lifts

Ledges

Clovers   Oaks   Elms

Willows   Meadows   Pines

Mount Snow Country Club / Golf School

Route 100

Mountain Bike Touring Center. Rental Shop. Pumkin Patch Nursery. Ski Rentals.

Vacation Center

Main Base Lodge

Ski / Gift Shop

Tavern Restaurant, Cafeteria, Lounges. Mount Snow Real Estate (Winter)

Birches   *Spruces*   *Cedars*

Maples

SnowTree Amenities Bldg.

Snow Den Inn

Outdoor Pool

Tennis Courts

Yankee Clipper Quad Chair

Mixing Bowl Double Chair

Snow Lake Road

Beaver Triple Chair

Sundance Triple Chair

Sundance Base Lodge

Handle Road

Tennis Courts

Lower Sundance Double Chair

Ski Trail

Townhouse Village

A

Q   L   K   J   C

P   O

Snow Barn Night Club (Winter)

Real Estate (Summer)

Lakeside Dining Room, Indoor Hot Tub & Sauna, Spiral Lounge, Fitness Center, Boutique

Snow Lake Lodge

G   Outdoor Pool

N   I   B

H   Sports Center

D   A   C

M   F

Seasons Condominiums

E   Paddle Tennis

Tennis Courts

Handle Road

B

Deer Creek Condominiums

Ski Trail

Flashing Light

Route 100

Fairway Double Chair

Ski Baba Double Chair

Carinthia Base Lodge

Carinthia Double Chair

Outdoor pools and tennis courts operate during the summer season only.

Mount Snow Country Club (See Insert) 2½ miles
Cupola Ski Shop 1 mile
Wilmington 9 miles

Snowboarding

Snowboarding is allowed on both mountains. Lessons are available through the ski school. Rentals are available at the Mt. Snow Rental Shop, Cupola Ski shop in West Dover and the Timing House in Wilmington. No leash required in the state of Vermont.

Cross-country

There are four major ski touring centers near Mount Snow. The largest is Hermitage Cross-Country Touring Center on Coldbrook Road in Wilmington; 464-3511. It has 50 kilometers of trails that form a circle from the warming hut out to Mount Snow and back. Sitzmark Ski Touring Center (464-5498), Timber Creek (464-0999 and the White House Touring Center (464-2135) are others offering more than 60 km. of trails skewed toward the intermediate Nordic skier.

Ski school (92/93 prices)

The Mount Snow Ski School offers two-hour group lessons for $21. Private instruction costs $50 an hour for one student; additional students pay $25. A two-hour introduction to skiing program is $41 including beginner lifts and equipment.

Children have a SKIwee program organized, which offers a five-hour daily lesson including lunch, for $63 for one day; $114 for two days; $162 for three days and $259 for five days. The half-day program costs $76 for two days; $105 for three days and $164 for five days.

In addition to traditional two-hour class lessons, Mount Snow offers an EXCL ski school program for intermediate and better skiers. The student skis through a free skier analysis area, where an instructor videos and critiques. The skier then receives a card showing what skills need improvement. Should the skier decide to take a lesson, this analysis lets groups be matched for ability. No group has more than three skiers, and lessons last 45 minutes, allowing plenty of free time for skiing.

For beginners, Mount Snow offers a 5-day guaranteed learn-to-ski package for $220 that includes lifts, daily lessons and rentals.

Lift tickets (92/93 prices)

Adult full-day tickets are $41 on weekends and $37 on weekdays; children, 12 and under, pay $23 a day. Two days cost $72 for adults and $40 for children 12 and under; three days, $101 for adults and $54 for children; five days, $160 for adults and $83 for children.

Accommodations

Lodging at Mount Snow ranges from sprawling mountain lodges and smaller mountain inns, to quaint bed-and-breakfasts and condominiums. At the immediate base of the mountain there are a group of condominium projects and three lodges which all have shuttle service to the slopes. Most of the other accommodations line Rte. 100 between the slopes and the town of Wilmington, with some tucked on side roads back into the foothills. All rates given are per person, non-holiday, based on double occupancy. The midweek rates and the five-day rates are only for Sunday through Thursday nights. On Friday and Saturday nights the weekend rates apply. The weekend package rates include two breakfasts and one dinner unless otherwise noted.

The Inn at Sawmill Farm, on Rte. 100 in the center of West Dover, 464-8131. Considered one of the nation's top country inns, it is in a class by itself here. Entry is through a portion of the former barn, which has been artfully restored. The rooms are spacious and feature dressing rooms off the baths. There are also small fireplace cottages which are actually small country apartments with sitting room and bedroom. The main sitting room provides a panorama over the surrounding countryside. The dining room serves some of the best meals in the valley.

The atmosphere is quite formal, with gentlemen required to wear jackets in the public areas and restaurant after 6 p.m. Children under ten years of age are not allowed. Weekend 91/92 rates: doubles $270 including breakfast and dinner for two; cottages, $290 including breakfast and dinner for two. The Inn at Sawmill Farm does not take credit cards.

Snow Lake Lodge, 199 Mountain Road; (800) 451-4211, or 464-7788. This sprawling 92-room mountain lodge is right at the base of the main skiing area. This is nothing fancy—just good basic skier accommodations. Rooms all have cable TV and there is a fitness center, sauna, indoor hot tub, outdoor Jacuzzi, and entertainment each evening après-ski. Skiers can actually throw their skis on their shoulder and walk 300 yards to the Sundance lift or ride the free shuttle. The Snow Lake Lodge is excellent with children as well. Room rates: two-day weekend package $149 with breakfast and dinner. Three-day midweek package $156 with breakfast and dinner. Five-day ski week package $265 including breakfast and dinner.

Andirons Lodge, Rte. 100, West Dover; 464-2114, or (800) 445-SNOW. This lodge has about 60 rooms and is just off the highway, only two miles from the lifts. These are simple paneled rooms with double beds and some rooms with additional twin beds for children. There is a full-sized indoor pool, and a sauna, game room and large function room. The attached Dover Forge restaurant is also an excellent place for affordable meals. Rates: two-day weekend package is $88; the five-day package is $160.

Surrounding Mount Snow are a group of excellent country inns all with 18 to 26 rooms. They excel at providing family-owned service, hearty meals and a true New England ski experience.

Matterhorn of Dover, on Rte. 100, West Dover, 464-8011. This is the granddaddy of Mount Snow mountain inns and has been lodging skiers for over 20 years. The lobby features a two-story stone fireplace and the rooms are simple paneled rooms, most with two double beds. All rooms have cable TV and the lodge also provides a sauna for after skiing relaxation. Rates: Two-day weekend package $112 including breakfast and dinner; five-day package is $199 with breakfast and dinner.

Nordic Hills Lodge, 179 Coldbrook Road, Wilmington; 464-5130. This inn has 27 immaculate rooms, some with paneling and others recently redecorated with floral print wallpaper. All rooms have cable TV and there are two separate lounge and fireplace areas. Rates: Two-day weekend package is $115 with breakfasts and dinner; five-day packages are $199 with breakfasts and dinner.

Gray Ghost Inn, on Rte. 100, West Dover; 464-2474. This large country inn is operated by a British couple who have been improving the property for the past six years. Some rooms are decorated with a country touch and others are paneled with mountain wood. Many rooms have smaller beds and bunk beds for children. There are three separate TV viewing areas and large lounges as well as a sauna. Rates: two-day weekend package is $90 with breakfast; five-day ski week package is $150.

Trail's End, Smith Road, Wilmington; 464-2727. This small inn has only 18 rooms. Each is tastefully decorated in country style. The owners reportedly are among the most attentive innkeepers in the valley. Meals are served family style at three round tables, which guarantees visitors will return home with new friends. Rates: two-day weekend package is $100; and the five-day ski week is $200; each package is with breakfast only.

Old Red Mill, Rte. 100 in the town of Wilmington about 15 minutes from the slopes; 464-3700, or (800) 843-8483. This inn, created from a former sawmill, is the bargain champion of the area. The rooms are small, most only about 7x12 feet with a double bed, toilet and shower. All rooms do have bath and TV and larger rooms are available for families. The common areas, bar and dining rooms are rustic Vermont. Rates: two-day weekend package is $80 room only; five-day package is $100.

Mount Snow also has a group of charming and elegant bed and breakfast establishments. These B&B's are smaller, most with less than ten rooms.

The Doveberry Inn, on Rte. 100, West Dover; 464-5652. Each room is individually decorated with flowered wallpaper, dried flowers and antiques. It is run by the Rossi sisters, graduates of the New England Culinary Institute, who lavish attention on visitors. This is a quiet inn with no children under 8 permitted, frequented mainly by couples. TVs and VCRs are in each room and the inn maintains a free video library for guests. Two-day weekend package is $110 including breakfast; five-day ski week package is $225 with breakfast.

West Dover Inn, Rte. 100, West Dover; 464-5207 or (800) 732-0745. A historic country inn built in 1846 with eight elegant rooms furnished with antiques, hand-sewn quilts, color TV's. There are also two luxury suites with fireplaces and whirlpool tubs. B&B rates: two-day weekend package is $110; five-day ski week package is $193.

The Red Shutter Inn, Rte. 9, Wilmington; 464-3768. This 1894 country home has been converted into an inn at the edge of Wilmington about 9 miles from Mount Snow. It provides an elegant country atmosphere. There are only nine guestrooms. B&B rates: two-day weekend package $88; five-day ski week is $176.

The Nutmeg Inn, Rte. 9W, Wilmington; 464-3351. Built in a 1770s home in the town and decorated with country accents and quilts, this B&B has ten rooms and three fireplace suites. B&B rates: two-day weekend package is $115; five-day ski week package is $238.

The White House of Wilmington, Rte. 9, Wilmington; 464-2135. This is an upscale luxury inn serving breakfast and dinner. There are only 12 rooms (five with fireplaces). Rates: two-day weekend package is $190; five day package, $350. Prices include breakfast and dinner.

Condominiums are also plentiful in the Mount Snow area. **The Mount Snow Condominiums**, (800) 451-4211 or 464-7788, are huddled at the base of the lifts; only the Seasons complex is actually ski-in/ski-out and is the most highly recommended. These condos have an excellent athletic center with indoor pools, saunas and Jacuzzis. A two-bedroom, two-bath, linens included, two-day weekend package will cost $540; the three-day midweek package costs $360; the five-day ski week costs $480. The Seasons complex prices are slightly higher.

Timber Creek Townhomes, (800) MTSNOW or 464-2179, are luxury condos located directly across Rte. 100 from the ski area; they have an excellent athletic center with pool, steam room, saunas and racquetball courts. There are 18 km. of cross-country trails just outside your door. Shuttlebuses run between the complex and the ski area. A typical 2BR/2Bath condo including linens two-day weekend package will cost $720; the three-day midweek package costs $615; the five-day ski week costs $820.

Greenspring at Mount Snow, (800) 247-7833 or 464-7111, are upscale condos only a mile away from the slopes across Rte. 100 from Mount Snow. This complex also has the best athletic center in the area with indoor pool, sauna, fitness center and spa. A typical three-bedroom, two-bath, linens included two-day weekend package will cost $795; the three-day midweek package costs $645; the five-day ski week costs $860.

Horizon Inn, 464-2131, Route 9 in Wilmington has recently been remodeled and has an indoor heated pool, whirlpool and sauna. The two-day weekend is $85 with no meals, and five-day ski week is $100 with no meals. A bargain any way you look at it.

The Lodge, (800) 451-4289 or 464-5112, at the base of Mount Snow has two-day weekend rates of $126 with breakfast and dinner; five-day ski package is $195. Kids 12 & under stay and eat free midweek, excluding holidays.

In addition Mount Snow has several special packages that include lodging and skiing. For a complete vacation planner with descriptions of most area properties , write: Mount Snow, 105 Mountain Road, Mount Snow VT 05356, or call 1-800-MTSNOW .

Dining

The top dining experience and the most expensive is the **Inn at Sawmill Farm** (464-1130) which has 21,000 bottles in its wine cellar and gourmet continental dining with appetizers ranging from $6 to $14, and entrées between $22 and $30. As noted above, dining here is somewhat formal and jackets are required on all male guests (if you didn't bring one they do have a selection of blue blazers which may be borrowed). No credit cards.

The Hermitage (464-3511) serves excellent meals at less stratospheric prices. This country inn has a very large dining room where some tables are surrounded by over-stuffed chairs. The walls are covered with the world's largest collection of hanging Delacroix prints. The wine cellar claims 40,000 bottles of 2,000 different labels. All game birds and venison are raised on the premises and jams, jellies and maple syrup are homemade as well. Entrées run from $14 to $25.

For other fine dining try **Betty Hillman's Le Petit Chef** (464-8437), **Two Tannery Road** (464-2707), and **Capstones** (464-5207) adjacent to the West Dover Inn. **Doveberry Restaurant** (464-5652) is small and intimate with a chef who is a graduate of the New England Culinary Institute.

The Deerhill Inn and Restaurant, (800) 626-5674 or 464-3100, on Valley View Road in West Dover is operated by a British couple. They serve American cuisine. One dining room has a mountain view the other a fireplace. Dinners are $15-$25.

The **Roadhouse** (464-5017) has a wonderfully rustic dining room with rough-hewn beams and barnboard walls. Complete meals here are $16 to $25 with a choice of three different salads, soups and deserts all served with homemade bread. **Fennessey's Parlor** (464-9361) according to locals serves up consistently good food. Decor is turn of the century. You dine for less than $30.

For economical family places try **Poncho's Wreck** (464-9320) with an eclectic dining room serving Mexican food, steaks, lobsters and fresh fish. Poncho's is a local institution. **B.A.'s Red Anchor** (464-5616), under the same ownership, serves its famous ribs and seafood specialties.

The Vermont House (464-9360) on Wilmington's main street, serves good food for cheap prices and is one of the local's favorites. **Deacon's Den** (464-9361) is a good place for pizza, burgers and sandwiches right after skiing. **TC's Tavern** (464-9316) serves up good Italian food. **Guiseppe's** (464-2022) across from Poncho's in Wilmington cooks the best pizza in town. And for sandwiches and deli fare try **Elsa's** (464-8624)on Rte. 100 in West Dover.

Child care

The Pumkin Patch is one of New England's largest day-care centers. It provides care for children from six weeks to eight years. There are separate rooms for infants and toddlers. Reservations are required; call 464-8501.

Kids six weeks to eight years, $45 all day with lunch, or $185 for five days. Rates are higher during the holidays .

Getting there

Mount Snow is the closest major Vermont ski resort to New York and Boston. It is on Route 100, nine miles north of Wilmington, Vermont. Mileage/driving time from major cities is: Boston, 127 mi./2.5 hours; New York City, 213 mi./4.5 hours; Albany, 68 mi./1.5 hours; and New Haven, 139 mi./2 hours, 45 minutes.

The closest airports are Albany and Hartford's Bradley International, both about a one-and-a-half hour drive from the resort.

Information/reservations

Contact the Mount Snow Vacation Services for one-stop reservations for everything from airline reservations to car rentals and lifts—(800)245-SNOW.

For snow conditions, call 464-2151.

Local telephone area code is 802.

Stowe, Vermont

For most of the 1980s, Stowe seemed intent to live off its reputation as a titled member of the New England skiing aristocracy. It displayed both an undeniable blue-blood lineage as one of the oldest and most distinguished east coast ski resorts, and perhaps a touch of arrogance. As is so often the case with royalty in these modern times, however, the castle and surrounding estate began to look a little timeworn when compared to some of its *nouveau riche* neighbors. The lifts seemed a little old, and the lift lines were not just a little too long. The slopeside facilities had also crossed that invisible but unmistakable line separating quaint from antiquated. Those of us who have always appreciated the unique atmosphere of Stowe could only stand by and watch, hoping that someone would reverse its fortunes before Stowe fell into disrepute, a once proud prince with threadbare regalia.

Happily, our hopes are well on their way to being answered. Last year saw the culmination of the first stage in a three phase facelift for Stowe, the most comprehensive workover the resort has seen since it was originally founded in 1940. The idea is to iron out some of the wrinkles of old age without sacrificing the regal bearing and atmosphere. Judging from the early returns, the prognosis is good.

First, a word about that atmosphere. For those of you who are not familiar with the area, Stowe is not a New England village nestled at the foot of a large ski mountain, with pubs and restaurants and boutique shopping cluster-

Stowe Facts

Base elevation: 1,300'; **Summit elevation:** 3,660'; **Vertical drop:** 2,360 fee.
Number and types of lifts: 10—1 super quad chair, 1 four-passenger gondola; 1 triple chair, 6 double chairs, and 1 surface lift
Acreage: 378 skiable acres **Percent of snowmaking:** 67 percent
Uphill capacity: 10,000 skiers per hour **Bed base:** 5,000+

ed around a village square. The 200-year-old village of Stowe is perfectly nice in its own right, with a number of fine shops featuring handmade crafts by local Vermont craftsmen, as well as Shaw's General Store, a fixture since 1895. But the town lies about seven miles away from the skiing at Mt. Mansfield and adjacent Spruce Peak. Strange as it may sound, the special atmosphere most people associate with Stowe derives in large part from that seven-mile stretch of scenic road: Strung along it like gems along the base of a crown are some of the most romantic inns in New England.

Those inns give Stowe its special magic. It is worth noting, however, that to truly enjoy that experience and all this area has to offer, you either need to stay slopeside at the Inn at the Mountain, or you need to have a car. While there are shuttles running between the village of Stowe and Mt. Mansfield, they do not run frequently enough or at convienent enough times at night to trust your vacation to their schedule.

As for the facelift, its most obvious manifestation is the spanking new, sparkling red, fastest-of-its-type-in-the-world gondola that sits ready to whisk skiers up the right side of Mt. Mansfield, at 4,393 feet the highest peak in Vermont. Commissioned in December 1991, this 8-passenger, high-speed gondola is reminiscent of those more common in Switzerland, and it has already been nicknamed "the vortex" by locals for its ability to suck in hordes of skiers and transport them up the mountain at the rate of 2,400 an hour (up from 900 for the previous lift). That has cut average waiting times at peak periods from roughly 50 minutes to between 8 and 12, going a long way toward answering complaints about lift line times heard in recent years. The skiing from the top is generally intermediate, with good grade and broad runs. The exception is a twister expert slope called Chinclip. More on the skiing later.

Besides the new gondola, the first phase of renovation also included the recontouring of 30 acres of trails to lessen bottlenecks, eliminate double fall lines, and generally speed the flow. Admirable constraint was shown during this effort, with those involved first having dusted off an old trail map as a blueprint so as to remain true to Stowe's lineage, which goes back to 1915, when the first skied descent of the moutain was made by a Dartmouth College librarian named Nathaniel Goodrich. That means you won't see the wide, sweeping autobahn cruisers of many more modern resorts, such as Stratton Mountain. The runs at Stowe generally tend to be more narrow, twisting, and cut closer into the surrounding forests.

The rest of the first phase of the facelift centered on improving snowmaking on the mountain. The number of snow guns were increased from 146 to 300, 28 percent of the ones were upgraded and repositioned, and 60 new hydrants were added. What all that means to you is that the snow conditions, always a concern in New England, will at least be of less concern at Stowe than in past years. With these improvements, Stowe's snowmaking system can blanket 72 percent of its slopes.

The skiing

Part of the legend of Stowe revolves around its Front Face, and the fact that it features some of the steepest and most difficult runs in skidom. "I've skied the Front Four at Stowe" is spoken like a badge of honor by northeast skiers, and deservedly so given the nature of Goat, Starr, Liftline and National. Besides being steep, they are frequently draped with vintage New England ice, and moguled liberally.

Experts who are gunning for all four should begin with National and Liftline. Last year the resort bought a new winch cat that allows groomers for the first time to prepare the steepest trails such as National. Thus, this is a good place to get used to the considerable steepness of the Front Four. Starr is generally not groomed, and the view from the top of this run as it disappears in a steep dive and you see the base lodge area far, far below is one you won't forget. End your extreme skiing adventure with Goat, a steep, moguled gut-sucker that is no more than three to five bumps wide.

Other suggestions for the experts, who will find roughly 25 percent of the mountain catering to their desires, include a short but lovely little moguled path through tight trees called Centerline, just to the right of Hayride. Also, there's a very nice section of glade skiing through well-spaced trees just off of the top section of Nosedive. Chinclip from the top of the gondola is long, moguled, and moderately narrow. It does not, however, have quite the steep grade that the Front Four boast.

Intermediates will find that 59 percent of trails at Stowe marked for their maximum enjoyment, including much of Spruce Peak. At Mt. Mansfield, ski to the right or left of the Front Four. Advanced intermediates will probably want to chance the tricky top part of Nosedive for the pleasure of skiing the long, sweeping cruiser with excellent grade that beckons further down. Going left from the top of the Forerunner Quad, take Upper Lord until it leads you to a handful of long, excellent intermediate runs all the way to the bottom in Lower Lord, North Slope, Standard and Gulch.

To reach the intermediate skiing under the gondola offers a small problem. The connection between the intermediate trails is not convenient unless you are an advanced intermediate willing to take a run named Nosedive. Basically, true intermediates have a choice of skiing the runs from Chair D or down from the gondola. It's a hike from Chair D area over to the gondola, or you can take the Crossover trail, which allows skiers to traverse directly across the Front Four and leaves them at the gondola base. If you want to work your way back from the gondola to Chair D, take the Cliff Trail, which eventually hooks up with Lower Nosedive and dumps you at the base of the high-speed chair. Across the parking lot there is also Spruce Peak with a small network of intermediate trails. If you feel as if you need a little elbow room after too many tight New England trails, try Perry Merrill or Gondolier from the gondola, or cut turns about as wide as you want down Main Street on Spruce Peak.

A short word about Spruce Peak: it is perhaps the coldest chair lift on the mountain, The runs face south, so they lose snow earliest in the spring, and there is no snowmaking at the top of the mountain or on the long intermediate Sterling trail. Skiing upper Spruce Peak is like all skiing was in the old days—no snow from heaven, no skiing. When the snow is good and the wind isn't blowing, though, the mountain can be a cruiser's delight.

Beginners will find themselves at the base area of Spruce Peak and probably will work up to the intermediate trails off the Little Spruce double lift and then advance to the Big Spruce double and the gondola runs. Advanced beginners looking for a little scenic adventure should ride to the top of the Forerunner Quad, and take the winding, gentle Toll Road trail down through forested slopes to the bottom. At over four and half miles, it is the longest trail on the mountain.

Snowboarding

While snowboarding has not yet caught on at Stowe to the same degree it has with some western resorts, "shredders" are welcome. As a welcome mat, Stowe has built a 600-foot half-pipe.

Cross-country

Stowe has one of the best cross-country networks in the country. Four touring areas all interconnect to provide over 160 kilometers of trails.

The Trapp Family Lodge (253-8511) organized America's first touring center and has 97 km. of trails with 58 groomed km. and 48 km. of tracked trails. The fee is $10 a day.

The Edson Hill Touring Center (253-7371) has 42 km. of trails with 20 km. trails set. Elevation varies from 1,400 feet to 2,100 feet. The fee is $7 a day.

Mount Mansfield Resort (253-3000) has more than 50 km. of trails, with 30 km. groomed. The daily fee is $10.

The Topnotch Resort (253-8585) has 40 km. of trails.

Ski school (91/92 prices)

Stowe has an innovative group of ski lesson programs. There is a special Front Four workshop concentrating on Goat, Starr, National and Liftline; a Drills for Skills workshop, which focuses on balance and timing; a Mountain Experience week works on mastering varying snow conditions with video; snowboarding lessons open a new sport; and the Young Adult Workshop offers programs designed for intermediate teens.

Private instruction is available for $45 an hour, with $15 for each additional person. A full day of private instruction costs $210, and for two to five people, $310. Group lessons range from $24 for one lesson to $85 for a five-lesson package.

The special workshops are: Front Four (9:30 a.m. to 2:30 p.m.), $45; Mountain Experience for a week, $115.

Telephone extension for the ski school is 2229 at Mount Mansfield Ski School and Ext. 221 at Spruce Peak.

Lift tickets (91/92 prices)

Prices change with the seasons—but the Regular season is from mid-December through the end of March.

Regular season prices follow: Full day, $39 for adults, $21 for children six to 12 years; half day, $31 and $18; two consecutive days, $69 and $38; three consecutive days, $99 and $55; five consecutive days, $155 and $85.

Accommodations

Stowe lodging ranges from small country inns and large resorts to hotels in the old New England tradition.

Ye Olde England Inne, on the Mountain Road; 253-7558. This is a favorite because it is bigger than a country inn and smaller than a full-fledged hotel. Recently restored, Ye Olde England is now considered one of the best lodgings in Stowe. It has been redone with an English country motif and lavish Laura Ashley touches. Since every room is decorated differently, call for specific differences. Room rates normally include breakfast, après-ski cider or tea and dinner. Just off the lobby is Mr. Pickwick's Polo Pub with a selection of more than 100 beers, eight available on tap. The pub also has a full selection of pub grub ranging from steak-and-kidney pie to haggis. Rates (all with private bath): $85-$135 per person.

The Green Mountain Inn, Main Street; (800) 445-6629. This has the flavor you would expect of an old inn in the middle of a town. The wide-planked floors are pine, as is the furniture, with many old four-poster canopied beds. The only drawback may be the hotel's location on Main Street: modern traffic has replaced the clatter of passing stagecoaches. The hotel also has an annex that is not quite so quaint, but is off the main road. Room rates (room only): $40-$71 per room; add $34 per person for breakfast and dinner.

Butternut Inn, Mountain Road; 253-4277. A country inn in the classic sense. Of those we visited, the Butternut was our favorite in Stowe. It reflects the eccentricities of the owners, transplanted from Texas. The inn strictly forbids smoking and no children are allowed. Every aspect of the inn is done nicely: its rooms are all different, guests are pampered, dinners are prepared only for the inn guests and include Angus beef and Tex-Mex, which alternate with more traditional New England fare. Anyone who wants everything done beautifully will appreciate the Butternut. Rates: $55-$75 per person double occupancy with breakfast and après-ski snacks.

Ten Acres Lodge, Luce Hill Road; (800) 327-7357, or in Vermont 253-7638. This country inn was converted from an 1840s farm house. As with all country inns, rooms vary in size. Rooms in the main lodge are relatively simple, but the common areas on the first floor are beautiful. Ten Acres Lodge also has a group of eight modern units, called the Hill House, tucked into the woods behind the old farmhouse. These units all have fireplaces in the rooms and share an outdoor hot tub. Room rates, including breakfast: $75-$135 per room double occupancy.

The Gables Inn, on Mountain Road; 253-7730 or (800) GABLES-1. Gables is what all friendly country inns should be. Not a quiet, stuffy place with antiques and Mozart playing, where you're afraid of breaking something, this is a real lived-in house, which helps everyone have a good time. The breakfasts are among the best in Stowe and its guests wouldn't think of eating anywhere else—for dinner either. Weekday room rates, based on double occupancy are $80-$100 per person with breakfast and dinner.

The Resorts

When the Trapp Family lionized in *Sound of Music*, their everlasting fame was guaranteed. **The Trapp Family Lodge** (tel. 800 826-7000) that they established near Stowe on arriving in the United States, however, is a legend in its own right. Unfortunately, the original building burned down in the late 1970s, and was completely rebuilt between 1980 and 1983. It is still the most popular and upscale place to stay in the area, and it is still in the family (now run by a granddaughter).

The motif as you walk through the lobby of the large main building of the lodge is rustic Austrian. This is virtually a self-contained resort with an excellent cross-country center. The collection of restaurants are among the best in the area, and a modern pool and fitness center provide excellent amenities. Make reservations early because this lodge is normally full throughout the season (Christmas reservations should be made about a year in advance). Rates, including breakfast and dinner: $110-$125 per person, based on double occupancy.

In a category just below the Trapp Family Lodge, but much closer to the lifts and the town, is the **Top Notch at Stowe** (800-451-8686; in Canada 800-228-8686; in Vermont 802-253-8585), which proudly boasts the most extensive fitness center and spa in the area. The Top Notch offers rooms as well as condos, and has excellent meeting facilities. It also boasts the only four covered tennis courts in Stowe. Rates, including breakfast and dinner: $125-$245 per person; junior suites, $140 per person without meals. Condos are rented by the unit without any meals. Rates: two-bedroom, $225-$350; three-bedroom, $450.

The Inn at the Mountain, part of the Stowe Mountain Resort, is 4-diamond rated by AAA, and we have no argument with that accolade (tel. 800-253-4SKI). This beautiful inn and the surrounding condominiums (available through the same telephone number) offer the only ski-in/ski-out facility in Stowe. The flavor is old world New England warmth. The story behind the Broken Ski Tavern in the Inn is that it was here that the founder of Head Skis first introduced the steel ski. An early prototype is sitting in pieces above the fireplace. At breakfast in the mornings guests create their own omelets to order, and enjoy bread from the Inn's own bakery.

While the ambiance in the Inn may be old world, the Fitness Center (free to all guests) across the parking lot is ultra-modern. There's universal weight training, free weights, work out rooms, aerobic classes, Stairmaster, Lifecycle and rowing machines, as well as a sauna and hot tub. Rates, based on double occupancy and including breakfast and dinner: double or queen, $195 a night; suite, $230. Condominium rates, which do not include meals, are: one-bedroom, $245; two-bedroom, $330; three-bedroom, $385. Packages run $346 for three days of lifts and lodging,.

The best family accommodations in Stowe are at the **Golden Eagle Resort Motor Inn**; (800) 626-1010. This sprawling complex has more than a dozen buildings and facilities, from motel rooms with kitchenettes to apartments. Along with an excellent restaurant, The Alpine, the complex offers an excellent fitness center with pool and hot tub facilities. It is all unpretentious and affordable. Featured is an innovative series of packages with breakfast and dinner plans that allow guests to eat in several different restaurants in town. There are dozens of pricing options. The best bet is to contact the property and explain what you are looking for. One-room efficiencies run between $99 and $129; one-bedroom suites from $110 to $189; and two-bedroom apartments from $160 to $225.

The Stoweflake, (800-253-2232) down the road a bit from the Golden Eagle, is more upscale and has a pool and fitness center. Rates with breakfast and dinner based on double occupancy are $45-$80 a night. There is also a group of very nice townhouse condominiums with studios going for $145-$180 a unit; two-bedroom units for $190-$230; and three-bedroom units for $320-$370.

The Vermont Ski Dormitory at the foot of Mount Mansfield offers bunk-style sleeping with shared bathroom facilities. Rates are about $35 a night with breakfast and dinner. Call (800) 866-8749 or 253-4010.

Dining

Stowe has long been famous for its cuisine. **Ten Acres** and **Isle de France** are considered by most to be the top gourmet spots in the area. Entrées at both restaurants range between $17 and $24. **Villa Tregara** south on Route 100 has good upscale Italian meals. **Stubb's Restaurant** also repeatedly gets good reviews.

The Trapp Family Lodge puts on an excellent meal for a fixed price of about $25 per person. There normally is a choice of about a dozen entrées.

For alternatives that aren't budget-busters, try the **Stowe-Away** for Mexican food, and try **The Shed** for prime rib and steaks. **Foxfire** has good Italian food, as does **Trattoria La Festa**. **The Whip** in the basement of the Green Mountain Inn is a good place for a light dinner or sandwiches. And **Mr. Pickwick's Pub Grub** is excellent. When your steak sandwich almost melts in your mouth, they're doing something right.

H.H. Bingham's, in the Inn at the Mountain, at the base of the Toll House lift, serves moderate continental cuisine with entrées in the $12 to $18 range.

A breakfast favorite is **McCarthy's** in the Baggy Knees complex. Also, the breakfast at **The Gables** shouldn't be missed, especially on weekends. **The Shed** now also serves an excellent breakfast buffet.

Après-ski/nightlife

It's difficult to say exactly what ingredients go into making the perfect après-ski bar, but for our money they are all there in just the right measure at the **Matterhorn Bar**. Located a few miles from the ski area on the mountain road, this raucous little roadhouse is packed and rollicking after the slopes close. There's a dance floor, a disc jockey, loud music, a rectangular bar that makes for easy circulation, pool tables, big-screen TV—yep, all the ingredients! There's a more low key après-ski meeting place at the mountain in the rustic **Broken Ski Tavern** at the Inn at the Mountain.

You can count the hot spots on one hand, and still have fingers left over. For loud—very loud—rock and roll, dancing and college crowds, head to the **Rusty Nail**. For a slightly older group and dancing, the place to be seen is **B.K. Clarkes**. **Mr. Pickwick's Polo Pub** at the Olde England Inne gets a good pub crowd, and the bar at the **Stowe-Away** seems to be a good singles meeting place.

Child care

The day-care program takes children from one month through 12 years. The ski school has children's programs for those three to 12 years. The children's centers are at the Spruce Peak area.

Kanga's Pocket handles infants from one month to three years. A full day costs $40 and a half day is $28.

Pooh's Corner Children's Day Care Center takes kids three to 12 years. Full days cost $40 and half days are $20. Five-day programs are $180. For children interested in skiing, the Pooh's staff offers full-day programs with lifts, lunch and lessons. The program fee with one class is $40; with two, $52. Five-day programs with one daily lesson are $180.

Young novice to expert skiers between seven and 12 have their own mountain adventure classes for $62 a day or a five-day program for $250. Teens (13-16) have a similar program for $72 a day or $250 for the week. The price includes instruction, lifts and lunch.

Other activities

There are health clubs and spas at the Mt. Mansfield Resort, Village Athletic Club, behind the Green Mountain Inn and at the Golden Eagle Health Spa.

Indoor tennis can be played at the Racquet Club on the Mountain road. Four Deco Turf courts are available for hourly fees as well as lessons.

Jackson arena has an Olympic-sized ice skating rink.

Snowmobiles are available at Nichols Snowmobiles (253-7239) or from Farm Resort (888-3523).

Horse-drawn sleigh ride reservations can be made through the area association at (800) 24-STOWE. Sleigh rides take place at Edson Hill Manor (253-7371), Stowehof Inn (253-9722) and Trapp Family Lodge (253-8511).

The East of Eden winter park, a short drive in the direction of Morrisville, offers an ice skating pond, snowshoe hiking tours, and toboggan rides.

Ben and Jerry's ice cream factory is just down the road in Waterbury and offers tours every half hour from 9 a.m. to 4 p.m. Monday through Saturday. The cost is $1 per person and includes samples. Afternoon tours fill quickly, so plan accordingly.

Stowe Winter Carnival normally takes place the second half of January; the Stowe Challenge Cross-Country Races kick off in February; the mogul contests normally take place in March; and in April there is a Sugar Slalom and the traditional Stowe Snow Beach Party.

Getting there

There are numerous flights into Burlington airport, which is only 45 minutes from Stowe. Shuttle service is by Vermont Transit for $20 each way or $34 round trip. All major rental car companies have offices at the airport and most hotels have a transfer service from the airport. You can make transfer arrangements when you make your hotel reservations.

For skiers located in Washington, D.C., Philadelphia or New York, the perfect prelude to the New England charm of Stowe is a romantic trip aboard Amtrak's Montrealer. This experience is like stepping back into an

Agatha Christie novel, with comfortable private berths, helpful attendants to bring cocktails to your room, and the incomparable sensation of watching as the moonlit landscape of New England whirls past your window to the lonely call of the train's whistle. The train arrives in Waterbury (only fifteen miles from Stowe) early in the morning in plenty of time for skiing a full day. Dinner and breakfast are included in the price, which will vary depending on place of origin. Reservations required.

Driving time to Stowe from Boston, 3.75 hours; Montreal, 2.5 hours; New York, 6.5 hours; Washington, D.C., 10.5 hours. The resort is a few miles north of Waterbury off I-89.

Information/reservations

For the Stowe Area Association, call (800) 24-STOWE. Representatives can take care of almost everything starting from the Burlington airport.

For slopeside accommodations, namely, the Mount Mansfield Resort, call (800) 253-4SKI.

Round-the-clock snow conditions: call 253-8521 or (800) 63-STOWE.

Local telephone area code is 802.

Sugarbush
Mad River Valley
Vermont

The Sugarbush and Mad River Valley offer extensive and varied skiing with accommodations in everything ranging from condos to rambling country hotels to quaint country inns and is coupled with one of the best collections of restaurants in American skidom. It offers both the modern resort environment and the traditional town experience. More than any other resort area in Vermont, the Sugarbush/Mad River Valley offers something for every level of skier at every level of accommodation luxury.

This area has a blend of the modern ski condo village clustered at the base of Sugarbush South, and the simple, timeless Vermont villages anchored by Waitsfield and Warren. Although buses shuttle between the Sugarbush South base area and Route 100 approximately every 45 minutes nightly from 5:30 p.m. to 12:15 a.m., this is a resort where you will need a car to move between accommodations, restaurants and nightlife.

The skiing

The skiing is on three distinct mountains—Sugarbush South and Sugarbush North in the Sugarbush area and

---

Sugarbush Facts

Sugarbush North: Base : 1,535; Summit: 4,135'; Vertical drop: 2,600 feet
Number and types of lifts: 7—1 superchair, 2 quad chairs
2 double chairs, 2 surface lifts,
Sugarbush South: Base : 1,575'; Summit: 3,975'; Vertical drop: 2,400 feet
Number and types of lifts: 9—3 triple chairs, 4 double chairs, 2 surface lifts
Acreage: 392 skiable acres **Percent of snowmaking:** 46 percent
Uphill capacity: 15,018 skiers per hour **Bed base:** 6,000, (2,250 on mountain)

Mad River Glen up Route 17 from Waitsfield. Each area provides a different experience for skiers, but one negative factor common to most areas is the plodding lift system. A local once told me that the lifts went at one speed: slow. I would amend that to two speeds: slow and very slow. But lift lines aren't a problem, so one doesn't much begrudge the extra time spent on the lifts.

That slow-lift problem has been addressed at least on Sugarbush North with overkill. From one of the slowest systems in the East, Sugarbush North now has three new quads—one high-speed superchair that replaced the Mountain Double and two fixed-grip lifts replacing the old Summit and Inverness. These new lifts have almost doubled the uphill capacity.

Sugarbush South is serviced by nine lifts and has varying terrain. As you face the mountain, the runs to the left are generally the most difficult and those to the right are designed for beginners and lower intermediates. The runs served by Castlerock lifts are very black and no place for beginners or timid intermediates.

For an intermediate a good start would be to take the Sugar Bravo triple chair, then traverse to the Heaven's Gate triple and the top of the mountain. From here, take Upper Jester, rated intermediate blue, (but barely more than a beginner's green; then choose from Downspout, Domino, Snowball, Murphy's Glades, or Lower Jester, to complete the run to the base. The most fun for intermediate skiers on this part of the mountain would probably be to use the Sugar Bravo lift and go either right or left to explore the intermediate terrain. Warning: there is a long runout at the bottom of Jester—be ready with your pushing technique. The far right side of the area is served by the Gate House double chair, then a surface lift, which takes skiers even higher. Here intermediates will have relatively wide runs and good cruising. Beginners will want to stick to this section of the mountain, practicing on Pushover and Easy Rider and then graduating to Slowpoke and Sleeper.

Experts will find plenty of challenge. The entire Castlerock area offers narrow New England-style steeps, and if you are lucky the Castlerock run will occasionally be groomed, making for a heavenly smooth steep. Note that the Castlerock lift is one that qualifies for very slow:

even when the resort is nearly empty at midweek the wait is eight to 10 minutes.

From the top of Heaven's Gate experts can drop down a trio of short steeps directly below the lift or descend Organ Grinder with its tricky double fall line. To the left, experts will find the legendary Stein's Run with its steep, moguled face and a trio of slightly less challenging expert runs.

Sugarbush North is more modern in the sense that there are wide-open cruising runs here that a skier won't find at South or at Mad River Glen. The main skiing area is served by three new quad lifts we mentioned. This is an intermediate playground. Sugarbush North used to be less crowded than South before they put in the new quad lifts, and a bit colder, according to locals. Sugarbush North also has more extensive snowmaking than Sugarbush South, which means better coverage on the intermediate trails.

On the map, the intermediate runs from the top of the Summit quad chair seem relatively short, but the map is misleading. The Rim Run connecting to Northway and then to either Which Way, Cruiser or North Star is one of the classic cruising runs in the United States. The other intermediate section is Inverness, which is served by a quad chair and offers a good training area. Beginners have an excellent area just to the left of the base area with a T-bar and a short double chair.

Mad River Glen is a totally separate ski area. Mad River Glen prides itself on being tough (even the beginner trails here might be graded intermediate at Sugarbush), traditional (where else do you find the original single chair lift still operating from the late 1940s?), natural (no snowmaking, combined with plenty of tight tree skiing), daring (can't imagine any other ski area with so much "out-of-bounds" skiing) and homey (the last hamburger I had, before here, that was squished together by hand and cooked to order was prepared by Mom). Yeah, Mad River Glen is a different animal.

Mad River Glen Facts

Base elevation: 1,637'; Summit elevation: 3,637'; Vertical drop: 2,000 feet.
Number and types of lifts: 4—3 double chairs, 1 single chair.
Acreage: about 95 skiable acres Percent of snowmaking: 15%
Uphill capacity: 3,000 skiers per hour Bed base: 6,000

Experts, real experts (forgive me Hegel)—have one goal: the top of the single chair. Yes, the lines do get long—very long. The ski patrol and lift operators scan the line and attempt to weed out beginners and lower intermediates who would have no business at the top. Meanwhile, the real experts happily wait. For them, this is what skiing in the East is all about.

From the top of the single chair experts can immediately drop down the Chute or the Fall Line, or if they are with a guide or local madman they can venture into the area called Paradise, entered by dropping down an eight-foot waterfall. Real experts: ask around for Octopus's Garden and the 19th and 20th hole. If you look like you know how to ski, a local may direct you there.

From the top of the single chair the Antelope and Catamount trails offer a relatively moderate alternate route down the mountain for most intermediates. Upon reaching the single chair midstation, tree skiing beckons through the Glades on one side of the lift line and Lynx on the other. More timid souls can traverse on Porcupine and drop down the wide-open Grand Canyon or thread through the narrow Bunny Run.

This brings skiers to the section served by the Sunnyside double chair. Upon reaching the top of this sector, intermediates can turn to the left and drop down Quacky to Porcupine, Grand Canyon and Bunny; or they can go below the lift and to the right down a short series of expert trails, Panther, Partridge, Slalom Hill and Gazelle, most of which empty into Birdland.

Birdland is ostensibly the beginner's area. Granted, there are Duck, Lark, Robin, Wren and Loon on which to train beginners, but there are also more intermediate tight runs like Snail and Periwinkle. The point being, if you find yourself going through this area remember that even though there are green circles at every fork in the trail, real intermediates can have plenty of fun here too. Suffice it to say, if you learn to ski here, nothing will daunt you elsewhere.

Mountain rating

Experts head to Mad River Glen, the Castlerock section of Sugarbush South, and the short-but-steep Black

Diamond and Upper FIS, plus Exterminator and Bravo at Sugarbush North.

Intermediates and cruise hounds will have the most fun at Sugarbush North. If the intention is be challenged for the entire day, strike out for Mad River Glen, and if you are just entering the intermediate ranks, test Jester and the Gate House area of Sugarbush South.

Beginners have their best area at Sugarbush North, and acceptable sections of Sugarbush South near Gate House. Never-evers should not start at Mad River Glen— head there after at least a week of lessons.

Cross-country (91/92 prices)

The Sugarbush Inn cross-country area has 25 kilometers of prepared trails across from the inn. Trail fees are $8 a day with reductions for guests. Equipment rentals are $12. Private lessons are $25 an hour and group lessons go for $12 an hour. Other nearby cross-country areas are: **The Tucker Hill Touring Center** with 40 km. of mostly intermediate trails connecting four country inns along Route 17; **Blueberry Lake** with 30 km. of beginner and intermediate trails; and **Ole's** (near the airport) with 35 km., and the most varied terrain in the area.

Snowboarding

Shredding is allowed everywhere at these resorts. Sugarbush South has a halfpipe, called The Wave, built on the Spring Fling trail, and Tsunami curving down Easy Street at Sugarbush North.

Ski school (91/92 prices)

Here the Sugarbush resort excels. The Sugarbush Ski School is tightly integrated into the Sugarbush package. It is considered to be one of the top ski schools in the East.

Daily ski school rates for classes are $24, with no discounts for juniors or children. Private lessons are $45 an hour with a limit of three skiers per instructor. An all-day private lesson from 9 a.m. to 4 p.m. is $225 and $310 for two to four skiers. Sugarbush also promotes a beginner's special, including the lower lifts, a two-hour lesson and rentals, for $38.

The Centered Skiing Program, a three-day holistic approach to skiing instruction, is designed to help the intermediate/advanced skier overcome the mental barriers that limit confidence. $339 per person includes 20 hours of instruction, three-day lift ticket, a video to take home and daily continental breakfast. Classes are limited to no more than 20 skiers with a student teacher ratio is 5 to 1.

Mad River Glen (92/93 rates) has a ski school that, like the area, marches to its own drummer. Mad River offers only private lessons with a maximum of four skiers per instructor. There are Mad River's Mountain Classes for experts only, which cost $20 a day on weekends and $15 mid week, and there are Mogul Classes for only three or more for the same rates.

One-hour private lessons on weekends cost: one person, $30; two people, $45; three people, $60. Weekday rates: one person, $20; two people, $30; three people, $40.

Two-hour lessons on weekends cost: one person, $50; two people, $65; three people, $80.

Beginner ski packages for first-timers are limited to three people. All-day cost: $45 on weekends and $35 weekdays. Half-day lessons are available weekdays for $25; on weekends for $35.

Mad River Glen has a special program for children between six and 12 years. Half-day packages cost $20 on weekends and $15 on weekdays. Full-day programs: $35 (weekends) and $25 (weekdays).

NASTAR racing programs are offered throughout the season. When opened, two runs through the timed race course cost $5, with a dollar for each additional run.

Lift tickets (91/92 prices)
At Sugarbush, including Sugarbush South and Sugarbush North:

Feb. & Mar. Weekend/Holiday rates: One-day, $38 for adults and $20 for juniors seven to 13; two-day, $74 and $38; three-day, $109 and $55.

Feb. & Mar. Midweek rates: One-day, $35 for adults and $20 for juniors seven to 13; two-day, $66 and $38; three-day, $94 and $55.

Value season (early Dec and late March and April): One-day, $28 for adults and $20 for juniors seven to 13; two-day, $54 and $38; three-day, $78 and $55.

Seniors 65-69 pay the junior rates. Children six years and under and seniors 70 and over ski free. There is a special midweek, pre-packaged rate; ask about it if making week-long reservations.

The "Ski Vermont's Classics" features an interchangeable lift ticket for Stowe, Sugarbush, Smuggler's Notch and Jay Peak. Prices (90/91) for the Vermont Classics interchangeable lift ticket are: three days out of seven—$109; five days out of seven—$159. Vermont Classics tickets are available to guests of participating hotels (most are in the Burlington area) and at the ticket windows of the four mountains. Program begins after Christmas and runs through April 1st. For more information on the Vermont Classics Ski Pass, call 863-3489.

Mad River Glen (92/93 prices):

One day adult is $26; $20 for juniors 16 and under; two days, $50 and $38; three days, $74 and $56. Children 5 and younger will be issues a free ticket when skiing with a paying adult.

Accommodations

The Sugarbush/Mad River area has some of the finest country inn accommodations in Vermont. Topping off the list of inns is the newly restored **Round Barn Farm** a mile from Route 100 across the wooden bridge on East Warren Road. The farmhouse has been made into an elegant ten-room bed-and-breakfast, four of the suites are new thie year. It is peaceful and quiet, strictly no smoking, children discouraged. Room rates range from $90 for a small room with shower and private bath to $155 for the new Richardson Room with Bermont-made pencil post queen bed, skylights, oversized Jacuzzi and steam shower.

Tucker Hill Lodge (496-3983) and the **Waitsfield Inn** (496-3979) also have excellent bed-and-breakfast accommodations but with more rooms and restaurants; the intimate, quiet atmosphere of the Round Barn Farm is lost. Both Tucker Hill and the Waitsfield Inn are better suited for children. Tucker Hill Lodge prices, which include breakfast and dinner are $69 midweek and $84 weekend, per person based on double occupancy.

The most luxurious full-service hotel property is the **Sugarbush Inn** located on the access road. It underwent complete renovation this last summer. Rates at the Sugarbush Inn, per person based on double occupancy, were $54 during the week and $61 on weekends. Call (800) 53-SUGAR. The inn has a 25-km. cross-country trail system, indoor swimming pool, fitness center and saunas.

In the more moderate category, **Olde Tymes Inn** (496-3875) is hard to beat. The rooms have been restored, the bar downstairs is becoming a town tradition, the restaurant is one of the best in the village, breakfast is fabulous and the prices are only $43 a night per person on weekends and $34 a night per person during the week. It fills up regularly, and rightfully so.

Another favorite is the **Weathertop Lodge** on the Rte. 17 between Waitsfield and Mad River Glen (496-4909). Rates during peak season: $37 for one person midweek and $49 weekend.

Mad River Barn (496-3310) has a reputation for spacious rooms and some of the best lodging food in the valley and heaping portions as well. Staying here is a step into a wonderful 1940's ski lodge.

Families will want to check into the **Madbush Falls Country Lodge** on Rte. 100 (496-5557) or the **Hyde Away** (496-2322). All are great spots for children and are close to the slopes. Otherwise, check into a condo.

As for condominiums, all at the Sugar-bush base area are managed by Sugarbush Village Real Estate; (800) 451-4326 or (802) 583-3000. The most luxurious are the **Southface Condominiums** with hot tubs in each unit; the condos are a shuttlebus ride away from the slopes. Rates per night for a two-bedroom unit are $222 midweek and $291 weekend.

The Snow Creek condos are ski-in/ski-out, but you will have the noise of snow guns out your back window during snowmaking. The **Paradise** condos are newer but a good walk from the slopes; however, they have good shuttle service. Snow Creek and Paradise rates: two-bedroom, $265 a night. **The Summit** and **Castle Rock** condos are the same price. Castle Rock has a better location close to the slopes and the Summit has more room. Rates: three-bedroom, $311 a night. **Unihab** looks like boxes stacked on one another, and **Middle Earth** condos are 10 minutes from the lifts and small, with two-bedrooms, $170 a night.

All units have access to the Sugarbush Sports Center for an additional fee. The Sports Center has an indoor pool and indoor tennis, racquetball and squash courts.

For families, an advantage of the Sugarbush village is the proximity of the children's center.

Almost as close to the lifts as Sugarbush Village units is the newly completed **The Bridges** complex. This complex has racquetball courts and an indoor pool. Rates: two-bedroom, two-bath unit costs $136 midweek and $180 weekend per night. For reservations, call (800) 537-8427.

Skiers heading primarily for Mad River Glen should check into the **Battleground** condos. Battleground prices: per night: two-bedroom, $195 weekday and $225 weekend. Reservations: call (800) 537-8427 or (802) 496-2288.

Ask the rental agents about the possibility of renting a house right on the Mad River slopes. If you are a dedicated skier, you couldn't be in a better spot.

Dining

With over 40 eating establishments in the valley, this area boasts a very high excellent-restaurant-per-skier ratio. The only other competition is the Mt. Washington Valley in New Hampshire.

The top of the line is **Chez Henri** in Sugarbush Village at the base area of Sugarbush South. Chez Henri is a touch of France transplanted to Vermont. Created in the basement of the new condo development, the restaurant manages to capture a true European bistro feeling. It is romantic and cozy, with low ceilings and a flickering fire. The owner, Henri Borel, personally greets guests and makes them feel at home. The wine selection is excellent and supervised by Borel. The restaurant is open from noon until 10 p.m. Henri features lunch, then fondue in the late afternoon. Entrées range from $12.50 to $19. Call for reservations in the evenings; 583-2600.

The Common Man has attracted an excellent clientele and developed a reputation for good food. Four years ago the original restaurant burned to the ground and was recreated by moving an old barn from Moretown to Sugarbush. The atmosphere is great New England baroque barn with crystal chandeliers. Entrées generally range from $10 to $16; 583-2800.

Olde Tymes is an old country inn on Route 100 in Waitsfield. The home-style dining room is decorated with a fascinating collection of turn-of-the-century photographs of Waitsfield. Entrées range from about $12 to $19; 496-3875.

The Waitsfield Inn offers an excellent Italian menu in elegant surroundings with main courses in the $6.95-18 range. It's located on Route 100 in the center of Waitsfield. Reservations are recommended; 496-3979.

Tucker Hill Lodge on Route 17 between Waitsfield and Mad River Glen has one of the best reputations for dining in the valley. The menu changes every night of the week. Expect to pay between $16 and $24 for entrées. Reservations are suggested; 496-3983. The downstairs lounge at Tucker Hill is called Flatbread. Here they serve a variation on pizza baked in a primitive earthen oven and garnished with a wonderful selection of herbs and spices. Try the flatbread without tomato sauce for a change. Prices range from $10-$14 for a 14-inch flatbread that easily serves two.

Sam Rupert's down a driveway to the left as you approach the Sugarbush parking lot has developed lots of fans and offers an eclectic menu.

The **Terrace Room** at the Sugarbush Inn is more intimate with similar prices and continental dining. The menu changes daily depending on what foods are in season. The **Grill Down Under** is a more casual dining spot in the Sugarbush Inn and **Knickers** in the clubhouse at the Sugarbush Cross Country Center is enjoyable.

The Bass Tavern on the access road serves basic meals around a giant fireplace with entrées from $9-$16.

Mad River Barn Restaurant has a popular Saturday buffet for $15, and from Sunday through Friday dinners are served 6:30-8 p.m. Meals are prepared by chefs from a neaby culinary school, Mary's in Bristol.

Locals also seem to gravitate to the **Beggar's Banquet**, which is very affordable, and seemingly has a bit of everything. For families out to stretch the budget and still get good fare, number one is The **Hyde Away** on Route 17. Or for simple quick food, stop in at The **Den** on the main street of Waitsfield, or **D.W. Pearl's**.

For breakfast, head to the **Pitcher Inn** in Warren, open only from 7 a.m. to 11 a.m. weekday mornings or 8 a.m. to 12 noon on weekends. **D.W. Pearl's** and the **Hyde Away** have a great basic breakfast. **Pepper's Restaurant** at Pepper's Lodge has a hearty and moderately priced breakfast.

The Mad River Barn lays out excellent homemade muffins and jams and serves only real maple syrup.

Après-ski/nightlife

Après-ski starts at the base lodges, which seem to do booming business just at the bar as the lifts begins to close. Or head to **Chez Henri** where the bar fills up with people quietly drinking beer or wine. The **Blue Tooth** has a lively, younger crowd. A bit down the road, the **Bass Tavern** often will get rowdy with its happy hour. One or the other Sugarbush base lodges will usually have a live band for après-ski. On weekends try the **Sugarbush Inn** for a slightly more upscale crowd. If you are coming from Mad River Glen, the only place to stop is the **Mad River Barn**. The bar there looks like an old Vermont bar should look: Moosehead hanging over the fireplace, hunting scenes on every wall, big couches and stuffed chairs, wood paneling and a choice of bumper pool or shuffleboard.

In the evenings, **Gallagher's** has dancing with a mix of music from rock to country-rock and an interesting crowd. **Chez Henri's** disco at Sugarbush South attracts an upscale, slightly older group.

Child care

The Sugarbush Day School is the first child-care facility ever established at a ski resort. No child is too small to be admitted to the nursery. Two emergency medical techs and a registered baby nurse are in residence, and blankets, sheets and cribs are provided. Toddlers and older children have a choice of playing in the snow, learning to ski or playing games and reading in the center.

Hourly rates are $6; with lunch, add $3. Full-day program with lunch is $40. Family discounts are available for those with more than one child.

The MINIBEAR program is for children four and five years old. The full-day program, including lunch, costs are $50 for one day, $95 for two days, $140 for three days, and $215 for five days. Half days are also available.

The Sugarbear program is half-day only for children between six and 10.

Mad River Glen has the Cricket Club Nursery for children 18 months to six years. Rates run $25 a day for the first child and $20 a day for the second child. Ski rentals for children five and under are free through Tuckerman's.

Other activities

The Sugarbush Sports Center provides an indoor pool, three tennis courts, two squash courts, two racquetball courts, free weights, steam bath, massage, Jacuzzi, Nautilus, and the list goes on, 583-2391.

Bridges Resort and Raquet Club offers indoor tennis, squash, swimming, Jacuzzi, sauna and exercise room.

Snowshoe treks are available from the summit of Sugarbush North to Sugarbush South. Call 583-0381.

Horseback riding, sleighrides and Skijoring can be arranged at the Vermont Icelandic Horse Farm in Waitsfield. Tel. 496-7141. Other farms offering sleighrides are the Lareau Country Inn (496-4949) and Whispering Winds Farm in Moretown (496-2819).

Sledding is available at the base of Sugarbush South. Sleds may be rented for $3.

Ice skating rinks are at Tucker Hill Lodge, Sugarbush Inn and Warren School.

Getting there

The resort is off Route 100, about 20 miles south of Waterbury. From Burlington—take Exit 10. From Boston—take Exit 9, then follow Route 100B to 100.

Burlington airport is only an hour away by taxi or bus.

Information/reservations

Call central reservations for just about everything. They will arrange all phases of your trip: (800) 53-SUGAR.

For condominium space in Sugarbush Village only, call Sugarbush Village Condominiums: (800) 451-4326 or (802) 583- 3000.

Snow phone: for Sugarbush call (802) 583-SNOW; for Mad River Glen call (802) 496-2001 or in VT 800-696-2001.

For Mad River Glen information call (802) 496-3551.

Lake Placid
Whiteface
New York

"And the riders are zigging," comes the announcer's voice over the loudspeaker system. "And they're zagging." Experiencing my first run down an Olympic bobsled track, sandwiched between a professional driver and brakeman, I have to confess that this rider was not only zigging and zagging. He was also yelling. At first they were only little yelps of surprise as we climbed up the wall through the Zig ("Woooow!") Zag ("Ahhhhh!") turn. By the time we hit the straightway before the final 120-degree turn in front of the grandstand, however, the sled has gained nearly 50 mph forward thrust, and my involuntary exclamations assume a deeper, more primal tone. The rattling of the bobsled's slats on the hard ice make everything look exactly like one of those shaky camera shots on Wide World of Sports, and all I can think of is the "Agony of Defeat" clip. As the bobsled soars high into the final curve, the spectators don't need a loudspeaker to know what this rider is doing ("WooooOOOHHHAAAAHHHHH!").

As an area that would sit somewhere in the middle of the pack of northeast resorts based on its skiing alone, Lake Placid stands out and apart as a winter sports mecca. There's no doubt that the 1980 Winter Olympics were instrumental in establishing that reputation; nonetheless,

---

Lake Placid Facts
Base elevation: *1,200';* **Summit elevation:** *4,416';* **Vertical drop:** *3,216 feet*
Number and types of lifts: *9—2 triple chairs, 7 double chairs*
Acreage: *about 158 acres of terrain* **Percent of snowmaking:** *93 percent*
Uphill capacity: *10,115 skiers per hour* **Bed base:** *5,000*

plenty of past Olympic host sites have retreated into relative obscurity (skied Sarajevo lately?). At Lake Placid, the folks have taken the flame, so to speak, and run with it. To fulfill the promise of Lake Placid so evident during the Olympics, the Olympic Regional Development Authority (ORDA) was formed to operate the multi-facility recreational area.

Because probably more world-class winter sports athletes still train and compete here than anywhere else in the free world (more than 8,000 a year) Lake Placid still has something of the feel of an Olympic village. Groups of young athletes are everywhere, and there always seems to be one championship or another underway. Even the athletes themselves revel in watching the daring, if demented, souls who soar off the Olympic jumping ramps.

On top of being an open training camp in the scenic Adirondacks, Lake PLacid urges you at every turn to *participate*. In addition to the bobsled run and one of the most extensive and well-prepared cross country ski circuits anywhere, you can experience the luge run at the Mt. Van Hoevenberg Olympic sports complex about eight miles away (this was the site of the 1983 World Luge Championships). For the uninitiated, bouncing off the walls of a luge track is not unlike being in a pinball game played by unseen Nordic giants, with you as the ball. You have to experience it at least once. Of course, no one in their right mind would *want* to experience firsthand the thrill of being launched off a 90-meter ski ramp, but you can get a breathtaking perspective on that particular madness by taking the glass elevator 26 stories to the top. The $5 ticket, thankfully, is round-trip.

Back on Main Street, the town itself is dominated by the arena where the America watched its Cinderella hockey team enter the history books in 1980. Wonderfully situated on Mirror Lake, the town is full of charm, if standing just one standard motel away from being truly "quaint." For a relaxing afternoon away from the slopes, take a dog sled ride across the lake for the sheer novelty of it. At night many visitors will find both relaxation and exercise on the Olympic Oval (where Eric Heiden won five gold medals), lulled into an easy rhythm by the sharp scrape of their skates in the crisp night air. My personal favorite, however, are the nighttime toboggan runs. As many as six of your entourage can ride clutching, and yes, yelping together as you shoot down the lighted ramp and spill suddenly out onto the darkness of frozen Mirror Lake with a giddy sense of both fear and elation. It's another one of those winter sports that had always *looked* or *sounded* like a lot of fun, but which you never quite got around to doing. Like so many other visitors, you'll find yourself running out of excuses at Lake Placid. "Come on," this area seems to beckon, "Just do it."

The skiing

With the greatest vertical drop of any mountain in the East (3,216 feet), Whiteface Mountain has some of the most worthy expert runs this side of the Mississippi. There's also a Medusa's head of excellent advanced and advanced-intermediate runs snaking down the forested slopes of Little Whiteface (a shoulder of the same mountain), and nearly all the bottom third of the mountain is wide-open and gentle—just right for advanced beginners.

Like many Eastern mountains, Whiteface stands un-shielded, lording it over a vast valley of forests and frozen lakes. That makes for some of the most spectacular views in the world, but winter winds do seem to whip across that valley and climb up the walls of Whiteface with predictable regularity. For many veteran Eastern skiers, the complaint about Whiteface has been that it's too often wind-blown, cold and icy. Having been there three times now, I would say that from my own experience Whiteface is, well, frequently wind-blown, cold and icy. You can't fault any area for unpredictable weather, and on an ideal day Whiteface comes close to being as good as it gets in the East. The local officials have also made a good-faith effort at countering icy slopes with increased snowmaking (now covering fully 93 percent of the mountain).

Beginners on Whiteface have a secluded area—off to the right looking up from the base, above Kids Kampus—reserved in their honor. The bronze, silver and gold runs off the Cliff are all gentle. The wide-open runs down to the bottom from the mid-station are all suitable for lower intermediates, giving you a free run of half the mountain.

Intermediates should take the G-lift from the mid-station up to the top of Little Whiteface. An observation platform just off to the left at the top of this double chair gives you an unparalleled view of the lakes and valley. Then try the snaking Excelsior run, which twists back down to the mid-station. You can cut the rounded corners of this baby like a bobsled, choosing your own pace. After that warmup, tackle the new Paron's Run all the way from the tip-top of Whiteface (Lift F—Summit Triple). Before this run was added three years ago, intermediates had no way to enjoy either the awe-inspiring view or best-in-the-East vertical available from the top of the mountain. Advanced skiers should also not miss the Empire and MacKenzie runs from the top of Little Whiteface. They're officially black, but under good conditions manageable.

Experts will want to spend most their time on Cloud-spin and Skyward, the men's and women's downhill Olympic runs respectively, at the top of Whiteface. These are sweethearts with plenty of pitch and moguls even for the hotdogs. Most of the runs down from Little Whiteface are also black, and they all have good grade.

Mountain rating

Whiteface is one of those rare mountains that has more to offer experts and beginners, with less in the middle range for true intermediates. Experts will find much of the upper half of the mountain challenging, though anything below the mid-station is generally a wide-open cruise with very gentle grade. Beginners will find anything below the mid-station much to their liking. Intermediates will probably feel bored by most of the lower half of the mountain, and stretched by much of the upper. If you are ready to push yourself into the advanced stage, however, you'll find Little Whiteface much to your liking. Special Note: It's about a ten-mile drive to both Whiteface (downhill) and Mt. Hoevenberg (cross-country) from the center of Lake Placid. There are regularly scheduled buses, but this is one place where it's nice to have a car.

Snowboarding

Snowboarding is permitted on all trails and lifts of the mountain. Complete ski school services are available to shredders, and rentals are found in the base area.

Cross-country

Here again, the folks at Lake Placid have built strongly on the foundation laid by the 1980 Winter Olympics, and the Mt. Van Hovenberg complex offers cross-country skiing you are unlikely to find elsewhere—50 km. of marked trails that average 15 ft. wide, regularly groomed and patrolled; bridges built especially for cross-country skiers so you don't have to worry about traffic while crossing roads; snowmaking (5 km.), and emergency phones.

Within the 50-km. complex there are ten specially marked loops offering three novice, six intermediate and one expert tour. There's also additional expert skiing on the Porter Mountain racing loops. The start/finish stadium at the sports complex also features a ski shop, waxing room, a small snack bar and a warming room. Trail fees are $7 for adults, and $6 for juniors 12 and under, and seniors over 62. Children under six ski free.

Ski school (92/93 prices)

The Whiteface Mountain Ski School staffs over 75 instructors, and is affiliated with the Professional Ski Instructors of America (PSIA). They will tailor instruction to your particular needs, ranging from race packages, ski weeks and individual lessons, to special programs for juniors and children.

Group lessons begin at 9 a.m., with hour-and-a-half group lessons scheduled at 10 a.m. and 1:30 p.m. daily. The cost of a lift pass with morning or afternoon lesson for adults is $51 a day; $90 for two days; $130 for three days; and $211 for five days. Ski week packages begin with a wine and cheese party, and end with a race and party. Classes are limited to 8 students.

Private lessons $35 an hour, with $20 for one extra person (limit of two). A half-day private lesson costs $85 (three hours), with $40 for one extra person (limit of two).

Race programs are offered through the Whiteface Alpine Training Center, and operated through the New York Ski Educational Foundation (NYSEF). They include electronic timing, bibs and printed results. You have to book at least two weeks in advance, however, by calling the NYSEF at 946-7001.

Parents with children should consider the Play & Ski packages offered at the Kids Kampus (just to the right of the main lodge area). The supervised program for children 3-6 includes indoor and outdoor activities, with instruction and regular nursery services. There's an easy drop-off area with adjacent parking. Half-day programs are 9 a.m. - 12 p.m. and 1 p.m. - 4 p.m. ($20). A full-day program costs $38 (including lunch). Children 6 and under who can already ski can ride free on Whiteface's three lower lifts (for more about the children's program, 946-2223).

Lift tickets (92/93 prices)

On weekends and holidays: Full-day $33 adult/$20 children (12 and under) and seniors (62 and over); two-day $60/$38; three-day $85/$56; four-day $115/$72; five-day $136/$85.

During midweek, nonholiday: Full-day $28 adult/$17 children and seniors; two-day $53/$32; three-day $78/$47; four-day $101/$61; five-day $119/$72.

Early season specials run until December 22, with adults paying $20 per day and juniors $14. The same rates apply in late season (after March 15).

Accommodations

Some of the larger hotels centered around the town of Lake Placid tend to be of the more modern, franchise variety. Not so, however, the singular **Mirror Lake Inn** (523-2544), a traditional lodge right on the lake shore, and probably the finest overnight in the area. The quaint New England-style exterior continues inside with antiques, chandeliers and mahogany walls. Don't let all that rustic atmosphere fool you, because the inn also offers such modern amenities as Jacuzzi, sauna, health spa, and game room. There are also two cocktail lounges and one of the best restaurants in town with candlelight dining overlooking the lake. A two-day weekend including dinner and breakfast runs $233 (per person, double occupancy); a weekday costs $75 with breakfast and dinner per person double occupancy.

The **Holiday Inn** (523-2556) in the center of Lake Placid is the largest hotel in town (209 rooms). It features great views over the lake, a large indoor pool with two-story ceiling and adjacent fitness center; and one of the town's most popular nightspots, Cristy's Nightclub. A two-day weekend with dinner and breakfast runs $144 (per person, double occupancy); three-day weekends for $216; and two days midweek for $66-$86 per room.

The **Best Western Golden Arrow** (523-3353) overlooks the lake with spectacular views and has indoor pool, Jacuzzi, as well as sauna, weight room, and racquetball courts. Rates are $118-$128 per room with lake views; three-night package is $122 per person, double occupancy; and five night package is $200 per person, double occupancy. Also boasting every amenity is the **Lake Placid Hilton** (523-4411), complete with two indoor pools and private balconies for each room with a view of the lake. Two-day midweek rates are $94 per person, double occupancy with dinner and breakfast. There is also a **Howard Johnson** (523-9555) here.

For a romantic getaway slightly outside of town, try the **Whiteface Inn Resort** (523-2551). This is actually a collection of typical Adirondack lodges, each with its own fireplace. There's also 20 km. of on-site cross-country skiing, as well as a ski shop, cocktail lounge and fireside restaurant. A two-day weekend including breakfast and dinner runs $101 per person, double occupancy; three-day weekend $145; and two days midweek $79.

Skiers on a budget should try the **Edge of the Lake Motor Inn** (523-9430) $68-$90; **Town House Motor Inn** (523-2532) $65-$90 **Alpine Air Motel** (523-2180) $42-$60 weekends; the **Econo Lodge** (523-2750) $80-$100 weekends; and the **Wildwood** on the Lake (523-2750) $68-$100 weekends.

The nearest RV park is KOA in Wilmington, NY.

Dining
Considered the best restaurant in the area, **Placid Manor** (523-2573, serves continental cuisine. Also upscale and excellent is the **Hungry Trout** (946-2217), specializing in, you guessed it, fish and beef (entrées $12.95 and up). If your taste runs to the rich and continental, with plenty of sauces, try **Lindsay's at the Woodshed** (523-9470). This cozy, woodsy restaurant with its fireplace in the entrance alcove next to the bar offers excellent atmosphere and a

central location. **The Charcoal Pit,** (523-3050) open for about 30 years, charbroils lots of steaks and chops.

Solid German fare is available at slightly more moderate prices at the **Alpine Cellar** (523-2180). A full menu of schnitzels, sauerbraten (marinated and roasted beef) and Rippchen (smoked pork) are available starting around $10.95 per entrée. **Villa Vespa** (523-9959) features authentic Italian fare in the same price category. A personal favorite is the **Artist's Café** (523-9493) which features a prime location overlooking Mirror Lake, as well as steak and fish at reasonable prices: after a chilled dog sled ride on the lake, take a break with a bowl of their excellent onion soup. And no skiing town is complete, of course, without an inexpensive Italian restaurant featuring pizza or carbo-heavy pasta. Try **Mr. Mike's Pizza** (523-9770) for the pizza part (no pasta), or the **Great Adirondack Pasta Company** (523-1629).

Après-ski/nightlife

Lake Placid is large enough to generate its own heat as a nightlife center, drawing not only the gypsy moths from the out-of-town vacationers, but also the local variety from the surrounding countryside. Because Whiteface lies separated from the town, however, most of the après-ski action is in the base lodge. **Steinhoff's** and **R.J. McDougall's,** just down the road from Whiteface are also good for an après-ski drink.

At night, the young and hot of foot head to **Mud Puddles,** on the side street next to the speed skating oval. All the high-tech disco gear is on full display around the dance floor. Most of the other nightlife action centers around the main hotels. My favorite was **Cristy's** at the Holiday Inn, which features a large bar and even more generous dance floor, with music spun by a DJ (drink specials on Wednesday nights). **Roomers** at the Best Western also offers dancing to a DJ, or for a live band, try **Dancing Bears Lounge** at the Hilton.

Couples looking for a kinder, gentler nightspot should head for **The Cottage,** across the street from the Mirror Lake Inn. The fire's always going, and at sunset there's an excellent view of Mirror Lake and the surrounding mountains.

Child care

When they opened the Bunny Hutch (formerly Olympic Acres) two years ago, Whiteface officials gave children their own lodge and congregating area on the mountain. There's a children's drop-off, adjacent parking for parents with children, a large nursery, children's rentals and an outdoor terrain garden.

The nursery is open daily for children aged 1 to 6, and the cost is $3 an hour per child, with lunch extra (supervisors can arrange for a variety of hot meals). Nursery service is offered daily 8 a.m.-4.30 p.m. If your child is ready for the slopes, you can enroll him or her in the Play & Ski programs (9 a.m.-12 p.m. and 1 p.m.-4 p.m.). The charge is $20 for a half day, and $40 for a full day with lunch.

Getting there

Commuter flights from several northeast cities serve Adirondack Airport, 16 miles from Lake Placid on Route 86 in Saranac Lake. Private planes can land at Lake Placid Airport.

There's a local rail stop at Westport on the New York City to Montreal line, and then shuttlebus service for the 40-minute ride to Lake Placid (523-4431 for the bus). There are special Amtrak Ski Packages, including rail fare, hotel accommodations, lift tickets and all transfers. Contact North Star Tours at (800) 338-8898 (in New York), or contact a travel agent. North Star also offers Fly-Drive packages.

Because the Lake Placid area is spread out, I recommend bringing a car. From the south, take Exit 24 (Albany) off the New York State Thruway (I-87). Take Northway (still I-87) to Exit 30, follow Route 9 north two miles to Route 73 and continue 28 miles to Lake Placid. From the west, take I-90 (NY State Thruway) to Exit 36 (Syracuse) for I-81. Follow I-81 north to Watertown, then east on Route 3 to Saranac Lake. Then take Route 86 east to Lake Placid.

Other activities

Lake Placid is nothing *but* other activities. The bob-sled rides at Mt. Van Hoevenberg Olympic Sports Complex are Tuesday through Sunday, 1-3 p.m., and cost $15 (including commemorative Olympic Bobsled Run pin).

Luge rides are offered on Saturdays and Sundays, 1 p.m.-3 p.m., and cost $10 (for more information on both, 523-4436).

Tours of the Olympic Jumping Complex, including chair lift and elevator ride, cost $5 for adults, $4 for children and seniors.

The Olympic Speed Skating Oval is open 7 p.m.-9 p. m. daily, and 1-3 p.m. on weekends (523-3325).

Operating hours for the toboggan run on Mirror Lake are Wednesday, 7-9 p.m.; Friday, 7-9 p.m.; Saturday, 12-4 p.m. and 7-9 p.m., and Sunday 12-4 p. m. The charge is $3 for adults, $2 for children, and $3 for the toboggan rental.

Information/reservations

For reservations contact the Lake Placid Commerce and Visitors Bureau, Lake Placid NY 12946 (800-44-PLACID or 523-2445).

The Olympic Regional Development Authority, Olympic Center, Lake Placid NY 12946 (523-1655, 800-462-6236 nationwide).

Local telephone area code is 518.

Hunter Mountain and Ski Windham New York

These are the two closest large ski areas to New York City, only a two and a half hours drive north. These resorts are in the midst of the rugged and rocky Catskills Mountains— home to legends such as Rip Van Winkle and the headless horseman of Sleepy Hollow. As far as skiing goes, the area only woke up a little more than a decade ago. Today it is one of the East's most popular skiing areas.

Both Hunter Mountain and Ski Windham have the same amount of vertical and they are only ten miles apart. Hunter is by far the bigger operation—it is major league. It has become the snowmaking champion in the Northeast, shooting out mountains of snow and continually upgrading the system. Ski Windham offers good skiing but is not quite in the same league with Hunter.

Hunter's skiing is primarily intermediate with some advanced flair. It has some of the toughest short runs in the East but most of Hunter One is mellow. Hunter with a

---

Hunter Mountain Facts
Base elevation: 1,600; Summit elevation: 3,200'; Vertical drop: 1,600 feet
Number of lifts: 16—1 quad chair, 2 triple chairs, 8 double chairs, 5 surface lifts
Percent snowmaking: 100 percent
Uphill capacity: 18,000 per hour

Ski Windham Facts
Base elevation: 1,500'; Summit elevation: 3,100'; Vertical drop: 1,600 feet
Number of lifts: 7—4 triple chairs, 2 double chairs, 1 surface lifts
Percent snowmaking: 97 percent Total acreage: 220 skiable acres
Uphill capacity: 9,800 per hour

far larger lift system can handle about twice as many skiers as Windham.

Windham has a strong intermediate flavor. Its advanced trails are not as tough as Hunter's but will keep skiers happy for a few days.

Snowboarding

Snowboarding is allowed on the entire mountain at both Hunter and Ski Windham. There are snowboarding lessons including packages for never-evers, and Small Class Sessions that meet three times a day. Rentals are also available at the mountain.

Ski school

Hunter: The Ski Free with Me program lets skiers take several runs with a pro every day except Christmas and New Year's at 11:45 a.m. at the top of Snowlite Express.

Hunter offers beginner packages that include everything one needs to learn to ski, except natural ability . . . and they try to teach you that. The cost is $52 for Alpine skiing and $53 for beginning snowboarders.

Normal lift/lesson packages with an hour and a half of lessons cost $46. Special two-hour high-performance skiing clinics for a minimum of two students and a maximum of five cost $35.

Small Class Lessons meet at 9:45 and 11:45 a.m. and 1:45 p.m. for one-and-a-half-hour sessions. They cost $20 for one session and $35 for two sessions.

Private lessons cost $45 per hour for one and $64 for two, with each additional skier paying $19. A two-hour private lesson will cost $45 with a two-person minimum. All-day private lessons are $210 for one and $265 for two.

Children's ski school is part of the SKIwee program. It is open to children 5-12 and includes lifts, lessons, rentals, box lunch and supervision. Rates for the full day are $49; half day, $40.

The Top Cat program for children 6 to 12 meets from 9:45 a.m. to noon and/or 12:45 to 3 p.m. The program costs $39 for lifts and lessons or $31 for lessons only.

Pee Wee School is for those 3 to 5. It meets for a.m. and p.m. sessons. Each session costs $17, or take two for $28.

Windham: (92/93 rates) This resort has a full ski school program as well. Private lessons run $40 an hour for one person; $70 for two; $90 for three. Group lessons are $18 per one-and-three-quarter-hour session, or $80 for a book of five sessions, $160 for a book of ten lessons. The resort also has a full range of programs for children four to 13. These cost $33 for a half day, $55 for a full day with lessons, lunch and supervision.

Lift tickets

Hunter: Full-day lift tickets cost $38 adult/$26 junior (12 and under); half day is $24/$18; two days cost $70/$50; five days run $165/$115; and ten days will be $320/$220. These lift tickets are good *anytime during this season,* — they do not have to be used consecutively nor within a specific number of days.

Midweek/non-holiday lift tickets cost $66/$46 for two days; $155/$105 for five days; and $300/$205 for ten days.

Seniors (65 and over) pay the junior rates.

Windham: (92/93 prices) A full-day ticket costs $35 adult/$28 junior (12 and under) on weekends, and $26/$23 on weekdays. You can build your own ski week. The first day costs full price and each subsequent day can be purchased at a $2 disount.

On non-holiday weekdays, Juniors (12 and under) rfeceive a free lift ticket whcn accompanied by a paying adult (one child per adult). children six and under ski free anytime when acompanied by a ticketed adult.

Accommodations

Hunter pioneered a bed-and-breakfast program which now has about 30 country inns participating. These B&Bs have prices starting at about $25. The program includes lift tickets and combined with the Kids Ski Free program becomes a real money-saver.

Ski Windham also has a reservation service with packages that include lifts, lodging and many discounts.

Other hotels in the area are the **Vatra Vegetarian Lodge** (518-263-4919) only a mile from Hunter mountain featuring vegetarian meals with rates (per person double occupancy) of $95 on weekends and $70 wekdays.

Han's Country Line Motel (518-678-3101 or 800-867-HANS) is virtually next to the area and has shuttles to Windham. Rates are $60 per room per night on weekends; $55 per room weekdays.

Howard Johnson has two lodges within striking distance, one at Exit 19 of I-87 (914-338-4200) and the other at Exit 20 of I-87 (914-246-9511). Call (800) 654-2000 for reservations.

Green Mountain View Inn (518-589-5511) is three miles from the area and features complimentary continental breakfast. It is near nightlife.

Pine Hill Arms Hotel (914-254-9811) is located in the Catskills in the hamlet of Pine Hill. The inn features 28 rooms and a Jacuzzi. Rates are $40 for standard room and $50 for deluxe based on double occupancy.

The **Red Ranch Motel** (518-678-3380), about 10 miles from the resort, charges $55 per room on weekends and $40 per night per room on a five-day midweek package.

The following are within three miles of Ski Windham (call 800-729-SKIW for reservations and information):

Albergo Allegria—$105-$115 per room per night weekends; $65 a night midweek.

Cave Mountain Motel—$56 a room per night weekends; $49 per room weeknights.

Windham Arms—$85 a room per night weekends; $60 per room weeknights.

Evergreen at The Thompson House—$95 a room per night weekends; $70 per room weeknights.

Christmas Windham House—$88 a room per night weekends; $66 per room weeknights.

Dining

Scores of restaurants are in this region. If you have lots of money to spend try **Auberge des 4 Saisons** in Shandaken (914-688-2223) for French cooking; **Chateau Belleview** in Tannersville (518-589-5525) also prepares fine continental cooking such as beef Wellington; try **Brandywine** (518-734-3838) for Northern Italian creamy cooking; **La Griglia** in Windham (734-4499) also does a commendable job with Northern Italian cuisine; or dine at **Redcoat's Return** (518-589-6379) for British flair.

More moderate restaurants are **Marie's Dream House** in Westkill (518-989-6565) for Austrian/German cooking; **Fireside** in Hunter (518-263-4216) for steaks; or try **Hans County Line** in Palenville (518-678-3101) for good all-round meals. **Thetford's** in Windham (518-734-3322) has great steaks and seafood.

Those on a budget should check out **The Frog's House** (518-734-9817) and **Point Lookout** (518-734-3381) both near Windham. **Alfredo's** in Hunter (518-263-4271) prepares inexpensive Italian food. **P.J. Larkins** in Tannersville (518-589-5568) and **Garbino's** in Windham (518-734-3914) have reputations as good family places.

For a heaping breakfast head to the **Pioneer Pancake House** in Catskill (518-678-9275) .

Child care

Hunter has a Kids Ski Free program which allows children 12 and under a free lift ticket when skiing with a parent or guardian with a paid one-day Hunter Mountain lift ticket. This offer is good any Monday through Friday only—holiday periods are excluded. Only one free junior ticket will issued per adult.

The child-sitting program has been expanded dramatically, doubling this season to handle 40 children. This service is for children who have not yet begun to ski. It costs $22 for a full day (9 a.m. to 4 p.m.) or $4 per hour. A book of five days will cost $75. Lunch is not included. It can be purchased for $2.50 per day per child.

Windham: The Children's Learning Center ofers non-skiers and skiers a variety of activities. Full day/half-day programs are $40/$25 for non skiers and $55/$33 for skiers with higher prices on weekends.

Getting there

The best access for both ski areas is up I-87 120 miles north of New York City. For Hunter Mountain, take Exit 20 at Saugerties and follow Rte. 32 to Rte. 32A then onto Rte.23A to the area. To reach Windham turn north on Rte. 296 off of Rte. 23A or if coming on the New York Thruway take Exit 21 in Catskill and go west on Rte. 23 for 25 miles.

Once you get to the resort area, many inns and lodges provide shuttles to the slopes, but a car is mandatory in order to get around at night to restaurants and nightlife.

Information/reservations

Hunter has a central reservation system which handles thousands of rooms in the region from B&B's to modern motels and condominiums. Call (518) 263-3827.

Windham also has a lodging service office at (800) 729-SKIW.

Canadian Rockies

Once upon a time, in a land not so far away, a fairy tale kingdom was discovered by people who liked to ski. They found majestic castles, enchanted forests, frosted looking-glass lakes. They skied through the forests, and skated on the lakes. And they stayed in the castles—the grand hotels of Canadian Pacific Railway. You see, it's not a fantasy.

This is the heart of the Canadian Rockies, National Park country with mountains of such grandeur that UNESCO has given them World Heritage status, shared with a handful of spots on the planet like the Galapagos and the Pyramids, where God or man outdid himself. Lake Louise, Sunshine and Mt. Norquay comprise a fine trio of ski areas located a two hours west of Calgary and 35 miles from Banff, with another, Marmot Basin at Jasper, three hours up the Icefield Parkway, one of the world's most spectacular drives. With such a hearty offering, Alberta takes its place in the fabled ski country of the western world.

The mountains here are no higher than the U.S. Rockies, but they're closer, looming, with a lower tree line (8,000 feet compared to 11,000 in the U.S. Rockies), which gives them the aspect of the Alps. Far younger than the U.S. Rockies, they are also sharper, formed of limestone, sandstone and shale in sedimentary deposits uplifted. This shapes them as sawridges, or castellates (buttressed walls with craggy crenelations) or dip slopes (the steeply tilted opposite sides of the castellate walls), which most of the ski mountains are.

Threading through the mountains as if in some great plan to connect the ski areas is a glacier-carved valley (the last Ice Age blew through here a mere 10,000 years ago), and an abundance of wildlife—elk, deer, bighorn sheep, moose. Add to that the magnificence of the grand railway hotels, mountain towns, landscape for sleigh rides, and morning lakeside walks under the honks of Canadian geese, and you have ski country with a purely Canadian character.

The weather here tends to be more variable than in the U.S. Rockies: in January, chinook winds may bring springlike temperatures, and in July there may be fresh snow on the mountaintops. The average temperature, over 30 years, is 24 degrees F. in December, 21 in January, 31 in February and 37 in March. Clearly, the chinooks operate to raise the average, but the climate is generally dry, which means more comfortable ski conditions and more lasting powder.

Prices in this section are all from the 91/92 winter and are given in Canadian dollars. They do not include the G.S.T., Canada's Goods and Services Tax of 7 percent.

Sunshine Village, Banff

The Great Divide Chair charges up the flat incline of a typical Canadian Rockies dip slope called Lookout Mountain, a tilted wedge with rocky cliffs on all sides. At the top, you will have crossed into British Columbia. All around are snowy peaks and somewhere near your ski tips is the Great Continental Divide itself. If you throw a snowball over your right shoulder, it will melt and find its way to the Pacific. Over your left, it will become one with the Atlantic, occasion for one snowflake to say to another, "There but for fortune go you or I. Adieu." Scenery like this encourages such musings on fate and the cosmic wonders of North American geology.

It also encourages you to point your tips down and let that other cosmic force, gravity, take over. The dip slope is wide, with an infinite number of ways down, some smooth, others more moguled, all exhilarating. In part, it must be the removed, top-of-the-world feeling that causes such abandon.

After all, you got here by an unusual route: up a narrow canyon in a six-person gondola from the parking lot, around a sharp left turn ("No way!" you say as you board. "Gondolas don't turn." But there are more things in heaven and earth, Horatio, than are dreamt of in your ski dreams—this one turns!) and then fifteen more minutes up another drainage, and *then* you're at what feels like a ski area base village. You can ski down all the way to the bottom, but it's here at the Village that the play really starts, around a lodge, rental shop, general store, restaurant

Sunshine Village Facts

Base elevation: 5,440'; **Summit elevation:** 8,954'; **Vertical drop:** 3,514 feet
Number of lifts: 12—1 gondola, 1 quad superchair, 1 triple chair,
4 double chairs, 5 surface lifts
Percent snowmaking: none **Total acreage by trails:** 780 acres skiable terrain
Uphill capacity: 15,000 per hour **Bed Base:** 10,000 in Banff

and the highest on-hill accommodation in the Rockies. Surrounding all this a half dozen lifts and tows take off in all directions. Most people never ski all the way down until the end of the day; some not until the end of their vacation. Morning waits at the gondola base may be extensive.

The longest ski season in the region, sometimes even into June, and the most snow (360 inches as opposed to 120 and 140 at the other areas) are Sunshine's strong points. Its reputation is based on its dramatic views—if it's clear weather. Sunshine is family-oriented; with such a centralized on-mountain village no one can get lost, yet people can spread out to play wherever the terrain suits them. The quieter, more remote on-mountain living experience suits some, while Sunshine's location 15 minutes from Banff makes town life after hours accessible.

And Banff is a gem of a town, not just a fabricated purpose-built village, but a real community with real people, real stores instead of "shops" and galleries, a handful of museums with a history to fill them, and an Edwardian manor growing out of the trees—the Banff Springs.

The skiing

Most of the lifts splay out in three directions from the on-mountain village at the top of the gondola, which is more for morning transport than for continuous skiing.

You'll find the most exhilarating skiing on the Great Divide Chair. Take Angel Express to get to it. Intermediates should first try the new run down the face of Angel, called Ecstasy—just to get ready for the high country.

From the top of Angel Express, it's wide open, above tree line skiing, with views of the Great Divide. Intermediates working up to blacks will find a bonanza there.

The most challenging route from the Great Divide is far to the right as you head down. Don't forget there's a cliff edge. The appeal in getting as far out along the cliff edge as you dare, of course, is virgin snow, less trafficked. If you stay on the edge, you have to dip down a drop innocuously called The Shoulder. It's the only thing on the mountain labeled a black which should be a double black. To avoid it, turn left and you'll negotiate only blacks, and find some great tree skiing.

Mogul runs can be found off the Teepee Town Chair. If that's mild for you, take the WaWa T-bar on the opposite side of the Village up to a ridge with a left-hand dropoff called Paris Basin that doesn't even look like a run, but they ski it. Once up there, if you decide against it, you have a long traverse and a lot of poling.

Come to think of it, poling is something to watch out for in other places at Sunshine—most notably at several spots on Highway One, familiarily dubbed "Tuck 'n Pole" by locals. If you don't tuck, you pole. Be sure to look far ahead coming off the Great Divide when you're headed back toward Strawberry Chair or you'll get caught on an up-slope.

The three-mile run at the end of the day from the Village down to the parking lot is a long, luscious trip for beginners, but a lovely end-of-day cruiser for intermediates with occasional drops to the left for experts, but they're short and eventually rejoin the ski-out.

To find powder just after a storm, head immediately to ByeBye Bowl (left, facing down off the Divide), but it gets blown off quickly. The day after a storm, try Paris Basin.

To stay in the sun, ski Standish Face in the morning and Lookout Mountain (Great Divide) in the afternoon.

A ski tour takes off from the upper gondola terminal at 9:50 a.m. and 12:50 p.m. daily. Many of the hosts are Canadian flight attendants from all over Canada, who like to stay with their groups more than the allotted one-hour mountain familiarization.

Mountain Rating

With a whopping 60 percent of Sunshine's terrain marked intermediate, this a cruiser's mountain, without hair-raising chutes or mogul-mania drops.

The remaining 40 percent is divided evenly between beginner and expert.

One run loved by snowboarders and early intermediates is Dell Valley, a natural halfpipe where the g-forces will have you swooping up one side of a gorge, turning to gain momentum on the down-slope to swoosh up the other side—just like the skateboarders do.

Cross-country

There are some lovely easy loops along the Bow River. Take Banff Avenue to the end of Spray Avenue, or turn left and cross the river. Trails wind through the whole area.

Banff Springs Golf Course Clubhouse offers ski and skate rentals. Touring ski rentals are Cdn$10 a day. Group lessons are Cdn$8 per hour at 10:30 a.m. Private lessons are $12 per hour. Maps and information on more challenging trails are available at the Clubhouse.

Snowboarding

Snowboarding is permitted and rentals can be had at Sunshine for Cdn$25 a day, Cdn$20 half day. One snow-boarding instructor is certified. Private lessons with him are Cdn$40 an hour, $70 for two hours, $100 for three hours, with an additional $15 for extra skiers.

Ski School

Sunshine encourages the traditional Ski Week, an on-mountain stay of a week, by providing appealing packages including classes with the same instructor for the whole time. Groups can be divided by ability level or by family, and the package includes evening activities as well. For two people, six-day packages range from Cdn$840 to $1,340, depending on time of season and room.

Group lessons are Cdn$20 ($5 for never-evers). A never-ever package includes a longer lesson (two hours and a half), rental equipment and lift ticket for $40. Short Turn Clinic or lessons for moguls and steeps are $25.

Private lessons are $43 per hour (plus $16 for an additional person), $75 for two hours (plus $21 for additional person), and $107 for three hours ($32 for extra person).

Instruction for children comes in two packages. The Wee Angels is for 3-5 year olds just venturing onto the slopes; boots and skis are included with lesson from 1:00 p.m. to 2:30 for Cdn$10. The Young Developers (aka Little Devils) is for 6-12 year olds just starting or well on their way. The price of Cdn$38 for full day includes lunch; $22 half day; $65 for two days. (All rates plus GST)

Lift tickets (91/92 prices)

Adult all-day tickets are Cdn$35; half day $30. Student with ID $30 full day. Children 6-12 are $13. Seniors 65 and over are $30. Children up to six years ski free. (Rates include GST)

Multiday passes up to six days discount tickets up to 15 percent off regular costs. They must be used consecutively and there are no refunds. An adult two-day pass is $67; three-day is $95. Student two-day pass is $57; three-day is $80. Child two-day pass is $21; three-day is $26.

Sunshine participates in Ski Adventure, a program of consecutive lessons with the same instructor and group, but skiing at three resorts. Lift line privilege is a big appeal. See Lake Louise ticket section for specifics.

Accommodations

The **Sunshine Inn** is the only lodging on the mountain and offers rooms ranging from Cdn$70 (low season) or $97 (regular season) to suites from Cdn$95 (low season) to $147 (regular). There is no discount for stays of more than one night. Lift tickets, a daily 90-minute lesson and complimentary day care (19 months to 4 years) are all included in the daily room rate with minimum five night stay. Children 4-12 are $18 a day, which covers lodging, lifts, lessons and day care if required. Meals are optional and are Cdn$38.50 daily for adults and $25 for children for three meals. No rooms have kitchenettes. (800) 661-1676.

All other lodging is in Banff. The **Banff Springs Hotel**, dating back to 1888 although it wasn't completed until 1928, is the town's jewel. A $50 million restoration has returned the baronial Canadian Pacific Railway Hotel to its Old World Scottish charm. This *is* the great brick monolith you've seen in many classic photos, the cinnamon walls and steep roofs rising nine stories out of the evergreens with dramatic peaks behind it and not another building to be seen. 2,000 people a night can stay here. Its public areas are expansive, designed for turn-of-the-century mingling. We're talking a ballroom for 16,000. Ski season is the off-season and the rates plummet to a third of their summer prices. (800) 828-7447.

Banff Park Lodge and Conference Center, which hosts many cultural activities, is an expanse of cedar buildings in a wooded area two blocks from downtown. A room for two is Cdn$99 (800) 661-9266.

Cascade Inn on Banff Avenue gets a fair amount of street noise but has an exceptionally good restaurant. Rooms for two are Cdn$99 to $140.

The Inns of Banff Park, a modern, multi-level lodge with balconies in most rooms, is a 15-minute walk from downtown. On-site ski rentals and repairs. For two people, rooms range Cdn$65 to $150 (800) 661-1272.

High Country Inn on Banff Avenue is the most budget lodging in town. Rooms for two range from Cdn$55 to $99.

For information about other lodgings, contact Banff Reservations, Box 1628, Alberta T0L 0C0 (403-762-5561).

Dining

At Sunshine Village, the **Eagle's Nest Dining room** in the Sunshine Inn serves a sit-down lunch of croissants, soups, salads, pastas, ribs and steak sandwiches. **Trapper Bill's** serves burgers. **Day Lodge Cafeteria** serves chili, stew, soup and pizza.

At the Banff Springs, you have 16 restaurants to choose from. **The Samurai** serves Japanese cuisine including Shabu-Shabu, a healthy fondue broth. **The Pavilion** serves Italian dinners and **Grapes** is the wine bar, originally the writing room. It only seats 26 and is a one-man restaurant, a cozy corner in the cavernous hotel serving fondues, soups, and salads; wine tasting, too. **Downstairs,** a 24-hour deli, packs picnics.

In the town of Banff, the **Bow View** is warmly personal, the Ticino is a long-standing reliable establishment serving Italian and Swiss cuisine. **La Fontaine Dining Room** in the Cascade Hotel has good food in lovely furnishings. **The Bistro** has a varied menu with pastas and salads.

Après-ski/nightlife

The Happy Bus shuttles skiers to night spots around Banff until midnight for Cdn$1.50. **The Mt. Royal** has a lively bar for après-ski. Next door is **The Rose and Crown,** an English-style pub with draft ale and darts. Those wanting a quieter atmosphere will be more comfortable at the **Cascade. Bumper's Loft Lounge** has a casual crowd, with live entertainment and ski movies. **Joshua's Pub** has Old Banff atmosphere, good food and Calgary's Big Rock ale on tap.

At the Banff Springs Conference Center, **Whiskey Creek** is a hopping bar, attracting many locals as well as tourists. In the Hotel proper, the **Rob Roy Room** has dining and dancing and the **Rundle Lounge** is a lounge with quiet music for hotel guests. At the **Waldhaus** at Banff Spring

Golf Course, Happy Hans and Lauren, on accordion and trumpet, get everybody singing and oompahing.

Child care

Kids Kampus Day Care is for children 19 months to 6 years. Available 8:30 a.m. to 4:30 p.m. for Cdn$5 per hour, plus $4 for lunch, to a maximum of $30 per day. Reservations recommended. (403) 762-6560.

Other activities

Around the Banff Springs Hotel, tobogganing, skating, and sleigh rides are part of the tradition. The Mountain Mushers provides dog sledding, 678-5742. The rink is lit for night skating until 9 p.m. Toboggans are available at the Waldhaus.

The Whyte Museum of the Canadian Rockies houses a collection of historic and contemporary works of art and maintains several historic homes. The Luxton Museum is a tribute to the Plains Indians, and the Natural History Museum traces the geological evolution of the Rockies.

Getting There

Calgary Airport is served by major airlines. It is possible to ski Banff and Lake Louise without a rental car by using Happy Bus shuttles ($1 a ride) in the area and Pacific Western Transportation (403-762-4558) or Brewster Transportation (403-762-6700) for regularly scheduled buses between the airport, Banff, and the ski areas.

Banff is 130 miles west of Calgary on the Trans-Canada Highway (#1), an hour and a half drive. The Sunshine exit is five miles west of Banff; then it's five more miles to the Sunshine Gondola base parking area.

Information/reservations

Sunshine Village, Box 1510, Banff, Alberta T0L 0C0; phone (403) 762-6500, or (800) 661-1676, (800) 661-1363 in Canada for Sunshine Inn reservations. Ski report number is (403) 762-6543.

Ski Norquay, Banff

It's called the New Norquay now. The Old Norquay, actually the oldest ski resort in the Rockies, consisted of plunging, deeply moguled expert runs, and off to the side some good beginner terrain, with nothing in between. Now, with the opening of 70 additional acres of intermediate terrain, and two new quad chairs as well, Norquay is experiencing a renaissance.

Some things remain the same, however. Ski Norquay still has those mogul plunges right down its face, bump ribbons which seem to hang right over the main street in Banff. Norquay still is the closest resort to Banff, only four miles away. And Norquay still has the most spectacular view of Banff and the Bow Valley from the North American chair, a lift scrambling up those bump ribbons. If the prospect of the run down puts your heart in your throat, you can ride back in the lift. Many do.

The skiing

Lone Pine is the name of that double-black mogul belt stretching up a 35-degree pitch. It's where the photos are taken, where the intrepid launch themselves with a hope and a prayer, and where lunchers at Norquay and Cascade Lodges watch their every move. Each year the area has a contest to see who can make the most consecutive runs in seven hours (Club 3,5000) on this 412-meter, skeleton-jarring wall. Both men and women have done more than 20 trips, which says a lot for local physical fitness.

Ski Norquay Facts
Base elevation: 5,350'; *Summit elevation:* 7,000'; *Vertical drop:* 1,650 feet
Number of lifts: 5—1 quad superchair, 1 quad chair, 2 double chairs, 3 surface lifts
Percent snowmaking: 90 percent of skiable terrain
Total acreage by trails: 162 acres skiable terrain
Uphill capacity: 6,300 per hour *Bed Base:* 10,000 in Banff

From the base Norquay looks like a haven for mogul maniacs and that only, but the terrain unseen from the base on the Mystic Express Quad, mainly intermediate, is groomed well. Three runs there, Excalibur (a black), Illusion and Knight Flight (blues) are only partially groomed, leaving skiers a choice of packed snow or powder. Also, there are several fall lines for each run.

The Norquay management asserts that "there is still a lot of adventure skiing in our area." They don't want their expansion to dilute anything for the skier who loves expert drops. For example, the two blacks on Mystic Express—Black Magic and Ka-Poof—are groomed regularly, whereas the blacks off North American are rarely groomed. Another appeal for the adventure seeker is a chute on Ski Norquay called Valley of the Ten, a narrow drainage perfect for avalanches and elevator skiers. To get to it, skiers at the top of North American chair drop off (correct terminology) to the left into a drop-out (accurate again) called Gun Run, the steepest thing on the mountain.

For first-time visitors up Ski Norquay—the peak, not the resort—the easiest way down, still a black, is Memorial Bowl. It's so steep they have stock fences staggered at the top of Memorial Bowl to force people to do wide traverses getting into it. "We think that's damn nice of us," they say. They also say, in lower, more serious tones, "You'd better be ready for North America chair."

To ski smart take the high intermediate from Mystic or Spirit back into the main base area on Speculation, a lovely run otherwise. The most popular run off Spirit, Abracadabra, also tends to ice up because of its high traffic, however the resort is taking steps to limit the skiers.

Skiers wanting to stay in the sun all day have a challenge. Since at midday none of Mystic gets sun except the front two runs, Black Magic and Ka-Poof, both blacks, they'd better learn to ski bumps. The capricious ski gods smile devilishly when they remember that the bump drops of Ski Norquay get more sun.

Mountain rating

Whereas the Old Norquay had 50 percent expert runs and 35 percent beginner, with the intermediates squished in between, the New Norquay claims 11 percent beginner,

45 percent intermediate, 28 percent advanced and 16 percent expert. Be aware, however, that what is considered advanced in the U.S. is often intermediate here.

Intermediates will find their neck of the woods on the two new quads, Mystic Express and Spirit. What's left for beginners is to poke around the base.

Cross-country

See Sunshine section for Banff area trails.

Snowboarding

The North American Snowboarding Championships were held here in 1988, so Norquay is a great supporter of the sport. However, snowboarders cannot use the North American chair.

Ski school (92/93 prices)

Learn-to-Ski packages for beginners are Cdn$30 for an hour-an-a-half group lesson, two lifts and equipment.

Adult group lessons are Cdn$20 for a two-hour lesson. Children pay Cdn$15.

Private lessons are Cdn$35 per hour for adults, each additional person is Cdn$10 per hour and Cdn$15 for two.

For children 6-12, full day lessons (2 hours in the morning and two hours in the afternoon) are Cdn$25, which includes lunch. A Learn-to-Ski lesson, either morning or afternoon, is Cdn$30 including lift and rental.

Ski Norquay participates in Ski Adventure, a program of consecutive lessons with the same instructor and group, but skiing at three resorts. Lift line privilege is a big appeal. See Lake Louise ticket section for specifics.

All ski school rates are plus 7% tax.

Lift tickets (92/93 prices)

Adult all day is Cdn$30; half day $23. That includes night skiing on Wednesday. Night skiing only, 4 to 9 p.m. is $11. Students 13-25 (with student ID) are $23 full day; $17 half day. Children under 12 are $11 full day; $5 night skiing. Seniors 65 and over are $17 full or half day. Children five and under ski free. (Rates include GST)

Dining

There are three restaurants in the Cascade Lodge, the large new building. Lone Pine Restaurant has healthy lunches, full meals with hot entrées such as seafood crêpes and steaks. The Cafeteria and Deck have a wide array of food and drink. Early Bird breakfasts are served from 8:30 to 9:30 for Cdn$3.45.

The Old Norquay Lodge at the base of Ski Norquay Chair serves soups, sandwiches and drinks. It is open weekends, holidays and when booked for special events.

Accommodations

There's no lodging at Ski Norquay. Banff has 43 hotels and motels. See Sunshine for Banff choices.

Child care

Children aged 19 months to 6 years are taken on a drop-in basis for Cdn$3.50 per hour per child, daily 9 a.m. to 4 p.m. Additional options include plans for lunch and combination snow play and ski instruction. Children have a "mini-mountain" all to themselves for snow play.

Getting there

Norquay is the closest major ski area to the town of Banff, ten minutes away. Free shuttles pick up skiers at 11 Banff hotels and the bus depot, as well as from the four Lake Louise hotels via the bus depot in Banff.

Information/reservations

For more information, write Ski Norquay—Banff, Box 1258, Banff, Alberta T0L 0C0, or phone (403) 762-4421. Calgary Snowphone is (403) 221-8259.

Lake Louise Ski Area

"As God is my judge, I never in all my exploration have seen such a matchless scene," said Tom Wilson, surveyor for the Canadian Pacific Railroad and the first white man to see Lake Louise. Now every skier from beginner to expert can see it from dozens of runs on Mt. Whitehorn across the valley, with the eternal white majesty of Victoria Glacier dipping down behind it from 11,360 feet, but with one major difference: At its edge stands the monumental Chateau Lake Louise, fitting in size the grandeur of the surroundings.

Lake Louise Ski Area is Canada's largest, comprising two mountains and four faces. That means dozens of bowls and a variety of snow conditions with some slopes always in the sun. Although there are 50 named runs on the ski area's 17 square miles of serviced terrain, there are probably another 50 still unnamed: 65 percent below treeline for snowy days when you want to stay more protected, 35 percent for clear days when, from the alpine heights, you feel you can see into Alaska.

The expansiveness, together with the efficient lift system, allows skiers to get to the far reaches of the mountain quickly—If you can't get out of the base area on one of its three lifts in ten minutes, you get your ticket price refunded. To date, no one has claimed it.

The skiing

The three front-side lifts and the gondola give access to mostly beginner and intermediate terrain; more confident

---

Lake Louise Facts
Base elevation: 5,400'; Summit elevation: 8,650'; Vertical drop: 3,250 feet.
Number and types of lifts: 11—3 superchairs, 2 triple chairs,
3 double chairs, 3 surface lifts
Acreage: 4,000 skiable acres   Percent of snowmaking: 40 percent
Uphill capacity: 23,955 skiers per hour   Bed base: 2,500 within 10 minutes

intermediates take Top of the World to access the Back Bowls, Larch Area and the Summit Platter, three separate areas each having their special appeals.

Now the Platter: first off, realize that it used to be a T-bar until they decided the steepness demanded concentration, not conversation, so it's one up at a time now. The skiing here is nicely moguled, above tree line, wide enough so you could stay up here all day and never cross your own tracks—almost all black diamonds with a touch of blue.

Either from the Platter or Top of the World Chair, you can dip down into the Back Bowls, especially in the morning because it will be in the sun. Most of the advanced Alpine skiing is found here in Paradise Bowl, but there are intermediate ways down the back as well. Paradise Bowl is not at all ill-named, with Paradise Chair waiting on the backside to hoist you up again.

Or if you'd rather, you can use The Ski Out for a spell and explore the sister mountain, Lipalian, and the Larch Area runs, some for all levels of skiers. There's great tree skiing directly under the lift between Larch and Bobcat runs. From the top of the Larch Chair, you'll see that some powder freaks have hiked up to the 8,900 foot summit to leave tracks down Elevator Shaft Chute, between two rock outcroppings, a bit out-of-bounds but skiable.

For a more modest thrill in a less travelled area, exit left off Larch Chair, then stay right and high on a gladed traverse and you'll find a deep powder bowl under Elevator Shaft. Called Rock Garden, it's not labeled on the map but it's in bounds, a hidden playground of loops and swoops, moguls and Cadillac-sized rocks. Albertans have recently renamed the spot Dances With Rocks. When you get through dancing down, it's time for nachos and chicken wings at Temple Lodge directly below, near the base of Larch Chair and Ptarmigan Chair which access both front and back sides of Whitehorn.

If you want sun all day, you can stay on the front, which faces south—rare for ski slopes, but this is far enough north that it keeps its snow until mid-May and is covered with snowmaking. If you want sun all day *and* want to ski the whole mountain, head into the Back Bowls in the morning, ski Larch midday and end up on the Face.

And if this is too much to remember, take advantage of Friends of Louise, the mountain's renowned snow host program, a crew of 150 volunteers ranging in age from 30 to 74, professionals in a variety of fields who love Louise and people so much (and so equally) that they take great pleasure in bringing the two together. The eight Ski Friends on mountain meet their new friends at 9:30 a.m., 10 a.m. and 1 p.m. at the north end of Whiskyjack Lodge.

Mountain rating

A key factor in Louise's 60 years of skiing history is that skiers of all abilities have terrain suited to their skill level from all lifts except the Summit Platter. The ratio is divided 25 percent beginner, 45 percent intermediate, 30 percent advanced, so everybody's happy.

For beginners, start on the Sunny T-Bar; it's the area used by instructors for beginning classes. Then progress to the Friendly Giant for your first big mountain experience on Wiwaxy, a two-and-a-half-mile cruiser. If that's getting to feel easy, venture up higher on the mountain on Eagle Chair and take Pika, long and meandering around the back, or Deer Run and Eagle Meadows down the front.

Intermediate skiers should not miss Meadowlark on the front or Gully from Top of the World, but will find routes suited to them on all faces. With a mountain so large, there's plenty for everyone.

Advanced and experts will love the platter lift, the Back Bowls, and the tree skiing.

Cross-country

There is plenty of groomed cross-country skiing around Banff. Lake Louise has about 60 miles of groomed trails and access to hundreds of miles of back country trails. The ungroomed, well-marked trail to Skoki Lodge, a rustic log cabin (meaning no electricity, no plumbing, wood-burning stove), begins just above Temple Lodge at the Ski Area and heads up the valley and over Boulder Pass, seven miles one way. If you're not up for skiing so far into the wilderness, follow the gentle Shoreline Trail starting in front of Chateau Lake Louise, an easy mile and a half one way. Skiing on Lake Louise is not recommended.

A complex 13-mile network called Pipestone Loops is accessed four miles west of the Lake Louise Overpass on the Trans Canada Highway. Although all are marked beginner, some are suitable for the intermediate.

There are probably a half dozen other trails in the area comprising a total of 50 miles of groomed touring. Rental shops, especially the one in Chateau Lake Louise which also rents clothing, can furnish trail maps.

Before setting out on any of the trails, check trail conditions at a park warden's office or by phoning 762-4256. Be aware that trail classification is done by healthy Canadians in good shape.

Snowboarding

Yes, everywhere on the mountain. There's a highly visible halfpipe right under Friendly Giant, the express chair on the Face. Snowboard rentals are Cdn$31 a day and lessons are Cdn$32 for one hour, usually with only you and maybe your buddy in the group.

Ski school

Group lessons (an hour and three-quarters in the morning, two hours in the afternoon) begin at 10:15 a.m. and 1:00 p.m. for Cdn$22. Private lessons are Cdn$50 per hour, reduced to Cdn$32 if taken at 9 a.m. or 3 p.m. Extra skiers, Cdn$16 each.

Beginner's Special is a Cdn$32 one-day package including a one-and-three-quarter-hour lesson, equipment rental, beginner area lift ticket and a half-price discount on the next full-day, all-area lift ticket. "You'll be skiing by the end of the day or we'll teach you again the next day free." Arrive well before lesson to pick up equipment.

The Club Ski Program operates at Lake Louise, Sunshine and Mt. Norquay. Groups of similar interest and expertise ski together with the same instructor for four hours a day at each of the three areas. This allows for maximum improvement through continuity and lets you make new skiing friends, learn the best runs at each resort for your particular ability level, and cut into lift lines. A three-day program costs Cdn$184.

Lift tickets

Adult tickets (including GST) are Cdn$38; half day Cdn$33; from 2:30 on, Cdn$19. Children 6-12 are Cdn$10 all day or part. Youths 13-17 are Cdn$34 full day; Cdn$30 half; Cdn$14 from 2:30 on.

Two-day tickets are Cdn$72 for adult, Cdn$63 for youth; three-day are Cdn$105 and Cdn$84; 4 days of 7 are Cdn$139 and Cdn$112; 5 days of 7 are Cdn$172 and Cdn$138; 6 days of 7 Cdn$204 and Cdn$164; 7 days Cdn$235 and Cdn$191.

Children under 6 ski free.

Accommodations

Two properties are the supreme lodgings in the area, but oh, so different from each other: **Chateau Lake Louise** and **Post Hotel**.

The Chateau is lodging in the grand manner of the old railway hotels. Skiers get a break: since summer is high season, winter rates are a fraction of the summer prices: Cdn$95-Cdn$160 for what those poor fools who don't ski pay Cdn$145-Cdn$295 for in summer. Some 500 guest rooms, several restaurants, 32 shops, in-hotel Nordic ski center, ski clothing rental, masseuse, and complimentary ski bus service make this 100-year-old Lady of the Lake right up to date for skiers. Reservations (800) 828-7447.

The Post Hotel is a cozy, beautifully furnished 93-room log lodging with great views on all sides and fireplaces in 38 of the rooms, two of which are lovely riverside cabins with heated slate floors. Newly expanded and thoroughly renovated, it's personal, quiet, with the warmth and elegance personally attended by Swiss innkeepers. The buffet breakfast is a groaning board of tasty delights (including cinnamon baked apple rings, yum!) for Cdn$12 and it's right on the way to the slopes. Except for Christmas, rates are in the Cdn$105-Cdn$225 range, higher for suites with kitchen. Five minutes from the lifts; free shuttle. (800) 661-1586.

Lake Louise Inn is a moderately priced family hotel with a noisy bar. Cdn$85-Cdn$145. (800) 661-9237.

Deer Lodge, near the Chateau, is everything the Chateau is not in terms of a full-service hotel: No phones, no television, rustic, but great rooftop hot tub. Old but kept up well. Cdn$110-Cdn$130. (800) 661-1595.

The Canadian Hostal Association is opening hostal accommodations next to the Lake Louise Inn this season.

Dining

In the **Chateau**, the most elegant dining room is the **Edelweiss**, serving such entrées as salmon and duckling for Cdn$15-Cdn$20. The most popular restaurant is the Walliser Stube Wine Bar serving Swiss cuisine such as raclette and fondue. It's romantic and dark with a cherry wood bar, and winds around the lower level of the hotel with great views out tall windows. **The Poppy Room** is a family restaurant, cheery and light, the only one open for breakfast in winter. Entrées Cdn$12-Cdn$16, sandwiches Cdn$7-Cdn$9. **Glacier Saloon** has a western theme, with steak sandwiches (Cdn$15), finger food and salads.

The Post Hotel is generally recognized as serving the finest cuisine in Lake Louise and is well known throughout Alberta. Continental, in the best Swiss tradition. Go here for a special occasion.

Deer Lodge has homemade breads, patés, fish, veal and beef dishes as well as innovative specials and pastries.

Lake Louise Lodge is a good spot for families often serving a hearty Italian buffet.

Après-ski/nightlife

Lake Louise has ten licensed bars, several of them in the Chateau. **The Glacier Saloon** has a lively atmosphere and dancing. For a cozier, quieter time, the **Walliser Stube** has a warm feel, and serves cappucinos and the Canadian Pacific Hotel chain's traditional blueberry tea (actually Earl Grey tea with Grand Marnier and Amaretto). In the Lake Louise Inn, **The Saddle Lounge** is quiet and **Charlie II's** is noisy. In the Post Hotel the **Outpost** has a pub atmosphere and the **Beehive** in the Samson mall is quiet.

Child care

Chocolate Moose Park serves children 18 days to 12 years with a variety of ski and play programs including a hot lunch. Infants under 19 months require reservations. Babies cost Cdn$21 per day or Cdn$4 per hour, Cdn$3.75 per hour for toddlers. Day-care for kids 3-6 is Cdn$3.50 per hour.

The **Kinderski** program, ages 3-6, provides supervised skiing and lessons with indoor and outdoor play at beginning and end of day. Cost is Cdn$31 (including two lessons) or Cdn$27 (one lesson).

In the **Kids Ski** program, children are guided around the mountain with instruction along the way. Cdn$19 for the morning; Cdn$33 for full day. Children's lift ticket, Cdn$10, must be purchased additionally. Optional lunch is Cdn$6.

Other activities

Skating, snowshoeing, tobogganing and sleigh rides are all available near the Chateau Lake Louise. Equipment is rented on site.

Getting there

"Only a few yards from the Trans Canada Highway," they say, once they're there. Lake Louise Village is 115 miles west of Calgary and 36 miles west of Banff. Direct or one-stop flights connect Calgary with most major North American cities via seven airlines.

Regular bus service is available from the airport direct to most hotels and the Lake Louise ski shuttle is free and operates from most hotels to the base of the ski lifts.

Information/reservations

For central reservations and ski area information, call (403) 256-8473.

Skiing Louise, Ltd. (Suite 505, 1550 8th St. S.W., Calgary, Alberta T2R 1K1) will send you loads of information. Phone: (403) 256-8473. Information about the surrounding area is available from Alberta Tourism, Box 2500, Edmonton, Alberta T5J 2Z4.

Marmot Basin
Jasper, Canada

Jasper is a winter vacation spot in the fullest sense of the word, with loads to do other than skiing, in a classic Canadian mountain setting. The largest of the Canadian Rockies National Parks, Jasper is studded with lakes, threaded by cross-country trails and spectacular drives such as the Icefields Parkway. But since Jasper Park Lodge, the old Canadian National Railroad hotel, now a CP hotel, has been open in winter for only three seasons, relatively few people outside Alberta know much about Jasper's Alpine ski area, Marmot Basin.

Being in a national park, Marmot Basin has developed slowly, a feature to its advantage today, for it still has a hidden feel, this far into the northland and separated from the hustle of Banff by the three-hour panoramic drive. It's far enough north, and far enough from a major airport (three hours from Edmonton) that people aren't here by mistake. They come for the scenery, the remoteness, the wonder of a herd of elk outside one's chalet, the call of Canadian geese swooping over Lac Beauvert in the spring while the ski area still has winter snow.

They call Marmot Basin "The Big Friendly," and indeed it aims to be skier conscious, with a good host program and convenient services.

The townsite of Jasper sprang up from a tent city in 1911, when the Grand Trunk Pacific Railway was laying

---

Marmot Basin Facts
Base elevation: 5,640'; **Summit elevation:** 7,940'; **Vertical drop:** 2,300 feet
Number and types of lifts: 18—1 quad superchair, 1 triple chair,
3 double chairs, 2 surface lifts.
Acreage: 800 trail acres **Percent of snowmaking:** 1 percent
Uphill capacity: 10,080 skiers per hour **Bed base:** 5,500

steel up the Athabasca River Valley toward Yellowhead Pass, and its growth was rather helter-skelter. Hugging the Athabasca River and nestled against the train station, the town is relatively nondescript, consisting of clapboard cottages, a steepled Lutheran church, stone houses and lodgings with no single architectural scheme. It has a Great Plains small town feel rather than a resort atmosphere. It's human, without a shred of glitz.

The skiing

Two peaks, a handful of bowls and a wide ridge consti-tute the ski area. The lower peak, Caribou Ridge, which takes two chair lifts to get to, is only 7,525 feet high. "We let the scenery, not the elevation, take your breath away," locals say. Even so, it climbs above the tree line, a notably low topographical feature determined by the last Ice Age. Marmot has the best glade skiing in the Canadian Rock-ies, and much of it is off the triple chair and Kiefer T-bar which service Caribou Ridge. Directly below are black mogul runs, negotiable by a strong intermediate when groomed (an event that takes place every Friday) but off to the right, facing downhill, advanced skiers can play in the trees in a black area misnamed Milk Run. Don't let the ti-tle fool you. It's fast.

By staying high to the right, skiers can take another lift, Knob Chair, to gain 500 more vertical feet on Marmot Peak. Here the lift doesn't climb to the summit, but that doesn't stop hardy Canadians from hiking up, as their tracks on upper slopes testify. It's all Alpine bowls up here, and it feels like Switzerland. Even intermediates can negotiate The Knob by a sinuous route down, but experts will want to drop into the fine powder in Dupres Bowl, a true scooped-out hollow, outrageously large, with Dupres Chute dividing it from Charlie's Bowl, even steeper and further away that untracked longer. Here's where knowing skiers head for. It should be a double black; try telling that to Canadians. The most horrendous bump runs are just to the right of the Knob Chair—Knob Bowl and Knob Hill.

By staying high and even farther to the right from The Knob facing down, experts have an entirely different play-ground all to themselves, a ridge wide enough that some parts are treeless, like Thunder Bowl, others gladed, like

Chalet Slope. Here is where powder lasts the longest, because it takes three lifts to get there.

Mountain Magic Tours are available, free, weekends and holidays. Tours leave from the Lower Chalet; check with Guest Services for times. There's a mechanical dual slalom race course on Dromedary (lower mountain; accessed by Eagle Express) used weekends and holidays. Register at the Ski School. Cost: $4 for two runs and a pin.

Be aware that only one chair lift, Eagle Express, accesses all but beginner terrain. That makes it a wait sometimes; don't come all the way down during peak loading times, like mornings before 9:30. There's rarely a wait on Caribou Chair, on the lower mountain far to the right, and it has terrain for all abilities.

Mountain rating

Many levels of skier can ski together, riding the same lifts, a factor which makes Marmot good family skiing. The terrain is nearly evenly divided, with 35 percent beginner, 35 percent intermediate and 30 percent expert. Beginners have expansive mountain access with 1,100 vertical feet on Eagle Express after they master terrain from the Red T-bar. They can even head up to Caribou Ridge for an above-tree line thrill where a high, wide trail, Basin Run, brings them safely back to the lower slopes.

Cross-country

This is prime ski touring country, and even if you've only done downhill, you'll want to try it. The scenery's guaranteed to draw you into the sport.

Jasper Park Lodge trails, nearly 16 miles of them, are unparalleled for beauty and variety—lake shores, Alpine meadows and forests. They're gentle and groomed and easily accessible. The easiest is Cavell, a three-mile lope with the elk. The perimeter loop samples a little of everything the Jasper Park Lodge trails offer.

Near Jasper Townsite, a good beginner trail is Whistlers Campground Loop, short of three miles, level and lit for night skiing. Pyramid Bench Trail, rated easy, overlooks the Athabasca River Valley. Patricia Lake Circle, three and a half miles and rated easy, provides several stunning views of Mt. Edith Cavell, the region's most prominent and dramatically sloped peak.

Trail maps are available in most lodgings. Guided cross-country excursions on weekends in February and March are offered by Parks Canada. Call Canadian Parks Service Interpretation, (403) 852-6146.

A full day's ski over Maccarib Pass from the Marmot Basin Road on the north shore of Amethyst Lake leads skiers to Tonquin Valley Lodge and hearty, home-cooked meals and welcome beds. Contact Tonquin Valley Ski Tours, Box 550, Jasper, Alberta T0L 1E0; (403) 852-3909.

Snowboarding

Snowboarding's come to stay at Marmot. Inside Edge Snowboard Cup is held in the spring and a halfpipe will open this season. Lessons and rentals are available.

Ski School (91/93 prices)

Adult lessons are Cdn$19; two sessions are $36; three sessions are $53; four sessions are $72.

Lessons for children four years and up are Cdn$14; two lessons are $26; three lessons, $38; four lessons $52.

Never-ever lessons which include lift pass and equipment cost Cdn$32 throughout the season.

Ski Improvement Weeks include five 2-hour sessions, Monday to Friday, video, a fun race and a Jasper Night Out. Adults are Cdn$87. Children 6-12 are $62.

Private lessons are Cdn$35 for an hour, $125 and $150 all day. Additional skiers, $15 each per hour.

Lift tickets (92/93 prices)

Ticket prices are based on time of year. Early season is November 27 to December 18; holiday season is December 15 Jan; regular season is January 4 to April 28.

Adult:	Regular	Early
full day	Cdn$33	Cdn$28
afternoon	28	24
3-day	94	80
5-day	149	126
Youth (13-17)		
full day	$27	$23
afternoon	22	19
3-day	77	66
5-day	122	104

Children under 6 ski free.

Accommodations

Although **Jasper Park Lodge** is now part of the Canadian Pacific Hotels, it's not in the style of a baronial manor like the region's two others. Rather, it's a grouping of traditional log cabins from the 1920s and new cedar chalets with spacious, modern suites. All buildings are connected by a pathway along Lac Beauvert to the main building, a Canadian hunting lodge style. Elk graze the meadows and golf course and the haunting call of Canadian geese will tell you for sure that you're in Canada. Only open in winter for three seasons, it's a relative newcomer in Canadian Rockies winter lodgings. Standard rooms to December 20 are Cdn$70, during the holidays $98, and $79 the rest of the season. Larger rooms run Cdn$95 to $165, with suites ranging from $147 to $195 depending on the time during the ski season. Nordic and downhill ski packages are available; write Jasper Park Lodge, Box 40, Jasper, Alberta T0E 1E0, or call (403) 852-3301 or (800) 828-7447. On the grounds, **Milligan Manor** is a newly restored eight-bedroom deluxe cabin overlooking the fairway and its resident elk herd. It's a special place for groups, family reunions or weddings.

All other lodging is in Jasper Townsite. **The Astoria** is a small hotel of character with elegantly renovated guest rooms, (403) 852-3351. **Chateau Jasper** has suites renting for Cdn$180-$250. Indoor pool and whirlpool, dining room, cocktail lounge and heated underground parking; (800) 661-9323. **The Athabasca Hotel,** one of Jasper's original lodgings, is close to the bus and VIA RAIL station. Rooms are Cdn$48-75; suites $170-$185 (403) 852-3536. Marmot Lodge has rooms with kitchens and fireplaces; indoor pool, sauna and whirlpool on the premises. No charge for children under 12. Rooms range from Cdn$50 to $135; (800) 661-6521. **Pyramid Lake Bungalows** has skating and cross-country trails at your doorstep. Located five miles from the Townsite, it has a lovely view, private whirlpools, kitchenettes and fireplaces, as well as a restaurant on the premises. Bungalows range from Cdn$50 to $120; (403) 852-3536.

An RV park is located 12 miles from the ski area.

Dining

At Jasper Lake Lodge, the **Beauvert Dining Room** overlooks the lake, is expansive, able to seat 800, but the Edith Cavell is the flagship restaurant, with white-glove tableside service, mahogany and silver touches and a harpist playing. French veal and shrimp in a pastry are specialties. **The Moose's Nook**, open only until New Year's, serves Arctic char (a landlocked salmon), buffalo and elk (domestic game), pheasant and duck. For breakfast, **The Meadows** features wholesome food in a country setting; food service continues all day.

In town, **Villa Caruso** (852-3920) serves steaks, prime rib, barbequed ribs, seafood and Italian dishes. Live music, beautiful view; make reservations. **The Palisades** (852-5222) serves barbeque chicken and ribs under an atrium roof in a refined atmosphere of wingback chairs by the fireplace. The **Amethyst Dining Room** (852-3394) serves light and healthy cuisine (beef, local fish) in an up-tempo, casually elegant restaurant. Breakfast features omelettes and a skier's buffet. **Mamma Teresa Ristorante** in Athabasca Hotel serves traditional Italian cooking in informal surroundings. A lovely buffet brunch on Sunday can be had at the Chateau Jasper's **Le Beauvallon Dining Room** (852-5644). Make reservations.

Mountain Foods Cafe, (852-4050) a sit-down or takeout restaurant, has affordable prices for its deli items. Pizza is at **Jasper Pizza Place** (852-3225), Greek cuisine at **L&W Restuarant** (852-4114), Japanese entrées and sushi bar at **Tokyo Tom's** (852-3780).

On the slopes, Marmot Basin has two food service areas. Upstairs in the Lower Chalet, **Country Kitchen** features pasta, sandwich bar and the local tradition, Marmot Basin Edible Soup Bowl—a delicious, hearty novelty. **Paradise Chalet**, mid-mountain, has a cafe and lounge. On busy days, lunch before 11:45 or after 1:15.

Après-ski/nightlife

Jasper is not known for rocking nightlife, but many of the in-town hotels have lounges. The Atha-B Club in Athabasca Hotel has the liveliest dancing in town; it also has O'Shea's, an Irish pub. Echoes Lounge in Marmot Lodge has nightly entertainment. Jasper Park Lodge's Tent City nightclub recalls the history of the area.

Child care

Little Rascals, the indoor nursery serves children 19 months through five years. It's Cdn$3 an hour, with no lunch service, so parents have to retrieve their children from 11:30 to 12:30. Reservations: (403) 852-3816.

Other activities

Heliskiing in Valemount, British Columbia, 56 miles away along a scenic drive, is available mid-February to mid-April. The price of $299 includes 4 runs (about 10,000 vertical feet) on Mt. Robson with licensed guides. Contact Robson HeliMagic at (604) 566-4700 or (800) 661-1931 for reservations and information for car rental to the pickup site, an hour from Jasper.

Valemount Snowmobile Tours operates three-hour tours in the high back country, stopping at a warm-up cabin. From January through mid-April, rates are $115 for one, $140 for two. Call (403) 852-3301, Ext. 6110.

Canyon Crawls is the ominous name of guided Maligne Lake Tours where visitors walk 1.2 miles through a 6-20 foot wide gorge on the frozen river, with naturally sculpted ice falls on both sides. Insulated hiking provided. It takes three hours, and it's like a deep freeze in the caverns, but it's one of those once-in-a-liftime activities that you'll brag about afterward. Only available in January and February.

Sleigh rides are available at Jasper Park Lodge for Cdn$10 an hour; 852-3301, Ext. 6052. Skating, too.

A drive on the Icefields Parkway (Highway 93) is a spectacle not to be missed. The highway winds through lodgepole and spruce forests, craggy peaks with crenelations on one side and dip slopes on the other, and along the Athabasca River, to the breathtaking Columbia Icefields nosing down into the valley.

Getting there

Four major carriers fly into the closest city, Edmonton: Delta flies from Los Angeles and Salt Lake; American from Dallas; America West from Las Vegas and Phoenix; and Northwest from Minneapolis. New this season, CAIR Western Airlines has service from Vancouver, Calgary and

Edmonton to Hinton, just outside the park. For information call (604) 270-6767. Private planes land at Hinton.

From Edmonton, Jasper is 270 miles west on Highway 16, a three-hour ride. By prearrangement, Jasper Park Lodge will send in a van for groups, even of four to five, for a price of Cdn$15 to Cdn$20 each, depending on the size of the group. The ski area is 12 miles south of Jasper via Highway 93, 93A and Marmot Basic Road.

VIA RAIL operates service to Jasper from Edmonton, Vancouver and Banff. Call (800) 665-8630 for information. Greyhound operates daily service from Edmonton and Vancouver; (403) 421-4211. Brewster Transportation operates the Banff-Jasper Ski Bus and the Marmot Basin Bus Service from Jasper; (403) 852-3332. The Edmonton Journal Ski Bus operates day return trips to Marmot Basin from Edmonton; (403) 448-1188.

Information/reservations

For ski area information, write Marmot Basin Ski-Lifts, Box 1300, Jasper, Alberta T0E 1E0, (403) 852-3816. Snow phone at Travel Alberta is (800) 661-8888.

Jasper Park Chamber of Commerce, Box 98, Jasper, Alberta, T0E 1E0 (852-3858) will provide information on activities outside Marmot Basin. There is no central reservations number.

Whistler/Blackcomb Canada

The greatest dual-mountain show in North America is happening in British Columbia in the coastal range 75 miles north of Vancouver. A tremendous surprise to the uninformed, these slopes charge up the ridges, some over 5,000 feet, of these sister mountains Whistler and Blackcomb, to a 360-degree panorama of alpine whitecaps. That's the greatest skiing vertical in North America. If you don't believe it, try it nonstop top to bottom—your ears will pop. It's so vast you'll lose your sense of where you are on the mountain. The runs seem to roll on forever in white-carpeted ribbons fanning out from a series of above-treeline bowls, themselves having nearly a 1,500-foot vertical.

Whistler Mountain began in 1966 as a rugged ski area served by bad roads, few lodges and essentially no grooming, but ever since Blackcomb's opening in December 1980, it has made leaps in improvement. Still, not many skiers from the U.S. have crossed the border to taste what Canadians have quietly kept to themselves.

Whistler Facts

Base elevation: 2,140'; **Summit elevation:** 7,160'; **Vertical drop:** 5,020 feet
Number of lifts: 13—10 passenger gondola, 3 super quad chairs, 3 triple chairs, 2 double chairs, 4 surface lifts **Percent snowmaking:** 7 percent
Total acreage by trails: 2,182 acres skiable terrain
Uphill capacity: 22,295 per hour **Bed Base:** 8,000+

Blackcomb Facts

Base elevation: 2,214'; **Summit elevation:** 7,494'; **Vertical drop:** 5,280 feet
Number of lifts: 13—4 super quad chairs, 5 triples, 1 double chair, 3 surface lifts
Percent snowmaking: 28 percent **Total acreage by trails:** 3,340 acres
Uphill capacity: 23,850 per hour **Bed Base:** 8,000+

Whistler Village, serving both mountains, is a low-lying hamlet of carefully designed plazas and walking lanes lined by European-style architecture: gables, turrets and clock towers house restaurants and shops with lodging above them. Everything is smack-dab in front of the lifts—cozy, yet elegant, with 80 percent of the lodging ski-in/ski-out. Both the village and the extensive interconnecting ski areas contribute to the feel of a European resort.

Where to ski

Ski both mountains; part of the appeal is to stand on one summit or ridge and look across the steep Fitzsimmons Valley at the runs of the other—to chart out where to go or gloat over where you've been. Of the two mountains, Blackcomb has the most high-speed superchairs. On weekends be ready for long, long lines to get up on the mountain. Once you are up and out of the village area, the skiers spread out and there are few long lines except at the Peak Chair on Whistler on sunny days and the Seventh Heaven superchair at the top of Blackcomb.

It's a good idea to start at the ten-person gondola, Whistler Express, at the village and take a speedy ride up 3,800 vertical feet to Roundhouse Station. Ascending over so much terrain, you'll think you're at the summit when you get out, but one glance out the gondola building reveals a series of five giant bowls above the treeline. These spread out sideways left to right: Burnt Stew Basin, Harmony Bowl, Whistler Glacier, Whistler Bowl and West Bowl, all served by lifts and T-bars. The view is heady. Far to the left you see only part of the skiing waiting for you at Blackcomb. In a circle stand a ring of rugged peaks.

Expert skiers will pause just long enough to enjoy the view and then head off on Peak Chair to the 7,160-foot summit, turning left along the ridge to drop into Glacier Bowl. Or they'll do the wide mogul apron, Shale Slope, in upper Whistler Bowl, rest awhile at the ridge and then have another go below Whistler Glacier. There are no definitive runs here—just ways down: it's wide open. Be creative and let fly. Expert skiing off this summit is in West Bowl, but there are two intermediate ways down. One is high and wide, to the right of West Bowl, keeping to the ridge instead of dropping into West Bowl. The other is

Burnt Stew, high and wide off to the left of Harmony Bowl. Reached by a long cat track looping behind the bowls, this is one of the great classic runs of North America because of its alpine views dominated by the imposing Black Tusk peak and the exhilaration of the open terrain.

For those wanting to know what skiing a distance of five miles feels like, take the Alpine T-bar from Roundhouse Station and turn right to find the bronze plaque identifying Franz's Run, the longest run in North America. The run turns and pitches and rolls and goes forever. Intermediates love it.

Beginners won't be able to experience the upper bowls, but will find numerous easier routes down from the Roundhouse, which is, after all, more than 3,800 feet above the village.

If that's not enough, there's another whole mountain. Fitzsimmons Chair at the village gives access from Whistler Gondola area to Blackcomb. The fastest way up Blackcomb Mountain is on the speedy Wizard Express, a sleek quad with an aerodynamic plexiglass windscreen. At the top, 2,230 feet higher, you're still not halfway up the mountain. Hop on Solar Coaster, adjacent, for another 2,000 feet, and here at Rendezvous Restaurant there are numerous routes down for all abilities.

To get into the wide open above-treeline territory, take Expressway, a lazy beginner's traverse, to Seventh Heaven Express, where at the Mile High summit, a free guided exploration of this upper terrain for intermediate and advanced skiers is available daily at 11 a.m. During the uphill ride, off to the right you'll see the blacks of Xhiggy's Meadow. But once at the Mile High summit, the routes off the backside into Horstman and Blackcomb Glaciers give the feeling of being hundreds of miles into the wilderness. While going down the spine off the backside, keep to the left and peer over the cornice over into the double black diamond chutes. Just seeing the abyss—or seeing someone hurl himself into it—gives quite a rush.

The best-known of these severe, narrow chutes is Saudan Couloir, named for Sylvain Saudan, a European extreme skier. The entry requires a leap of faith—and skill. Unbelievable though it may be, once a year Blackcomb hosts a race down Saudan Couloir. Nearby is Cougar

Whistler/Blackcomb - Canada

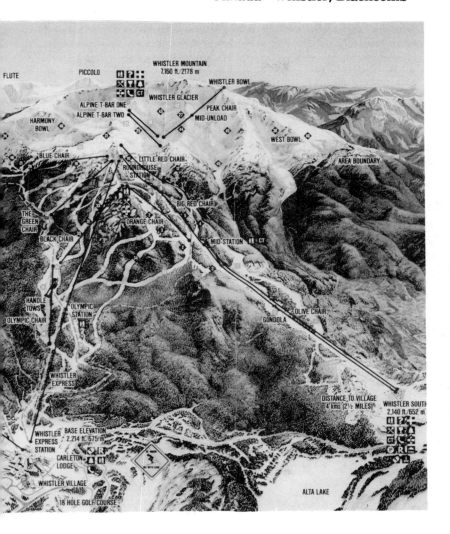

Chute, also a double black, which usually has better snow than Saudan because it's not as skied out.

One of the most difficult chutes on the mountain is Pakalolo, which is very narrow and steep with rock walls on either side. "You don't want to miss a turn," a local says. Another, called Blowhole, drops from the trail leading to the Blackcomb Glacier from the Horstman Glacier.

You can ski over the next ridge into Garibaldi Provincial Park. But that's extreme skiing, advisable only with a guide knowledgeable about conditions.

A surprise for beginners is a sinuous run called Easiest Route for those needing encouragement. The run takes off from the upper terminal of Seventh Heaven Express and follows the natural contours of the mountain from top to bottom on trails groomed daily. It's a thrilling way for beginners to do big mountain skiing, but getting down down down may take all day.

Mountain rating

This is a resort that has plenty of terrain for all levels of skiers. When you ask locals which mountain they prefer, you get mixed responses. Even super experts have reasons for enjoying both, and intermediates will have a field day on either set of slopes. Generally speaking, both Whistler and Blackcomb have their most challenging terrain above tree line, which should only be attempted by advanced and expert skiers—that means at the top of the Peak Chair at Whistler and from the top of Seventh Heaven superchair at Blackcomb. The bottom half of the mountain provides plenty of intermediate terrain interspersed with mellow runs for beginners, as well as steep mogul fields for energetic advanced skiers.

Cross-country

Lost Lake Park is within a half mile of Whistler Village. It's not enough to keep a good cross-country skier content, but it's fine for a day's alternative from downhill. Be aware that it has a shorter season because of its low elevation (2,200 feet).

Most avid cross-country skiers take BC Rail to the Cariboo and the 100 Mile House. For information on offerings, contact BC Rail Passenger Services, Box 8770,

Vancouver, B.C. V6B 4X6, or call (604) 984-5426 or Great Escape Vacations at (800) 663-2515.

Snowboarding

Snowboarding is allowed on the entire mountain. There is a halfpipe on Whistler Mountain and snowboarding lessons and rentals are available on both mountains.

Ski school (91/92 prices)

Each mountain has its own ski school, and there is a dual-mountain ski school/ski host program called Ski Esprit.

At Whistler, the rate for a two-hour group lesson (10:30 a.m. or 1 p.m.) is Cdn$38, Cdn$60 for a private, one-hour lesson and Cdn$90 for a two-hour private lesson. First-time skiers pay Cdn$38 for a two-and-a-half-hour lesson, rentals and lift ticket. At Blackcomb, the rate for an hour-and-a-half group lesson at 10:30 a.m. is Cdn$31. Private lessons are Cdn$60 for one hour, Cdn$150 for a half day. First-time skiers pay Cdn$39 for a two-hour lesson, rentals and lift ticket.

Both mountains offer adult workshops in parallel skiing, bumps, powder and racing. a two-and-a-half hour course is Cdn$38. At Whistler, Stephanie Sloan's Women Only ski programs are offered six times a season. They stress self-motivation, fitness and nutrition. Three-day programs are Cdn$165, plus Cdn$96 for a lift ticket, four-day programs are Cdn$210, plus Cdn$128 for a lift ticket. At Blackcomb, the Ladies Unlimited program for intermediate or advanced skiers is Cdn$150 for a two-day session and Cdn$190 for a three-day session, plus lift tickets.

For those wishing a series of consecutive lessons, Ski Esprit is a blend of ski instruction, including video analysis, dual-mountain guiding, recreational race and après-ski activities beginning every Monday. Three-day programs cost Cdn$145 and four-day programs are Cdn$150.

Ski Scamps is the children's instructional program at Whistler. Wee Scamps (2-3 years) $48, provides lunch, snacks and skis. At Blackcomb, Kids Kamp operates Wee Wizards for 2-3 year olds for Cdn$44, including lunch and ski equipment rental. Kids Kamp for 4-12 year olds, Mini Masters for 7-10 year olds, and Pepsi All-Stars for 10-13 year olds are all Cdn$35 a day, with half days and multidays available. All children's lessons are from 9 a.m. to 3:30 p.m., except weekends and holidays when they begin at 8:30 a.m

Lift tickets (92/93 prices)

Though each mountain has its own pricing, the dual-mountain lift ticket is the only one which makes sense for destination skiers.

Dual-mountain lift tickets for three days are Cdn$129 for adults (19+); Cdn$114 for youths between (13 to 18 years of age); and Cdn$60 for children (7-12). Five-day, dual-mountain tickets cost Cdn$200 for adults; Cdn$175 for youths; and Cdn$88 for children; nine of ten day lift tickets are Cdn$351 for adults; Cdn$306 for youths; and Cdn$148 for children.

Full-day tickets at Whistler and Blackcomb, as individual mountains, (1991-92 prices) are Cdn$40 for adults, Cdn$32 for youths ages 13-17, Cdn$17 for children ages 7-12 and Cdn$20 for seniors over 65. Children up to age six ski free.

Accommodations

Skiing at Whistler is clearly limited not by the mountain, but by the accommodations. Chateau Whistler is the latest jewel in the crown of impressive French chateau-style Canadian Pacific Hotels (owners of Chateau Lake Louise and Banff Springs Hotel) with 350 rooms in 13 stories, an expansive sun deck stretching below the high turrets, several restaurants, night club and extensive health club. Rates: Cdn$140 to $375.

Other than the Chateau, the largest deluxe lodging is Delta Mountain Inn, with 300 rooms, 30 percent of which are kitchen-equipped suites. Hotel rooms are Cdn$185-Cdn$350, studios are Cdn$235-$295, one-BR suite is Cdn$295-$375.

There is also the Glacier Lodge, decorated in pale plush. One-bedroom condominiums are Cdn$145-$285; two-bedroom, Cdn$215-$375. Lodge rooms are Cdn$110-$180. The Nancy Greene Lodge, operated by the 1968 Olympic Gold Medal winner, has 140 rooms from Cdn$120. Cozy common areas around the fireplaces give a European feel. Families who don't mind a slightly longer

[handwritten margin notes: La Chamoix · 245/nt +17% Tax. / London Lune — 19 r. 2 km. 5 side w. Mtn. Kitchen FP. 28. $175 +tx No ht.]

walk to the village center may find the large two-bedroom condominiums at Tantalus Lodge suitable for Cdn$260.

The Fairways Hotel, Hearthstone Lodge and Listel Hotel would be considered moderate, offering rooms for Cdn$99-Cdn$169. More medium-priced units are available at Mountainside Lodge, mini-kitchenette studios for Cdn$85-$180.

The least expensive accommodations are located outside the walking village at Shoestring Lodge offering rooms for Cdn$57-$90. Whistler Resort and Club has rooms for $80 a night. There are three dormitories, BCIT Lodge, Fireside Lodge and UBC Lodge with beds for Cdn$12-Cdn$16 a person.

Whistler also has upscale B&B's, usually owned and operated by families and sharing a central common area. These are located in residential areas and usually have no more than six rooms. Most have private baths. Rates vary from Cdn$69 to Cdn$150 and include breakfast. Ask for those with "BC Accommodations" approval.

Central reservations; (604) 932-4222; (800) 944-7853.

[handwritten: 800 663-8964 771 / World Cup Down hill.]

Dining

For years locals have said the Rimrock Cafe and Oyster Bar (932-5565) in Highland Lodge is the best restaurant in town. It is not in the village center but in Whistler Creek, a short ride away. Well-prepared seafood, especially lobster and poached British Columbia salmon, is complemented by an extensive wine list.

Val d'Isère (932-4666) located in the heart of Whistler Village features fine French cuisine. Umberto Menghi, a flamboyant Italian chef whose TV cooking show is popular in Canada, is well known for his restaurants in Vancouver and three in Whistler—Trattoria Di Umberto (932-5858), Umberto's Grill (932-3000) and Il Caminetto Di Umberto (932-4442). Continental cuisine is featured. At Myrtle's Restaurant (932-5211) they call the food "funky nouvelle cuisine," only they serve hefty portions rather than the modest amounts common to nouvelle. A favorite appetizer is ceviche, made with salmon and scallops. The house specialty is pepper steak flambé. Planter's Restaurant (932-1133) is a surprise jungle of silk plants and dusty rose tablecloths serving an international menu, featuring the biggest rack of lamb in Whistler, as well as

Thai vegetarian curry and chicken tandoori. Its buffet breakfast makes for a good, quick meal and an early start on the mountain. Ambrosia's (938-1921) in the Nancy Greene Lodge serves excellent meals and extensive buffet breakfasts at mid-range prices as does Twigs (932-1982) in the Delta Mountain Lodge. The Keg (932-5151) has good steaks and other basic American-type cooking.

On the Blackcomb side of the village the top dining spots are the Wildflower (938-2033) in the Chateau Whistler, La Fiesta-Hot Rock Café (938-2040) serving Mediterranean cuisine, Monk's (932-9677) at the base of the Wizard Lift with great lunches, and McQueen's (932-2779) in the Chamois building, for dinner with piano.

With more Japanese skiers than any other North American resort, Whistler also has excellent Japanese restaurants: Sushi Village (932-3330) and Irori (923-2221). For steaks cooked at your table Japanese steakhouse-style, it's Teppan Village (932-2223).

Moderate-priced dining is also available. Jimmy D's Roadhouse (932-4451) across from the conference center has affordable steaks, chicken and pasta. For light dinners and creative lunches, Cafe Presto (932-6009) is situated conveniently at the gondola base. Peter's Underground (932-4811) is a family self-service restaurant serving large portions—pizzas, pasta, burgers, chicken and steaks, as well as Greek specialties and filling breakfasts. A&W Rootbeer in the Cornerstone Building across from the conference center has good cheap breakfasts from 8 to 10 a.m. and basic burgers all day long.

A short walk from the village area along Fitzsimmons Creek in the Fitzsimmons Lodge, The Border Cantina (932-3373) serves decent cheap Mexican fare for poco dinero.

Après-ski/nightlife

Après-ski spills out onto the snow from Longhorn Pub at Whistler Village gondola base and Merlin's at Blackcomb. Both are of the beer-and-nachos variety with lively music. Citta in the center of Whistler Village is also a good spot to spend après-ski time and to meet new freinds.

For a quieter environment at the Whistler base area, Nancy Greene's Piano Bar from 3 p.m. to 6:30 p.m. hosts specialty coffees and guitar and piano music to help create a warm, gentle atmosphere. Creative aperitifs are mixed up at Planter's Lounge. On the Blackcomb side, The Mallard Bar in the Chateau Whistler provides quiet piano music après-ski.

Later in the evening, the reggae and rock at Buffalo Bill's starts at 9 p.m. and gets rocking by 10. Another disco is the Savage Beagle, and behind the Beagle you'll find Tommy Africa's with a young crowd. The locals seem to congregate at Garfinkle's which has beer by the pitcher, TV's on almost every wall and a well-used dance floor.

Child care

The only community licensed preschool, Dandylion Day care, charges Cdn$22 for full day and Cdn$15 for half day for children ages 3-5. Call 932-1119. Whistler Resort Association operates a referral service for babysitting. Call 932-3928.

Other activities

Dog-sledding, mornings or afternoons, takes off on groomed or ungroomed trails through an ancient cedar grove. After you try to keep up with the two Alaskan malamutes, Mya and Skeena, you're served lunch in the Cougar Lake Facility, a small log cabin in the woods. Price is Cdn$85 for a four-hour ride. Call (604) 932-4086.

Heli-skiing for strong intermediate or advanced skiers costs Cdn$255 for three runs (8,000-10,000 vertical feet) or Cdn$280 for four runs. Call Tyax Heli-Skiing (932-7007), Whistler Heli-Skiing (932-4105) or Canada Heli-Sports (932-2070).

Scenic flights offered by Whistler Air (932-6615) feature the option of landing on a glacier.

Getting there

Canadian Airlines and Air Canada fly to Vancouver. From there, the most scenic way to travel the 75 miles north to Whistler is to board BC Rail's passenger trains, which have schedules designed to accommodate skiers. Trains leave North Vancouver at 7 a.m. daily, arriving at 9:20 a.m. They depart Whistler at 5:30 p.m. and return to North Vancouver at 8 p.m. Fare is Cdn$12 one way. You'll need a taxi to get from Vancouver Airport to the train station.

Also, Perimeter Transportation leaves directly from the Vancouver Airport and goes to Whistler three times a day and four times a day on weekends, with the last bus leaving at 10 p.m. Fare is Cdn$24 one way. Reservations are required. Call (604) 261-2299.

Maverick Coach Lines operates from the downtown Vancouver bus depot, Dunsmuir and Georgia, and charges Cdn$12 one way. Call (604) 255-1171. You'll need Canadian currency.

Airport Express shuttle operates between the airport and bus depot; call (604) 255-1171.

Allow plenty of time in the Vancouver Airport, both arriving and leaving, for customs declarations and currency exchange.

Tourist information

Travelers from the United States should bring a birth certificate or passport. Currency can usually be exchanged in lodges, and often merchants take U.S. currency without charging an exorbitant surcharge. It's best to have Canadian currency for transportation services.

For specific information about each mountain, contact Whistler Mountain Ski Corp., Box 67, Whistler, B.C. V0N 1B0; Call (604) 932-3434 or (604) 685-0521. Blackcomb: Blackcomb Mountain, Box 98, Whistler, B.C. V0N 1B0; 687-1032 or 935-3141.

For general information about the Whistler area, contact Whistler Resort Association, 4010 Whistler Way, Whistler, B.C. V0N 1B4; (604) 932-3928 or toll-free in the U.S. (800) 634-9622.

Ski report number is (604) 932-4211 for Blackcomb.

Heli-skiing

This is the best recreational skiing in the world. Ski films show hotshots coming down through waist-high powder, and in a typical week a good amount of powder skiing will be done. But one of the joys—as well as challenges—of heli-skiing is that you meet all kinds of conditions and terrain: various snow textures, depths, ice, crust, trees, valleys, glaciers, and steeps. Three long runs are made each morning, lunch is helicoptered in for outdoor eating, and three long runs are made each afternoon. Each descent is over a fresh, untouched surface.

Many wonder whether they are good enough skiers to take part in heli-skiing. Stamina and strength are more important than skiing style or ability. If a skier can go down the black runs at a well-known resort with fairly decent form and has a flexible, spirited approach, he will probably do well. In track terms, this is a half-miler's sport; people with flashy turns and guts may have trouble if they lack wind. Although many more men than women turn out, a good female skier would really enjoy this activity.

Is this kind of skiing dangerous? Potentially, yes: operating in high, remote winter territory is inevitably going to bring on some tense situations and setbacks. However, the hazards are handled well by this experienced and knowledgeable oufit. And just by themselves, the chopper rides between peaks and onto precarious perches are outstanding adventures.

Heli-skiing operators

More than 30 years ago, **Canadian Mountain Holidays (CMH)** began as a rugged backpack operation that took venturesome skiers as far into unskied territory as abandoned logging roads permitted. Then came snowmobiles, then the quantum leap to helicopters.

Jet-powered Bell 204 (nine-passenger, single-engine) and Bell 212 (11-passenger, twin-engine) helicopters take skiers into areas with 600 to 1,000 miles of skiable terrain—the equivalent of 40 major ski areas.

Seven-day packages, operating from Saturday to Saturday and running from early December into May, include meals, lodging, guides and at least 100,000 vertical feet of skiing. The price ranges from Cdn$2,602 to Cdn$5,300 (including GST), depending on the week and location. For information, contact **CMH Heli-Skiing**, Box 1660, Banff, Alberta TOL OCO. Call (800) 661-0252 or (403) 762-4531, fax (403) 762-5879.

After CMH, **Mike Wiegele Helicopter Skiing** is the next best known company. It takes skiers to the Caribous and Monashees of British Columbia onto hundreds of runs in a 50-mile radius. The season is early December to mid-May, and weekly rates go from Cdn$3,100 to Cdn$5,000 (GST included). For information, write Box 249, Banff, Alberta TOL OCO, or call (403) 762-5548 or (800) 661-9170.

Also operating in western Canada are: **Purcell Helicopter Skiing Ltd.**, Box 1530, Golden, British Columbia VOA IHO; (604) 344-5410; and **Selkirk Tangiers Heli-Skiing Ltd.** Box 1409, Golden, British Columbia VOA IHO; (604) 344-5016).

In the United States, **North Cascade Heli-skiing**, Box 367, Winthrop, WA 98862; (509) 996-2148

Telluride Helitrax, Box 1560, Telluride CO 81435; (303) 728-4904.

Colorado Heli-ski, Box 64, Frisco CO 80443, (303) 668-5600.

High Mountains Heli-Skiing, Box 2217, Jackson WY, 83001; (307) 733-3274, into the Grand Tetons.

Ruby Mountain Heli-Ski, Box 1192, Lamoille NV 89828; (702) 753-6867, into Nevada's Ruby Mts.

Sun Valley Helicopter Guides, Box 978, Sun Valley ID 83353; (208) 622-3108, fly within a 35-mile radius.

Utah Powderbird Guides fly from Park City. Contact them at: Box 1760, Park City UT 84060; (801) 649-9739.

The **Wasatch Powderbird Guides** operate out of Snowbird. Box 57, Snowbird UT 84092; (801) 742-2800.

Alyeska, Alaska

Alyeska, 40 miles southeast of Anchorage, is an unusual ski resort mountain. The mountain rises from sea level to 3,939 feet, and 2,850 feet of its vertical is skiable. The lower half of the mountain is forested and the upper portion is above the tree line. The altitude of the base is only 270 feet above sea level, the lowest of any major ski area in the world. This, coupled with upper mountain snow accumulations reaching 750 inches a season, can make for rare conditions: on a recent visit in mid-April there was still 20 feet of snow on the upper mountain and the temperature at the top of the lifts was just 30 degrees.

Impressions of Alaska tend toward ice, sled dogs, Eskimos and construction of the oil pipeline in subzero weather. Anchorage reality is much different; warm Pacific currents cause winter temperatures to average 10 to 30 degrees Fahrenheit. But plenty of snow does fall, and with the mountains dropping right into the sea, the avalanches along the road skirting the edge of Turnagain Arm are normal. Snow control cannons trigger slides over the road, and a drive to Alyeska can take you through more than a half dozen cleared avalanches.

The resort itself has a small base area with normal ski area amenities. There are no high-rise buildings, no super luxury units, no bustling shopping or village centers, just a quiet ski community. You will find most Alaskans surprisingly open and chatty; be prepared to tell and hear some good stories. It's hard for Alaskans to stay in touch with family members in the "Lower 48," so they'll chat freely with visitors.

Alyeska Facts
Base elevation: 270'; **Summit elevation:** 3,160'; **Vertical drop:** 2,850 feet
Number and types of lifts: 7—2 quad chairs, 3 double chairs, and 2 surface lifts
Acreage: 1,200 skiable acres **Percent of snowmaking:** none
Uphill capacity: 5,000+ skiers per hour.

Change is coming to this sleepy corner of Alaska. Seibu Corp. of Japan, has already built a high-speed quad and new Daylodge. And Spring 1994 is the target for opening a 307-room luxury Alyeska Prince Hotel, a 60-passenger tram and a new upper mountain restaurant.

The skiing

Two double chairs and the superchair provide access to the upper mountain, opening 2,500 vertical feet; the top half iswide-open, above tree line skiing. The only other U.S. resort with similar terrain may be Arapahoe Basin. The entire 2,500 feet of vertical is skiable in one continuous run, with intermediate to super-expert pitch depending on your choice of route.

Alyeska also has a unique combination of open bowl skiing and trails through the trees directly under Chairs 1 and 4. Beginners will stick to the area served by Chair 3 and the surface lift. Intermediates can take the new quad chair and drop into the bowl and ski whatever they can see. It won't take much judgment to figure out whether you are getting in over your head, and in this bowl there is plenty of room to traverse out of trouble. The bowl funnels into Waterfall and ends on Cabbage Patch before reaching the base area.

For intermediates taking the Spirit Quad to the top of the resort, it best to follow the Mitey Mite: swing left when you get off the chair. This takes you past the Skyride snack bar, and back to the Quad by three intermediate routes, or tip down South Face (very steep and ungroomed).

From the Quad, experts can go right and drop down Gail's Gully or Prospector and take a gully left or right of Eagle Rock, then back to the Quad. Experts willing to work can take the High Traverse from the Quad, arcing through The Shadows between Mt. Alyeska and Max's Mountain, dropping down through new snow and open steeps; or continue over the ridge to find good steeps and a short section of gladed skiing on Max's Mountain (when opened by the Patrol—it's avalanche-prone until March).

Mountain rating

Alyeska has a small beginner area, but we wouldn't suggest this as a place to learn to ski unless you're athletic.

Intermediates will have a field day, especially with the wide-open bowl skiing and spectacular views from the top of the Quad. Experts have some good drops but the real challenge of Alyeska is the tremendous variety of terrain and snow conditions from top to bottom. Snow may be groomed, cut up or untouched. Often there is powder at the top moistening to mashed potatoes at the bottom.

Cross-country

The Nordic Skiing Association designed and prepared the 10-kilometer Winner Creek trail, which leaves from Alyeska's Nugget Inn and wanders through woods, across meadows and up and down gentle hills. The trail is not groomed. You can also skinny-ski around nearby Moose Meadow area—locals will point you there; it's not marked.

There are hundreds of kilometers of groomed cross-country trails in Anchorage at Kincaid, Russian Jack and Hillside Parks. The Chugach State Park hillside trails are easily accessible (with a 4-wheel-drive) wilderness areas. There's a Nordic resort at Hatcher Pass (an hour and a half north of downtown Anchorage) and more cross-country trails at Sheep Mountain Lodge, 50 miles north of Palmer.

Ski School (92/93 prices)

You will meet some very interesting people teaching skiing. The half-dozen full-timers, all PSIA-certified, build houses, drive boats and catch salmon in the summer. Part-timers might be pharmacists, lawyers, pilots, mothers, purchasing agents, or firefighters.

Ski school adult group lessons (age 11 and up) are 10:45 a.m.-12:30 p.m. and 2:15-4:00 p.m.

Adult group lessons cost $35. Juniors 11-13 and seniors 60+ pay $25. Special beginner programs combine beginner lift and rentals for $35/$25. Lessons with full lift ticket cost $55/$35; with rentals, cost is $73/$45.

Private lessons are $40 an hour, $20 for extra students.

Alyeska has a weekend children's program for ages 4-10 with 2-hour lesson, or full-day program including cafeteria lunch with the instructor. It is often overbooked, so always try to make reservations (783-2222). SKIwee group prices are $15 for a two-hour lesson or $40 for a full day. Beginner package costs $25 for two hours and $50 for a full day. Packages including all mountain lifts cost $30 for two hours and $55 for a full day.

The Challenge Alaska Adaptive Ski School, a chapter of National Handicapped Sports, provides skiing for the disabled with support from Alyeska Resort. All disabilities, all ages, by reservation only. A skier with a disability, and ski buddy, may purchase discount lift tickets and rent adaptive ski equipment. Open Tuesday-Sunday, usually December 15 to April 15. Challenge Alaska also has information on wheelchair-accessible accommodations and amenities in the area. Call: Challenge Alaska, Box 110065, Anchorage AK 99511-0065, fax (907) 561-6142.

Alyeska Ski School phone 783-2222.

Lift tickets (1992/93 prices)

Adult full day (10:30-5:30) or late day (12:30-9:30) all mountain: $26 weekday, $30 weekend/holiday. An adult three-day pass costs $70. Juniors 12 and younger and seniors 60+ pay $15. Children under 7 pay $7 all lifts, any time. Chair 3 beginner lift is $15 any age, day/night. Night skiing (4:30-9:30): Adults—$14, Juniors and Seniors—$10.

Child care

Here, Alyeska has a problem. Little Bears Playhouse day-care center is near the resort (783-2116), but it is normally full with local children. The staff may recommend other baby sitters who live in the valley.

Accommodations

The only accommodations at the base of the resort are in the resort's **Nugget Inn**, to be replaced by a 307-room Alyeska Prince Hotel in 1993; and privately owned condominiums which may be rented through management agencies.

Nugget Inn rates are $85 single; $95 double; $105 for four adults. Call 783-2222 for reservations.

About 50 condominium units are managed by two firms, **Vista Alyeska Accommodations**, Box 1029, Girdwood AK 99587 (30 units), 783-2010, fax 783-2011. A condo sleeping six costs $175-$250 a night, a condo sleeping four costs $125 to $200 depending on amenities. Some have fireplaces, whirlpools, hot tubs and wet bars. Fireplace use is not restricted by air quality regulations.

Alyeska has a few bed-and-breakfasts. See Visitors Guide B&B section under "Alyeska" alphabetic listings.

The larger bed base is in Anchorage, a 35- to 55-minute drive depending on weather. Major hotels include the Regal Alaskan, Hotel Captain Cook, Hilton, Holiday Inn, Sheraton and Westmark. There are many smaller hotels and motels, and hundreds of bed-and-breakfast rooms (some with spectacular views) available through the B&B reservation services. See the Visitors Guide.

Dining

Alaska is casual about dress, and you'll see suits and long gowns in the same dining room with blue jeans. Ski-wear is always acceptable. These are some of our favorites; see the Visitors Guide for more selections.

Alyeska & vicinity: Perhaps the best restaurant in the area is the **Double Musky Inn**, a mile from the lifts on Crow Creek Road. It's mind-boggling to find great Cajun food in Alaska. Entrées from $18 to $30. No reservations, opens at 5 p.m.

Turnagain House, a white-tablecloth restaurant looking out on Turnagain Arm halfway to Anchorage, has a reputation for fine seafood and other dishes with excellent service. Entrées $15 to $30. Reservations.

Chair 5, casual, less expensive, offers prime rib, halibut and a tasty, very spicy chicken jalapeño. Girdwood business district next to the Post Office.

The Bake Shop at the resort boardwalk has killer soups, huge buns, energy-filled buttered sticky buns with fruit filling, and sandwiches. Walk in, meals $5-$9. Lots of locals, ski instructors and patrollers here.

The Girdwood Griddle in the business district has some of the best homestyle breakfasts at modest prices.

Edelweiss, a three-minute walk from the Nugget Inn, has German cooking at modest prices.

At Alyeska Resort itself, the Nugget Inn has humongous nachos, hearty soups and American fare. Try the wonderful seafood chowder in its own bread bowl. The Daylodge cafeteria's specialty is spicy curly fried potatoes, plus burgers, chili and sandwiches.

Anchorage: For those with deep pockets and taste for the best, call the **Marx Brothers Cafe**, for inventive continental cuisine and impeccable service in a cozy framehouse setting which reminds us of a small New England inn. Reservations required. Most entrées $20-$30.

Likewise, the **Corsair**, with continental cuisine offered by owner Hans Kruger. The style is elegant—expect to spend the whole evening.

For Northern Italian, **Romano's** in midtown has a strong local following; no reservations. **Little Italy** in South Anchorage, closer to Alyeska, also are packed with locals, reservations taken and occasionally needed. Moderately priced, entrées $11-$21.

Also moderately priced with fresh seafood specials daily are **Simon & Seafort's Saloon & Grill** (livelier) and **Elevation 92** (quieter), around the corner from each other downtown. Also try **Jens' Restaurant & Gallery**, **Europa Cafe**, and **C'est La Vie** in midtown. Seemingly a hole in the wall, **Club Paris** is a intimate downtown steak house.

For great views, especially at cocktail time, try the topfloor **Crow's Nest** at the Hotel Captain Cook, **Josephine's** in the Sheraton or **Top of the World** in the Hilton. Reservations, bring $$$ if dining.

Many Japanese have settled in Anchorage, and good moderately priced restaurants such as **Akaihana, Tempura Kitchen, Daruma, Kumagoro, Shogun, Yamatoya** and **Ichiban** are the result. All offer tempura, sukiyaki and other cooked dishes as well as sushi and sashimi. **Thai Cuisine** has—obviously—Thai cuisine. **The Warsaw** offers Polish and **The Prague**, Czech and Eastern European cooking: tasty, moderately priced. There are good Chinese establishments and a few Korean. **La Paella** offers interesting Spanish dishes; get good directions as it's hard to find (in the lower level of a shopping center).

Families should head to **Sourdough Mining Co.** (great ribs, corn fritters) **Gwennie's Old Alaska Restaurant** (breakfasts, sandwiches, historic photos), **Hogg Brothers** (wow omelets for working people), **Red Robin**, the **Royal Fork**, **Peggy's**, **Lucky Wishbone** (the best fried chicken), and **Arctic Roadrunner** (super burgers).

For margaritas and Mexican cooking: **La Mex, Garcia's, El Patio, Mexico in Alaska**. Nice places, not great cuisine.

Après-ski/nightlife

For immediate après-ski, head to the **Nugget Inn Bar**, or to the **Daylodge Don's Bar** for Don's Ramos Fizz.

The **Double Musky** and **Chair 5** also have taverns. On the drive into Anchorage, the **Bird House** is a legendary sunk-in-the ground log building. Try a drink, an incredibly hot pickle, and some conversation while trying to sit up straight. Bring a business card: you'll find out why. Look for the "Bar" sign and bird head on the building.

Anchorage has a highly developed nightlife and cultural scene, a legacy of the pipeline days, the long winter nights, and generous doses of oil patch money.

For theater, opera, drama and movies, buy the local newspaper (Daily News). There's a Friday morning entertainment tabloid that's very helpful. You'll be surprised at the visiting artists and productions at the Alaska Center for the Performing Arts downtown, or the University of Alaska in midtown.

The Fly By Night Club puts on a zany, hilarious show called (depending on the season) Christmas in Spenard, Springtime in Spenard, or Whale Fat Follies. Call 279-7726 for reservations. This may be the only bar in the world where you can order Spam with champagne, or Spam nachos. After the show, there's dancing to the Spamtones. Mr. Whitekeys, the owner, sponsored a climber eating a can of Spam on the summit of Mt. McKinley.

For loud rock and dancing try **Chilkoot Charlie's**, "where we cheat the other guy and pass the savings on to you," or **Midnight Express**. **Grand Central Station** is less raucous. For quieter dancing and a slightly older clientele try **Legends** at the Sheraton, **Whale's Tail** at the Hotel Captain Cook, or the lounge at the Golden Lion Best Western. For country music head to **The Pines Club** on Tudor Road.

Women who want to see naked men: check out the Midnight Express for visiting male strippers. Men with opposite aspirations, try the **Great Alaska Bush Company** with an elegant frontier saloon atmosphere.

Other activities

For a dog sled trip, run by Bob Crockett's Chugach Express Dog Sled Tours, call 783-0887 for reservations; last-minute calls don't work. Trips and prices range from 30 minutes to 3 hours, $20 to $50+ per person.

The variety of other activities is staggering. This city of 250,000 is the business, cultural, transportation and to some extent government center of the state. Use your Anchorage Visitors Guide, buy a newspaper, ask locals on the chair lift for their favorite things.

Getting there

Alyeska is 45 miles south of downtown Anchorage. Get on Gambell Street south, which becomes the Seward Highway, Route 1, along Turnagain Arm. This spectacular drive is one of the best parts of the skiing experience at Alyeska, and if you see cars parked by the road near Falls Creek, stop—the drivers are watching Dall sheep. Toward spring you may see bald eagles as the fish return.

If you are driving on mountain roads, or on back roads in Girdwood, get a 4-wheel-drive vehicle. Locals do.

If you choose to stay at a downtown hotel, Alaska Sightseeing runs there is regularly scheduled transportation to the resort. Ask at the hotel desk.

Information/reservations

Alyeska Resort, Box 249, Girdwood AK 99587; (907) 783-2222, snow conditions tape 783-2121, fax 783-2814, tour/group reservations 561-2515.

The source for community information is the Anchorage Convention & Visitors Bureau, 1600 A St. #200, Anchorage AK 99501. Phone the main office (907) 276-4118, fax 278-5559, for a copy of of the encyclopedic Anchorage Visitors Guide. Request First Class Mail.

Questions and details: phone ACVB's Log Cabin Visitor Center (274-3531) or drop in at 4th and F downtown. There's also an Airport Visitor Center in the baggage claim area.

Mid-Atlantic Resorts

Snowshoe, WV (304) 572-5252
33 trails; 1,500 ft. vertical.
Snowshoe sits atop Cheat Mountain, topping off an inverted resort: the facilities are at the summit. Snowshoe's altitude of 5,000 feet is higher than Stowe or Killington in Vermont. The area often gets 200 inches of snow and has extensive snowmaking. This is the most elaborate and extensive resort in the South. The main problem is access: this resort is difficult to reach, at the end of a 10-mile car path, but once there, every skier can enjoy the mountain.

Blue Knob, Claysbburg PA
1,100 ft. vertical
This mountain is in a part of the Pennsylvania which gets more natural snow than the Poconos. The mountain has the lodge at the top, like Snowshoe. At the top of the mountain you'll find the beginner areas and towards the bottom the pitch becomes steeper. The resort is 150 miles from Philadelphia and 100 miles east of Pittsburgh. Take the Bedford Exit off the turnpike, then follow Rte. 220 north to Pavia and follow the signs.

Elk Ski Area, Union Dale PA (717) 679-2611
17 trails; 1,000 ft. vertical
This mountain is, for Pennsylvania, a tough skier's mountain. The slopes are good for advanced skiers and solid intermediates who want some practice. Even the beginner trails are difficult. There is no real "resort area," but the region has about 50 hotels. Elk is on the northeast corner of Pennsylvania, near Scranton. From New York take I-80 to I-380 then turn onto I-81 and drive until Exit 63. From Philadelphia head north on the turnpike extension to Exit 37 which connects with I-80.

Seven Springs, Champion PA (814) 353-7777
30 trails; 970 ft. vertical.
Hidden Valley, Somerset PA (814) 443-6454
16 trails; 610 ft. vertical
These resorts are about three and a half hours from Baltimore and Washington and an hour from Pittsburgh. Seven Springs offers the best base facilities and Hidden Valley offers quieter surroundings. Trails at these two resorts will keep beginners and intermediates happy for a day or so. Seven Springs has the more difficult trails.

Camelback, Tannersville PA (717) 629-1661
25 trails; 800 ft. vertical.
This is the largest and busiest Poconos resort. All trails are blanketed with manmade snow. It barely qualifies as a destination resort, with only 250 townhouses located at the base of the ski area. A 150-room hotel, The Chateau, overlooks the trail network. The resort is an easy 100-mile drive from New York City or Philadelphia—if at all possible avoid it on weekends.

Wintergreen, Wintergreen VA (804) 325-2200
10 trails; 1,003 ft. vertical
Located less than an hour south of Charlottesville along the famed Skyline Drive. While natural snow is limited, the manmade variety is religiously pumped out day and night. The lodge is rather upscale with boutiques and antiques. Most skiing is mellow, but The Highlands offers a thousand feet of bumps with limited crowds, thanks to good control by the ski patrol.

Whitetail, Mercersburg, Pennsylvania (717) 328-9400
10 trails; 995 vertical.
This is the newest Pennsylvania resort, in fact the newest major resort to be built in the nation in more than 10 years. The owners have spent $20 million on start up costs, installing three quads (including one high speed detachable), building a beautiful Deer Valley inspired base facility and getting ready to give Eastern skiers an upscale ski experience. With 100 percent snowmaking, covering its 100 acres of trail, a children's center and 4,000 per hour skier capacity, just two hours from the White House.

Midwestern Resorts

The biggest of Midwestern ski areas may not have the great verticals of major mountains to the east and west, but they've got enough terrain, fine facilities, and uphill capacity to tune up anyone for bigger adventures. The following are the best Midwestern ski destinations. Expect lift prices to range between $25 and $30 a day for these resorts. And check with them for details on their stay-and-ski packages.

✔ Michigan's Lower Penninsula:

Boyne Highlands and Boyne Mountain,
Harbor Springs and Boyne Falls MI
800-GO-BOYNE; 34 trails; 520 ft. vertical.

Near the bustling resort communities of Petosky and Harbor Springs, **The Mountain** and **The Highlands** are about about 30 minutes apart and exchange lift tickets.

The Mountain's steep chutes and mogul fields are legendary among flatlanders; Hemlock has long been the standard-bearer for Midwestern steep. The Highlands is a Michigan classic, with wide, sweeping bowls and New England style trails that slice through the woods. The Highlands added a high-speed quad lift last year to provide quicker access to its more demanding runs. Each resort has an uphill capacity of around 19,000 skiers per hour (tops in the Midwest). Boyne's snowmaking capabilities are legendary. Boyne Mountain will routinely stay open on weekends through April.

Nubs Nob is just across the valley from the Highlands. Nubs offers the best trio of advanced slopes in the Lower Peninsula. A chair lift on the back opens intermediate and beginner slopes.

Sugar Loaf, Cedar MI
(616) 228-5461; (800) 748-0117; 20 trails, 440 ft. vertical.

With the backdrop of Michigan's blue-gray waters and the Manitou Islands nestled off the coast, it"s hard to keep your eyes on the slope. In addition to some great cruising runs, it boasts some of the best steeps.

Crystal Mountain, Thompsonville MI
(616) 378-2911; 22 trails, 375 ft. vertical
This is the "Little Big Man" of Michigan skiing. It skis much bigger than its 375-foot vertical. It's a great family area that offers some good advanced intermediate slopes and lots of beginner to low intermediate trails. As testament to its appeal, Crystal ranks annually among the top 10 resorts nationally for NASTAR participants. There is a variety of lodging available and a new indoort pool and fitness center.

Shanty Creek Schuss Mountain, Ballaire MI
(616) 533-8621; (800) 348-4440; 30 trails, 450 ft. vertical
This resort offers a nice weekend retreat. They are two separate resorts about five miles apart that are now operated as one with interchangeable lift tickets. Shanty has the nicest lodging, but Schuss has the best skiing. A good skier will get bored quickly at Shanty.

✔Michigan's Upper Peninsula
This is a rugged land of dense forests, long winters, deep snows and a collection of ski areas called "Big Snow Country." The region receives over 200 inches of snowfall annually. About a six to seven hour drive from Chicago, it is near Ironwood. Between areas there is enough variety to keep any skier happy for a weekend or midweek trip.

Indianhead Mountain, Wakefield, MI
(906) 229-5181; 800-3-INDIAN;18 trails, 638 ft. vertical
Indianhead runs are wide boulevards. It's an intermediate's dream . . . long, smooth runs, but they all look the same. The skier that likes a good challenge might get bored here but it is a great family area. The lodge and compact ski area sit atop the mountain. Runs fan out into the deep forests below, but all the lifts funnel back to the lodge on top.

Blackjack, Bessemer, MI
(906) 229-5115; 800-848-1125; 16 trails, 465 ft. vertical
Just down the road with slightly less in vertical drop (465 ft.), but it more variety of trails. It appeals to the intermediate and advanced skier. Both can explore some of the wide bump runs or the narrow chutes and trails that fan off from the boulevards. The Black River peacefully meanders through the valley.

Big Powderhorn Mountain, Bessemer, MI
(906) 932-4838; 800-222-3131; 23 trails, 600 ft. vertical
   Big Powderhorn offers a good variety of trails. They offer the most slopeside lodging, restaurants and aprés-ski activity. Powderhorn is in the 600-foot club, and with 24 slopes and trails to choose from there is enough variety to keep even the diehards busy. There are tree-lined trails, open bowls, long rambling trails and narrow chutes to explore.

Whitecap Mountain, Montreal, WI
(715) 561-2227; 32 trails, 400 ft. vertical
   Just across the border in Wisconsin, it is not long on frills, but offers some of the most interesting skiing in the area. The lodge is plain and simple, and many of the chair lifts are made of plywood. But the trails are an interesting mix of difficulties. They fan off three peaks in just about every direction. It's the one place where a trail map will come in handy. On a clear day from the top you can see Lake Superior in the distance. It may have the smallest vertical drop—a little over 400 feet--but it has the best mix of trails.
   To obtain information on the three-to-five day interchangable lift ticket and other lodging in the area, contact the Gogebic Convention and Visitors Bureau at 906-932-4850.
   Porcupine Mountain about 45 minutes north of Indianhead, offers some of the most stunning Lake Superior views. It's almost perched on the shoreline, and the lake is in evidence on every run. The skiing is quite good, with 600 feet of vertical drop. A new triple chair has been added for this season, which will help ease the weekend liftline. Being state-owned, it offers the best lift rates in the area.

✔ Minnesota

Blessed with superb ski terrain and consistently cold temperatures, northern Minnesota has some of the best snow conditions to be found east of the Rockies, and the northwoods scenery is spectacular.
   What's here? Three excellent ski areas with big vertical drops (for the Midwest)—Giants Ridge 550 ft., Spirit Mountain 700 ft. and Lutsen 800 ft. You won't find a

collection of bigger peaks anywhere in the Midwest. They are around Duluth and within an hour or so of each other.

Lutsen (218-663-7281) about an hour north of Duluth, is the closest thing to true mountain skiing in the Midwest. It has the only gondola in the Midwest. It will remind you of a New England ski area...three mountain peaks; long rock-ribbed trails flanked by birch and pine; tight headwalls and breathtaking views of Lake Superior. Part of the fun is exploring the many trails found here. Moose Mountain offers some of the best and longest cruising runs in the Midwest.

Spirit Mountain (800-642-6377) within the city limits of Duluth, has everything a Midwestern resort could ask for...good vertical, long runs, snowy winters and some breathtaking views of Duluth and the harbor perched on the Superior shoreline. Plus, it has the historic port city to explore. Runs are long intermediate runs without much variation in pitch and few twists and turns. A high-speed covered quad accesses a couple of advanced runs.

Giant's Ridge (282-865-4143) about an hour's drive northwest of the city, is not as crowded as the other two. The trails soar off the crest and are varied in pitch, with a headwall here, a bowl there. The day lodge is first class, and so is the cross-country skiing. It's well worth the drive for a day of skiing either from Duluth or Lutsen.

✔ Wisconsin

Resorts here have gradual, groomed, cruiser friendly runs. You won't find deep powder here, endless forests or exceptionally steep terrain, but it does have a certain ruggedness.

Devil's Head (800-DEVILSX) is long on intermediate cruising runs, but short on advanced terrain. In the Baraboo Bluffs, it boasts a decent vertical of 500 feet. All the natural contours and rolls have been graded out. The runs lack variation . . . too much sameness. It has some of the best beginner and intermediate terrain, with long runs. Weekend crowds and lift lines can be huge.

Located just down the road is **Cascade** with 460 ft. vertical and a wide variety of skiing. It's straightforward skiing , with few twists and turns, and solid cruising with hefty faces for the bumps. It has more uphill capacity than Devil's Head (12,000 per hour). Weekend lines can be long.

Rib Mountain (715-845-2846) near Wausau has the biggest vertical drop in the state, at 634 ft. It's an intermediate mountain with a few headwalls that offer some steep. Most runs are great for cruising.

La Crosse (800-426-3665) overlooking the Mississippi, is a skier's mountain with 516 ft. vertical drop and some of the steepest runs in the Midwest. Most of the runs are cut through rocky bluffs with headwalls and chutes. It sits high atop a rocky, rugged bluff along the Mississippi River. It has the only true double-black slope in the Midwest . . . Damnation.

✔ Iowa and Illinois

These states offer a couple of good areas to consider for a weekend trip . . . **Chestnut Mountain** (800-397-1320) near Galen and **Sundown** (800-397-6676) near Dubuque. They sit about 30 miles apart on blufs above the Mississippi River. Both have 475 ft. drops and offer a good variety that will apeal to all abilities. Sundown is perched on a bluff in an Iowa "Field of Dreams" setting overlooking a river valley. You can see Wisconisin 28 miles away. **Chestnut** is perched on a bluff overlooking the mighty Mississisppi. The biggest drawback is the amount of natural snow. You are often skiing on the only ribbons of white. Both do an adequate job of snowmaking with 100 percent coverage, but they are subject to a lot of freeze and thaw.

Part of the experience of skiing either of these areas is staying in the historic old river towns and exploring them. They have some of the finest B & B's, quaint Victorian and country inns you'll find anywhere.

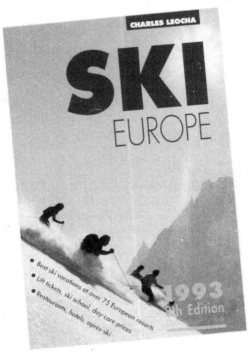